SUSAN ELEANOR HIRSCH

After the Strike

A Century of
Labor Struggle
at Pullman

UNIVERSITY OF ILLINOIS PRESS

URBANA AND CHICAGO

Library of Congress Cataloging-in-Publication Data
Hirsch, Susan E.
After the strike : a century of labor struggle at Pullman /
Susan Eleanor Hirsch.
p.   cm. — (The working class in American history)
Includes bibliographical references and index.
ISBN 0-252-02791-4 (cloth : acid-free paper)
1. Labor movement—United States—History.
2. Pullman Strike, 1894.
3. Pullman Incorporated—Employees—History.
4. Labor—United States—History.
5. Working class—United States—History.
6. Industrial relations—United States—History.
I. Title. II. Series.
HD8072.5.H57   2003
331.7'62523—dc21   2002007705

To Lew

Contents

Acknowledgments

Every book begins with a spark of inspiration, and for me that spark was Jan Reiff. One day Jan invited me to the Newberry Library in Chicago to see if I would be interested in the papers that the library had recently acquired from the Pullman Company. We went on to create the computerized databases of payroll and employee service records, work our way through the then–not catalogued collection, and become good friends. Over the years we have written papers together, read each other's work, and exchanged every arcane tidbit about Pullman that we could find.

While we compiled databases and wrote papers, the writing of this book often languished. But in that time many people have assisted me, making it a different and a better book than I would have written a decade ago. I want to thank Margo Anderson, Jim Barrett, Lew Erenberg, Walter Licht, and Jan Reiff, all of whom read at least one draft (and some more) of the entire manuscript, for their excellent suggestions. Nick Salvatore and Shel Stromquist helped me hone the early chapters. Thanks also to Eric Arnesen, Liz Cohen, Lyn Hughes, Greg LeRoy, and the economic history seminars at Northwestern University and the University of Chicago for leads to sources, critical analyses, and encouragement.

I have been fortunate to have the assistance of many people in compiling the databases and in other research tasks. Thanks to David Blanke, Brian Coffey, Greg DeBenedictis, Robyn Draper, Robin Einhorn, Michelle Harris, Mark Long, Camille Minton, Andrew Miz, Beth Myers, Dorothy Neville, Ilana Pergam, Manjula Rathaur, Tina Reithmeier, Sarah Rude, Melinda Schlager, Matt Seeberg, Janice Slupski, Anne Spurgeon, Adam Stewart, Andres Tapia, and John Walsh.

The Newberry Library allowed me access to the Pullman collection before it was catalogued, and John Aubrey helped me find my way through it. Without such assistance I could not have begun this study, much less completed it. Archie Motley and Linda Evans provided me, as they have every scholar who uses the Chicago Historical Society, with wonderful guidance to its many collections. I also want to acknowledge the aid of the staffs at the Catherwood Library, Cornell University; the Reuther Library, Wayne State University; the National Archives, both in Washington, D.C., and in Chicago; and the Richmond (California) Public Library. Harris P. Shane, former vice president for industrial relations at Pullman Standard, and an employee of the Pullman Company who preferred to remain anonymous consented to be interviewed, and I thank them for providing information not available elsewhere.

No project of this scope is accomplished without financial support. The National Endowment for the Humanities and the National Science Foundation funded the creation of the computerized databases. The Newberry Library provided a Lloyd Lewis Fellowship that helped me begin the first draft. Loyola University granted me a travel grant for research and two leaves of absence that allowed me to complete the writing of this book.

Finally, I want to thank my family members for their support and their patience. To my mother, Margaret Hirsch, who is always encouraging; to my sister, Barbara Hirsch, who is always inspiring; and to my children, Jesse and Joanna Erenberg, who grew up with this project. My greatest debt is to Lew, my most devoted editor, my strongest supporter, and my best dancing partner.

AFTER THE STRIKE

Introduction

Pullman workers appear in the narrative of American history at two critical junctures: in the confrontation between capital and labor in the 1890s and in black workers' challenge to discrimination from the 1920s to the 1940s. In both instances the actions of Pullman workers shaped the development of the U.S. labor movement and the evolving balance of power between capital, labor, and the state. Yet historical accounts have segregated these episodes and failed to explore why Pullman workers assumed such important, if disparate, roles in U.S. history.

In 1894 Pullman's four thousand railroad car builders sparked a national rail strike that pitted the American Railway Union (ARU), the first attempt by U.S. workers to organize a national industrial union, against a coalition of twenty-four railroad corporations.[1] After immense disruption to commerce and industry, the railroads persuaded the government to intervene. A federal court granted an injunction that made the strike illegal, and President Grover Cleveland sent troops to move the trains. Widespread violence broke out, and the workers were defeated. This nationwide confrontation transfixed the general public with the specter of class warfare and shaped industrial relations in the United States for decades. The railroads achieved their aim of destroying industrial unionism, and until the 1930s most U.S. workers eschewed industry-wide unions for craft-based organizations. ARU president Eugene Debs sought political power for workers by forming the new Socialist Party, while U.S. corporations found that the courts continued to help them break unions and strikes. But national outrage about the intransigence of the companies and the violence of the mobs also induced Congress to pass the first federal legislation that extended even minimal government regulation to labor-management relations, the Erdman Act of 1898.[2]

After the strike Pullman car builders disappear from the narrative of U.S. history, but in the 1920s Pullman's black porters emerge as the vanguard of the African American struggle for economic and civic equality. Led by A. Philip Randolph, they formed the Brotherhood of Sleeping Car Porters, which struggled not only to improve their jobs but also to spread the concept of working-class organization among newly urbanized and industrialized African Americans. In 1937 the Brotherhood became the first black union to wrest a contract from a major corporation. At the same time it consistently fought racism within the white-dominated craft unions of the American Federation of Labor (AFL). During World War II Randolph and the union demanded government action to end segregation in the military and discrimination in employment. Using Brotherhood locals as an organizational base, Randolph created the March on Washington Movement that spurred President Franklin D. Roosevelt to issue the first order banning job discrimination in war industries. In this way the Pullman porters played a critical role in the genesis of the modern civil rights movement.[3]

Historians interpret the 1894 Pullman strike as part of the broader struggle of white craft workers to maintain control of their work and resist de-skilling in the face of management efficiency drives and technological change. They view the Brotherhood of Sleeping Car Porters, on the other hand, as a key manifestation of the "New Negro," who sought opportunity in urban industrial America. I contend that we cannot fully understand either the strike or the Brotherhood in isolation. Nor can we understand why Pullman workers played such critical roles in U.S. history without seeing the strike and the Brotherhood as part of a larger struggle—that between the company and its multiracial, multiethnic, and gendered workforce. The corporation's national scope, its unusual mix of railroad and manufacturing operations, and its large number of black employees gave it a unique role in the U.S. economy and its workers a pivotal position in the U.S. labor force. The social division of labor in the company—the segregation of jobs by race and gender—profoundly shaped workers' struggles. Analyzing how that division of labor originated and why it changed is key to illuminating the influence of Pullman workers on the U.S. labor movement.

This study must address a variety of issues that scholars have raised about the development of labor-management relations, the nature of working-class organization and workers' activism, and the roles of race, nativity, and gender in shaping the paid labor force. How, for instance, did the company develop its labor relations policies? Company goals—maximizing profit and maintaining a free hand to manage labor—remained relatively constant, but the techniques for achieving these goals changed over time. U.S. corporations and labor relations experts developed a variety of strategies based on modes of supervision, applications of technology, and provision of nonwage benefits as they sought to control and exploit workers.[4] Fashions in labor management changed over time and varied by industry. To what extent was the Pullman Company a follower or an innovator in labor relations policies and what effect did its dual role as manufacturer and railroad have on policy creation? Historians have also shown that employers could use divisions between workers based on race, ethnicity, and gender in their struggle for control.[5] This study must also ask, therefore, if and how the Pullman Company used such divide-and-conquer techniques.

Understanding Pullman workers' struggles also entails asking what spurred them to action, how they viewed the economic and social order, and what forms of organization they chose. Scholars have documented a variety of sources for workers' activism, from concerns about conditions on the shop floor to a working-class community's culture to identification with a racial or ethnic group. The basis for union organization also varied from craft to community to industry, and organizations propounded a wide range of ideologies. What was the source of Pullman workers' activism and what types of union structures and ideology attracted different groups of Pullman workers at different times? Moreover, most workers, including most Pullman workers, did not create unions but joined pre-existing organizations as vehicles to achieve their goals. Tensions between the rank-and-file and national union leaders could and did weaken the organizations.[6] What influence did Pullman workers have on the unions that they joined, and how did the national unions' policies affect Pullman workers' struggles with management?

Workers and employers were not the only participants in labor struggles, however. Since the 1890s the state has played an important, if changing, role in labor-management relations and the development of the labor movement. Government policies reflected not only the relative power and influence of capital or labor but also the concern of state officials to maintain domestic peace.[7] Understanding the labor struggle at Pullman involves asking how state policies toward railroad and manufacturing workers shaped the capacity of different groups of workers to organize and affected their choice of unions. Moreover, beginning in World War I, the federal government intervened in labor relations not only by developing and implementing labor law but also by attempting to promote racial and gender equity in employment. What influence did government policies on race and gender have on the social division of labor at Pullman and hence on the workers' struggles?

My analysis of the social division of labor at Pullman is grounded in the premise, confirmed by the vast literature on occupational segregation, that until recently individuals did not compete for jobs equally but found opportunities to be hired or promoted within separate niches of the labor market. Prejudice against European immigrants operated in many instances, but the opportunities open to different groups varied from company to company or from region to region.[8] The American-born sons of European immigrants faced much less prejudice and had access to a much greater range of jobs. Discrimination based on race and gender was much more pervasive and much longer lasting, and therefore these are the primary focus of this study. Nonwhite men and all women experienced systematic occupational segregation, and, before the Civil Rights Act of 1964, change rarely led to integration. During the two world wars, for instance, women were recruited into "men's jobs" in heavy industry, only to be expelled from those positions after the conflict ended. Usually, change simply shifted the boundaries between white and black or men and women. The feminization of clerical work in the late nineteenth and early twentieth centuries and the opening of unskilled, but not skilled, manufacturing jobs to men from racial minorities during the 1910s and 1920s are examples of new opportunities that left segregation intact. But discrimination was not uniform across the United States, and regional differences in racial hierarchies also shaped opportunities. Before the 1940s, for instance, white westerners expressed more hostility to Asians than to African Americans.[9] Did the Pullman Company follow national patterns of sex-typing jobs and regional patterns in ethnic and racial hiring? If not, this analysis must explain why it diverged from the norm.

I also use the concept of labor market segmentation that connects skilled, semiskilled, and unskilled manufacturing jobs to service and clerical work within the same framework of analysis.[10] From this perspective employers "segment" the labor market by creating different classes of jobs and restricting movement from one to another in order to undermine worker unity. Jobs in the primary segment provide high wages, fringe benefits, and opportunities to advance, while those in the secondary segment offer low wages, no stability, and few avenues of upward mobility. Most scholars show that women and racial minorities are concentrated in the least desirable jobs, but they presume that management focused on creating segmentation and that segregation was an afterthought or a consequence of noneconomic forces.[11] In contrast, this analysis reveals that at Pullman the social division of labor by race and gender was an integral part of the segmentation of jobs, not merely a consequence of it.

Those who have explored the social division of labor or labor market segmentation often note that only a company-level focus can bring all the critical factors and actors together, because both segregation and segmentation are products of decisions made at the level of the individual firm.[12] Lack of access to company records has limited the number of studies of this micro level. When it went out of business, the Pullman Company donated its records, including the correspondence, memos, and policy statements of management and the employee service records of hundreds of thousands of individuals, to the Newberry Library. This archive allows documentation of both what management hoped to accomplish and what actually occurred. The Pullman Company is particularly useful for analyzing segregation and segmentation because, as a corporation with both railroad and manufacturing divisions, it hired workers for an exceptionally broad range of occupations—clerical, craft, manufacturing, and service jobs. It also operated throughout the nation and had access to workers from every ethnic and racial group in the population. Furthermore, along with the rest of the railroad industry, it was subject to early government regulation of labor-management relations. With Janice Reiff I created a computerized database of payroll and employee service records from repair shops in Wilmington, Delaware; Chicago; and Richmond, California, that I use to compare opportunities for workers of different nationalities, races, and sexes in three regions of the country. (I describe this database in detail in the appendix.) Thus I can link individual workers, their social backgrounds, and their job histories to the collective issues of company policy, government regulation, and labor union formation.

My analysis extends previous scholarship on the social division of labor in several ways. Many scholars examine racial or gender segregation in isolation, but employers always considered race and gender simultaneously when defining the qualifications for jobs. Thus we must ask how race and gender interacted in decisions about whom to hire for what jobs and on what basis managers made their decisions. To what extent did Pullman managers follow their own prejudices? Did they defer to workers' preferences for racial or gender segregation? To what extent did management manipulate the social division of labor as it struggled to control the workplace? Although most investigations of job segregation ignore workers' attempts to unionize, labor historians have paid more attention to the influence of race, nativity, and gender on union organizing.[13] Yet few have examined the actual development of the workforce and the social division of labor in relation to workers' struggles.

This study documents the long history of racial and sexual discrimination by corporations and unions that continues to shape the capacity of U.S. workers to resist exploitation. It also illuminates the significance of race for the development of the U.S. labor movement by revealing how complicated the relationship among racial groups, company policy, and unions became from World War I on. I challenge the interpretation of historians who have presumed that once workers lost their post–World War I strikes, corporations easily reimposed management control of the shop floor. The Pullman Company reclaimed the upper hand at its repair shops and yards only by using a complex labor-management strategy that included manipulating the racial division of labor in response to regional differences in the militancy of white craftsmen. In the 1920s most U.S. manufacturers hired more African Americans and other racial minorities, and this study suggests the important role that integrating the shop floor played in dividing workers, weakening AFL unions, and imposing management authority.

This analysis also questions interpretations of the development of U.S. unions during the depression and World War II that do not recognize race as a central issue in the process. The unions of the new Congress of Industrial Organizations (CIO) welcomed all workers regardless of race, national origin, or gender and, unlike AFL unions, were not tarnished by a history of racism. The bitter contest between the AFL and the CIO for the allegiance of Pullman workers revolved at least as much around issues of race as it did around whether workers believed that craft or industrial unions would be more efficacious. The ability, and in many cases the desire, to build racially egalitarian unions continued to elude most Pullman workers, and they and the U.S. labor movement paid the price in failed organizing attempts and stunted unions.

1 Working for a Monopoly in Formation

In the months after the 1894 Pullman strike, President Grover Cleveland bowed to a frightened public and appointed a commission to investigate the causes of the violent confrontation. The U.S. Strike Commission concluded that George Pullman's policy of cutting wages but refusing to lower rents for company-owned housing was the primary source of dissatisfaction. This finding minimized fears about endemic class warfare by focusing on what was uncommon about the Pullman situation—that its workers lived in a company town. Yet the testimony given by Pullman and railroad employees revealed other motivations for the strike. Like many skilled workers in the late nineteenth century, they were engaged in a bitter struggle with management for control of their work. Indeed, the factors that led to the 1894 strike emanated from labor policies that were common in U.S. industry.

Although George Pullman, who founded the Pullman Palace Car Company in 1867 and served as its president for thirty years, was known in business and labor circles for his autocratic style and bad temper, his chief motivations were similar to those of other entrepreneurs. His unwillingness to surrender any decision-making power to outside arbiters seemed extreme to members of the U.S. Strike Commission, but many employers whose success in creating their own companies reinforced their belief in their own infallibility shared this characteristic.[1] Pullman had to cut labor costs to achieve his goal of creating a monopoly in sleeping-car service and this, far more than personality, lay behind the development of his workforce and his labor policies.

As Pullman built his monopoly, he pursued strategies to limit labor costs that set the groundwork for company policy in the twentieth century. He followed the lead of the railroads and began to build a bureaucratic structure for labor management, but he also pioneered two strategies of his own, one racial, one environmental. The policy of segmenting jobs on the basis of race held down labor costs for decades. The environmental policy, which rested on the belief that craft workers would allow management to abrogate their standards and autonomy in exchange for nice living conditions, produced the strike of 1894. The failure of Pullman's environmental policy led his corporate successors to search for new methods of cutting costs that profoundly changed the nature of Pullman workers' struggle.

Creating a Monopoly in Sleeping-Car Service

As a young man, George Pullman left upstate New York for the rapidly growing city of Chicago to make his fortune by taking advantage of whatever opportunities arose. Eventually, he made his fortune from the railroads, by designing sleeping cars that markedly improved the comfort and luxury of long-distance train travel just as tourism and business travel began to boom. Pullman sought to profit as other nineteenth-century businessmen did, by creating a monopoly. His company would own the sleeping cars and lease the full service—cars plus attendants—to all railroads in the United States.

To build a monopoly Pullman had to win over railroads and travelers, control his workers, and defeat his competitors. Many railroad officials believed that each railroad should own and operate its own sleeping cars, and his competitors also understood the possibility for profit in sleeping-car service.[2] But Pullman's financial acumen and advertising flair enabled him to best most of his competition. Although he obtained his first contracts in the Midwest, Pullman realized that the greatest need for sleeping-car service would be on the western railroads that covered the longest distances. He participated in financing these railroads and soon secured the most important contracts in the West. His role in rebuilding the southern railroads during Reconstruction ensured that he would dominate that region as well. In the East, where railroads had developed earlier, Pullman faced his strongest competitors and made the slowest progress.

In every region Pullman needed to create public demand for his product in order to trounce the competition. Long before most business leaders understood the role of public relations in creating brand-name identification, he had an extensive program of wooing journalists and opinion makers and disseminating favorable information about the worth of Pullman service through the media.[3] In 1870 he decided to manufacture his own cars, both to maintain that standard and to provide the innovations that would keep his service in the public eye. Pullman sleeping cars were the first to use electric lighting, for instance, and Henry H. Sessions, manager of the Pullman Car Works, invented the vestibule that allowed passengers to move easily and safely between cars.

By 1890 Pullman was well on his way to obtaining a monopoly of sleeping-car service; his company provided service on three-quarters of the track mileage in the United States and held contracts in Mexico and Canada too. His only competitors remained in the northeastern United States. The Pullman workforce numbered ten to fifteen thousand people, scattered from the Chicago headquarters to district offices, rail yards, repair shops, and manufacturing plants throughout North America. In his drive for monopoly Pullman was careful not to undermine the financial strength of his company, keeping large cash reserves and always paying a quarterly dividend of at least 2 percent. This financial depth allowed the company to weather depressions, finance large orders for railcars that railroads could not pay for without credit, and, when the need arose, to survive long strikes.[4]

Yet Pullman had reason to be concerned about profitability: his manufacturing operations often ran a deficit. Soon after he decided to manufacture sleeping cars, Pullman also entered the competition for building railroad cars, producing day coaches, dining cars, freight cars, and streetcars. He sought to monopolize that industry too, and by the mid-1880s he had destroyed some of his competitors by underbidding on orders and taking losses. Long-term contracts with the railroads and increasing numbers of passengers provided the sleeping-car service with large and steady revenues that offset deficits from manufacturing. But even here Pullman's income was not secure; he had to fight threats from the states and the federal government to regulate his service and its prices. As Americans began to demand government regulation of railroad rates in the 1870s and 1880s, they also questioned the high Pullman fares. Although the Pullman Company escaped regulation at that time, it could not easily raise fares further for fear of public displeasure. For Pullman profitability came to depend on containing labor costs in both the sleeping-car service and manufacturing.

Segmenting the Workforce

As he struggled to complete his monopoly, maintain the company's financial strength, and contain labor costs, Pullman made several innovations in labor recruitment and management. His first, in 1867, entailed dividing his workforce into two segments.[5] Race was the rationale for this segmentation, as Pullman hired white people for managerial, clerical, and craft work and black people for service work. The racial division of labor appeared on every train as Pullman divided the work into two parts: conductors collected tickets, sold berths en route, and dispatched telegrams, whereas porters made up berths, carried luggage, and provided other personal services to travelers. Conductors also supervised the porters. Following railroad precedent, Pullman hired white men as conductors but black men, often the newly freed slaves, as porters. Within the close confines of each train, porters could learn the conductor's job easily, and this might have been a path of upward mobility for African Americans. But no porter ever became a conductor.[6]

Differential pay scales further distinguished the two segments of Pullman's workforce: jobs for white men paid "white men's wages," whether monthly salaries or daily wages, while porters received only a pittance. In 1879, for instance, porters earned on average $10 per month, while conductors earned $65. No porter could support himself, much less a family, on his wage. Instead, like waiters and other service workers, porters had to rely on tips. Some could make a good living, but it was always insecure—dependent on working the trains with the big tippers and on a servile performance that pleased white patrons. With this wage policy Pullman pushed more of the cost of his service onto the public and his workers. Because porters comprised about one-sixth of Pullman's workforce, underpaying them significantly enhanced company profits.

Pullman established this segmented workforce on the basis of common conceptions about race and occupation that evolved in the first half of the nineteenth century as the North industrialized while black slavery expanded in the South. Most white Northerners believed that black people were their inferiors, and this belief justified reserving supervisory jobs, both managerial and clerical, for white people. At the same time white Northerners accepted the image produced by slavery's supporters, that black people made especially good servants. Racial hierarchy was less clearly demarcated in crafts transformed by industrialization. As David Roediger has argued in *The Wages of Whiteness*, black slavery shaped the ideology of white craft workers who feared dependency on wage labor and chafed at the constraints of factory discipline. In their struggle against "wage slavery," the white craft workers defined the working class itself in racial terms. Policing the color line became especially important because Southern employers assigned black slaves to skilled jobs and demonstrated that no natural barrier existed between free and slave labor, white and black labor. After the Civil War most craft unions institutionalized white racism through white-only membership criteria. Railroad craft unions all insisted that their work was the province of one race—white—and one gender—men, and they fought for decades to eliminate black workers from skilled jobs on southern railroads. Whether they believed that black people could perform skilled work or not, northern employers could afford to discriminate because they had an alternative, relatively inexpensive source of labor in European immigrants. What set the Pullman Company apart from most northern corporations was that it employed large numbers of people in both service and manufacturing jobs and thus had large numbers of both black and white employees.[7]

The sheer number of black men who worked for the Pullman Company created a complicated relationship between the company and African Americans. As Pullman porters traveled across the United States, the excellent service that they provided reinforced the idea that African Americans were particularly suited to being servants. Yet despite the low base pay and lack of opportunity for promotion, many black men found the job attractive. Lack of alternatives pushed black men toward Pullman employment, but being a porter also had positive features. It allowed black men to travel freely throughout the United States, protected from white hostility by their uniforms, at a time when their physical safety might otherwise have been in jeopardy. Furthermore, tip income could be considerable, and many men traded the certainty of a low daily wage at unskilled labor for the possibility of higher earnings.[8]

While Pullman clearly exploited the situation created by discrimination against black workers in U.S. industry, he did not speak or write at length about his views on race, leaving historians to interpret his actions. Pullman, a staunch Republican, acted on the bifurcated legacy of the party of Lincoln—promoting both civil equality for African Americans and economic inequality in general. He had close ties to party leaders, and Robert Todd Lincoln, the Great Emancipator's son, became a director of the Pullman Palace Car Company in 1880. After passage of the 1875 federal Civil Rights Act, Pullman ordered that tickets were to be sold without regard to race, and his sleeping cars were integrated even in the South until the passage of Jim Crow laws later in the century. Pullman contributed large sums to "Negro causes," and he could believe that he helped the newly freed slaves by employing them. Yet he also took advantage of white racial stereotypes to build his business. In a Pullman car each white passenger had his own black servant, something most could not attain in "real" life. The efficient and courteous porter became the symbol of Pullman travel, part of the luxury of the experience.[9]

As his company grew, Pullman left hiring practices to local managers, who followed his racial guidelines, the lead of other railroad companies, and the constraints posed by regional labor markets. District supervisors took advantage of the low wages paid to women, racial minorities, and new immigrants to contain labor costs for maintaining another part of the standard of Pullman service—the cleanliness of the cars and linens. Pullman cars were first-class hotels on wheels, and they required laundry workers and an army of car cleaners stationed at rail yards around the country. These jobs required few skills, had little status, and paid only laborer's wages. In northern cities, where European immigrants provided the bulk of unskilled labor, most Pullman car cleaners and laundry workers had been born in Europe. In southern cities, where black Americans predominated in unskilled labor, most Pullman car cleaners and laundry workers were African Americans. In the West, Asian immigrants worked as Pullman car cleaners, and the yards there probably hired Mexicans as well. Pullman yards also reflected Victorian gender conventions that defined women's work in terms of the domestic sphere: women usually cleaned the inside of cars, as they might other people's homes, while men cleaned the outsides. Women also did the bulk of the laundry work for Pullman, as they did for their own families, commercial laundries, and private employers. Like other employers, the Pullman Company followed the conceit that women's wages merely supplemented male support and paid women much less than men. Through its yards and laundries the Pullman Company tapped the full potential of U.S. hierarchies of race, nationality, and gender for producing inexpensive labor.[10]

If the porters, car cleaners, and laundry workers labored for low wages, the same was not true of Pullman's skilled workers. By the 1890s the Pullman Company had repair and manufacturing facilities in Chicago; Detroit; Ludlow, Kentucky; St. Louis, Missouri; and Wilmington, Delaware, that together employed about seven thousand people, mostly skilled workers. Other craft workers were stationed at Pullman rail yards where they did routine maintenance and emergency repairs. Virtually all these skilled workers were white men, who, regardless of their ethnic background, commanded much higher wages than did unskilled laborers.[11] In a southern city like Wilmington, where most men were native-born Americans, Pullman's skilled workers were too. In northern cities like Chicago, where immigrants from northern and western Europe dominated the ranks of craftsmen, most of Pullman's skilled workers also had been born abroad.[12] The only less expensive craft workers at Pullman factories, repair shops, and yards were the small number of white women employed to sew and repair curtains and linens, tasks that were considered appropriate industrial work for women because they developed from women's customary household tasks. Like the women car cleaners and laundry workers, Pullman seamstresses labored for about half of what men in comparable tasks (upholsterers) earned.[13]

In the nineteenth century Pullman and his managers used women and racial minorities as inexpensive labor but only in jobs considered appropriate by most white Americans. When he tried to lower labor costs in the 1880s, George Pullman did not alter these patterns but instead followed two other paths, one marked out by the railroads and one his own. Railroads created bureaucratic forms to control far-flung employees and lower costs, and Pullman followed suit in the sleeping-car service. In the manufacturing division Pullman made his second innovation in labor management: building the company town of Pullman, Illinois.

Bureaucratic Forms of Labor Management

In the late nineteenth century railroad companies faced two major problems in managing their workers: how to supervise employees spread across large areas at many different sites and how to cut the cost of high-priced skilled workers like locomotive engineers. In the 1870s, when on-train workers—engineers, locomotive firemen, conductors, and trainmen—organized for higher wages, shorter hours, and seniority systems to eliminate favoritism and insecure tenure, the stakes for management increased. The interaction of managers who struggled to extend their supervision and skilled white men who wanted good pay and secure jobs created the new bureaucratic forms of labor management that began in the railroad industry and spread to all large corporations in the twentieth century.[14]

When railroad managers found that they could not easily replace skilled workers with machines or laborers, they sought control by codifying work processes in order to monitor workers' activities and increase efficiency. They specified technical knowledge and prescribed behavior for each occupation so that supervisors could judge the quality of work and punish or reward accordingly. Workers resisted this extension of management oversight, and fairness in judging performance became critical to workers' acquiescence to the new regime. To achieve fairness managers created new bureaucratic forms—centralized personnel records; standardized rules for hiring, firing, layoffs, and promotions; and grievance and disciplinary procedures. Most important, they eliminated the discretionary power that first-line supervisors had exercised to hire and fire at will. This was the origin of the modern personnel department.

Railroad managers then used their new knowledge of work process-es to educate men for skilled jobs in the expectation that expanding the supply of labor would drive down wages. Managers created internal la-bor markets within each company: rather than seek already-trained work-ers from outside the corporation, management educated employees for better jobs as a reward for good performance. Workers could expect up-ward mobility as a reward for faithful service, as job ladders became com-mon in much of the railroad industry. Increasing the supply of skilled workers created downward pressure on wages, yet individuals found some opportunity for advancement. Companies also encouraged long careers by expanding positive incentives like bonus systems and fringe benefits such as free passes for travel, shipping privileges, and company housing. Internal labor markets had important consequences for the railroad craft unions: they could no longer rely on restricting knowledge of how to do the job to a relatively small number of white men as leverage against the companies. Instead, they insisted that union-controlled seniority as well as satisfactory work be the basis for assignments, layoffs, and promotions.

With its continental scope the Pullman Company faced even great-er challenges in supervising employees than most railroads did, and it adopted the bureaucratic solutions too. The company first instituted the punitive aspects of the system as it sought to ensure that its conductors and porters were people who would not pocket fares en route and "to whose care might be entrusted women, children, and invalids."[15] Man-agement wrote rules for conductors and porters and sent out "spotters" to report on their performance. District supervisors kept records of any infractions and assessed fines based on these records. Along with nega-tive sanctions, the company created the positive incentive of job ladders but only for the conductors. By the mid-1880s Pullman had three levels of pay rates for conductors, and those at the highest level could then move up to supervisory positions in the district offices. Although the compa-ny extended the bureaucratic forms of punishment to the porters, it did not give them the rewards. Porters could never move up and become conductors, much less clerical or managerial employees at the district offices, because this would violate the racial rationale for the segmenta-tion of porter and other jobs. The only step up for the porter was to be-come a porter-in-charge: when the number of sleeping cars on a train was too few to necessitate a full-time conductor, one porter became the porter-in-charge, assuming the conductor's duties temporarily for a fraction of the conductor's pay. Racism compromised the bureaucratic system's fairness, and the disparity between jobs in each segment increased.[16]

Managers soon found that they could use separate and unequal job ladders to pit workers against each other and undermine workers' movements. In the Pullman Company conductors feared replacement by the lesser-paid porters, and the porters envied the higher wages paid for skin color alone. In 1890, when a group of Chicago porters demanded a minimum wage of $40 per month, the company responded by threatening to replace the black porters with white men. Insisting that "there will be a chance to do away with the tipping evil. . . . We would pay the white porters living wages," an unnamed Pullman official told reporters that "if the 'coon' wants to go and go for good, all he has to do is strike."[17] Using both bureaucratic methods and segmentation enabled the Pullman Company to maintain a nonunion workforce on its sleeping cars. Pullman conductors did not join the Order of Railway Conductors, and the company easily defeated the porters' sporadic attempts to organize.

If race became the basis for separate and unequal job ladders in train service, gender assumed that role in the office. For the managers, supervisors, clerks, and ticket sellers at the central and district offices, George Pullman followed railroad practice and hired white men, usually American-born men. He also paid them monthly salaries commensurate with industry standards. Before the invention of the typewriter, men dominated clerical jobs in all businesses because these positions were a form of apprenticeship for management. In the 1870s some U.S. employers used the new technology of the typewriter to carve out a job for white women, who could be paid lower wages. Because Americans believed women should not supervise men or make careers in business, the position of typist did not lead upward.[18] Over time managers created more such positions for white women and effectively segmented the clerical workforce on the basis of gender, with women in the lower-paying, dead-end jobs. The Pullman Company and the railroads created clerical positions for women, but they did so more slowly than corporations in most other industries because the railroad industry clung to the traditional view of the male railway clerk as a manager in training.[19]

The Pullman Company, like the railroads, extolled the possibilities that it provided for white men and prided itself on the supervisors and managers who came up through the ranks. Thomas H. Wickes, the second vice president of the company and its primary spokesman during the 1894 strike, was an exemplar. He was twenty-three when he joined the company as its agent in East St. Louis, Illinois, and he made a career within one company, something that American men were only beginning to do on the railroads.[20]

In the late nineteenth century few American workers had either the job security provided by a seniority system or the possibility for upward mobility that internal labor markets afforded. By using these practices, the railroad industry was the first to create a comparatively stable workforce of long-term employees. By respecting the concept of seniority throughout the sleeping-car service, the Pullman Company encouraged long-term employment even from workers in the least desirable jobs that were subject to seasonal layoffs. Pullman traffic peaked in the summer months and around Christmas; the service required many fewer conductors, porters, and yard workers in the intervals between those times. A seniority system for layoffs and rehiring promised older workers steady employment and allowed newer workers to plan their unemployment and arrange for temporary jobs that would allow them to return to Pullman. Coupled with job ladders, this ensured that workers could have very long "careers" with the company. For instance, one white woman who began as a car cleaner at the Cincinnati yard in 1886 stayed with the company for twenty-eight years. She was recalled after layoffs, promoted to seamstress at the yard, and then to head of the female yard workers.[21]

The Environmental Approach

Initially, the Pullman Company did not extend these bureaucratic forms to its repair shops and manufacturing facilities. Repair shop workers and car builders came from a great variety of crafts, from blacksmiths and carpenters to tinners and upholsterers. Their skills made them useful in many industries, and men in these trades had long formed craft unions and insisted on union wage scales. When railroads sought less costly skilled workers, they usually isolated their repair shops in rural towns, where wages were low and craft unions absent.[22] They expected that these environments, dominated by merchants and farmers, would inhibit formation of the collectivist perspective necessary for union organization.

Pullman officials followed a similar strategy in 1886 when they closed a repair shop in Elmira, New York, to find less expensive labor in Wilmington, Delaware, an old industrial city in a border state. Wilmington's civic leaders lured northern companies with the promise of low wages and hostility to unions. The city offered a large pool of unemployed railroad car builders who could staff the shop, because Pullman's strategy of taking orders at a loss ruined most Wilmington railcar manufacturers. Pullman encouraged its Elmira workers to move to the new location, but those who did found their wage rate reduced to $2 per day from the $2.50 that they had received. The workers contacted the Knights of Labor in nearby Philadelphia, who helped them hold out for $2.25 per day.[23] Even so, the company forced a 10 percent wage cut on its relocated workers and hired new employees for 20 percent less than it had paid. U.S. businessmen like Pullman perfected the tactic of the "runaway shop" in order to cut labor costs long before the globalization of industry in the twentieth century.

In 1879, when George Pullman decided to expand his manufacturing business, he thought in slightly different terms about how to attract unorganized skilled workers at lower rates. Rather than relocate his Detroit factory to an existing community like Wilmington, Pullman made his second innovation in labor management. He decided to create the perfect environment for producing unorganized skilled workers by building a new town.[24] Pullman had built his sleeping-car service on the concept that "people are very greatly influenced by their physical surroundings. Take the roughest man . . . and bring him into a room elegantly carpeted and furnished and the effect upon his bearing is immediate."[25] He decided on a site only fourteen miles south of Chicago on Lake Calumet, where he could buy hundreds of acres of farm- and wasteland inexpensively without sacrificing access to good transportation. The property was close enough to a major city to attract skilled workers, but miles of farmland would separate them from the city's working-class districts, with their union organizers and union wage scales.

Not surprisingly, Pullman built the town in the image of his sleeping cars—beautiful, clean, substantial, planned, and orderly—and named it for himself. He expected the surroundings to compensate workers for working conditions and wage rates that they might otherwise contest. He did not view himself as a philanthropist, nor did he expect merely to create a skilled but unorganized labor force. Pullman believed that through the rents charged for housing, the town, like his sleeping cars, would make a profit. It would be a modest profit, though, in keeping with his idea of fairness to workers. Pullman also realized the public relations value of the town for the company's image and used it as advertising for his products and service.

Visitors from around the country and the world came to admire Pullman, Illinois, with its brick housing, flower beds, and clean streets. The company town, which had a population of 14,702 by 1892, was one of Chicago's premier tourist attractions, not only on its own merits but because Pullman advertised it extensively through the newspapers and a tour guide.[26] His fame came to rest as much on his image as a town builder and enlightened employer as it did on his luxurious sleeping cars. The town revealed what planning could accomplish, as it contrasted so sharply with Chicago's slums and haphazard working-class neighborhoods. With water and sewer lines installed before building began, the town of Pullman had none of the pollution and associated health problems of the city. It won international competitions and was heralded as an example of enlightened industrialism.

Consistent with Pullman's vision of the main purpose of his town, the Pullman Car Works, including the main car-building shops, a large repair department, and administrative offices, stood at its center. From its opening in 1882 the factory produced day coaches and freight cars as well as sleeping cars; the railroads bought about 70 percent of its production. In 1886 the company added a streetcar division, and by 1900 the Car Works was the country's largest producer of streetcars. With four to five thousand employees, it was one of the largest manufacturing establishments in the United States, and in 1892 *weekly* production capacity was 240 freight cars, twelve coaches, three sleeping cars, and a large number of streetcars. In 1880 Pullman's old plant in Detroit had employed one thousand workers to produce only 114 cars—all sleeping cars—in an entire year.[27] The entire Illinois factory complex, consisting of nine buildings covering thirty acres, reflected Pullman's penchant for monopoly, in this instance in the form of vertical integration. Pullman, like other manufacturers, wanted not only to monopolize the market for his product but also to control every component necessary for its manufacture. As a result the town housed a rolling mill to produce iron and steel, a foundry, a wheel-making factory, and huge lumberyards and drying houses. This range of activities meant that, from the outset, workers of all skill levels could find jobs at Pullman.

In race and nativity, workers in the model town resembled those in Chicago. That no black men labored at the Pullman Car Works reflected not only racial ideology but also their small numbers in the area: African Americans comprised only 1 percent of Chicago's population in the 1880s. Most Pullman workers, like the majority of Chicago's craftsmen, were immigrants from northern and western Europe, though the ethnic mix at Pullman was distinctive.[28] As table 1 reveals, men born in Ireland and Germany were much less likely to work at Pullman than they were to live in Chicago, while those born in Scandinavia or Holland were much more likely to work in the model town than to live in the city. This disparity was more a product of happenstance than ideology, even though many Americans, including some Pullman managers, had come to believe

Table 1. Nativity of Pullman Workers (1892) and Chicagoans (1890)

Birthplace	All Pullman Workers	Foreign-Born Pullman Workers	Foreign-Born Chicagoans
United States	28.4%	—	—
Scandinavia	22.5	31.4%	16.0%
Germany	11.6	16.2	35.7
Holland	11.9	16.6	1.2
Great Britain[a]	8.4	11.7	8.7
Ireland	6.4	8.9	15.5
Canada	4.2	5.8	5.4
Poland	1.8	2.6	5.3
Italy	1.6	2.2	1.3
Russia	0.2	0.3	1.7
Hungary	0.2	0.2	0.4
All other	3.0	4.1	8.6

Sources: Pullman statistics are from Mrs. Duane Doty, *The Town of Pullman: Its Growth with Brief Accounts of Its Industries* (Pullman, Ill.: T. P. Struhsacker, 1893), 35. Chicago statistics are from U.S Census Office, *Population of the United States at the Eleventh Census: 1890* (Washington, D.C.: Government Printing Office, 1895), 670–73.
    a. Includes England, Wales, and Scotland.

the claims of scientific racism that there were distinct "races of Europe" with different aptitudes. Duane Doty, who managed the model town, told George Pullman that he thought Germans, Englishmen, and Scandinavians were industrious, intelligent workers but inferior in "executive ability" to those born in the United States. He found the Irish undesirable because he felt that they were more inclined to engage in politics than in "honest work."[29]

While prejudices like Doty's might explain the relatively small number of Irish working in Pullman, they cannot explain the relative paucity of Germans or the large number of Scandinavians and Dutch. Immigrant settlement patterns rather than the preferences of Pullman management created these disparities. The primary German community in Chicago developed on the North Side of the city, a location that precluded commuting to Pullman for work. On the other hand, the Dutch pioneered the farming community of Roseland long before George Pullman decided to build a model town next door. Newer Dutch immigrants continued to locate in Roseland, now attracted to factory work in neighboring Pullman.[30]

The environment that George Pullman created had to mold workers from diverse cultures whose attachment to the United States, much less to the model town, was by no means clear. Many Pullman residents were not American citizens, and each month they sent thousands of dollars through the Pullman post office to family members in foreign countries. A large number of these workers may have been migrants who looked forward to returning to their families and homeland once they earned sufficient money. Like most heavy industries in the United States, Pullman factories employed many foreign-born men who lived singly. Some were bachelors, but others had left families behind in their search for work. Throughout the 1880s and 1890s adult men outnumbered adult women in the town of Pullman by a ratio of 2 or 3 to 1.[31] Despite its image as a family neighborhood, the "Pullman experiment" had to cope with large numbers of single men.

Pullman expected to mold these men into a tractable labor force through their experience in the model town. Good homes were the foundation of that experience, and Pullman insisted on controlling the housing to create a proper environment. He refused to sell homes to his workers, and the town manager issued extensive rules for renters. This often alienated the men, who wanted to own their own homes or found rules, like that discouraging them from sitting on the steps in their shirtsleeves when relaxing after work, restrictive of their personal freedom. Pullman also believed that favorable neighborhood life would create better workers, and this would be especially important to molding single men. The model town had excellent athletic facilities, a library, theater, and meeting halls but no saloons. Although Pullman expected to shape his workers through these institutions, his stress on luxury and profit precluded such an outcome. The library was decorated like a gentleman's club, but it was not free and few workers joined.[32] Furthermore, what George Pullman did not provide, his workers themselves often supported. Saloons sprouted like weeds right outside the boundaries of the model town.

Two areas, sports and religion, best reveal the limits of Pullman's environmental strategy and the alternate influences on workers. Pullman encouraged men to use the town's extraordinary athletic facilities, and the company provided equipment and, in some cases, hired coaches for teams in baseball, cricket, football, soccer, track and field, cycling, rowing, and shooting. But virtually all the surnames of Pullman worker-athletes appear to be English or Scottish, and only a few are clearly German, Dutch, or Swedish. On the other hand, German *turnverein*—gymnastic associations—met frequently in the neighborhoods surrounding the model town. Immigrant workers often preferred to participate in organizations defined by their ethnic identities, which they created and controlled. As they did elsewhere, the English and Scots felt more comfortable joining organizations with native-born Americans.[33]

Workers' desire to define and control their own community organizations shaped the development of religious institutions too. George

Pullman was a Universalist and had little sympathy for doctrinal differences. This, coupled with his desire to create luxurious facilities at minimal cost, led him to construct one substantial church. Pullman expected all to share it, because no single congregation could afford the high rent. From the beginning, Pullman workers wanted their own churches, and many congregations met in rented rooms in commercial buildings. An 1885 census estimated that as many as three-quarters of the town's residents professed the Lutheran or Roman Catholic faiths. Workers preferred services in their native languages, so the town had a Swedish-speaking Baptist congregation as well as an English one and German Lutherans as well as Swedish Lutherans. As these congregations grew, Pullman workers rejected Pullman's vision and built churches outside the confines of the model town.[34]

Pullman could not keep his workers from escaping the environment that he created, because within a few years the manufacturing workforce exceeded the capacity of the town's housing. At that point Pullman decided against building more housing himself, and suburban development of the farmland around the model town began. The company did not force workers to live in the town, but it did give preference in hiring and layoffs to its renters. By the early 1890s more than two thousand Pullman workers lived outside the model town.[35] Increasingly, workers used the surrounding towns of Roseland, Kensington, and Gano to express their own vision of neighborhood, family, and cultural life. In making choices and creating institutions that George Pullman did not control, workers developed an autonomous space in which they could, if they chose, come together. Pullman controlled much, but not all, of his workers' lives. In comparison to those who lived in company towns in mining areas or the textile mill villages in the Appalachian Mountains, Pullman workers had much freedom and much contact with others. Furthermore, barely a decade after the town of Pullman was built, Chicago annexed it along with the rest of Hyde Park township. Even so, Pullman expected the town to be the answer to his problems with skilled manufacturing workers, and he gave much less attention to what happened on the shop floor in the Car Works.

Building and Repairing Pullman Cars

More than 60 percent of Car Works employees were skilled workers, but they plied their trades in a very different setting than the traditional artisan shop.[36] Car building necessitated coordinating the work of many different crafts, whose members had to follow precise instructions to ensure standardized production of each batch of railcars. Pullman insisted on manufacturing every part that a car required, so the Car Works was actually an assemblage of individual craft shops for prefabrication of specific parts, plus large erecting sheds where all the pieces came together. Planning was the first step in production: designers made detailed drawings, and supervisors ordered all the materials needed, down to the number and quality of bolts and screws. Next, Pullman's lumber mill and Union Foundry provided the basic materials—wood beams and planks and bars of iron and steel—that different groups of skilled workers then shaped into specific parts for the cars. In one department woodworkers prefabricated structural items like window frames and doors, while in another cabinetmakers and carvers produced car furnishings such as wall panels, bunk or chair frames, and cabinets. Iron machinists made sure that the wheels were truly round and then pressed them onto the axles; blacksmiths made nuts, bolts, and small forgings; brass workers produced curtain rods, door knobs, and cuspidors; glass workers made window panes and mirrors; and upholsterers and seamstresses made seat cushions, carpets, drapes, and linens.

Construction itself also required a variety of crafts and further coordination, because the typical passenger car was built in sixteen separate steps. One group of carpenters built the bottom of each car onto its undercarriage, and then other carpenters put up the frame and completed the body of the car. A third group of woodworkers followed them and put on the roof, which tinners then covered with metal. Work on the inside of the cars required coordinating the activities of trimmers, who installed moldings and cabinetry; electricians, who wired the cars; and plumbers, who put in the heating equipment. Finally, each car went to the painters, who needed a month or more to complete the entire paint job—inside and out.

Oversight and coordination were the keys to successful production, but workers objected to various aspects of their employment from the very beginning. Unfortunately for Pullman's reputation, nothing the town offered assuaged them. Pullman craft workers labored to specifications provided by management, but they did so by hand, according to their own methods and using their own hand tools. Those who built cars had the same skills as those who repaired them, and Pullman workers judged their wages and conditions by the standards set by fellow craft workers in railroad repair shops.[37] Like the repair shop workers, the car builders resisted deviations from those standards by withholding their labor. Some quit and looked for other jobs, while others engaged in short strikes and some joined craft unions. In the 1880s they created a tradition of activism that was based on common experiences on the shop floor, the support of their community, and the encouragement of the wider Chicago labor movement.

A management style that exacerbated workers' sense of exploitation created discontent almost as soon as the Car Works opened. Department foremen did not directly supervise skilled workers but negotiated a price for a particular prefabrication or construction project with craftsmen called gang bosses. These inside contractors supervised small groups of skilled workers whom the company paid every two weeks at the rates that the gang bosses and foremen set when they negotiated the contract. When the work was complete, foremen inspected the cars and approved payment to the gang bosses of what was left of the overall price for the job. This residual was the gang bosses' profit. In theory a gang boss profited based on his ability to negotiate a good price and to obtain the cooperation of his men. In fact, coordination between departments also determined what remained after wages were paid. When cars, parts, and materials did not arrive in a timely fashion, gang bosses found it difficult to make a profit. Foremen often failed to effect the necessary coordination between departments, and the gang bosses complained bitterly about the mismanagement. As leaders of small groups of men who chose to work for them, the gang bosses communicated their dissatisfaction with Pullman management to the entire workforce. Furthermore, in order to maximize profits Pullman insisted that foremen recompute the rates paid to skilled workers for each new contract to reflect variation in the difficulty of any particular job because of new specifications. Whether the new rates were fair or not, frequent changes created numerous occasions for workers to wonder whether they were being short-changed. Rapid turnover of supervisors further exacerbated the suspicion between workers and management. George Pullman's emphasis on cost cutting led the superintendent to fire quickly foremen and managers who did not produce the desired results.[38]

By 1885 car builders, cabinetmakers, carvers, wood machine workers, blacksmiths, hammer smiths, and freight-car builders had all expressed their discontent by joining craft unions and threatening or staging strikes. Because the company used spies to identify organizers and then fired and blacklisted them, the unions usually held secret meetings. The halls of Roseland and Kensington, especially those attached to saloons, provided the safe places that men needed for organizing. As more Pullman workers moved outside the model town, the supportive space for union organizing increased.[39]

Pullman workers reached out to and were courted by all elements of the Chicago labor movement, from traditional craft unions to a strong socialist movement, the International Working People's Association (IWPA), which was termed anarchist by the capitalist press. In Chicago socialist craft unions, composed largely of Germans and Bohemians, challenged older craft unions in many fields, including metalworking, cabinetmaking, and tailoring. Pullman workers joined unions of both persuasions, and although few commentators thought that many were anarchists, the IWPA leaders Albert Parsons and Michael Schwab spoke frequently at halls in Roseland and Kensington to large crowds that cheered all denunciations of the Pullman Company.[40]

In the mid-1880s many Pullman workers also joined the Knights of Labor, which became the largest labor organization in the United States through its openness to workers of all skill levels and its vision of re-creating U.S. society around the dignity and independence of "producers." The Knights organized workers into district assemblies based on community residence, and in Chicago as elsewhere many skilled workers joined a district assembly while remaining members of their craft unions. The Knights' vision of creating a "cooperative commonwealth," in which workers would own and control economic organizations and no longer be beholden to capitalists, built on the traditional value that U.S. skilled workers attached to independence from wage labor. While advancing this long-term goal, the Knights counseled arbitration (meaning negotiations) rather than boycotts or strikes, the major weapons of craft unions. In the mid-1880s, as Knights of Labor membership soared nationwide, the order chartered a second district assembly, #57, for the South Side of Chicago and its suburbs, including Pullman. The Knights appointed an organizer for the Car Works, who recruited about eighteen hundred Pullman workers in 1885. Pullman workers were attracted to the Knights by the example of both other Chicagoans and large numbers of midwestern and western railroad workers who joined the organization. As the membership grew rapidly, an ideological rift developed in the order. Along with many other assemblies, #57 began to ignore the counsel of national leaders and supported boycotts and strikes by its members.[41]

Before 1886 Pullman workers were not united despite their activism. In part, divergent philosophies on organizing or politics divided them. The company also deliberately staggered rate cuts among the different crafts to avoid creating a sense of common grievance. Language differences further impeded solidarity, as speakers at union meetings had to deliver speeches in German, Dutch, and Swedish as well as English. The divergence in personal goals between the many migrant workers and those for whom the United States was home, whether by birth or choice, could also hinder unity. Migrants, regardless of nationality, often ignored organizing appeals and accepted lower wages than union members wanted. Strikes interfered with migrants' ability to make as much money as quickly as possible and to return to their homelands or support family members left behind.[42]

Despite these barriers to solidarity, shared experiences created a basis for unity among Pullman workers by 1886. They all faced the managerial regime that exacerbated their sense of exploitation, and as craftsmen, whether European or American trained, they expected that their skill would command respect, a just wage, and control over their labor. In early 1886 the company created another shared grievance when it changed its policy on disability. Previously, the company paid medical bills and wages for those injured at the Car Works. Now management insisted that only workers who could prove that they were not personally negligent would receive benefits. Few workers could prove their innocence, and most were thrown back on their own resources. In all probability the company changed its policy because of the scale and therefore the cost of claims: injuries and deaths abounded at the Car Works. Even the commissioners of the state bureaus of labor statistics, who published a laudatory report on the model town, noted the relatively high number of deaths from industrial accidents. Injuries were endemic. An 1888 newspaper article detailed the work-related injuries at Pullman during only one week: three people lost fingers, one bruised a knee, one was wounded in the groin, one suffered crushed toes, two people broke arms, and one broke a foot.[43]

These common perspectives and concerns increasingly unified Pullman workers as a community, although most were new to the area and of diverse backgrounds. They lived side by side regardless of national origin, except for the Dutch, who had created a tight-knit, ethnically distinct community in Roseland well before George Pullman built his new town. Pullman's Dutch workers had a strong and well-organized allegiance that competed with that based on the issues originating in the factory and the model town.[44]

The First Big Strike and Lockout

The issue that finally brought Pullman workers together in common action was their dislike of long hours. The typical workday lasted ten or eleven hours, and Pullman's excellent facilities for recreation only heightened workers' awareness of how limited their time for leisure was.[45] The issue of shorter hours galvanized workers throughout the nation in 1885–86, and unprecedented numbers joined unions and planned a general movement for the eight-hour day. District Assembly #57 endorsed the most radical position on limiting hours—the eight-hour day for ten hours' pay—which had first been proposed by the socialist unions. On May 1,

1886, workers across the nation walked out in support of the eight-hour day; in Chicago as many as sixty thousand left their shops. At the Car Works the Knights began to strike first, but each day the number of strikers grew as the company refused to consider a shorter workday. On the evening of May 4 a large crowd of Pullman workers resolved to strike for ten hours' pay for an eight-hour day, and the next morning the entire Pullman workforce walked out.

Although the strikers belonged to different union organizations, they united as a community under the direction of the Knights. Pullman workers appropriated the public spaces of the model town, holding huge rallies on the baseball and soccer fields to keep up morale. They were undeterred by the attacks on unionism and strikers that followed the Haymarket bombing, which occurred in Chicago just as they made their decision to strike. Probusiness newspapers trumpeted denunciations of radicalism and blamed Chicago anarchists for the bombing, while across the country employers used the occasion to paint unionists as dangerous radicals and crush their strikes. Pullman workers created a "Law and Order League" to ensure that no violence or disorder spoiled their image as respectable workingmen, and they condemned anarchists too and praised the police. They did not escape the antiunion hysteria completely, however, when Chicago newspapers used headlines such as "Hunting Dynamite in Pullman."[46]

Like many other employers, George Pullman rejected his workers' demands for higher pay and shorter hours, and he set a precedent for how the company would deal with strikes in the future by threatening to lock the workers out for sixty days. After two weeks with no progress in negotiations, the workers decided to end the strike as they began it, as a community. At another mass meeting more than two thousand workers resolved to follow the advice of organizers from the Knights of Labor and go back to work together rather than to straggle back as individuals. Many, if not most, striking workers returned to the shop on the company's terms, and Pullman workers endured ten- to eleven-hour workdays until 1902. Yet defeat did not turn Pullman workers away from organization, and many continued to belong to unions, including the Knights of Labor.[47]

More problematic for George Pullman was that his workers had created an ethos of working-class militancy based on community that would sustain them in the future. In the nineteenth century workers relied on the encouragement and support of their neighbors to challenge their employers, who sought to ensure that those neighbors believed in individualism and spurned collective actions. The weakness of Pullman, Illinois, from a management perspective was that it failed to stem the creation of a working-class culture that supported militant collective action even as company policies spurred skilled workers to organize.

That weakness was manifest in 1886, but it would be impossible to ignore after the 1894 strike, which occurred because of the conjunction of economic depression with the underlying turmoil and discontent in the Car Works. In order to increase profits the Pullman Car Works, like other U.S. manufacturers, began to transform production techniques and hence the nature of work. Management sought to replace expensive craft workers, who used their knowledge to control how and at what pace work proceeded, with machinery and less skilled, and thus less expensive, employees. Everywhere, the craft unions that regulated production methods and controlled access to jobs were on the defensive, as managers appropriated workers' knowledge, introduced new machinery, and hired those whom they could train in the new techniques. Factory towns became sites of almost constant struggle, but increasingly skilled workers and their craft unions faced giant corporations whose resources dwarfed their own. Though their surroundings were more pleasant than most, the men and women of the Pullman Car Works were enmeshed in the same struggle.

In many industries companies replaced high-priced and relatively autonomous craftsmen with machines tended by semiskilled workers (operatives), and technical knowledge became the purview of a few engineers and toolmakers and became embodied in the machines themselves. The people who took jobs as machine operatives were often men who were newly arrived from eastern and southern Europe; sometimes they were women and children. By the 1890s this process had revolutionized the steel industry, and skilled workers comprised only about one-third of the workforce. At that point steel manufacturers were able to break the major craft union in the industry, the Amalgamated Association of Iron and Steel Workers, in the Homestead strike of 1892.[48]

The process of change at the Pullman Car Works, compared to that of the steel industry, was still in its infancy. Pullman managers reorganized the woodworking departments in the passenger car and repair divisions, so that by 1893 both departments employed one highly skilled toolmaker along with scores of semiskilled wood machinists. In other departments management introduced no new techniques but forced workers to specialize in one task or aspect of their craft. Builders of passenger cars became body builders, bottom builders, roofers, trimmers, or inside finishers. Painters in the passenger car division worked on the exterior body, interior body, ceilings and headlining, bunks and sash, or small objects. Within these groupings existed further specializations, such as the ornamenters and stripers, who were the highest paid among the painters in exterior bodywork.[49]

The new systems had their greatest influence on the production of freight cars, which had never required as great a range of skilled workers as the passenger cars. Managers used unskilled workers for many tasks, confining craftsmen to those aspects of their jobs that demanded significant training. They also planned the timing of work assignments to keep the pace as fast as possible. By 1893 unskilled laborers comprised almost one-third of the workers in the freight car division, although skilled workers still comprised a majority of workers in each division of the Car Works.[50]

Because they had not yet figured out how to eliminate most skilled workers, Pullman managers sought other methods to reduce labor costs. Except in the repair division, they eliminated inside contracting and replaced the gang bosses with foremen, who now hired, fired, and disciplined without intermediaries. Most skilled workers no longer labored for day rates but for piece rates that they negotiated individually with their foreman and that the company hoped would force them to work harder for less.[51] But increasing the power of foremen proved as ill suited to maintaining an efficient, inexpensive, and docile labor force as inside contracting had been. Some foremen were fair, but others played favorites, demanded kickbacks, and cursed and hit workers. They did not have to follow seniority in layoffs and recalls, and the mere fact of variation in treatment rankled. Nor were the new foremen necessarily better managers than the old ones. Some still failed to coordinate their efforts, and the resulting inefficiencies in production now hurt the workers directly, because they labored for piece rates and earned less when they had to wait for work.

Pullman's attacks on skilled workers' customary control of the labor process triggered confrontations in individual departments. Wood carvers struck in 1887 when managers gave part of their work to cabinetmakers and again the next year when the superintendent assigned the carvers a foreman whom they had not chosen. When the company experimented with new methods of mass production in its lumberyards and in freight car building, workers in these departments responded with strikes too. Workers called numerous small strikes because of the actions of individual foremen, but the superintendent of the Car Works almost always supported his staff.[52]

Management initiatives reflected a deep ideological disjunction between employers and craft workers, who believed that their skills entitled them to high wages and autonomy.[53] Mrs. Duane Doty, the wife of Pullman's town manager, exemplified management attitudes in her guidebook to Pullman. She rejected the principle that underlay skilled workers' perspective—the labor theory of value. While workers believed that their labor was the most important factor in production, she viewed it as only one of many factors, some of which, like capital, were more vital to modern industry. She asserted that inventors and managers were superior to all workers, and despite the theories of anarchists she was sure that even skilled workers could not produce highly complex products like railroad cars without supervision. While she noted with pride that skilled workers predominated at Pullman, she saw them as intermediate in a hierarchy between inventors and managers on the one hand and "dextrous" (semiskilled) and "rude" (unskilled) workers on the other.[54]

Doty coupled her analysis of the hierarchy of skill with the belief that every man's occupation reflected his innate abilities. She opined that "we have never had any patience with the oft repeated dream of Rousseau, that 'All men are created equal, etc.,' for every philosopher knows that the first great law of nature is in the inequality of man. Human beings are born with aptitudes fitting them for widely different positions in life." This philosophy, which reflected the Social Darwinism popular among U.S. business leaders, shaped management's response to workers' demands. If each man achieved only what he was capable of, the Pullman Company was not responsible for low wages or unemployment.[55]

The struggles between Pullman workers and management reflected these ideological differences but also that, like other heavy industries, building railroad cars remained the preserve of adult men. George Pullman never envisioned using women and children to build railroad cars; he planned his town so that women could keep good homes and children could go to school. As they transformed work processes, Pullman managers continued to define car building as "men's work," and they employed fewer than one hundred boys, who were apprentices learning crafts, or "boys"—a designation for youngsters doing errands and odd jobs for various departments. Several hundred women and girls labored at the Car Works but in a narrow range of occupations: most worked in the sewing rooms or in the laundry that cleaned the linen for trains originating in Chicago. These were traditional women's jobs, and the company moved the laundry to the model town in 1885 specifically to provide what Pullman considered appropriate paid work for women. Many women at the Car Works were, like other U.S. workingwomen of the time, literally girls—aged fifteen to twenty-five, the daughters of current or former Pullman workers.[56]

As Pullman managers transformed production, they found little for women to do. Because sewing was traditionally a female occupation, managers believed that women had nimble fingers and excelled at jobs requiring fine motor skills. Managers also believed that women lacked the physical strength of men and could be employed efficiently only for relatively uncomplicated, small-scale assembly work. These notions produced only a few new jobs for women: twenty-two women became glass embossers; four women made push buttons and assembled batteries in the electrical department; and a few others finished small objects like wine racks and step ladders in the "girl's room" of the paint department. Pullman managers shared the conviction of other Victorians that women should be shielded from the rough world of men and that if women entered public spaces dominated by men, like factories, they required a separate, protected space. In the Car Works women worked together in their own areas, separate from men, and could not move freely around the factory.[57]

Because few paid jobs were open to women and children, families found it difficult to make ends meet when men suffered layoffs or injuries. Households needed a second earner to cushion these blows, but the relatively isolated model town did not provide many job opportunities for women and children. Most supplemental earnings that families received came from housewives' taking in boarders and roomers: almost half of Pullman's housewives worked for money in this fashion. As long as the economy was good, most Pullman families enjoyed a middling standard of living based on the combined income of husband and wife or teenage children.[58]

The Pullman Strike of 1894

In 1893 the country plunged into the worst depression of the nineteenth century, and more than three million workers lost their jobs. The Pullman Company closed its Detroit manufacturing plant completely, and between May 1893 and May 1894 the Car Works laid off more than one thousand workers, almost one-fourth of the labor force. The biggest decline occurred in the freight department (45 percent), while the repair department stayed at full strength. Management put many remaining employees on shorter hours and slashed wage rates an average of 28 percent. Although it was company policy to lay off bachelors before married men, this did not spare Pullman families from want. As single men left town to look for work elsewhere, the supply of boarders dwindled, and housewives could no longer generate income. Between lower wages and layoffs at the Car Works and the loss of boarders, more and more families were plunged into poverty.[59]

The inability to support their families troubled Pullman men, who, like other American craftsmen, believed that husbands should be the primary, if not sole, breadwinners for their families. Craftsmen expected wives and daughters to contribute to the household but only to supplement male support. Since the early nineteenth century, U.S. craft unions had predicated their wage demands on what a male breadwinner needed in order to provide his family with a respectable standard of living. Being the breadwinner could make a man vulnerable to management pressure, but it also spurred craftsmen's militancy. During an 1891 strike at the Car Works, a striking painter noted that the foreman "thinks that because we are married men we can be bulldozed into anything he wishes us to do."[60]

This refusal to be cowed, coupled with the inability to support a family, coalesced in the spring of 1894. As a freight car builder wrote to the Rev. William H. Carwardine, a local pastor who sympathized with the strikers: "I have a wife and four children, and it was for them that I struck, as I think that when a man is sober and steady, and has a saving wife, one who is willing to help along, and after working two and a half years for a company he finds himself in debt for a common living, something must be wrong."[61] The leaders of the Pullman strike framed their appeal for support from railroad workers in terms of a gender ideology that prized wives more for their emotional and moral qualities than their wage-earning ability. They painted a picture of a morally well-ordered community of working-class families headed by respectable workingmen: "In all these thirteen years no word of scandal has arisen against one of our women, young or old. . . . We are not desperate to-day, because we are not hungry, and our wives and children are not begging for bread."[62]

As the depression deepened and Pullman workers faced deeper pay cuts and more layoffs, what they perceived as the company's lack of fairness intensified their anger. At the same time that workers suffered, the company did not cut managers' salaries, and it paid stockholders the usual 8 percent dividend. On top of this, George Pullman refused to lower the rents for company housing, because he viewed the town and the factory as separate businesses, each designed to turn a profit. With their pay drastically reduced and their boarders leaving, however, the one-third of Pullman workers who leased housing from the company could no longer afford such high rent.[63] The lack of fairness not only provided a common grievance for workers but it also made the general public sympathetic to Pullman workers. Although George Pullman rejected the idea that he was a philanthropist for building his town, most people expected him to give his workers a fairer deal than other employers might and not to be bound by the cold calculation of profit and loss.

In the early months of 1894 Pullman workers again organized, and this time they joined a new union, the American Railway Union (ARU), the first industrial union with a national scope. ARU leaders believed that when all workers banded together, their power could equal that of the huge railroad corporations. The leadership saw craft unions, which bound workers together across many industries but divided them within any one, as powerless against corporate capital. Yet the organizational form of the ARU respected craft distinctions because it developed from rail-road workers' experiences in the Knights of Labor and craft unions in which they had attempted to form system federations. In each rail system workers formed union locals along craft lines, but the locals created a federation to present unified demands to management. Furthermore, like the railroad craft unions, but unlike the Knights of Labor, the ARU was not truly inclusive—the membership voted to bar nonwhite workers, although it welcomed the small number of women who worked in the industry. This action reflected the intensification of racism throughout U.S. society in the 1890s. Southern states legalized segregation and disenfranchised African Americans, while the biracial unionism that had existed in the 1880s disappeared, except among miners and longshoremen. ARU policy meant that although Pullman manufacturing workers, conductors, and white yard and repair shop workers could come together in the same union, they would be divided from the black Pullman porters and car cleaners.[64]

Virtually all the employees of the Car Works joined the ARU, except for the Dutch workers, who lived apart in their own ethnic enclave and whose ministers spoke out strongly against unions. The Dutch joined the ARU only after the strike began and they found themselves locked out. Even then they insisted on forming a separate local, defined by their nationality rather than their crafts. Unlike the Dutch, the 125 women workers who joined the "girls" local of the ARU were active union supporters from the beginning. Jennie Curtis, head of the local and a seamstress in the repair division, was a prominent speaker at the ARU convention. She decried the "abuse and tyranny of forewomen whose delight it has been to make the girls' lives one of discontent, humbling and crushing them in spirit, forcing many of them to become pliant tools and debased informers of a merciless, soulless, grasping corporation."[65]

Like many workingwomen, the Pullman "girls" took part in labor struggles and joined unions because of their own grievances and the standards of justice that they shared with workingmen. But women maintained their customary separate space. They did not join the same locals as men in their departments (upholstery, glass, electric, and paint) but grouped together on the basis of their gender, as was common in other unions. This allowed women to have their own leaders and meetings and to define their own grievances, but it also assured that the overall leadership of the ARU would be male and that the masculine identity of the industry continued.[66]

The Pullman Company was aware that most of its workers had joined the ARU, because it had an extensive spy system built up over the years as part of its antiunion activities. Several weeks before the walkout, newspapers reported that the company had transferred repair work to its shop in St. Louis, Missouri, in expectation of a strike in Chicago.[67] Management also may have tried to undercut discontent by co-opting some union organizers. The leader of the ARU local in the freight department, Merritt Brown, told the U.S. Strike Commission that, "as I took quite a prominent part there last January and February, trying to get the freight shop organized, I do not see why it was, unless it was to get me out of the way, they made me an inspector, unless it was that I had some influence with the men and they thought if they gave me that position there would be no strike."[68] But in May, when the leaders of the ARU locals at the Car Works presented their grievances about wages and supervision to George Pullman and other officials, management showed no sympathy nor did the officials propose any positive solutions. After foremen laid off several rank-and-file leaders, the workers decided to strike, and on May 11 more than three thousand employees walked out of the Car Works. Following the strategy that had succeeded in 1886, the company immediately locked the workers out and prepared to outlast them.

The American Railway Union was less the instigator of the Pullman strike than the vehicle by which workers organized themselves. The national leaders of the ARU wanted to strengthen their organization before confronting the railroad companies, and they counseled the workers to wait for a more propitious time to strike. Just as members of the Knights of Labor had acted in defiance of that organization's official policy against strikes, Pullman workers acted in 1894 despite the advice of ARU leaders. Both the Knights and the ARU were what Shelton Stromquist has termed "strikers' unions"—movements that workers joined when they were ready for action, regardless of what the putative leaders thought. As Thomas Heathcoate, chairman of the Pullman strike committee, explained: "We do not expect the company to concede our demands. We do not know what the outcome will be, and in fact we do not care much. We do know that we are working for less wages than will maintain ourselves and families in the necessaries of life, and on that one proposition we absolutely refuse to work any longer."[69]

Given its deep financial reserves and the paucity of contracts for new cars, the company was in a strong position to outlast the strikers. Additionally, the ARU's racial bar, which alienated Pullman's two thousand black porters, limited the strikers' ability to pressure the company. Had the porters been striking too, Pullman service might have been crippled. The Pullman strikers, however, never questioned the racial exclusivity of their union, their strike, their jobs, or their community. If the white car builders did not recognize the strength that might have come from biracial unity, the company seems to have. As the strike neared, management instituted the first positive benefit for porters, offering to pay for uniforms for men with ten or more years of service. Pullman porters stayed on the job, and some African Americans volunteered to work for the company in place of strikers, but management was content with the lockout and did not hire any replacement workers for the Car Works.[70]

Preparing for a long lockout, the strikers organized a relief fund and, as they had eight years previously, guards to keep order and avoid property damage. Chairman Heathcoate curbed radical speakers at the nightly meetings of strikers. This behavior elicited widespread praise, and the U.S. Strike Commission commented that "such dignified, manly, and conservative conduct in the midst of excitement and threatened starvation is worthy of the highest type of American citizenship."[71] The chief representatives of the Pullman workers were the type of skilled workers whom the American middle class did not disdain as "rabble": white, native-born (or like Heathcoate, English-born) craftsmen and family men. Jennie Curtis, a working-class daughter forced by her father's death to support herself, represented the small number of women who labored at the Car Works. Generally overlooked was that most Pullman strikers were European immigrants from diverse cultural backgrounds; that many men lived singly and did not have families with them; and that only one-third paid rent to the company.

During the first month of the strike, Pullman workers found support from many Chicagoans, not only the 100,000 union members in the city but also members of the middle and business classes. The strength of the working class and its perspective in Chicago and the respectable demeanor of the Pullman workers meant that many people saw the strikers as having just grievances and as sober, responsible citizens. The new Civic Federation of Chicago offered to arbitrate the strike, a proposal that the strikers accepted but George Pullman refused. The inability of the federation to forge a compromise signaled the disjunction developing between the concept of public interest held by many in the middle and upper classes and the goals of big corporations. This public valued labor peace, but it also believed that workers had real grievances that employers should address. Although only one Chicago newspaper sided with the strikers, even the most hostile believed that Pullman was wrong to reject arbitration. Pullman maintained his absolute opposition to recognizing unions or negotiating with them, because this would have undermined his ability to build company profits through downward pressure on wages. Like other well-financed corporations, the Pullman Company could refuse wage concessions, accept long shutdowns, and ignore public opinion.[72]

Although ARU leaders had counseled against the walkout, they supplemented worker militancy and community support by sanctioning the strike and using the union's resources to help the strikers withstand the lockout. ARU leaders solicited relief funds from railroad workers nationwide, worked with the Civic Federation arbitrators, and organized Pullman repair shop workers in St. Louis, Missouri, and Ludlow, Kentucky. Support for the Pullman strikers extended to more direct action by western railroad workers too. Only three days after the strike began, railroad workers in St. Paul, Minnesota, refused to handle Pullman cars—that is, they began a boycott. Pullman strike leaders thought that a national boycott might be necessary to force the company to negotiate, and they welcomed this action.[73]

When the ARU held its annual convention in Chicago in mid-June, Pullman workers had been on strike for a month with no settlement in sight. They appealed for help from ARU members, who were ready to register not only solidarity with Pullman workers but also dissatisfaction with the railroad corporations. Railroad workers had experienced drastic wage cuts on top of long-standing grievances too. By coordinating their labor policies, the western railroads had given their workers the commonality of experience that underlay their solidarity with Pullman workers. Despite warnings from the ARU leadership that this was not an opportune moment, the membership voted to begin a sympathetic boycott of trains carrying Pullman cars on June 26. What had been a local strike quickly engulfed the nation's railroads.

The boycott proved effective throughout the Midwest and West; workers refused to handle Pullman cars, and repair shop workers on many railroads walked out. Workers struck at Pullman's St. Louis and Ludlow shops and at the Illinois Central's large Burnside repair shop near the Pullman Car Works. Shelton Stromquist has shown how the foundation for this unity developed in communities in the Midwest and West where railroad "boomers" brought their craft union traditions as they moved to new towns and nurtured pro-union working-class communities where none had existed previously. In Ludlow, Kentucky, a suburb of Cincinnati dominated by rail yards and repair shops, Pullman shop workers struck in conjunction with workers from the Cincinnati Southern Railroad yard. The local community supported the strikers, and Thomas Wickes, the company spokesman, asserted that the Pullman Company felt compelled to close its shop there when the police did nothing to protect its property and the strikebreakers it had hired initially. In St. Louis daily meetings at the Central Turner Hall rallied the five hundred Pullman workers and another one thousand railroad workers, while the high level of community support in Chicago made it difficult for the Illinois Central and other railroads that tried to recruit strikebreakers. ARU members everywhere used the claims of worker and community solidarity to create such cohesion. Rallies and assistance to strikers reinforced working-class community cohesion, but sabotaging railroad property and intimidating strikebreakers also helped maintain solidarity. Although workers in Pullman's model town usually were portrayed as blameless in the violence of early July because none of it took place in the town itself, some participated in acts of sabotage and intimidation and in the mobs that burned railcars in nearby yards.[74]

The Limits of Worker Unity

In response to the boycott, the General Managers Association, which coordinated policy for western railroads, recruited strikebreakers and sent out hundreds of armed private marshals to protect them. The ARU's color bar alienated black railroad workers in the South, but most of the strikebreakers were white easterners, unemployed railroad workers who had never been drawn to the union. The vast majority of the ARU's members lived in the Midwest and West, while the railroad craft unions—the brotherhoods of conductors, locomotive engineers, firemen, and trainmen—had more strength in the East. These unions viewed the ARU as competition and refused to support the strike. This lack of sympathy and coordination between labor organizations was not new; it had undercut railroad workers' strikes for several decades.[75] This regional split was manifest within the Pullman Company too, as workers at Pullman's only eastern repair shop in Wilmington, Delaware, worked through the strike, in part on cars that normally would have been repaired in Chicago.

The situation in Wilmington reflected not only the regional basis of the ARU but also the importance of autonomous working-class communities to worker militancy. In this respect the Pullman strike was similar to other nineteenth-century strikes that foundered on the problem of creating solidarity beyond the local community when the latter was the primary source of militancy and support. In the nineteenth century labor movements developed in places like Chicago, where workers had created an autonomous space for themselves and in which a working-class ethos legitimized labor organization. Wilmington workers were incorporated into a local culture dominated by resident manufacturers. Most employers ruled in a paternal manner. A son of the business class described them as viewing "the men" collectively as troublesome but as liking and trusting individual workers. Employers fired any worker attempting to unionize, but they also supported municipal government improvements during the depression of the 1890s to give work relief to jobless men.[76]

ARU organizers found that the majority of Pullman workers in Wilmington would not even listen to them. Only about two hundred attended the mass meeting held on May 27. The first speaker, the ARU leader L. W. Rogers, described the problems of Pullman workers in Chicago in much detail and in a tone that suggested how little communication existed between Wilmington and Chicago workers. Rogers appealed to Wilmington's primarily native-born workers by framing the strike in the familiar rhetoric of the American Revolutionary struggle—the plutocrats as royalty, the union members as patriots, and the strikebreakers as Tories (Loyalists). Yet neither this appeal nor that of H. B. Martin of the Knights of Labor was effective. Fifty or sixty of the seven hundred Pullman shop workers joined the ARU, but none walked out, even though they also experienced wage cuts and complained of incompetent and unfair supervision. The local newspaper reported that the company pressured workers by sending "spotters" to mass meetings and by hiring extra watchmen for the shop. One Pullman worker asserted that "if the men said that they were satisfied they lied, and if so they were afraid of being discharged. They had not the manhood to say that they were dissatisfied."[77] The depression had caused widespread unemployment everywhere, but workers in Wilmington did not have the type of unity that made the recruitment of replacement workers from among the unemployed difficult in Chicago, Ludlow, or St. Louis.

Wilmington workers had not developed an autonomous oppositional culture that legitimized strikes and rallied a working-class community behind strikers. Discontent among skilled workers surfaced sporadically in the city, but no strong craft organizations or large-scale strike activity resulted. The Knights of Labor had claimed a large membership in Wilmington in early 1886 but quickly lost a strike in the leather industry—the only major strike in the city in the nineteenth century.[78] In 1894 those local railroad workers who were organized belonged to the craft brotherhoods, and they scoffed at the ARU. One conductor was quoted as remarking, "The railroad men here aren't such——fools as the railroad men out West. We are in the orders for the insurance we get out of them and we would not quit work if the organizations ordered us to strike."[79]

The cultural dominance of Wilmington's manufacturers rested on the size and composition of the city's population. With only seventy-six thousand residents, Wilmington was small enough to have a unified elite. A relatively small group of successful manufacturers dominated not only the local economy but also Wilmington's government and social organizations. In larger cities the multiplicity of local elites reinforced the possibility for competing perspectives, and scale alone allowed for the development of semiautonomous communities. Moreover, in cities like Chicago with large immigrant populations, workers were less likely to accept the cultural authority of American-born manufacturers: language and culture reinforced class differences. In Wilmington the majority of workers were native-born white Americans who shared a common language and history with their bosses. The largest group of immigrants was the Irish, who were also English speakers. The Pullman workforce reflected local conditions: 80 percent were native-born white Americans and another 4 percent were born in Ireland. Although the city had some immigrant churches and cultural groups, no ethnic or working-class neighborhoods provided autonomous spaces in which workers could organize.[80]

Wilmington's paternal regime also rested on the ideology of white supremacy, which bound men together across class lines. Delaware had been a slave state, and in 1890 about 10 percent of Wilmington's population was black. The caste position of African Americans at the bottom of the social hierarchy underlay beliefs about citizenship, manhood, and status and provided the central conflict in local politics. Wilmington's white residents had legally segregated its public schools, and most public accommodations were segregated by custom. Race baiting figured in every election, and poll taxes disenfranchised many African Americans. Black men found jobs primarily as casual laborers; they had no opportunities for economic advancement and were barred from trade unions. When employers, such as Pullman's repair shop, followed the color line in hiring, they encouraged their white workers to see them as allies and accede to the paternal regime. Consequently, if white workers defied their employers, they had broken the alliance, and employers were free to transgress the color line. This is what Wilmington leather manufacturers had done in 1886. They broke the Knights of Labor strike by hiring black men as well as Polish immigrants as replacement workers.[81]

Breaking the First Industrial Union

The Pullman strike was a transitional strike in two senses. Workers relied on the supportiveness of local communities as they had throughout the nineteenth century, but many also displayed the industry-wide allegiance that would come to the fore in the twentieth century. The strike also revealed the crucial role that the federal government would come to play in the balance of power between workers and employers. Local public opinion could not control big corporations bent on breaking unions regardless of the cost to society. The federal government had the power to counteract major corporations, but in 1894 President Grover Cleveland took their side. Railroad officials and business leaders, especially the Chicago meatpackers, whose production had plummeted when the boycott disrupted rail traffic from the West, called for government help, and the national press began to portray ARU president Eugene Debs as a dictator with the United States at his mercy. Although union members made every effort to avoid interfering with the mails and to curb violence, the railroads persuaded the president that the strike threatened the nation. As the leader of the "Gold Democrats," the most conservative probusiness wing of the party, Cleveland responded as U.S. capitalists expected officeholders at all levels to do. The attorney general, Richard Olney, a railroad lawyer who continued his private practice while in office, secured an injunction against the union, making any attempt by ARU officials to continue the strike illegal.

As the federal government entered the dispute, authorities jailed Debs and other union leaders when they refused to call off the strike, and the president ordered troops to Chicago and other strike centers over the opposition of local Democratic officeholders. As troops began to shield strikebreakers, violence broke out in rail yards across the country. At the height of the strike more than fourteen thousand troops, marshals, and police were on duty in the Chicago area alone, where twelve people died in rioting and more than one thousand railcars were destroyed.

Under attack from the government as well as the corporations, the ARU looked for support from other unions. About twenty-five thousand Chicago workers struck in sympathy with railroad and Pullman workers, including several thousand butchers who walked out of Chicago packinghouses, combining their own demands for higher wages with the sympathetic action. The Chicago Building Trades Council called for a nationwide general strike if Pullman did not consent to arbitration. But most national unions, as well as the leadership of the American Federation of Labor (AFL), refused this call, because they feared that sympathy strikes would bring the full force of employers and government down on them too. Indeed, the meatpacking corporations decimated the butchers' union by hiring thousands of replacement workers.[82]

Because of federal intervention the Pullman boycott collapsed in the middle of July, but the Pullman strike continued. Rank-and-file leaders at the Car Works refused to call an end to the strike, even as the company reopened various departments under armed guard and advertised for new workers. By early August about eight hundred people were at work. Most were new employees from outside the area, but several hundred Dutch workers also broke with the union. Although initially most workers at the Illinois Central's Burnside repair shop stayed on strike too, community unity began to crumble. The strikers and a women's auxiliary composed of their wives, daughters, and girlfriends mobilized to turn back strikebreakers, but increasingly the situation seemed futile. Throughout August individual workers began to break with their neighbors and to accept Pullman's offer of re-employment if they would tear up their ARU cards and sign contracts pledging not to join unions. Perhaps as many as nineteen hundred did so, and by the end of August the labor force at the Car Works numbered twenty-seven hundred. While some workers chose not to return to Pullman, the company denied employment to others and blacklisted strike leaders like Heathcoate.[83]

The U.S. commissioner of labor estimated that three-quarters of the railroad workers who joined the boycott lost their jobs, although some may have found employment in later years by working under assumed names. Thomas Wickes, the Pullman spokesman, asserted that the company rehired only sixty strikers at the St. Louis shop and none from Ludlow. The company treated workers at these shops much more harshly than employees of the Car Works, perhaps because George Pullman continued to hope for a positive relationship with the residents of his model town.[84]

In crushing the strike the railroads, the Pullman Company, and the federal government also destroyed the American Railway Union. Although some ARU locals continued to exist in the West, Eugene Debs and other leaders dissolved the union in 1897. They decided that lack of political power was the workers' greatest weakness, and their solution was to create a new Socialist Party. But the strike also destroyed George Pullman. Many Americans now viewed him as the embodiment of arrogance and intransigence, not as an enlightened employer. The model town became an image maker's nightmare, a glaring example of the overweening power of big corporations. Furthermore, Illinois Democratic politicians had not forgiven the use of federal troops over their vehement protests, and the Illinois attorney general brought a suit against the Pullman Company, alleging that it had overstepped its charter and had no legal right to own a town. George Pullman spent his last years fighting this attempt to take away his creation.[85]

Pullman's environmental strategy failed because craftsmen cared more about controlling production and maintaining what they saw as just wages and working conditions than they did about modern housing and superior community facilities. Yet challenging workers' control and wages remained critical to increasing profits. After Pullman died, his corporate successors abandoned the environmental strategy and followed a new method for accomplishing these goals. In so doing, they divided Pullman manufacturing workers from railroad workers and channeled workers' activism in disparate directions.

2   Two Roads to the Open Shop

In the years after the 1894 strike the Pullman Company faced two challenges: replacing the failed environmental strategy for controlling manufacturing workers and coping with newly militant black and white workers in the sleeping-car service. Company officials looked to industry leaders for models of how to proceed, and they developed different strategies for different workers. In the sleeping-car service they followed railroad corporations in elaborating the bureaucratic structure of employment. Through a system of rules and routines that created a sense of fairness as well as possibilities for upward mobility and fringe benefits, they sought to create workers who would stay with the company for many years, accept the wages offered, and defer to the direction of supervisors. At the Car Works company officials still wanted to wrest control of production from craft workers and to cut labor costs, but now they followed the methods developed by metal manufacturers to accomplish these goals. These focused on using technology and industrial engineering to transform methods of production and eliminate craft workers, not on creating a bureaucratic structure of employment.

The company's strategies for labor-management relations enabled it to remain an "open shop," that is, to keep its workers from unionizing successfully. Officials found that they needed to tailor policies carefully to control their most troublesome workers, the Chicago repair shop workers, but they succeeded without resorting to the racial strategy that some railroads began to use to undercut strikes and unions—hiring black workers as strikebreakers and replacement workers.

From Environmental to Shop-Floor Strategies

When George Pullman died in October 1897, his family's day-to-day involvement in company management ended, and a modern corporate bureaucracy developed. But men who had worked for Pullman for years headed this bureaucracy, and the longevity of these corporate officers created continuity with much of his vision for the company in the decades after his death. At the top Robert Todd Lincoln, a company director and general counsel, succeeded Pullman as president, and Thomas Wickes, who had been in charge of "the detailed affairs of the company," continued as vice president. Although Wickes died in 1905, Lincoln remained president until 1911. John S. Runnells, who had been with the company since 1888, succeeded Lincoln and served until 1922.[1]

Lincoln began his tenure by pushing ahead with George Pullman's course of monopolization. In 1899 the corporation absorbed its last great rival, the Wagner Car Company of New York, which manufactured railcars and held the sleeping-car service contracts on Vanderbilt-owned railroads in the Northeast. Now the Pullman Company monopolized sleeping-car service nationwide and was one of the largest railroad car manufacturers too. J. P. Morgan, William K. Vanderbilt, and Frederick W. Vanderbilt joined the company's board of directors, integrating it even more firmly into the core of American capitalism. The expansion of service nationwide necessitated new offices, new yards, and a new repair shop in Buffalo, New York. By 1904 the company's workforce numbered more than twenty thousand, one-third larger than the prestrike high of fifteen thousand.[2]

While corporate officials pursued Pullman's policy of monopoly, they rejected his environmental strategy in favor of one that relied on changes in methods of production and supervision. The shift began almost immediately after Pullman's death, when the company stopped fighting the lawsuit that attacked its ownership of the model town. Although the company did not actually sell the houses and commercial spaces until 1907, Pullman's vision of molding workers through their environment faded quickly. Within a few years the company had filled in Lake Vista in front of the Car Works and converted most parks to industrial use. First to go were the old playing fields where workers had rallied in 1886 and 1894. These became storage and roundhouse spaces for the new Calumet Repair Shop that officials created when they separated the repair department from the Car Works in 1900. Pullman housing, now two decades old, deteriorated too, and in 1910 the census taker even reported "slum conditions" in the Pullman apartment blocks where ten or twelve people crammed into three or four rooms.[3]

As the company retreated from using the environment to mold manufacturing workers, management looked to changes in methods of production and supervision at the Car Works to wrest control from craftsmen. When the national economy rebounded after 1898, orders for railcars revived, and by 1904 employment at the Car Works stood at approximately seven thousand, almost twice what it had been in the early 1890s. Increasingly, these workers were helpers and semiskilled specialists. Product innovation also decreased the amount of sewing and ornamental wood and brass work required. The new methods of production had such a dramatic effect that in 1900 only 40 percent of the manufacturing workers were skilled, compared to approximately 60 percent in 1893.[4]

Many new workers, especially in specialist or semiskilled positions, were men from southern and eastern Europe. From the mid-1890s on, Italians, Poles, Hungarians, and Russians flocked to the South Side of Chicago for jobs in its many factories. Most newcomers took unskilled or semiskilled jobs, but those with skills also found the Pullman Car Works and the Calumet Repair Shop attractive. As one Polish carpenter wrote to his cousin: "I intend also in the future to get into a passenger carshop, for not far from me there is a big carshop in which thousands of carpenters are working. It is, I have heard, the main carshop for whole America, called 'Pullman.'"[5] At the Calumet Repair Shop almost one-fifth of those hired for skilled positions in the decade after the strike were from southern and eastern Europe, as were two-fifths of those hired for semiskilled jobs. Although the new immigrants met discrimination in some companies and individual foremen might have been prejudiced against particular groups, no corporate-level policy encouraged or sanctioned discrimination against any group of Europeans. Because the company assembled and repaired cars for its sleeping-car service in Great Britain and Italy, as well as Mexico and Canada, Pullman executives were well aware that no nationality had a monopoly on the skills necessary for car building and repairing.[6]

As they transformed production processes at the Car Works, Pullman managers still avoided the least expensive labor strategy—hiring women or children. Women remained in the sewing and laundry departments and in glass embossing, but they found no new avenues of employment.[7] Managers' concepts of appropriate work for women and children had not changed, and the continued influx of adult males from Europe who would labor for comparatively low wages meant that Pullman never faced a labor shortage severe enough to force the managers to rethink their position.

Nor had the time arrived when the Car Works would hire black men. African Americans had begun to move to Chicago in the 1890s, but their numbers in the local population remained small. The vast majority of Chicago manufacturers followed the color line, and only the meatpacking corporations had crossed it. Discrimination in housing also meant that few African Americans lived near the Car Works. What would become Chicago's black ghetto was developing just south of the downtown, miles from the model town and its employment opportunities. Many Pullman porters lived in the black ghetto, close to the rail yards and stations from which they worked, but as long as European immigrants flocked to the far South Side of the city, managers at the Car Works had no incentive to reach north to hire black Americans.[8]

The larger and more ethnically diverse manufacturing workforce and the specialization of jobs did not, in and of themselves, enhance company profits. Setting piece rates in ways that would drive workers to do their utmost for the least remuneration remained necessary but not easy. Many steps in the production process were carried out by small groups of people who could collude to slow the pace of their labor. Management expanded the supervisory ranks to counter such collusion by creating the position of "leader" for each major specialty or work group within a department. The leader worked along with a small group and kept the record of jobs completed, which determined each individual's earnings.[9]

If the new methods, supervisors, and workers increased profits, they did not bring labor peace, because the company maintained many practices that had caused the 1894 strike. Readjusting wage rates for each new contract continued, as did abuses by foremen. A seventy-year-old cabinetmaker, Orrin Lawrence, expressed his discontent in the most extreme fashion in 1901 when he shot his foreman, Gustave Doemling. Company spokesmen claimed that Doemling laid Lawrence off because he was too old to produce good work and that for five weeks he pestered the foreman for another job. Then, according to one newspaper, "Lawrence's pent-up grief of five weeks broke forth. Without a word he drew a revolver from a pocket, and, aiming at Doemling, fired."[10] Another newspaper concluded that Lawrence was less aggrieved than angry, and the cabinetmaker, who had been employed at the Car Works for eighteen years, asserted that he had long-standing complaints. When the company raised wage rates in the late 1890s in response to worker demands, Doemling had given him only a small increase, because "Mr. Doemling preferred young foreigners to me, an old, experienced Yankee workman."[11] Lawrence asserted further that Doemling had discharged Lawrence's grandson for a "trivial offense" and then rehired the young man at a lower wage, as part of a "general scheme of persecution against me." Lawrence's charges suggest how competition for jobs created or reinforced hostility toward immigrants. They also highlight the insecurity that older men and women faced in U.S. industry, because workers had no pensions to fall back on and supervisors often preferred the young on the presumption that they could work faster.[12]

The Limits of Skilled Workers' Power

Although the 1894 strike had been crushed, the American Railway Union (ARU) disbanded, and many less skilled, often immigrant, workers hired at the Car Works, Pullman car builders and repair shop workers continued to see themselves as craftsmen with common concerns and perspectives. By 1900 workers at the Calumet Repair Shop and the Car Works were organizing again. Beginning in 1898, union membership surged across the nation in industries from meatpacking and coal mining to the building trades. Craft unions affiliated with the American Federation of Labor (AFL) expanded quickly, and they had close to 250,000 members in Chicago by 1903. Pullman workers also turned to AFL craft unions, some of which, like the carvers' union, had members at the Car Works before the 1894 strike. Others, like the International Association of Machinists, were newcomers to the Car Works. At first, many employers acceded to union demands in order to maintain production during the economic expansion, but as workers' demands escalated, employers began to resist and strikes became the order of the day. At the Car Works, where management resisted wage increases, organizing also quickly led to new strikes. Passenger car builders struck in September 1901 for an increase in piece rates, and freight car builders and numerous Pullman craftsmen followed their lead in the next year.[13]

The working-class ethos of their community continued to bolster the activism of Pullman manufacturing and repair shop workers. Eugene Debs's new Socialist Party had its national headquarters in Chicago, and the Pullman area had one of the city's strongest Socialist ward organizations. While Scandinavian and German skilled workers were especially conspicuous among Pullman Socialists, the new immigrants employed by the Car Works were not immune to radical politics, either. Some Italians who settled in the Pullman area quickly formed their own socialist, syndicalist, and anarchist groups based on political ideologies that they brought with them from their homeland. Such diverse radical movements reinforced the local working-class ethos that had long supported opposition to employers, if not to capitalism itself. Radicals remained a minority, and Socialist candidates only once polled more than 20 percent of the vote in the ward that included Pullman. In 1903, when the Republican Party repudiated its own nominee for alderman because of charges of corruption, the Socialist candidate won the aldermanic seat with 37 percent of the vote. This one-term alderman, William Johnson, was head of the Pullman local of the International Carvers Association and an employee of the Car Works.[14]

By September 1902 journalists estimated that three-quarters of the workers at the Car Works and the Calumet Repair Shop had joined AFL unions. Despite the level of organization, no one big union brought everyone together. Men joined union locals across ethnic lines but on the basis of craft or department, and women organized separately, as they had in the past. After the defeat of the American Railway Union, few workers were attracted to the concept of industry-wide organizing. In Chicago the Amalgamated Meat Cutters and Butcher Workmen organized men and women of all skill levels and ethnicities, but such inclusiveness was unusual. Instead, most unions pursued their goals individually, leaving those workers who were most easily replaced at a great disadvantage.[15]

The seventy-five women laundry workers at the Car Works found the limits of such go-it-alone unions in 1903 when they struck for a nine-hour day at ten hours' pay. Unfortunately for the women, the company found them expendable, and it locked them out and sent their work to commercial laundries in Chicago. Officials eliminated the laundry at the Car Works, and consequently by 1904 the manufacturing plant employed women in only two areas—sewing and glass embossing.[16]

The laundry women were not the only unskilled workers who challenged Pullman management at this time. During the union ferment at the turn of the century, many unskilled workers organized, and for the first time Pullman yard workers struck. In 1902, 350 men who cleaned cars for Pullman in Chicago formed the United Order of Car Cleaners #1 and went on strike for Sundays off, higher wages, and an end to piecework. Car cleaning was still a "white job" in Chicago, and during the strike the company attempted to keep its sleeping cars running by using black men as well as some white male office workers as temporary cleaners. The company acceded to the strikers' demands, however, when the public complained about dirty cars. The Pullman Company, like most local employers, was not yet ready to permanently alter the color line in Chicago, and with business booming the company chose to give in to the demands of even its least skilled white male workers.[17]

Union locals at the Car Works and the Calumet Repair Shop soon posed a greater threat to management control when they joined with other unions in the Pullman area in 1902 to form the Calumet Joint Labor Council. This organization facilitated sympathetic movements within the community, and it decided on a common program demanding shorter hours and an end to Sunday work. The council successfully pressured area employers, including Pullman, the Illinois Central Railroad, and International Harvester, for the nine-hour day. Without recognizing the unions, Pullman management responded to the depth of worker dissatisfaction and agreed to ten hours' pay for nine hours' work. When the fifty-four-hour week replaced the sixty-hour week at the Car Works and the Calumet Repair Shop, the average hourly wage rose from twenty-five cents to thirty cents. The reduction in hours also forced the Car Works to hire more than one thousand additional workers to maintain the same level of production.[18]

Yet shorter hours alone did not satisfy Pullman workers or their neighbors, and in 1903 Pullman locals and those from the Illinois Central's Burnside repair shop planned a general strike to eliminate piece rates. Burnside workers had been the first to walk out in solidarity with the Pullman strikers in 1894, and railroad repair shop workers and manufacturing workers joined forces once more. With such far-reaching demands looming, the Pullman Company decided to fight. In December 1903 management closed the Car Works for several weeks. International Harvester closed its plants at the same time, and workers feared that this was the beginning of a joint lockout designed to break unions throughout the area.[19] Although a lockout did not materialize at this time, workers' suspicions were well founded.

By 1903 U.S. employers had combined to bolster their authority and combat the threat of the AFL unions. Their "open shop" drive sought to break union contracts through coordinated use of some old methods—lockouts, injunctions, and hiring strikebreakers—and one new one: a public relations campaign to educate the general citizenry about "union tyranny." The centerpiece of this ideological offensive was the defense of each worker's freedom not to join a union but to work as an individual.[20] The American workingman, unlike his counterparts elsewhere, had been enfranchised for a century, and his independence as a voter and citizen was a staple of political rhetoric. Accordingly, the proponents of the open shop asserted that the American workingman could meet his employer as an equal and negotiate the terms of his employment without outside interference. Unions, like monopolies, coerced individuals and therefore posed a threat to American democracy. That it might seem hypocritical for a corporate monopoly to label unions as monopolies did not seem to faze Pullman spokesmen.

Only the need to complete contracts for railcars restrained Pullman officials from acting decisively. Once the economy went into recession and contracts became scarce in the summer of 1904, the Car Works began mass layoffs. In September Pullman joined with other employers in what one newspaper called the "$1,700,000,000 Capital War on Unions." U.S. Steel, International Harvester, U.S. Rubber, the Pullman Company, and others either cut wages, which sparked strikes, or locked their workers out in a massive and coordinated open shop campaign. Pullman workers received written notice that "your services will be required no longer and you are requested to remove your tools at once."[21] On the South Side of Chicago, Pullman, the three Harvester plants, and the stockyards locked out more than twenty-six thousand workers.

Across the city and indeed across the country, the corporate offensive succeeded in breaking unions and cutting wages. Many companies found an old weapon, strikebreakers, not the new ideology, to be their most effective tool. Chicago meatpackers fought the two-month strike of their predominantly immigrant employees by hiring packinghouse workers from other cities and by importing thousands of black workers from the South. Yet the packinghouse owners did not reward most black strikebreakers with permanent jobs, despite their critical role in defeating the union. Only a few hundred remained in the plants, and many white strikers, now embittered against African Americans, returned to their jobs on the companies' terms. Locally, this strike was a watershed; it exacerbated racial tensions between white and black Chicagoans and revealed to other employers the utility of manipulating racial divisions.[22]

But the Pullman Company did not break unions at the Car Works and the Calumet Repair Shop by using strikebreakers, white or black. Rather, as it had in the past, it simply locked workers out and waited for hunger to force them back on company terms. Car builders and repairers, many of whom had already been laid off for several months, responded as they had to lockouts in 1886 and 1894: some left the area to look for work elsewhere, while others stayed but became disheartened by the company's ability to sustain a long lockout. Management announced the reopening of the Car Works and the Calumet Repair Shop after only a few weeks, and the Calumet Joint Labor Council, which was coordinating efforts by area unions, voted to allow Pullman locals to decide whether to order their men back to work. Like those who had organized with the Knights of Labor in 1886, Pullman workers decided to return together, and thousands asked for their jobs back. This democratic process reflected the belief, shared by most U.S. workers, that workers themselves should decide when to strike and when the price of militancy was too high.

Pullman car builders and repairers returned on the company's terms: lower wages for all skilled workers and a signed promise to "work as individuals." Yet the workers had not lost all that they had won in the preceding years. The company did not rescind the fifty-four-hour week or cut laborers' wages.[23]

In a year when stockbrokers heralded the corporation's earnings as the largest in its history, management locked workers out not because of simple financial need but to crush the unions before they became strong enough to demand recognition and the abolition of piece rates. If company officials now rejected Pullman's environmental strategy, they clung to his belief that unions undercut profits. Thomas Wickes reaffirmed that "the Company never has recognized labor unions and will not permit them to run its business. It will continue to control its shops and to determine the conditions under which they are operated."[24]

The Pullman Company defeated its workers more easily in 1904 than in 1894, because AFL unions were less capable of successfully challenging a national corporation than the ARU had been. Pullman conductors and porters continued to perceive no common interest with car builders and repair shop workers and remained on the job. Most organized railroad workers were not affiliated with the AFL, so none boycotted Pullman cars in support of Pullman strikers. Furthermore, a community-based association like the Calumet Joint Labor Council could not rally workers in other cities to strike in sympathy, as the ARU had done, and once again the company simply shifted repair work to other shops. Pullman's Wilmington workers had played a similar role in undercutting the 1894 strike, but workers at the St. Louis and Buffalo shops also remained on the job during the 1904 lockout. The St. Louis shop had rehired few of the 1894 strikers, and the new workers there, like those at the recently opened Buffalo shop, had not joined the AFL unions. The weakness of Pullman car builders and repair shop workers in Chicago and their allies at other local factories was not unique. During the open shop campaign major corporations defeated virtually all the AFL unions that had made inroads among their employees. Pullman workers had looked to craft unions and their local community, but these were powerless against united capitalists, who now needed no government troops or injunctions to win.[25]

The 1904 lockout signaled the end of an era: skilled workers had lost control of car building. Craftsmen did not disappear from the Car Works, but they never again led a plantwide movement to secure their vision of a just workplace. Although Pullman's environmental strategy failed, the company prevailed by joining with other manufacturing corporations in the open shop movement. Just as management created an open shop at the Car Works, however, employees of the sleeping-car service became more demanding.

Developing Bureaucratic Labor Relations

At the same time that Pullman manufacturing and repair shop workers organized in AFL craft unions, the conductors and porters also threatened to organize. Ironically, the federal government, which had broken the 1894 strike, was responsible for this development. The presidential commission established to determine the causes of the strike recommended that the railroad industry settle labor disputes through arbitration. In the Erdman Act of 1898 Congress not only established machinery for voluntary mediation of railroad labor disputes but also guaranteed railroad-operating workers the right to representation through craft unions. By supporting craft unions, the Erdman Act undercut any industrial union movement like the ARU, but it also began the process of making the federal government an arbiter in the class struggle rather than merely a tool of big capital.[26]

Although the Erdman Act did not apply to sleeping-car companies, the recognition that it provided for unions of railroad-operating workers nonetheless posed a threat to the Pullman Company's commitment to an open shop. Within a few years membership in the brotherhoods of railroad engineers, conductors, firemen, and trainmen soared, and they wrested real concessions from some railroads.[27] The Pullman Company refused to recognize the Order of Railway Conductors, and its largest group of on-train workers—the black porters—were shunned by the all-white railroad brotherhoods. But Pullman conductors and porters demanded wage increases and threatened to form unions every time unionized railroad workers won better contracts.

Company officials responded by incrementally extending George Pullman's policy of adopting the bureaucratic labor management strategies developed by the railroads. In 1902, after conductors and trainmen on the western railroads combined into a regional association and forced the railroads to negotiate the first multiemployer contracts with higher wage rates, Pullman conductors and porters demanded the same wages. The company responded by raising conductors' rates in a schedule tied to length of service. By linking wage increases to a seniority system, this policy discouraged turnover while it encouraged good work and obedience. The porters, though, were not as fortunate. The company instituted a minimum monthly wage of $25 for them, but most porters received no benefit because they already earned more. The company followed up on these steps by establishing a department of industrial relations at the Chicago headquarters to centralize record keeping and policy making for the sleeping-car service.[28]

The porters received less than the conductors did because they had much less leverage against the company. White railroad workers refused to allow the porters into their unions, and black men still found so few job opportunities in U.S. industry that the Pullman Company always had more than enough applicants for each porter position. But the militancy of the porters led the company to extend new benefits and policies to them even as it refused to address the basic inequity in their pay rates. Black porters found themselves more likely to wrest concessions from Pullman when they aligned themselves with the white railroad brotherhoods that rejected them, a situation that would plague the porters for decades.[29]

The federal government became more of a factor in Pullman labor relations in 1906 when Congress extended the oversight of the Interstate Commerce Commission (ICC) to sleeping-car companies. The company fought federal control up to the Supreme Court, but it lost. From then on the ICC determined the rates for Pullman service, just as it did for rail service generally. When the company no longer had sole control over rate setting, it concentrated harder on developing a system of labor relations that would keep wages down and profits up.[30]

In 1906 Pullman conductors and porters again demanded wage increases when the railroad brotherhoods did, and the Department of Industrial Relations responded by developing a new bonus policy tied to the old demerit system. In 1908 the company awarded a bonus of one month's pay to 2,617 porters and 1,153 conductors, the "roll of honor people," who had no demerits during the previous year. Sixty-eight percent of conductors and 59 percent of porters received bonuses that year. That fewer porters than conductors benefited may have resulted from discriminatory supervision that meant more porters received demerits. Yet considering how differently the company had treated conductors and porters in the past, the large number of porters who received a bonus reflects the extent to which color-blind practices grew with the expansion of bureaucratic methods. Pullman porters often pushed the company in this direction, and the company responded when they demanded that their wages increase with seniority as the conductors' did. By 1913 porters' base pay, though still inadequate, increased in stages too.[31]

The company also followed the railroads in instituting welfare policies for workers in the sleeping-car service, and it made them available regardless of race. Railroads led the way for U.S. corporations in developing benefits to counter the appeal of unions, and they sponsored a wide variety of educational, health, and social programs along with company newspapers, pensions, and insurance plans. They also contributed to nonprofit organizations in the communities in which their workers lived. When Pullman porters and conductors took up the call for pensions, the company established its plan in 1914. Although officials extended the pension plan to employees of the manufacturing division too, most new programs were exclusive to the sleeping-car service. These programs included a relief plan that provided full or half pay (depending on length of service) for up to two months in cases of sickness or disability for reasons not related to work.[32]

Although positive incentives proliferated and porters were among the few black workers in the United States to have access to such benefits, Pullman conductors and porters were not appeased. The porters never ceased to decry the low wages that made them rely on tips, and they objected to inadequate sleeping quarters and provisions for meals. In August 1914, when company officials held a lecture series in each district to encourage porters to give more friendly service, they heard these complaints. Some porters stated frankly that their smiles and politeness depended on how well the company met their demands for better conditions. In 1915 Pullman porters and conductors also testified before the Commission on Industrial Relations established by Congress to investigate the condition of labor in the nation's largest industries. They complained about low wages, long hours, and the lack of uniform policies for discipline. They asserted further, and Pullman officials agreed, that supervisors routinely fired union organizers, because the company did not tolerate "disloyalty."[33]

In the wake of the commission's hearings, porters and conductors expected wage increases, but these did not materialize. Instead, the company once more looked to less expensive benefits to quell dissent, offering its first employee stock purchase plan and sponsoring a convention of porter delegates from around the country to form the Pullman Porters Benefit Association, a fraternal order that would furnish insurance. Although porters and conductors remained dissatisfied, the bureaucratic policies enacted succeeded in shaping the Pullman operating force toward a model of long-term employment. By 1916 one-fourth of the nearly eight thousand porters had ten or more years of service with the company. Because the number of porters had doubled in the preceding decade, half the porters who had been on duty in 1906 still worked for the company a decade later.[34]

Although they extended similar benefits to conductors and porters, managers continued to exacerbate racial tensions between the two groups. Management maintained the policy that only white men could be conductors, encouraged conductors and porters to spy on each other, and provided separate and unequal sleeping facilities for their layovers. Keeping porters and conductors divided was critical to management's ability to best exploit both groups, because the company could not rely solely on white racism among the conductors to achieve that goal. If only out of self-interest, conductors who sought to unionize at this time also tried to help porters form their own union. Furthermore, despite their privileged position, not all conductors subscribed to a belief in white supremacy or the laws that enforced it. In 1911, for instance, the *Chicago Defender*, a leading black newspaper, applauded one conductor for violating Jim Crow laws in three southern states by refusing to expel Mrs. Booker T. Washington from a Pullman car traveling from Texas to Tennessee. The conductor asserted that he would do the same for "any respectable colored lady."[35]

Revolutionizing Car Building

The Department of Industrial Relations looked to other manufacturers, not to the railroads, for guidance on how to control car builders. The metalworking industries established few bureaucratic forms of labor management but instead used technology to control workers and cut costs. For the Pullman Car Works new technologies could serve not only these goals but also the public's demand for improved railcars. Because of public concern about fires in wooden cars, the company began to explore the possibility of producing steel car bodies and by 1910 had totally converted to steel construction. Then, as the company publicist Joseph Husband wrote, "At one fell stroke the old order changed to the new. The songs of the band-saw and the planer were stilled and in their stead rose the metallic clamor of steam hammer and turret lathe, and the endless staccato reverberation of an army of riveters."[36]

New technology allowed the Car Works to displace many of its old workers, as steelworkers and riveters replaced woodworkers by the thousands. The shift to steel accelerated the influx of Italians, Greeks, Hungarians, Russians, and Poles who were experienced steelworkers from their employment at the mills on the South Side of Chicago. By 1912, 40 percent of the combined workforces of the Car Works and the Calumet Repair Shop came from southern or eastern Europe; in 1892 fewer than 5 percent had. But the performance of the new workers did not always meet expectations, and foremen trained some old cabinetmakers and wood body builders for jobs such as steel cabinetmaking.[37] The changes in assembling and erecting proved harder for the older workers to endure because of the noise level, especially that endless staccato reverberation of riveting. Some men who had worked in erecting left the Car Works as bitter toward the men who replaced them as toward the company. When the social reformer Graham R. Taylor studied the Pullman neighborhood in 1912, old residents, who looked askance at the newcomers, told him that "Slavs, who 'don't seem to have any nerves,' take these jobs."[38]

The new technology and the extensive division of labor undercut the old crafts, but they facilitated learning on the job. With each contract for railcars foremen refigured wage rates, and as some men rejected the new terms, others took their places. The career of Girolamo Venturelli illustrates the way in which the Car Works attracted young immigrants and broadened their skills. Born in Italy in 1894, Venturelli became a laborer at the Car Works when he was eighteen. He did not remain in unskilled work but over the next five years held four semiskilled jobs—helper in body building, heater of rivets, bucker (a riveter's helper), paint scrubber—and one craft specialty, body fitter. In that time Venturelli was developing skill in steel body building, but the relatively short term of each contract ensured that he still needed to be flexible enough to take a lesser job in another department (paint scrubbing) to maintain steady employment at the Car Works.[39]

Tensions between ethnic groups increased as men from northern and western Europe, whose skills were in woodworking, were displaced. Prejudice against eastern and southern Europeans increased across the nation at this time, as even scientific studies proclaimed a hierarchy of races, with northern and western Europeans superior and southern and eastern Europeans above Africans and Asians but not by much. One Dutch tradesman from Roseland reflected this view when he told Graham Taylor that some of his fellow Hollanders no longer desired jobs at the Car Works because "no white man would now want to work in some departments of the shops."[40] Yet no evidence exists that the Pullman Company consciously replaced the old immigrants with the new as part of the divide-and-conquer strategy that many large manufacturers adopted at this time. Rather, the Car Works simply hired those available with the necessary skills.[41]

As the company introduced new technology and hired thousands of new workers, the old problem of increasing productivity and capturing the profits remained. Skilled workers continued to comprise about 40 percent of the workforce, and the Car Works was still an assemblage of small factories—a paint shop, brass foundry, machine shop, and the like—grouped around a large-scale fabricating and erecting plant. The proportion of skilled workers remained relatively high because the increase in semiskilled and unskilled workers in erecting was offset by the increase in skilled workers like steamfitters and electricians who installed the more sophisticated water, heat, and light systems in the cars. The ubiquity of hand tools further facilitated workers' independence. Men took tools to be sharpened whenever they judged it necessary and waited for that job to be done before returning to work. This enabled them to move around the shop relatively freely and to control the pace at which they labored. In these circumstances peer pressure could enforce any informal agreements about the pace of production, and foremen found it exceedingly difficult to establish piece rates favorable to the company.[42]

To address this problem Car Works management began the first major efficiency drive based on systematic investigation of work processes, following the latest trend in the metalworking industries, Frederick Taylor's "scientific management." Taylor expanded the role of the engineer in designing work processes and replacing the skilled worker and the craft-trained foreman as the arbiter of how tasks should be defined and accomplished. One of Taylor's associates, Carl Barth, consulted with Pullman management; by 1916 company president John Runnells proudly described for *System* magazine a method that combined Taylor's principles of scientific management with Pullman's "common sense" techniques.[43]

Throughout the Car Works new systems more narrowly specified the content of work and circumscribed workers' control of their labor. "Tool boys" supplied sharpened, repaired, or new tools so that workers did not have an excuse to leave their stations. Laborers known as "move men" facilitated the flow of work by bringing workers new materials and passing on the output to others, speeding up production but also further limiting workers' physical mobility. The redefinition of job content blurred old craft lines, and now workers could transfer among several departments to take closely related jobs that were also relatively easy to learn. Despite the scope of the innovations, like most employers, Pullman only selectively accepted advice based on scientific theory. In line with their notion of common sense and contrary to Taylor's prescriptions, for instance, officials instituted piece rates set on broad classifications of jobs rather than tailoring rates to individual workers. In passenger car building, management divided the tasks in each craft into two or more levels according to difficulty and established standardized piece rates for each level.[44]

Freight cars had always been less complicated to produce than passenger cars, and mass-production methods made their greatest inroads in this department. The company installed a track system for car construction—a simple assembly-line system of four tracks with thirteen stations each for progressive building. Yet the workers, not the machines, still controlled the pace of the line. A moving assembly line that allowed management to control the pace of work, such as Henry Ford installed at his automobile plant, was not feasible in railcar construction, and foremen and their common sense were always necessary to maintain productivity. On the freight car construction tracks the foremen encouraged a spirit of rivalry between the positions on each line so that workers at one position would try to feed cars to workers at the next station before the latter were ready for them. As Pullman managers recognized, men doing repetitive tasks sometimes welcomed such diversions and opportunities for achievement, and one supervisor characterized this method as "a game, a game that makes the time move faster and at the same time increases both the workman's pay envelope and the Company's production." In promoting competition, supervisors went so far as to sanction betting on which position on the four lines would finish a job first. A superintendent recalled "the action" on a big order of several thousand freight cars that took six months to fill. The men were "betting day after day, just like teams of ball players. Why, we figure on an average of twenty-one cars for a track a day, and one day competition got so hot they pushed up the record to thirty-three. And . . . a man's never too tired at night if there's a spirit of contest in his work."[45]

If new technology and scientific management promised greater productivity from less costly workers, they did not provide a safer work environment. The Car Works had never been a safe place to labor, and the new processes only worsened conditions. Among other hazards, steel cars, unlike wooden ones, required sandblasting that could produce lung disease. When the Illinois legislature passed the Occupational Diseases Act in 1911 as well as workers' compensation legislation, the Pullman Car Works became an object of state scrutiny. The next year Dr. Alice Hamilton, a leading advocate for workplace safety, investigated conditions at the Car Works for the Occupational Diseases Commission of Illinois. Louise deKoven Bowen, a leading Chicago reformer who was also a major stockholder in the Pullman Company, aided in acquiring information about the plant.[46] Hamilton and Bowen found a severe safety problem as well as industrial disease among those exposed to poisonous or irritating dust and fumes; the Car Works saw two hundred accidents per month but only one part-time doctor was on staff with no nurse to assist. Hamilton identified widespread lead poisoning in the paint department among Italians, Lithuanians, Greeks, and Russians. She noted: "Work of this kind is recognized as the worst the painter can do, and skilled painters are so familiar with the risks that they will not undertake it if they can possibly find anything else to do. As a consequence, many unskilled men were employed by the Pullman Company to do interior painting, some of whom had never handled a brush before. . . . Not one of these men had any idea that the work was dangerous, and if they were warned or instructed by the foreman they had not understood what he said."[47]

The new immigrants took the noisiest and most dangerous jobs at Pullman, just as they did throughout U.S. industry, but the pressure to improve conditions did not come from them or from the more skilled workers. Rather, the state and a prominent stockholder's public pressure forced Pullman to take safety issues seriously. Managers met the letter of the law by modifying some procedures and providing lunchrooms, washrooms, and special clothes for those handling poisons. They also switched to a safer paint, hired five physicians, and provided respirators and monthly lung exams for sandblasters, glass cutters, asbestos cutters, and metal polishers and buffers. After the company established its safety department in 1913, management took an active role in protecting workers.[48]

If workers did not protest safety issues, they did not necessarily acquiesce to the new order, and in 1916 the Department of Industrial Relations decided that it needed to explain and justify scientific management to the workers. It began publication of the first company newspaper, the *Pullman Car Works Standard*, whose articles hinted at workers' concerns. Descriptions of a new policy of encouraging workers' suggestions and rewarding them revealed the tension between scientific management and workers' desire to use their brains as well as their hands. The *Standard*, like most company newspapers, submerged such articles in the "feel-good" news of workers' clubs and sports teams, activities that dated to the foundation of the model town but now were linked directly to the factory. The Car Works had ten baseball teams comprising its own league, plus soccer, football, bowling, gymnastics, track, and basketball teams. Other articles touted benefits, including those that flowed from state safety and health laws, as company largesse—from more lavatories, showers, and locker rooms to a visiting nurse who cared for the families of workers. The newspaper, like the teams and health and safety benefits, was designed to create an aura of caring and cooperation, as its editor opined: "This is an age of better understanding between the employer and employee. Both have made mistakes but they were not intentional or deliberate."[49]

Yet other articles in the *Standard* revealed the continuing difficulty of molding thousands of workers into the efficient labor force that the company desired. A spate of articles in 1916–17 reported employee thefts of materials and tools from the Car Works and the Calumet Repair Shop and suggested that "stealing doesn't pay" by recounting the swift discipline to those who cheated the company.[50] Other articles revealed that Pullman managers continued to fight a battle as old as the factory system itself: the attempt to instill in workers the personal discipline necessary for higher production. Since the early nineteenth century U.S. manufacturers had sought to impress on workers that efficiency required promptness, consistent attendance, and sobriety. Traditional artisans who controlled the pace of their work had not exerted such rigid restraint, and Blue Monday—a day spent nursing a hangover from Sunday or extending its alcoholic spree—was a custom for many. An article in the *Standard* that alluded to employee drinking at the Car Works suggests that some Pullman workers had kept Blue Monday too: "Our Polishers call themselves 'Shiners,' saying: 'We shine for a living, and live to shine.' Some years ago a number of our 'shiners' were in the habit of coming into the shops on a Monday morning with a 'shine' on, but of course none of our present force belong to this class."[51] The company actively intervened to inhibit drinking among employees by launching a temperance crusade that included providing dining rooms and paying cash wages so that workers did not have to go to saloons to eat their lunches or get their paychecks cashed. All this was ancillary, however, to the predominant mode of labor control—the new production methods.

The Intersection of Two Systems of Labor Management

The dual strategies of the Department of Industrial Relations—emphasizing bureaucratic methods of labor management in the sleeping-car service and technical forms in the manufacturing division—faced their severest test in the repair shops. Repair workers, especially in Chicago, had been among the most active strikers and union members in all the movements of Pullman workers since the 1880s, and they provided the bridge between Pullman manufacturing workers and railroad workers. Company executives began to separate repair workers from manufacturing workers in 1900 when management transformed the repair department of the Car Works into the Calumet Repair Shop. The shop was just across the street from the Car Works, but it had its own manager, who reported directly to company headquarters, not to the superintendent of the Car Works.[52] In corporate terms repairs were clearly part of the sleeping-car service and the railroad industry, but, for decades to come, men and women and their skills would be transferable from the Car Works to the repair shops and vice versa. The Department of Industrial Relations thus melded its strategies in order to manage repair shop workers.

The company attempted to transfer some methods perfected at the Car Works to the repair shops, beginning with new forms of supervision. Replacing inside contracting and gang bosses with foremen and leaders proved relatively easy, but transforming production methods did not. Repairs could not be as easily standardized as construction could, and the majority of the shop force remained highly skilled. Furthermore, because so many older wooden sleeping cars continued in use, repair shop managers did not replace woodworkers en masse in 1910 with the advent of steel construction. Instead, shop forces included both woodworkers and steelworkers, although the number of the latter grew steadily through the 1910s and early 1920s as the old cars were retired.[53]

After the physical separation of the repair department from the Pullman Car Works, management used the Calumet Repair Shop as its testing ground for applying the new methods of manufacturing to repair work. With more than one thousand workers, the Calumet shop was the company's largest repair facility, and while proximity made it the logical test site for new methods, management had another reason to experiment there—the militancy and relatively high price of Calumet workers. These men and women had led all the union movements among Pullman shop workers since the 1880s, and union wage scales in Chicago forced the company to pay them higher rates than shop workers elsewhere accepted. New work processes could serve two purposes—decreasing the cost of production and disciplining skilled workers who insisted on unionizing. At shops where workers had not unionized and labor costs were lower, management did not tamper as quickly with the traditional structure of jobs. At Calumet management first pushed specialization of tasks. As table 2 shows, by 1911 the Calumet shop had one-third more job titles than the Wilmington shop, although the latter had almost as many employees and the same departmental structure. Other shops that posed no union threat, like the repair shop in Richmond, California, also escaped specialization. In 1911 the company chose Richmond as the site for its newest repair facility because of the town's open shop reputation.[54]

Table 2. Size and Structure of Pullman Repair Shops

	Number of Workers			Number of Job Titles		
	Calumet	Richmond	Wilmington	Calumet	Richmond	Wilmington
1906	1,005	—	882	137	—	126
1911	1,263	640	1,098	156	88	120
1917	1,219	450	819	205	102	127

Sources: Payrolls, Calumet, Richmond, and Wilmington shops, 2nd Half of Apr. 1906; 2nd Half of Mar. 1911; 2nd Half of Oct. 1917, PP.

Steel technology and an extensive division of labor attracted "new immigrants" to the Calumet Repair Shop just as they did to the Pullman Car Works. Between 1910 and 1917 more than half of those hired at the shop for skilled and semiskilled jobs and three-quarters of those hired for unskilled jobs were born in eastern or southern Europe. Men like Giovanni Ippolito, who had been born in Italy in 1888 and lived in Kensington, found new employment opportunities as the repair shop ceased to be a craftsmen's stronghold. In 1907 Ippolito first went to work at the shop on flooring, then became a roofer in 1913. Two years later he switched specialties again, becoming a helper in the body department.[55]

After 1910 the Calumet shop diverged further from the other repair shops as management instituted features of the efficiency drive underway at the Car Works. By 1917 Calumet managers had categorized the specialized tasks in each craft into two or three levels with different pay rates, so that they used the most skilled workers only for jobs requiring great facility and could use less skilled workers for routine tasks. Giovanni Ippolito was reclassified as a body builder 2. The Calumet shop now had twice as many job titles as the Wilmington and Richmond shops, whose job structures remained relatively unchanged (table 2).[56] Despite these innovations, the Calumet shop would always lag behind the Pullman Car Works in replacing skilled workers with less skilled ones because of the complexity and diversity of repair work.

Specialization at Calumet did not mean that its workers earned less than those at other shops did. Indeed, Calumet's skilled workers earned slightly more on an hourly basis than craft workers at Wilmington or Richmond did. Yet even though their skilled workers earned less, the Wilmington and Richmond shops shrank in size in the 1910s, while the Calumet shop remained Pullman's largest repair facility. This suggests that specialization succeeded in offsetting Calumet's higher wage rates and made the shop more profitable for the company. Pullman management certainly seemed to believe this, and in the decades to come the company did everything in its power to protect its methods of car repair from the attempts of workers and unions to change them.[57]

Although the company subjected the repair shops to many of the new job structures and methods of supervision that it developed at the Car Works, in one critical respect it treated them differently. As part of the sleeping-car service, the repair shops used seniority as the basis for layoffs and recalls, whereas the Car Works, like most manufacturing plants, did not. A seasonal pattern of layoffs in shop work developed by the early twentieth century, with a slack season of six weeks or more every summer that corresponded to the high point of rail travel. This predictability allowed repair shop workers to plan for unemployment and to find alternate jobs that they could leave to return to Pullman. Just as the railroads did, the company even allowed shop workers to take leaves of absence without loss of seniority. One Calumet upholsterer, for instance, took his sick wife to another city for a year and then returned to his job. Consequently, Pullman shop workers, like most railroad workers, made careers with one firm; the skilled workers who were hired at the Calumet shop between 1910 and 1917 averaged 25.5 years of service with the company.[58]

During the same period turnover at the Car Works was chronic, because management refused to respect seniority even though large fluctuations in the receipt of contracts for railcars made layoffs common. The most that the company promised was that "all workmen have the right to appeal to the Employment Manager when they feel there has been any unfairness in their transfer, lay-off or discharge."[59] The employment manager encouraged workers to accept lesser jobs at the Car Works when they were laid off in order to maintain the record of continuous service that they needed for pensions, and some did so. Many others preferred better wages elsewhere and often ignored recalls if they had jobs. As industries boomed in the neighborhoods around the Car Works and public transportation improved, workers had a much wider choice of jobs than formerly. Many Pullman car builders had erratic job histories; they might work at the Car Works for years but only intermittently for short periods. Even those like Girolamo Venturelli, who maintained steady employment for five years by accepting five different jobs, eventually tired of the situation. Venturelli looked for security elsewhere, at the Calumet Repair Shop. He worked there for three months in the fall of 1917 and then in 1919 returned to the shop in the body department, where he remained until he retired in 1957.[60]

The Open Shop

The reliance on technology and industrial engineering at the Car Works and the more mixed strategy at the Calumet shop succeeded in keeping unions out of these workplaces when a new union organizing drive threatened. By 1910 all railroad craft unions except the brotherhoods of conductors, engineers, firemen, and trainmen had joined the American Federation of Labor, which formed the Railway Employes' Department to establish national coordination among them.[61] Although these craft-based unions rejected the idea of forming one industrial union like the American Railway Union, they wanted to make joint demands on each railroad—that is, to establish the system federation concept that railroad workers had attempted to implement since the 1880s. In 1910 the six craft unions in the railroad shops, which came to be known as the "shopcraft" unions, began to build their memberships by organizing system federations. These unions claimed jurisdiction over Pullman repair shop and manufacturing workers, and all had adjusted to new methods in railroad and locomotive manufacture and repair by redefining *craft* to include specialists who used new machines or techniques. By their expanded definition of *craft*, as many as 50 percent of those who labored at the Car Works and 70 percent of those at the Calumet Repair Shop were eligible for membership.[62]

For Pullman management the new union movement began uncomfortably close to home at the Illinois Central Railroad's Burnside repair shop. In 1910, when the railroad tried to introduce scientific management, its workers formed a system federation, as did repair shop workers for the Southern Pacific and other railroads controlled by the financier Edward Harriman. The next year, when the railroads refused to negotiate with the system federations, workers for the Illinois Central and Harriman lines staged a joint strike for a broad set of demands.[63] Pullman manufacturing and repair workers and Burnside workers had organized and struck together in 1894 and 1904, but Pullman workers did not support the Burnside workers during the system federation strike. The Car Works was in turmoil from the new processes of steel production and the influx of large numbers of new immigrant workers, but the Calumet shop workers also were quiescent. After the 1904 lockout those who returned to the shop did not openly join unions, and no locals of the shopcraft unions appeared at either the repair shop or the Car Works.

The Illinois Central and Harriman railroads broke the system federation strike but only by taking huge losses and pioneering approaches that influenced antiunion strategy throughout the railroad industry. First and foremost, they shifted the color line, hiring black men in skilled jobs. Although the Illinois Central demoted black workers at the Burnside shop to helper-level positions after the strike, it retained them as permanent employees ready to be upgraded again if necessary. Northern manufacturers made greater use of black strikebreakers after the turn of the century, but the Illinois Central pioneered this practice among northern railroads. The shopcraft unions were not equipped to cope with racial change in the workforce, regardless of its origin, because they, like other railroad unions, excluded black men from membership. The Illinois Central introduced its second innovation for keeping unions at bay in 1912—a shop committee comprised of one representative from each group of skilled workers; it met monthly with the shop superintendent to "air views" and work on safety issues. The shop committee concept would evolve during World War I into the company union—U.S. management's new weapon in the fight against the AFL.[64]

The success of Pullman's dual strategies in maintaining the open shop continued into the early years of World War I despite the growth of labor unions, which had greater influence in the making of government policy. The political environment had become much more prolabor during the Progressive movement, and this made it easier for workers to achieve their goals through strikes and unionizing. In the 1914 Clayton Act, Congress attempted to relieve workers from the imposition of yellow-dog contracts and unions from the type of injunction that gave railroad corporations the upper hand during the 1894 strike. President Woodrow Wilson established the Department of Labor and vastly expanded government's role in mediating labor disputes. In 1916 the best-organized railroad workers—the four brotherhoods of conductors, engineers, firemen, and trainmen—even used a strike threat to force Congress to pass the Adamson Act, which gave them the eight-hour day. The shopcraft unions also made progress, and by 1917 about one-third of railroad repair shop workers labored under union contracts. Other craft unions made inroads into major manufacturing corporations, and the AFL promoted organizing on an industry-wide basis in steel and meatpacking.[65]

Despite the ferment around them, Pullman's manufacturing workers were too deeply divided by craft, skill level, and ethnicity to organize together. The hostility with which the old immigrants had greeted the new in the conversion to steel construction continued to fester. Although some immigrants from southern and eastern Europe held skilled positions, they virtually monopolized the unskilled and semiskilled jobs; northern and western European immigrants were still concentrated in the skilled ranks. This conjunction of skill level and ethnicity shaped the largest strike of the period at the Car Works, a two-week walkout in 1916 by twelve hundred laborers who struck when the company refused their demand for a five-cents-per-hour raise. The laborers belonged to no union but had decided on this action by themselves. The Industrial Workers of the World (IWW), which tried to organize the strikers, described the difficulties in its newspaper, *Industrial Solidarity*. The most radical elements of the U.S. labor movement had formed the IWW in 1905 with the goal of organizing workers to replace capitalist control with worker control. The IWW favored direct action, and it attempted to help workers who went on strike in any industry.[66]

In the pages of *Industrial Solidarity*, IWW organizers excoriated the Socialists at the Car Works for pandering to the primarily northern and western European skilled workers and trying to start a back-to-work movement. Charles Johnson, leader of the Socialists, exemplified these skilled workers. He was a Swede and an electrician who had begun work at Pullman in 1890, when he was twelve. Because of the critical role of laborers in expediting production under the new systems, the 1916 walk-out adversely affected skilled workers' productivity and therefore their earnings from piece rates. The skilled workers had a choice: support the laborers and strike too or try to get them to go back to work. They chose the latter.[67]

But the IWW organizers also found their task complicated by ethnic divisions that went beyond a simple dichotomy between northwestern and southeastern Europeans. Since the 1890s the increasing diversity and size of the immigrant population on the far South Side of Chicago had been accompanied by intensifying identification with ethnicity. Neighborhoods were more ethnically homogeneous, and the old model town itself had become an Italian enclave. Immigrants were not assimilating but instead establishing institutions to maintain their own cultures. IWW organizers found that English-speaking Lithuanian and Polish laborers at the Car Works willingly joined Car Builders' Industrial Union #500, which the IWW created. But the Italians, who comprised three-quarters of the strikers, refused. According to the IWW organizers, the Italians were "under the influence of a bunch of 'individualist' anarchist leaders, who opposed organization and did not believe in having strike committees, strike organization or strike discipline."[68] Italian anarchism and IWW syndicalism were not identical, and the Italian laborers followed their own leaders and their own ideas about how to run a strike. The Italian community in the Pullman area had an extensive organizational structure that reflected the diverse political and religious beliefs and social and economic needs of Piedmontese, Venetians, Sicilians, and Calabrese. Enmeshed in this larger Italian world, the laborers did not feel it necessary to defer to leadership by Americans or to give up their own ideas to cooperate with others. They ran the strike their way and held out for two weeks until management offered them a raise of two cents an hour.[69]

World War I and Racial Change

Pullman's two roads to the open shop contained worker challenges to management control for more than a decade. The Pullman Company had been able to maintain its traditional racial division of labor, even though some employers hired black workers to undercut white strikers and unions. World War I, however, induced Pullman management to rethink the company's racial policies, not as an antiunion measure but as a way to contain costs. When the U.S. economy boomed on the basis of exports to the European combatants and unemployment declined, wage rates increased and prices soared. Workers, both skilled and unskilled, found many job openings, and companies like Pullman, which gave wage increases only grudgingly, saw their employees go elsewhere. In the sleeping-car service workers in every job category—porters, conductors, shop workers, and car cleaners—resigned to take positions with better wages. Turnover at the Car Works reached 283 percent annually, as men left for higher-paying jobs at local shipyards.[70]

When Pullman and other employers looked for replacements for those who quit, they found immigration no longer supplied new recruits. The war in the Atlantic had halted emigration from Europe, and some resident aliens left the United States to fight for their homeland. To fill empty positions while holding down wage increases, companies began to alter patterns of job segregation by race and gender, hiring new workers for whom the wages offered were an improvement over what they usually earned. In Chicago and much of the industrial North, manufacturers opened their doors to African Americans and set off a massive migration from the South. The jobs that black migrants found were usually the least desirable from a white perspective, but unlike in the South these positions often provided equal pay for equal work. While employers welcomed the newcomers, white northerners generally did not. Residential segregation increased as white residents resisted living next to African Americans, even if they worked with them.[71]

The Pullman Company joined other large corporations in actively encouraging black migration by financially supporting the Urban League, which helped place African Americans in northern industry. The company's first concern was to ensure enough applicants for porter positions, but it soon saw a need for African Americans at the Car Works too. But to integrate the manufacturing plant the company had to ignore the wishes of the white residents of the greater Pullman area, including many of its employees. Among area employers, only the Illinois Central had already crossed the color line, when it broke the system federation strike. Some employers, like Wisconsin Steel and International Harvester's West Pullman plant, refused to hire African Americans until World War II. Discrimination at these factories reflected management acquiescence to popular racism in the Pullman area, where many social clubs were racially restricted, where minstrel shows that demeaned black people were popular, and where the residents of Lilydale, a small section of housing for the Illinois Central's black workers, lived in enforced isolation. Yet by

1916 management at the Pullman Car Works had decided to ignore local sentiment and hire black men. At any one time the Car Works never
employed more than five hundred African Americans in a labor force that
fluctuated from seventy-five hundred to nine thousand, but an important
line had been crossed. Management held out the possibility for long-term
employment, insisting that "no matter what your race or creed, the Company wants you to become a better workman, and to share in the opportunities for advancement. Don't forget that your progress depends on your
own effort."[72] African Americans had come to the Car Works to stay, but
they found no homes in the Pullman area and had to commute daily from
the black ghetto.

The new policy at the Car Works was a product of the declining appeal of Pullman manufacturing jobs. Racial barriers did not fall at all
Pullman facilities but only at those where jobs and wages failed to impress white workers. Pullman repair shops, which had a much higher
proportion of skilled jobs than the Car Works did, integrated much more
slowly or not at all. The Calumet Repair Shop did not hire its first black
workers until mid-1917, at least a year and a half after the Car Works did.
When initially faced with labor shortages, Pullman repair shop managers responded by increasing the number of helpers and specialists, and
the Richmond shop, which suffered from a particularly acute labor shortage, doubled the percentage of workers at the helper level. As one manager later recounted, "We had to go out and pick up anybody we could
and teach them to do something. We couldn't teach them a trade because
we didn't have time."[73] Yet shop managers continued to envision "anybody" as an adult white male, and at first they found such workers by
hiring more immigrants from eastern and southern Europe than they had
previously. Like other employers, they turned to black workers only after the supply of immigrants had been exhausted. This situation never
occurred at the Richmond repair shop, which did not hire any nonwhite
workers during the war, even though nearby Oakland, where many of its
white workers lived, had a sizable black population. The Richmond shop
also abided by the racial prejudices of white Americans in the West and
hired none of the several thousand Chinese and Japanese immigrants who
lived in the area.[74]

Although labor shortages in 1915 and 1916 created new opportunities for men who had previously been discriminated against, they did not
cause U.S. employers to re-evaluate the gender definition of most of these
jobs as "men's work." In Pullman repair shops and the Car Works a relatively small number of white women labored where they always had,
in sewing and glass embossing and in a few ancillary tasks in upholstery

departments, like hair picking. This remained true even though women still worked for significantly lower wages than men did. Where women found new opportunities at the Pullman Company and other corporations was in the office, as the shortage of men accelerated the feminization of clerical work.[75]

After the turn of the century Pullman, like the railroads, had begun to hire more women for clerical positions created by the new methods of worker control and supervision and the reorganization and mechanization of bookkeeping. In Pullman's central office, officials created both new low-paid jobs for women and hired women for "men's jobs" but paid them lower wages. Most corporations, including Pullman, also held down clerical wages through a policy of hiring only single women and firing those who married. The marriage ban decreased the number of long-term clerical employees and enabled companies to avoid the full consequences of the tradition of paying office workers higher wages based on tenure. The tight labor market during World War I induced Pullman to open many new clerical positions to women.[76]

The new women office workers in the United States were not only all single but also all white. By the early twentieth century U.S.-educated daughters of European immigrants swelled the ranks of office workers in many northern cities. Daughters of immigrant car builders and repair shop workers from the greater Pullman area took most of the newly opened clerical jobs at the Calumet Repair Shop and the Car Works or commuted by train to Chicago's central business district to work at Pullman headquarters. For Margaret Manson the war opened a job for which she qualified but previously had not been able to obtain near her home in Roseland. Born in 1891, this daughter of Scottish immigrants began work in 1908 as a seamstress in the Calumet shop. During the war she finally had the opportunity to become a clerk, a position that she held until she retired in 1951. Although corporations welcomed the daughters of immigrants, until the 1960s black women found clerical employment primarily in black-owned businesses.[77]

In the early years of World War I, Pullman managers made choices that shaped opportunities for women and racial minorities well into the twentieth century: they opened jobs in manufacturing to black men but not to women, while they offered more clerical work to white women but not to African Americans. Race and gender operated as distinct criteria in all hiring and together doubly disadvantaged black women, who found their greatest opportunities in the least desirable jobs. Most of these jobs at the Pullman Company were in the yards, as car cleaners. Although the southern yards had hired black men and women for car cleaning for many years,

Pullman's northern yards followed suit only during the war. In Chicago black men and women entered car cleaning in 1916 when white workers struck for higher wages. During the 1902 strike by Chicago car cleaners, the company had capitulated to workers' demands after a brief attempt to use black strikebreakers. Now that Chicago employers routinely hired African Americans, the yard superintendent could easily follow suit and permanently replace the white cleaners with black workers. Yet strikes by car cleaners were rare, and most frequently Pullman supervisors hired black workers when they could not attract competent white workers at the current wages. At Pullman's Philadelphia yard black men replaced white women when the supervisor could no longer find white women "of good quality (many of them drank)."[78] As the war progressed and the Philadelphia yard lost these black men to higher-paying industrial jobs, it hired black women in their places. The company's policy of keeping wages down and resisting unions gradually transformed car cleaning into a "black job" at Pullman. But during the war Pullman car cleaners remained a diverse group—immigrant and native born, all white at some points, all black at others, and integrated racially at still others.[79]

Despite the pressures created by the war-induced labor shortage, Pullman officials had maintained a relatively inexpensive labor force that did not challenge the open shop. By tailoring labor management strategies differently for the manufacturing division and the sleeping-car service and by loosening barriers to women and black workers in some jobs, the company had retained the upper hand. But Pullman workers were not content, and in the sleeping-car service the company's success would turn to defeat virtually overnight. Its workers would increase their wages and refashion their jobs and working conditions in ways unimaginable only a few years earlier. The key to this transformation was the federal government.

3   The State and Pullman Workers

The state played only a minor role in labor struggles at the Pullman Company after the strike of 1894, but U.S. entry into World War I in April 1917 soon transformed that situation. The federal government intervened in labor relations in war industries in order to maintain worker efficiency and morale and to minimize strikes. Under a prolabor federal administration, union membership in the railroad industry soared, workers attained many of their most important goals, and democracy seemed to have come to the workplace. Pullman officials now found themselves bound by national policies and their workers' demands. At the same time the war opened new job opportunities to women and minorities, who posed a problem for unions that excluded them from membership. Black workers, especially Pullman employees, challenged the racism of AFL unions and demanded more access to "the house of labor."

Federal intervention was only an emergency measure, however, and once the war ended a conservative backlash led to the withdrawal of state support for workers and unions. U.S. capitalists sought to return to the open shop, and their employees fought to maintain their unions and the gains that they had made. Many workers lost both. But federal intervention, especially in the railroad industry, had a lasting effect. The participation of twelve thousand Pullman workers in the railroad shopmen's strike of 1922 revealed how federal intervention and the wartime experience with unions altered the sources of workers' solidarity. Allegiance to national unions became a more important source of workers' militancy than the local community. Furthermore, although white racism had not disappeared, workers often crossed racial lines to stand together in strikes.

The State Intervenes

Federal agencies established to maximize production of munitions and supplies did not force companies to recognize unions, but they insisted that employers provide the fairness that workers desired. Bureaucratic methods of labor control—a workplace "rule of law" that covered wage rates, job classifications, criteria for hiring and firing, and grievance systems—became the preferred mechanism for establishing fairness, and they spread from the railroad industry into the manufacturing sector. The concept of industrial democracy, of shared governance of the workplace by workers and employers, legitimized these practices. To many Americans, particularly workers and federal administrators, this concept embodied U.S. war aims, which President Woodrow Wilson characterized as "making the world safe for democracy." A key component of industrial democracy was workers' right to a voice in decision making through freely elected representatives, and government administrators encouraged companies to establish systems of shop committees composed of management and worker representatives to settle disputes. The purview of such systems varied considerably, depending on how much control companies saw fit to relinquish, and most did not empower workers to the extent that union contracts did. Yet by opposing practices like yellow-dog contracts and blacklisting of union organizers, federal agencies helped unions to grow and in many cases to assume direction of these shop committees. Not surprisingly, union membership doubled between 1915 and 1920.[1]

In no sector of the economy did the government take more far-reaching action than in the railroad industry, and no unions benefited more from wartime policies than railroad unions. Fearing that the financially weak railroad corporations could not manage the transport of troops and supplies efficiently, the federal government seized major railroads in December 1917 and established the U.S. Railroad Administration (USRA) to coordinate and control rail operations. The underlying dissatisfaction at Pullman surfaced immediately as workers from both the sleeping-car service and the Car Works wrote to Washington, pleading with the USRA to include them in its jurisdiction. As one group of Pullman workers in Kansas City, Missouri, wrote: "We have had opportunities to work for other roads, which are now under the Government control. We think that owing to the fact that we stay with the Pullman Company, we should be taken care of by the Government, which we are loyal to. We have purchased Liberty Bonds, and we feel that if we are not under the Government Control, we shall have to look for other employment in order to pay for our bonds."[2] Pullman officials tried to avoid a government takeover by insisting that the corporation was primarily a manufacturing concern rather than a part of the railroad industry.

Nevertheless, the director general of the railroads, William McAdoo, seized the sleeping-car service because he deemed it vital for the transport of troops. In the next two years government control revolutionized labor relations in Pullman's operating service. McAdoo left the manufacturing division in company hands, however. The Car Works contributed to the war effort by making shells and freight cars but under the oversight of the National War Labor Board rather than the USRA. Unlike the Railroad Administration, the labor board did not directly manage the companies under its jurisdiction but only intervened in shop-floor relations when serious problems arose. The different effects of the state on the two divisions of the company solidified the breach that had developed between Pullman car builders and railroad workers after 1904.[3]

Working for the Government

One of the first problems facing the USRA was the possibility of massive strikes. Workers rushed to join unions after the government takeover. Membership in the Brotherhood of Railway Carmen (BRCA) increased fourfold, while the Sheet Metal Workers' International Alliance tripled in size. But most railroads refused to bargain with the unions. To keep the trains running McAdoo issued General Order #27 and its supplements in May and July 1918 to set labor policy for the railroads. These orders established a new level of uniformity in labor-management relations across the industry. At the same time the extent of union organizing and militancy among railroad workers ensured that these directives reflected the union definition of what workers wanted. Besides raising all workers' wages significantly (in some cases nearly double what they had been), McAdoo insisted that workers had the right to form unions and that railroads had to recognize and bargain with unions that represented a majority of their employees. Shopcraft workers also received the eight-hour day with time and a half for overtime, the right to abolish piece rates, and seniority as the basis for layoffs, rehires, and promotions with grievance procedures to ensure that the rules were implemented fairly. The orders assured workers a voice in critical decisions, even if they were not union members, by mandating that workers had the right to vote on such issues as whether to abolish piece rates. McAdoo also created boards of adjustment, comprised of equal numbers of union and management representatives, to handle differences in the interpretation and implementation of collective bargaining agreements. This mechanism for forestalling strikes was a step beyond the voluntary efforts at mediation and arbitration that Congress had fostered since the 1894 strike.[4] The USRA profoundly altered the balance of power between railroad workers and corporations, and it opened the door for unions to organize throughout the industry.

Despite its previous success in maintaining an open shop, the Pullman Company found workers in the sleeping-car service rushing to join unions too, once that service came under federal control. Indeed, the timing and scale of this movement suggests that only the company's well-developed antiunion methods had kept its workers from organizing earlier. In the first months of government control, complaints from Pullman workers flooded into Washington. They charged that the company had an extensive spy network, that supervisors fired those who joined unions or demanded the conditions granted by McAdoo's directives, and that officials refused to consider articles of agreement presented by unions. But with government support, Pullman workers persisted, and the conductors formed a union, the Order of Sleeping Car Conductors, in 1918.[5]

Pullman porters began organizing too, but they did not unite in one organization. The unions that they formed reflected the complexity of African American labor activism, framed as it necessarily was and would continue to be by both racial and class-based perspectives. In the early months of the war Chicago porters joined the Sleeping Car and Parlor Car Porters of America, organized by the otherwise all-white Hotel and Restaurant Employees International Alliance. Most porters did not follow their Chicago co-workers into this AFL union, however. They rejected consignment to segregated locals in white-dominated unions and preferred to form their own organizations. As long as most unions either excluded black members or offered at most admission to segregated, second-class locals, many black workers remained nonunion or organized on their own. Occupations in which black men predominated often spawned black craft unions, like the Brotherhood of Dining Car Employees. New York porters followed this model and formed the Brotherhood of Sleeping Car Porters' Protective Union. Yet other porters joined the Railway Men's International Benevolent Industrial Association, an industrial union established in 1915 for all black railroad workers who were excluded from equal membership in unions for their crafts. The association became the largest union of black railroad workers during the war as it challenged the labor movement to end discrimination and racism.[6]

Government control also opened Pullman repair shops and yards to the six AFL railroad shopcraft unions. By mid-1918 the Brotherhood of

Railway Carmen of America, which claimed jurisdiction over most of Pullman's skilled repair shop workers as well as the car cleaners, had made inroads at shops and yards that previously had shown no signs of organization, like the Richmond repair shop. As they had previously, Chicago workers led the organizing drive, and virtually every department at the Calumet Repair Shop had a union shop committee by the summer of 1918. Company officials viewed this shop as "the 'hot bed' of radical unionism . . . [that] graduated more radical labor leaders than any other branch of our service."[7] Calumet workers again took part in an organizing drive that swept through the greater Pullman area. Organizers for the federated shopcraft unions reached out to white shop workers of all ethnic backgrounds at the many railroad repair shops and yards in the region. Shopcraft workers responded on the basis of their shared occupational identification, just as workers had between 1898 and 1904. By the summer of 1919 nearly thirty-five hundred Pullman shop and yard workers nationwide belonged to the shopcraft unions, and Calumet workers called for the creation of a Pullman system federation. That system federation, #122, maintained its headquarters on Michigan Avenue in Roseland, just west of the old model town.[8]

Although Calumet workers flocked to the shopcraft unions, their neighbors who labored at the Pullman Car Works did not. Some skilled manufacturing workers joined the BRCA, which would claim jurisdiction over the Car Works for another two decades, but craft unions never attracted a majority of the workers. Some laborers and a few craftsmen belonged to the Industrial Workers of the World, but it never appealed to most car builders, either. Even the National Committee to Organize Iron and Steel Workers, which brought together a range of unions that claimed jurisdiction over the majority of Pullman manufacturing workers, could not unify the Car Works. The committee started organizing on the South Side of Chicago in the fall of 1918, but its success at local steel plants was not duplicated at Pullman. The committee attracted large numbers of immigrant steelworkers by building on wartime propaganda campaigns that identified industrial democracy as a manifestation of American political ideas. The Pullman Car Works saw its share of flag raisings and pledges of allegiance too, and Pullman's immigrant manufacturing workers, like their neighbors in the steel plants, were bombarded by appeals from local newspapers to become "Americanized" and uphold both democracy and the "American standard of living." But if most of those who labored at the Car Works did not see themselves as railroad shopcraft workers, neither were they ready to identify as steelworkers.[9] They were still fragmented and more strongly identified by skill level, craft, ethnicity, race, or political ideology than by employment at the Car Works. Pullman workers in the sleeping-car service, on the other hand, had a clear identity as railroad workers, a strong union movement to rally to, and a federal agency that could force management to accommodate their demands.

Workers in the sleeping-car service joined unions not merely because of long-suppressed pro-union sentiment but also because only unions could deliver what the government promised railroad workers. Although federal control profoundly affected every railroad, it did not do so instantaneously. The USRA relied on each corporate management to implement new policies, and companies that looked forward to a future without government control often refused to comply until unions lodged scores of protests with the federal agency. Pullman's central office would not order local supervisors to implement directives, and the company rejected any procedures that narrowed management prerogatives, such as those that mandated strict application of seniority. Some Pullman supervisors threatened workers with discharge if they asked for the new wage rates, and the company continued its war on unions by transferring repair work from the Calumet shop to the unorganized Car Works in order to lay off unionized workers. Because the company was so recalcitrant, unions played a major role in implementing government directives by appealing every deviation from the rules at the almost four hundred Pullman shops, yards, and district offices. At the same time F. L. Simmons, Pullman's assistant federal auditor, secretly counseled company officials on how to use every step of the grievance procedure through the boards of adjustment to slow down settlement of outstanding issues. Only strong unions could successfully fight grievances through this long appeals process, and increasing numbers of Pullman workers joined unions as they proved their worth in achieving the government-mandated standards.[10]

Pullman repair shop and yard workers wanted more than merely higher wages and the right to form unions; they wanted to turn back the clock and eliminate the specialties and use of helpers that had accompanied the application of new technologies and scientific management to repair work. Beginning with General Order #27, the USRA did just that by standardizing job descriptions for all railroad crafts. After classifying jobs in repair shops and yards into three broad levels—mechanic (skilled), helper (semiskilled), or laborer (unskilled)—and setting hourly wage rates for each level across craft lines, the USRA mandated job descriptions that accorded with union specifications. Pullman workers voted overwhelmingly against piecework to take advantage of the new hourly rates: sixty-eight cents for mechanics, forty-five cents for helpers, and forty cents for laborers. Getting supervisors to implement the new job descriptions would not be easy, however, because they had to reclassify all specialists as mechanics and pay them the same rate, regardless of whether they were fully skilled. Managers resisted every reclassification, and the company contended that much shop work was not skilled because of design changes and new processes. The USRA sided with the unions in so many cases that by 1921 every Pullman repair shop had virtually the same job structure with a relatively small number of distinct job titles. At the Calumet shop the number of job titles was halved, and the structure of all the shops once more resembled the craftsmen's domain of the 1890s.[11]

In contrast, the National War Labor Board rarely involved itself in issues of job classification or work rules, and it intervened in shop-floor relations only when workers struck or when a strong union brought employer violations of its policies to the fore. At this point Pullman manufacturing workers were not united enough to take such action. Thus Pullman repair shop workers and car builders had strikingly different experiences during the war. Manufacturing workers still endured piece rates and long hours, received no overtime pay, and lacked the job protection that a seniority system provided. Perhaps more important, while unions reversed the transformation from craft to mass production at the Calumet Repair Shop, Car Works' management had taken the new methods so far that many workers had never actually seen a completed car, only the pieces or stages on which they worked.[12]

The USRA managed Pullman's sleeping-car service and U.S. railroads until March 1920, and in the more than two years of its existence workers used the government agency to re-create the conditions of their employment. After the war ended, workers still expected the USRA to act on their behalf, and when cutbacks in overtime led to a sharp drop in earnings, shop workers again demanded higher wages. The USRA balked, and more than 100,000 railroad shop workers staged wildcat strikes in the summer of 1919. Union leaders counseled against these actions because they were afraid to undermine the government agency that so enhanced union power. Just as in 1894, workers ignored this advice in order to assert their demand for a living wage. In response to the strikes the unions and the USRA came to a compromise that set an important precedent for the railroad industry: the shopcraft unions scaled back their wage demands and received the first national agreements with the railroads. Every company subject to government control had to adhere to the same contract provisions, and for the first time the Pullman Company was bound by a union contract.[13]

Women, Minorities, and the USRA

From the perspective of the unions the period of federal oversight was an unmitigated success, and many workers who benefited from the new wages and working conditions agreed. Yet throughout the war some workers continued to leave the railroad industry for jobs that paid higher wages in shipbuilding and in making munitions. The USRA thus became involved in widening the pool of potential workers for railroad jobs. The strength of the women's movement induced the Wilson administration to encourage women's employment in war industries and to mandate equal pay for equal work. The USRA established a women's service section, headed by the feminist Pauline Goldmark, which urged railroads to apply scientific management principles to craft jobs to create new specialist positions for women. During the war women took not only more railroad clerical positions but also unskilled labor jobs in railroad yards and some semiskilled work as helper-level specialists in repair shops. Pullman managers hired more black and white women in car cleaning, more white women in clerical jobs, and a few white women in helper-level positions in the repair shops. Yet opportunities for women were still limited at Pullman, as virtually all the new helper-level jobs were in upholstery departments where women long had been employed as seamstresses.[14]

Most positions that Pullman officials initially opened to women were unremarkable, but yards in Council Bluffs, Iowa, and St. Louis, Missouri, had forewomen over mixed gangs of men and women car cleaners. At the Iowa yard a Pullman official told government investigators that he did not think it would work, "as the men won't like it and she probably will not keep them up."[15] At the St. Louis yard, however, an investigator for the Women's Service Section reported that the men had considerable respect for their boss. Perhaps her age and experience made the difference; she was sixty and had worked for the company for thirty-seven years.[16] These unusual situations arose because Pullman yards had hired large numbers of women car cleaners in the past and trained women leaders to supervise them.

Although the Pullman Company gave women some new opportunities, and in a few cases even authority, it resisted paying them equally with men despite the clear policy of the USRA. The woman who became a forewoman in St. Louis earned $50 per month less than foremen and only $5 a month more than the man who assisted her. Women in the lowest-paying jobs were the most likely to receive equal wages, but if a job commanded a high wage, the company fought through every level of the grievance procedure to deny it to women. Rather than pay seamstresses the mechanics' rate, supervisors laid them off and gave their work to male upholsterers or to women who would work for the low wages prevalent in the garment industry. Some seamstresses earned as little as forty cents an hour, just as car cleaners did. The USRA gave women an avenue to fight these injustices when it established the concept of equal pay for work of comparable value. In the fall of 1919 the Railroad Administration recognized the comparable worth of the work of seamstresses and upholsterers and awarded the Pullman women the mechanics' rate, with back pay to January 1918. After years of earning no more than male laborers or helpers, skilled women achieved a measure of equality.[17]

Like other federal agencies, the USRA did not match its concern for women with similar support for racial minorities. It had no special section to encourage their employment, nor did it mandate equal pay except in three job classifications (fireman, trainman, and switchman) in which southern white workers feared competition for employment by black men whom railroad managements hired at lower wages. The greater concern for women than racial minorities reflected the transformation of racial and gender ideologies during the Progressive era. Feminist demands articulated by white women found favor in U.S. society at the same time that racism increased. Furthermore, women in the North (primarily white) were gaining the vote and becoming a political force, but black men and women were losing political strength because of disenfranchisement in the South. Neither the USRA nor the Wilson administration challenged racist practices, and most managers and unionists continued to view railroad crafts as white men's work. At the Calumet Repair Shop black workers came to comprise about 7 percent of the workforce, but virtually all were laborers. Only a few, like a West Indian immigrant who took on a specialty as a painter of car bottoms, were upgraded to helper-level jobs. In Wilmington the Pullman repair shop hired more black men but only as laborers, while the Richmond repair shop remained all white during the years of USRA control.[18]

Pullman porters were especially disappointed by the USRA. For years they had demanded a living wage to free them from the insecurity and servility of the tipping system and had protested the lack of access to conductor positions. They hoped and expected that government control would help them achieve both goals, but it did neither. The USRA gave the porters a sizable wage increase, but because agency officials did not re-evaluate the base onto which they added the percentage raise, porters still had to rely on tips. Nor did the agency challenge Pullman's policy of reserving conductor positions for white men.[19]

African Americans' hopes for new opportunities produced only fleeting results at Pullman. Julius Avendorph, who supervised the porters in Chicago, encouraged company executives to open clerical work in the central office to black men, and in 1918 they hired eight young African Americans as office boys or beginning clerks. Pullman officials were well aware that some black men qualified for these jobs, because every summer, when the demand for porters increased, the company hired hundreds of black college students on a temporary basis. Yet in the past officials had refused to hire black college graduates permanently for positions suited to their education. Avendorph's own history with the company exemplified the barriers to black advancement. The Fisk alumnus had come to Chicago in the 1880s and, like many educated black men, found that racism blocked access to all but service jobs. He became an elevator operator in a hotel but then turned to local Republican politics and obtained a government job. In 1897 Pullman president Robert Todd Lincoln hired Avendorph, who was then a social leader of Chicago's African American community, to oversee the porters. During the next two decades hundreds of men got their jobs as porters or were reinstated on Avendorph's recommendation. Despite his powerful position, Avendorph's job title was messenger, and the company would not even accord him the title of clerk until 1921.[20] Pullman's white executives, like most other white men at that time, refused to acknowledge that a black man might in fact hold a supervisory position, even over other black men.

Pullman's white clerks objected to their new black co-workers and complained to the USRA that "the company have not only employed girls at a far less salary to take the place of men in the last year, but have also introduced negro clerks, at a smaller salary, to share our daily work, drinking and toilet facilities, etc."[21] During World War I white men faced simultaneous challenges to the gender and racial hierarchies that privileged them. Feminist pressure to open new jobs to women coincided with the migration north of thousands of black Americans looking for jobs and homes. Sharing work and facilities suggested equality between white and black men, but opening new office jobs to women did not necessarily change the relationship between the sexes. The hierarchy of gender was still anchored outside the workplace in the patriarchal family, and the expectation that women would be wives and mothers first and paid workers second justified their lower wages and confinement to dead-end jobs.[22] As thousands of black Americans headed to cities like Chicago in search of freedom from segregation and second-class citizenship, they contested the hierarchy of race inside and outside the workplace.

Pullman's experiment with racial integration in the central office was an exception, and in its district offices and repair shops supervisors did not breach the color line in clerical work. The experiment was also short lived, as the tenure of these eight men did not outlast the period of government control. That integration did not last at Pullman was hardly unique; the catalogue sales companies, Sears Roebuck and Montgomery Ward, hired black women for clerical work during World War I but laid off most of them afterward too. Yet the failure at Pullman reveals the complex relationship between race, gender, and jobs in the modern bureaucracy. The only way to keep black men from climbing job ladders that led from clerical work to management was to create a third classification of occupations—in addition to men's jobs and women's jobs—based on race. Pullman officials chose not to do this; white women would supply them with all the inexpensive labor they needed for the office.[23]

Race, Gender, and System Federation #122

Although women and racial minorities found only limited opportunities for new jobs in the sleeping-car service, they had a significant influence on the union movement in Pullman repair shops and yards. Historically, the shopcraft unions confined their membership to white men, but increasing diversity and militant workers challenged this criterion and eventually shaped Pullman System Federation #122 into a more inclusive organization. In early 1919 white seamstresses at Pullman's St. Louis repair shop made the first claim on the shopcraft unions when they asked for support in their protest against the shop manager's failure to give them the mechanics' rate. They asked to join the men's local of the Brotherhood of Railway Carmen, and the union's national office acceded to the men's request to bring the seamstresses in and fight their case. As women's employment on the railroads became more common, the BRCA changed its charter to allow white women membership. By the summer of 1919 seamstresses at most Pullman repair shops and yards had joined the previously all-male BRCA locals, but where they were numerous enough, at the Calumet and Buffalo shops, they formed their own locals.[24]

Pullman car cleaners posed the biggest challenge to BRCA membership criteria because so many were members of racial minorities. The BRCA welcomed white car cleaners, and at some yards women belonged to the same locals as men, while at others they formed separate locals. But the increasing number of nonwhite car cleaners were forced to look elsewhere. Just like other Pullman workers, car cleaners needed unions to force recalcitrant supervisors to pay them the government-mandated wages: forty cents per hour instead of the twenty-nine cents Pullman paid men or the twenty-eight cents women received.[25] The AFL offered to directly charter union locals not affiliated with existing labor unions that discriminated against black workers, but it excluded entirely workers of Asian origin and descent. The AFL called such union locals "federal labor unions" and ordinarily established them to "hold" workers before it decided which craft union had jurisdiction over their jobs. Using this structure to bring black workers into the AFL was fraught with ambiguity, because none of the railroad craft unions wanted them. Like the porters, the black car cleaners were divided about the best course of action. Some formed Car and Coach Cleaners Federal Labor Unions, some joined the Railway Men's International Benevolent Industrial Association, and others belonged to no union at all.[26]

The BRCA's history of racial and gender exclusion created a chaotic situation in Pullman yards, many of which employed white and black women and white and black men. At one St. Louis yard, where three white women worked, each belonged to a different organization—one to a women's local of the BRCA, one to a mixed local of the BRCA, and one to a Coach Cleaners Federal Labor Union. Florence E. Clark, an investigator for the Women's Service Section of the USRA, noted "the danger to the women of splitting the economic power of the white and colored women, the colored women assigned to colored mixed locals of men and women, and the white women forced into ineffective separate women's locals which are little more than women's auxiliaries to the Carmen's Union."[27] In such situations Pullman supervisors could play fast and loose with the rules, knowing that workers could not mount a strong appeal to the USRA.

Some yard supervisors consciously used competition for jobs to divide workers along racial lines, as another investigator's account of her discussion with a Pullman car cleaner from Council Bluffs, Iowa, revealed: "The whole gang was originally colored under a white forewoman. This forewoman began changing them to whites until all were replaced. Later, out of spite to some of the workers another forewoman took on these two colored women. It doesn't seem to her [the car cleaner] fair that colored women should be given white women's places!"[28]

Yet it would be inaccurate to emphasize only the ubiquity of racial and gender prejudices. The war was a liminal period, attitudes were in flux, and some workers saw unity as necessary, even desirable. Attempts to build inclusive unions of whites and blacks, men and women, like that of the Stockyards Labor Council in Chicago, ultimately proved unsuccessful, but they reflected the willingness of many to accept all co-workers as partners in the struggle for industrial democracy.[29]

Pullman workers in the St. Louis yards exemplified the range of attitudes and behaviors in the railroad industry. At one end of the spectrum stood the head of a BRCA local who told a government investigator: "The women belong to some sort of an organization which is trying to affiliate itself with us, but they have no *more right in our organization than the niggers.*"[30] At the very same time, however, white and black, men and women workers at two other Pullman yards in the city organized into one union, Coach Cleaners Local #16088, with a black leader, Jordan W. Chambers. A government investigator who spoke with Chambers reported: "Despite the activity of the Carmen to get the white cleaners, Chambers got most of them into the Coach Cleaners local. . . . The men argued . . . that the women should not get the same rate of pay as the men. Chambers told the Field Agent that he told them that 'he knew the men should get more than the women but unless they got the same rate for the women as they did for the men the Pullman Co. would hire more women than men and thus keep men out of work.'"[31] Chambers and the Coach Cleaners Local achieved equal pay for men and women, both black and white, at the two yards.

Although they were in many cases new to Pullman yards, the black car cleaners were anything but reticent about their demands. They protested to the USRA when the company denied them their due, and they rejected second-class status in the AFL and led the movement to abolish racial barriers in the shopcraft unions. Their campaign began at the AFL's annual convention in June 1919, where Jordan Chambers presented a resolution asking the organization either to charter an international union for black workers or to use its influence to induce unions to admit them. Garret Rice, head of Pullman's black car cleaners in Chicago, and representatives of other federal labor unions supported this resolution, but the AFL rejected it. At the next convention Chambers presented a resolution asking that the AFL prohibit any union from adopting racial lines in its constitution. He and Frank M. Phaire, head of Pullman's Philadelphia Coach Cleaners' Local, also supported another resolution that requested an international charter for a coach cleaners union to take jurisdiction away from the discriminatory BRCA. Chambers further proposed that the AFL sponsor a black organizer and mount an education campaign among both white and black workers to "convince them of the necessity of bringing into the ranks of labor all men who work, regardless of race, creed, or color." The AFL committee on organization responded by recommending that the BRCA eliminate the racial barrier in its constitution, and the head of the BRCA promised that he would place the matter before the union's next annual convention. When no action was forthcoming, Chambers introduced another resolution at the 1921 convention asking that the AFL suspend any union that failed to eliminate racial barriers to membership.[32]

Although the AFL again rejected Chambers's resolution, the BRCA finally acted. It adopted the strategy of segregation, amending its constitution to create separate lodges for black workers where their employment had "become a permanent institution." In the Pullman Company, where almost half of all car cleaners were black, the permanency of their employment was not in doubt. The structure of segregated lodges left union power in white hands, but some of Pullman's federal labor unions then joined the BRCA and System Federation #122. Others, including Chambers's integrated local, remained independent.[33]

Management Fights Back

Government controls over private industry were a temporary response to an emergency, and once the war ended wartime agencies disbanded. Corporations sought to re-establish prewar conditions by slashing wages, increasing hours, revising work rules, and undermining unions. A huge strike wave engulfed the nation in 1919 as more than four million workers walked off the job in an effort to maintain their wartime gains. The long and bitter steel strike, the Seattle general strike, and the Boston police strike appeared to many Americans as unprecedented threats to the established order, and they created fears of class warfare on a scale not seen since the Pullman strike of 1894. At the same time employers exacerbated public apprehension by equating state regulation and collective bargaining with communism and U.S. strikers with the newly triumphant Bolshevik revolutionaries in Russia. Attorney General A. Mitchell Palmer initiated a government crackdown on radicals that began the first "red scare" in the United States. Without support from the federal government or the general public, newly organized workers lost their strikes and their unions in industry after industry.[34]

As part of their effort to smash unions in 1919, many large manufacturers established shop committee systems, which gave workers an avenue for airing grievances and a voice in policy making on issues like safety. These systems, unlike those that the War Labor Board had encouraged manufacturers to establish, gave workers no voice over issues like wage rates that were crucial to management control. Furthermore, by restricting voting rights to longer-tenured workers and service as worker representatives to "trustworthy" employees, these representation plans denied the spirit of industrial democracy that had shaped the wartime shop committee systems. But used in concert with welfare programs and a policy of firing union members, employers expected these employee representation plans (ERPs) to keep real unions at bay. The Pullman Company first attempted to establish an ERP at the Car Works in the spring of 1919, but the workers rejected it. The next year F. L. Simmons, the assistant federal auditor for the USRA who had secretly counseled Pullman officials about how to avoid resolving union grievances, became supervisor of industrial relations, and he revived the plan. He insisted that Car Works employees had asked for another vote and that a majority approved the plan in May 1920.[35] Even though the company did not face a serious union challenge at the Car Works, it continued to follow the policies established by other manufacturing corporations, if only as insurance.

While most workers experienced defeat in 1919, railroad workers remained under the umbrella of the USRA, so re-establishing the open shop was much more difficult for railroad corporations. Railroad unions feared a return to private management and advanced a plan for government ownership of the railroads, which the AFL supported. Because members of Congress had been so impressed with the efficiency of consolidated management of the railroads in comparison to the prewar era of competition, they hesitated to return to private control without creating a mechanism for government oversight. Fashioning appropriate legislation took time, and the USRA lasted through February 1920. In the more conservative and antiunion political environment, however, Congress rejected the labor movement's call for government ownership and returned the railroads to private hands in the Transportation Act of 1920. In order to minimize rail strikes, the act established the Railroad Labor Board to determine wages in the industry and to arbitrate disputes about union contract provisions. This agency then created boards of adjustment modeled on the wartime ones to encourage negotiated settlements of disagreements. But the Railroad Labor Board was fatally flawed as a regulatory body, because Congress made compliance with its decisions voluntary. Furthermore, although Congress framed the new legislation with the expectation that unions would continue to represent workers, it did not specifically guarantee workers' right to unionize, as the USRA had done.[36]

When the USRA died, the Pullman Company and the railroads felt free to re-establish the prewar balance of power between labor and management, but the national agreements that they had signed during the war stood in the way. Companies looked for points of weakness and began ignoring and undermining contract provisions.[37] At the Calumet Repair Shop managers also sought to exploit the lack of protection for women workers under the Railroad Labor Board. When the Women's Service Section of the USRA disbanded, the new board made no special provision for ensuring gender equity. Although Pullman repair shops had provided few opportunities for women during the war, in March 1920, at the very moment of transition to private control, Calumet managers first hired women for jobs outside the upholstery department that previously were "men's work." They did so in search of less expensive workers. Women, like twenty-three-year-old Cecelia Daczkowska from Poland, entered an old helper-level specialty, paint scrubbing (washing down the outside of a car between coats of paint). The company paid women paint scrubbers the laborers' rate of forty-nine cents per hour rather than the helpers' rate of sixty cents. The shop also hired more women, like nineteen-year-old Maria Benicky from Czechoslovakia, for unskilled labor, channeling most of them into a "woman's labor gang" assigned to janitorial work. Immigrant women from nearby neighborhoods had few job opportunities that paid as much as forty-nine cents per hour, and women from southern and eastern Europe took most of these new jobs.[38]

Women who worked for lower wages, even in only a few positions, clearly threatened men, and System Federation #122 protested to the Railroad Labor Board the lack of equal pay for the women paint scrubbers. In July 1920, when the board granted shop workers' demands for higher wages, it also ruled for System Federation #122. In August the Calumet Repair Shop began to pay the women paint scrubbers, like the men, the new helpers' rate of seventy-three cents per hour. But the 1920 wage decisions revealed the declining influence of the feminist movement too: unlike the USRA, the Railroad Labor Board would not go beyond the concept of equal pay for the same work to attack the idea of a "woman's wage scale." When the board increased the mechanics' rate from seventy-two cents per hour to eighty-five cents, it left Pullman seamstresses behind. They now earned one penny less per hour than women paint scrubbers, who threatened men's jobs. Nor did System Federation #122 protest this discrimination between skilled women and men. At the end of the war the AFL shopcraft unions attempted to push women out of "men's jobs," and some men at Pullman repair shops and yards colluded with managers in expelling women from new positions. In this climate concern for equity for the seamstresses faded.[39]

Once the company had to pay women paint scrubbers equally with men, management began to phase out their employment, laying them off and not recalling them. Within a year all the women paint scrubbers and most women laborers were gone from the Calumet shop. Cecilia Daczkowska remained but only by becoming a seamstress. In the railroad industry generally, women made lasting inroads only in clerical, laundry, and janitorial jobs, and the belief that shopcraft work was "men's work" continued.[40]

Because the Railroad Labor Board still recognized the national agreements and sometimes supported union demands, Pullman executives looked for a new strategy to displace System Federation #122 and other unions in the sleeping-car service. Pullman's president, John S. Runnells, wanted to eliminate the new wage rates and work rules in the sleeping-car service that "made it difficult to operate with either economy or facility."[41] F. L. Simmons, now Pullman's supervisor of industrial relations, counseled that the company should follow the model used in the Car Works—establish an employee representation plan. Simmons designed an ERP for the sleeping-car service that divided workers into three groups: office workers, conductors, and storeroom clerical employees in one group, porters and maids in another, and yard workers, car cleaners, storeroom personnel, and minor supervisory forces in the third. He separated Pullman's repair shop workers from the sleeping-car service and placed them in the ERP for the Car Works. This split repair shop and yard workers and thus divided the constituency of System Federation #122. Simmons recommended his ERP as part of a larger strategy to re-establish the open shop. He further counseled Pullman executives about hiring an outside firm to disrupt the existing union organizations by putting men in the shops who would charge that union officials were making fortunes while using the workers as pawns and who would attempt to foment factions and stimulate disturbances.[42]

Workers throughout the sleeping-car service opposed the ERP because they recognized that the ERP was no substitute for a real union. When one district supervisor tried to force the plan on yard mechanics in New York, they protested to the Railroad Labor Board that "the record of our work as loyal citizens in war or industry either at home or abroad in the hope for true democracy has proven itself. . . . Employees of today prefer to have voice and assist in plans that govern their conditions."[43] The experience of the manufacturing workers strengthened suspicions about the true nature of the ERP. In 1921, when a foreman discharged seven men from the Car Works for poor performance, eighty others joined in demanding a hearing for them under the grievance system. The superintendent then discharged all eighty workers as unsatisfactory.[44]

Actually establishing the ERP in the sleeping-car service was not an easy task. After a year and a half of attempting to bring the conductors into the ERP, Simmons gave up and signed a contract with the Order of Sleeping Car Conductors. Recognizing this independent union may have seemed to be a worthwhile compromise, because it kept Pullman conductors out of the powerful Order of Railway Conductors. Porters also resisted the ERP; they protested deviations from wartime policies, and in 1920 another fledgling union, the Pullman Porters and Maids Protective Association, appeared in a few districts. Because porters were the single largest group of employees in the sleeping-car service, the success of the ERP hinged on their participation. Although supervisors continued to fire men whom they identified as leaders of protests or unions, intimidation alone would not bring porters into the ERP. Simmons began to use the Pullman Porters Benefit Association of America (PPBAA), which the company helped establish in 1915, as a positive incentive for acquiescence to the ERP. The company helped the organization to grow by paying its administrative costs, even though it did nothing similar for white workers. By 1922 the PPBAA had fifty-three hundred members, and the ERP also claimed to speak for the porters.[45]

In the yards and repair shops Simmons waged a two-year battle against System Federation #122; he held elections at one facility after another and in September 1920 had an early victory at the repair shop in Buffalo, New York. But it was a hard struggle elsewhere; not only white shopcraft workers but also black car cleaners rejected the ERP in election after election. The car cleaners' federal labor unions fought the ERP vigorously and solicited community support through the black press. Despite workers' rejection of the ERP, the Pullman Company proceeded as if its workers were not union members and as if it were not bound by the 1919 national agreement with System Federation #122. Managers discussed grievances with ERP officials rather than union representatives, and they fired or laid off union leaders. Yet Pullman shop and yard workers did not acquiesce to the abrogation of provisions in their national agreements. As Pullman workers had in the past, they acted, with or without union leadership, when they believed that management had treated them unfairly. When the manager of the St. Louis repair shop tried to withhold the prescribed wage rate from five lead burners in June 1920, a majority of the shop force walked out with them. The wildcat strike spread to other Pullman repair shops, and at its height more than three thousand workers, including virtually the entire Calumet shop force, was on strike. The walkout ended only when C. W. Pflager, mechanical superintendent at the Chicago headquarters, intervened and ordered the St. Louis manager to pay the wage rate specified in thc national agreement.[46]

Though workers for the railroads and the sleeping-car service struggled hard to keep their unions, their task was made more difficult when President Warren G. Harding appointed new members who had no sympathy for unions to the Railroad Labor Board. Now the board allowed railroads to contract work out to escape their unionized workers, and Pullman management took this option for some electrical repairs. Then, in January 1921, the board allowed Pullman to increase regular working hours in its yards and repair shops from eight to nine per day.[47] Workers' earnings declined when they ceased to receive overtime pay for the ninth hour, but they did not decline sufficiently to satisfy the company.

When officials sought an actual cut in wage rates, Simmons looked to the ERP to rubber-stamp the cuts, because on paper the representatives had the authority to make recommendations on "all questions which arise as to wages and working conditions."[48] The representatives for the repair shops and yards agreed to the wage cut in January and then again in June 1921. Both times, however, Simmons asked for a vote of the workers themselves to show that they accepted the ERP. Both times workers rejected the wage cuts.[49] In July 1921 the Railroad Labor Board rescued Pullman and the railroads when it cut the mechanics' rate from eighty-five cents per hour to seventy-seven cents.

The Railroad Labor Board further aided the railroads by disbanding its boards of adjustment at the corporations' request. Now unions had to appeal grievances directly to the agency, and the already time-consuming process slowed measurably. In June 1921 the chairman of System Federation #122, Harry Smith, accused the board of holding up a decision on the merits of Pullman workers' complaints until the company could smash the unions. At that point 150 grievances had accumulated. Pullman workers looked to the unions to achieve contract standards, and when these were violated, they wanted action. Yet the national leadership of the shopcraft unions insisted that the system federation work through the slow procedures. Pullman shop workers were becoming disillusioned with the unions, and the Richmond workers protested that "our patience is exhausted inasmuch as the Pullman Company has been allowed to continually violate the Transportation Act, while the employees have lived up to the law. . . . We demand that the U.S. Labor Board stop the Pullman Co. from further violating the Transportation Act. Further, we blame the Railway Employes' Department [of the AFL] and Harry Smith and all the other General Chairmen . . . for their delay in not taking earlier action."[50] In Chicago Pullman shop workers were looking elsewhere, and the secretary of the Calumet Joint Labor Council reported that "the streets are filled with men declaring they are going to join the I.W.W. and get direct action."[51]

In an attempt to force the Railroad Labor Board to act, Smith called for a strike vote, and more than 90 percent of the twelve thousand workers in Pullman repair shops and yards voted to walk out. The St. Louis shop began a strike, but the national leadership of the shopcraft unions refused to sanction the walkout and charged Smith with insubordination.

The union leaders believed their organizations were too weak to win strikes at that time and might be destroyed in such confrontations. Smith, like Heathcoate in 1894, led workers who believed that they should decide when to fight. The Department of Labor sent in a conciliator, and in September 1921 the Railroad Labor Board finally sided with the workers and ordered Pullman to negotiate with its employees. At this point the Pullman Company was not prepared to follow the lead of the Pennsylvania Railroad and simply ignore the board's rulings. The company signed a contract with System Federation #122 that recognized union-defined job classifications and seniority within each craft—a clear setback for management's effort to reimpose the methods of the prewar era.[52]

Within a few months, however, Pullman workers charged that shop and yard managers were again violating the contract by using intimidation and firing or laying off union members. Simmons continued to hold elections to get approval of the ERP, and a bare majority of workers at the Richmond repair shop voted for it in January 1922. Railroad officials generally were emboldened in their fight against unions when the Railroad Labor Board virtually abolished overtime pay and allowed the reintroduction of piece rates in late 1921. At Pullman Simmons's victories were real as the fight with the ERP took a toll on the system federation. In February 1922 John F. Nelson, the new general chairman of System Federation #122, estimated that membership was down to 60 percent of those employed.[53] Allegiance to the unions waned in part because managers refused to handle grievances brought by leaders of the union locals.

Nelson, a U.S.-born upholsterer, had worked at the Calumet Repair Shop since 1901, and he understood what would be necessary to reverse the company's gains. He asked the leadership of the six federated shopcraft unions to fund three organizers—Harry Smith of the Brotherhood of Railway Carmen, R. J. Smith of the International Brotherhood of Electrical Workers, and Garret Rice of the Federal Locals of Colored Car Cleaners—to make a nationwide tour to revive the federation. The composition of the organizing team revealed how important unifying black and white workers was to the system federation, as well as its willingness to include the black unions that had spurned second-class status in the BRCA. Nelson noted that the system federation could not finance this organizing drive itself, but he believed that virtually all workers would reinstate with or join the unions if the system federation reached out to them. The Railway Employees' Department agreed to fund one person, Nelson himself, to make a national tour. This not only minimized expenses but also facilitated resolution of grievances because many Pullman managers refused to discuss them with leaders of the individual shopcraft unions, especially Harry Smith, who was anathema for his part in forcing the company to sign a union contract.[54]

Nelson's tour renewed workers' loyalty to the unions again, because the company was not ready to openly defy the Railroad Labor Board, and the board insisted that local managers discuss grievances with him. ERP officials could not fight for the provisions of the 1921 contract, because the ERP was not a party to it, but Nelson could deliver. Furthermore, Nelson worked hard to unify black and white workers, and more of the federal labor unions of black car cleaners, including those in Philadelphia, Boston, and New York, became affiliated with the BRCA. By May, Nelson saw racial diversity as a threat to worker unity only at the few Pullman yards that employed car cleaners of Asian origin and descent, because they were not accepted into AFL unions. Nelson also worked on women's grievances, such as being replaced by men in violation of their seniority, and he encouraged the amalgamation of men's and women's locals to strengthen both, a process that many women demanded as a condition of reinstating with the system federation. Although the shopcraft unions on many railroads had turned against women's membership, the Pullman system federation had to be more welcoming when nearly two thousand women worked as car cleaners.[55]

Combating the ERP was as easy as Nelson expected it to be, because workers' loyalty to the ERP was superficial. At Pullman's Seattle yard, for instance, where almost all workers belonged to the ERP as late as mid-May 1922, Nelson persuaded the ERP chairman and two committeemen to rejoin the system federation and other workers followed their lead.[56] For public relations purposes the company pronounced the ERP a great success, but by June 1922 the system federation had strengthened itself enormously. Simmons declared: "A year without a strike or a lockout and with numerous grievances handled amicably, shows that we have reached the broader grounds of mutual understanding, mutual confidence and mutual respect."[57] The year without a strike or lockout was not over, however.

The Railroad Shopmen's Strike of 1922

Members of the shopcraft unions became increasingly restive as railroad companies abrogated contract provisions and ignored any pro-union rulings by the Railroad Labor Board. Wildcat strikes spread as workers lost faith in the unions' ability to enforce negotiated settlements. Yet railroad companies continued to complain that the wages that they paid were too high, and the board responded by cutting wage rates for shop workers even further: mechanics from seventy-seven cents per hour to seventy cents and helpers from fifty-four cents to forty-seven cents.[58] Members of the shopcraft unions ignored the advice of their leaders and voted overwhelming to strike when the wage cuts became effective. On July 1, 1922, 400,000 repair shop and yard workers began a three-month strike that seemed to repeat the confrontation of 1894. Unionized workers and railroad corporations faced off over non-negotiable demands, reached an impasse, and brought large sectors of the economy to a halt through their conflict. The federal government intervened on the side of the corporations, and workers once more lost their unions and often their jobs. Yet nothing was quite the same as it had been three decades earlier, except the determination of railroad workers not to meekly accept wages and conditions that violated their standards for just labor.

The strengths and weaknesses of the American Railway Union influenced the outcome of the 1894 strike, and the structure of railroad unions in 1922 shaped this strike too. The division between workers in different regions of the country that weakened the ARU had disappeared; the unions were truly national now. But the concept of an industrial union had also disappeared as workers now had much stronger allegiances to their individual crafts than to railroad workers as a whole. The six shopcraft unions agreed on united demands and action, but railroad workers as a whole were not ready to unite even in a structure of system federations that included all crafts. Thus, unlike the 1894 strike, this one did not shut down entire railroads because workers in other crafts did not walk out.[59]

As in 1894, the strike gave railroad corporations the opportunity to smash unions. The Pullman Company consciously planned such a strategy, using the weapon that had served it so well in the past, the lockout. Managers began laying off workers in the last weeks of June to secure an orderly shut down of Pullman repair shops. Then the company closed the shops on July 1 for ten days under the guise that this was "10 Days Holiday Given," an extension of the usual three-day closing over Independence Day. This was not, of course, a paid vacation, and System Federation #122 insisted that it was a lockout under the terms of the 1921 contract. As part of its strategy, the company did not announce the new wage cut before July 10, and thus it could claim that workers who refused to return that day were striking without cause and had ceased to have a claim on employment. Yet the company fully intended to implement the wage cut, as the minutes of the executive committee of the board of directors record: "Inasmuch as The Pullman Company has not reduced wages and will not do so until the strike is settled, the employes of the Pullman Company who walked out of the yards and shops voluntarily left the service of the Company, have been paid off, and therefore, are not in a position to demand consideration from the Company as to seniority or other rights after the strike is settled. This should enable the Company to take back the men it wishes and to refuse to hire objectionable men."[60] The Pennsylvania Railroad also used this strategy to divide and confuse workers, many of whom returned to its repair shops and yards on the tenth. But when Pullman managers tried to reopen that day, they found that their workers were almost completely united in support of the strike. Pullman repair shop and yard workers held huge meetings to vote on whether to return to work, and except for the Buffalo shop, no more than a handful of workers ignored the decisions of their shop mates to strike.[61]

Throughout the next several weeks the strike by almost twelve thousand Pullman repair shop and yard workers coalesced, and estimates of the percentage on strike ranged up to 98 percent. At each facility only a few mechanics, primarily older white men worried about losing their pensions, joined supervisory personnel to cope with emergency repairs. All the seamstresses struck, as did most black men who worked in the repair shops. Virtually all car cleaners—women and men, black, white, or Asian—walked out too, including those who belonged to federal labor unions rather than the BRCA. On most railroads co-workers supported each other through the strike regardless of their race, just as they did at Pullman. For instance, Japanese American and Mexican American workers, who had been employed in previous union-busting episodes at the Santa Fe Railroad's repair shop in Richmond, California, stood fast with white co-workers. Indeed, craft rather than race was the primary division during this strike. Pullman's white conductors, like railroad conductors, worked through the strike, as did Pullman's black porters.[62] Faced with solid opposition among its shop and yard workers, the Pullman Company closed its repair shops again and proceeded, as it had in previous strikes, to wait out its workers.

Pullman Workers on Strike

Shop workers throughout the country, including virtually all Pullman shop and yard workers, stayed on strike for three long months. The Railroad Labor Board was responsible in part for the length of the strike, because it encouraged companies to recognize seniority only for nonstrikers, a point on which the unions would not compromise. The ability to maintain this long walkout testified to the unions' strong organization, but the nationwide scope of the strike also revealed the changing sources of worker solidarity in the twentieth century. The strike transcended any regional or community base as workers stood fast with members of their system federations in other cities and towns. The USRA and the Railroad Labor Board were critical in strengthening attachments beyond the local level by giving the system federations such a pivotal role in improving wages and working conditions and by implementing national standards. This time, not only Calumet shop workers, both new employees and veterans of the 1894 strike, but also workers at all Pullman repair shops and yards stayed out for the duration of the strike.[63] Workers' ability to maintain a long strike reflected first the strength of their system federation; second, the level of militancy of other local shop workers; and, third, the type of community support that was crucial to strikers in the nineteenth century.

The declining importance of community solidarity was apparent even in Chicago. Virtually all railroad repair shops in the greater Pullman area were on strike, and railroads found they could not recruit strikebreakers locally but had to import them from elsewhere. The situation was so tense that the Pullman Company did not even attempt to reopen the Calumet Repair Shop during the summer. But employees at the Pullman Car Works did not join their neighbors and fellow workers on strike. Even those like Arthur Bernier, a French Canadian water fitter who had worked in the Calumet shop for six months in 1917, did not walk out in sympathy. Most manufacturing workers no longer felt the same solidarity with railroad workers that they had in the past, and only a small number who belonged to the Industrial Workers of the World struck in concert with the repair shop workers.[64] Yet despite the lack of support from their closest neighbors, Calumet workers maintained strike discipline for more than three months.

The militancy of Pullman's Wilmington workers further highlights the extent to which allegiance to national institutions replaced community support as the critical issue in strike militancy. Many Wilmington workers were long-term employees, and some had been the nonstrikers of 1894. George Herdman, a glazier who was secretary-treasurer of the strike committee, began work at the Wilmington shop in 1892 when he was sixteen. He had not gone on strike in 1894 but now was leading the action as a married man of forty-six. Like Herdman, most Wilmington shop workers were native born, often locally born, white men, and social activities, like the shop choir led by the foreman of the upholstery department, gave many a bond with management. If they shared a similar heritage with the 1894 shop force, by 1922 Pullman's Wilmington workers had a wholly new experience of working for several years under union contracts that brought them vastly improved wages and job security and reversed recent management attempts at undermining the crafts. That experience made them solid supporters of the strike, and the Wilmington shop's BRCA local even reached out to organize two small groups of Pullman yard workers in Baltimore and Philadelphia.[65]

Pullman shop workers in Wilmington defied their community's antiunion ethos, which had changed little, although the Du Pont Company rather than smaller manufacturers now controlled the city. AFL craft unions had small memberships locally, but none succeeded in unionizing any major workplaces. Not surprisingly, the 1922 railroad shopmen's strike was the only significant strike in Wilmington during the first three decades of the twentieth century.[66] Many workers there still had faith in employer paternalism. When the Pullman Company first announced that it was closing down the repair shop in preparation for the strike, the leaders of Wilmington's Central Labor Union contacted J. V. Weaver, a Pullman vice president who had been a general manager at a Wilmington shipyard. They asked him to intervene because "the labor body knows Mr. Weaver well, and believes his interest in Wilmington is intense, to a degree that would mean that his influence could be brought to bear in an endeavor to give constant employment to the Pullman workers here."[67] These union leaders seem to have envisioned a replay of 1894 in which Wilmington workers collected their paychecks while Pullman workers elsewhere starved. The leaders of the Pullman System Federation in Wilmington did not subscribe to this approach, and those who thought that local attachments might outweigh the needs of a multinational corporation were quickly disabused of the notion.

Pullman's Wilmington workers maintained their strike even in the absence of solidarity from other railroad shop workers in the city. The strength of each system federation determined how long the strike would last on any railroad, and by June 1922 System Federation #122 was at a peak. The largest repair shop in Wilmington belonged to the Pennsylvania Railroad, which led the industry's assault on the shopcraft unions and had been most effective in undermining its system federation. Pennsylvania shop workers had the lowest overall response to the strike call—barely half joined the walkout. Pullman workers in Wilmington picketed the Pennsylvania repair shop as well as their own, and they razzed the railroad workers who crossed their line.[68]

If community support no longer predicted whether workers would strike or their ability to sustain a strike, it was still helpful, and Richmond, California, residents bolstered the militancy of shop and yard workers there. In the decade since the opening of Pullman's Richmond repair shop, the predominantly working-class citizenry had organized, and the reign of the open-shop ideology ended. Union members no longer hid their allegiances, and Pullman workers opened their strike headquarters in the grill of the Pullman Hotel, next door to the repair shop. The repair shops of the Santa Fe Railroad and the Pullman Company were the second- and third-largest employers in the city, so the strike involved many residents. The *Richmond Daily Independent* reported that local merchants and businesses supported striking shop workers by selling goods at cost, extending liberal credit, and donating to the strike funds. A Methodist minister also publicly backed the strikers and urged his congregation to support them.[69] Capping this community support, the *Richmond Daily Independent* editorialized that this was "a justifiable strike" because the wage reductions were too drastic. The editor recognized that the strikers played an important role in the city and deemed them solid citizens, in much the same way that the Pullman strikers of 1894 had been termed "respectable": "They have purchased homes here, they take part in all of the activities that lead to the upbuilding of our city, they support our schools, churches and lodges and a fair day's pay for their efforts means prosperity for all of us. They are entitled to public sympathy, too, because there has been no disorder here. . . . The strikers have acted as high-minded Americans."[70]

The respect accorded Pullman and other shop workers, most of whom were recent arrivals, reflected the civic culture of northern California at the time. Cities in the East Bay area were relatively new and evidenced little division between old settlers and newcomers. In a California lifestyle that already relied on commuting, albeit by light rail, not automobile, workers often lived in one town and worked in another. Only half of Pullman's workers lived in Richmond itself, yet no one suggested that those who lived in nearby El Cerrito, Berkeley, or Oakland were not part of the same community. Nor did the hostility toward immigrants, which had flared during the war, revive to turn public opinion against the shop workers, although barely half the strikers at Pullman had been born in the United States. Strike leaders may well have shaped public perception, however, just as they had in 1894 in Chicago. Joseph P. Reeves, chairman of the Pullman strike committee, was a U.S.-born mechanic who had lived in the city since the opening of the shop in 1911.[71]

Although they received varying amounts of support from their neighbors, Pullman repair shop workers conducted their strike activities similarly in every city. They cooperated with other railroad shop workers and found rhetorical support from other unions but no sympathy strikes. Wilmington's Central Labor Union, for instance, compiled a list of "friendly merchants" so that union members could help by rewarding those who were aiding the shop workers. As strikers began to experience real hardship, they kept their spirits up with daily meetings, and men invited their wives to join them in order to shore up support at home for the loss of income. Activities to enforce strike discipline were critical to the success of the strike, and everywhere strikers engaged in mass picketing of their workplaces to discourage strikebreakers. Pullman workers at Wilmington, like railroad shop workers elsewhere, forced a few men who crossed their picket line to join the strike by heckling them and covering their homes with large yellow signs saying "SCAB." In some cities strikers' wives visited the homes of strikebreakers to urge them not to cross picket lines. Women's participation in this activity played such an important role in Richmond that the Pullman Company and the Santa Fe Railroad obtained federal injunctions that prohibited both union leaders *and their wives* from picketing the shops and from visiting other workers' homes.[72]

As the strike dragged on, violence escalated in many cities around the nation. While guards and police often beat up or shot at pickets, strikers perpetrated much of the violence as they attempted to stop others from breaking the strike. Crossing a picket line was always an incitement to attack, and the Wilmington newspaper reported that the handful of Pullman strikebreakers there walked one mile out of their way to enter the shop grounds where pickets could not get at them. Beatings of strikebreakers going to and from work and sabotage of railroad property became common, even in places like Wilmington that had not seen such activity previously, and some of those arrested for these incidents were Pullman workers. In Chicago, where many railroads imported strikebreakers from other cities, newspapers reported beatings, shootings, or riots virtually every day as strikers tried to keep repair shops closed. Gangs of "labor sluggers" roamed the Calumet region around Pullman, enforcing the strike.[73] Nor did strikers confine their attacks to outsiders. When picketing of local strikebreakers' homes began in Chicago, the *Chicago Daily News* reported that the strikers were "calling in a friendly spirit and had come to warn them of impending danger at the hands of other strikers."[74] The large size of the crowds that surrounded strikebreakers' homes reinforced the thinly veiled threats. Police dispersed the crowd that menaced the home of "an aged couple" who were car cleaners at one Pullman yard, but two Illinois Central workers' families were not as fortunate. According to the *Daily News,* a crowd of strikers and sympathizers, including many women, attacked and tried to burn their homes. The armed wife of one strikebreaker held off the crowd, reportedly saying: "You were all my friends once . . . but I'll kill the next one of you who throws a stone."[75] The shopcraft unions never sanctioned violence, but many union members saw it as a necessary and legitimate method of enforcing adherence to the strike.

Defeating the Strike

By late July the strike was exerting a devastating effect on the national economy. More and more railroad equipment broke down, and the disruption of transportation, combined with a coal miners' strike then in progress, produced shortages of fuel and raw materials for factories. Growers feared that the Pacific Coast fruit crop would rot in the yards. At this point the federal government again became critical to the success or failure of the workers' movement. Responding to the strike's economic effects, President Harding first proposed a compromise, but railroad executives refused to use it as a basis for bargaining, because Harding recommended recognition of the strikers' seniority rights. Subsequently, Harding put his full weight behind the railroads' and the Railroad Labor Board's open-shop drive. In a replay of 1894 the attorney general, now Harry Daugherty, obtained an injunction that denied the rights of free speech and assembly to the shop workers. The injunction was so extreme that it provoked widespread criticism in Congress and the press, and Daugherty retreated from fully enforcing its provisions.[76]

Yet this time government intervention was not decisive. The strikers continued to hold out, and in late August the Association of Railway Executives split when the Baltimore and Ohio, the Seaboard Airline, and the New York Central railroads led more than forty others in seeking a compromise. The leaders of the shopcraft unions, who had become increasingly dubious about the strike, agreed to abandon their demand for a national contract and to negotiate on a company-by-company basis. In September 1922 the federated shopcraft unions signed contracts with these railroads, which agreed to take back strikers with their seniority intact, albeit with the pay cut that had triggered the walkout. By the end of October 126 railroads had signed agreements with the unions. Although workers lost the strike and acceded to the wage cut, they maintained union recognition and their seniority on these railroads.[77]

The Pullman Company was not among those that sought compromise. Rather, it stood firm with the Pennsylvania Railroad and other hardliners and like them looked to break the strike by hiring new men. Companies recruited members of racial minorities to divide and conquer, although this tactic might require reaching out to new minorities to replace those on strike. For instance, the Santa Fe Railroad imported Native American workers from the Laguna Pueblo in New Mexico to try to reopen its Richmond repair shop, when Japanese American and Mexican American workers there stayed on strike with white co-workers. In other California cities railroads hired Japanese American mechanics where they had not been employed previously. In the East and Midwest railroads usually hired African Americans, and the Illinois Central once again used black strikebreakers at its Burnside shop. There, as in other shops that hired African American men, fears of race riots spread. It had been only a few years since such conflicts swept U.S. cities, but none resulted from the railroad shopmen's strike, because it created no clear racial divide.[78]

During the third week of August the Pullman Company also began to use a racial strategy in order to reopen its repair shops. For the first time the weekly reports made by shop managers on the progress of the strike began to specify the number of "colored" employed along with the usual totals by skill level. Management did not attempt to reopen the Calumet Repair Shop, but at the four other shops the number of workers increased slowly thereafter with the hiring of "colored" employees. Yet through the end of September none of the shops had returned to anywhere near their full employment levels.[79] Indeed, the resolve of Pullman strikers did not weaken until other railroads began to settle their strikes.

The decision by the national union leaders to negotiate with individual railroads divided workers against each other. The chairman of System Federation #122 wrote to the AFL's Railway Employes' Department to protest any settlement that did not include all railroad shop workers, but his plea was ignored along with those from other system federations. Strikers whose employers refused to negotiate felt abandoned by their fellow union members, and many gave up and returned to work. Pullman workers faced this dilemma as the company began to contract out repair work to railroads that had settled their strikes, so that Pullman repair workers were undercut by members of their own unions. Consequently, when the Pullman Company officially reopened its repair shops in October, about one-third of the strikers returned to work. Shop and yard managers were instructed to re-employ only those who agreed to "go along" with the employee representation plan. At the same time the shops hired significant numbers of African Americans to replace strikers who did not return promptly or would not renounce the unions. By mid-October the St. Louis shop had 419 mechanics, helpers, and laborers on the job; 311 were "colored." Pro-union communities like Chicago and Richmond continued to support the railroad shop workers with events like "Tag Days" during which women and children took to the streets to collect donations for strikers. But with union solidarity broken, many more Pullman workers returned to their shops in the coming months. The company had won the strike and refused the efforts of Department of Labor conciliators to effect a settlement with the unions. During the next year the AFL's Railway Employes Department admitted defeat and called off strike after strike as workers returned to their jobs.[80]

After the formal reopening of the Pullman repair shops, the leaders of System Federation #122 asked the national unions to allow Pullman workers to decide for themselves whether to remain on strike or to allow individuals to seek re-employment if they wished. They argued that if workers were allowed to vote on the issue many would retain their union memberships, and then the system federation could present claims to the Railroad Labor Board concerning the technical lockout and other contract violations. The national unions ignored this desire for democracy, but they also did not call off the strike. Pullman leaders remembered only too well the lessons of 1894 and warned them that "your refusal . . . will bring about the abandonment of the respective Organizations and the repetition of the strike in 1894, to the discredit of all responsible persons and the utter impossibility of any further attempt for at least a decade to reorganize."[81] If workers no longer relied as strongly on community support for their union and strike activities as they had in the 1890s, they continued to insist on making their own decisions. Just as they would not compromise beyond a certain point with their employers, they would not sacrifice beyond a certain point at the behest of union leaders. Thus in the winter of 1922–23 Pullman repair shop workers again returned to company employment without a union contract but now with a new group of co-workers—African Americans.

4   Restoring the Open Shop

After defeating strikes and unions in the immediate postwar years, U.S. employers set out to build another open-shop era. Yet many companies, especially in the railroad industry, found that remaining union free required struggle and compromise. The legacy of government intervention and union contracts limited the return to past practices. To achieve their goals Pullman and other companies used a combination of tactics from coercive to conciliatory. On the one hand, Pullman officials continued to hire spy services for surveillance of union activity, while managers recruited new, and they hoped, nonunion workers.[1] On the other, the company extended the structure of bureaucratic labor relations, expanding welfare benefits and establishing employee representation plans. But Pullman and increasing numbers of U.S. employers also pursued a new racial policy, integrating workforces that seemed vulnerable to union organizing. Race now played a dual role in the sleeping-car service: management relied on segregation to control porters and conductors but looked to racial integration to keep unions out of the repair shops and yards. In the manufacturing division the company perfected old policies like the application of technology and industrial engineering, but it also used racial integration where necessary to achieve its aims. Pullman, like most large corporations, re-established the open shop in the 1920s but only by developing increasingly complex systems of labor management. As it did so, its policies ensured that race would assume a central role in Pullman workers' struggles.

New Opportunities for Black Men

Only 40 percent of striking repair shop workers returned on the company's terms in the fall of 1922, and the large number that stayed on strike forced managers to hire new workers in order to reopen the repair shops. The Department of Industrial Relations advised shop managers that they could rehire strikers as long as the workers were willing to renounce System Federation #122, and the department encouraged workers to return by recognizing their pension rights. The company also replaced union benefits that were now lost to the returnees by extending its new group life insurance program, for which it paid all premiums, to the shop and yard workers. Although managers refused employment to the most active union members, they seem not to have discriminated on other grounds, like age, against those seeking reemployment.[2]

But the majority of strikers refused to return without a union contract and under the conditions that the company imposed. Following the policy approved by the board of directors at the beginning of the walkout, the company considered strikers to have quit voluntarily and took them back as new workers with no seniority. Officials did not abolish seniority but again allowed foremen discretion in its application. Furthermore, returning mechanics had to accept the reduction in their hourly rate to seventy cents, while the company continued to pay the few mechanics who worked through the strike the old rate of seventy-seven cents per hour. Management also insisted on reimposing the prewar job structure, and returning strikers who did not accept consignment to a single task had to leave. The Wilmington shop manager, for instance, discharged one returning painter in January 1923, noting on his service card that he "refused to do work instructed. Fighting with Foreman . . . and arrested."[3] On the railroads where the shopcraft unions still had contracts, the unions resisted any restructuring of the crafts, unless it was done with union cooperation, to ensure that workers as well as the company profited. Sharing the fruits of efficiency was not what Pullman officials had in mind as they reinstituted the old specialties.

When the majority of strikers refused to return on this basis, shop managers looked to black men to take their places. Rather than lay off the small number of black men they had hired in August 1922 and return to a white shop force, as most railroads did, the Pullman Company hired more African Americans. By mid-October the St. Louis shop had 419 employees, 311 of whom were "colored," and by the end of November black men comprised 39 percent of Buffalo shop workers. This proportion is explicable solely by active outreach by management because only 1 percent of Buffalo's adult male population was black. The shops took on large numbers of black men throughout 1923 until they were again at full strength. As table 3 reveals, half the men hired in rebuilding the workforce at the Calumet shop were black, as were one-third of those at Wilmington. The company recruited some new black shop workers from its force of car cleaners and porters, many of whom had skills that they had not been able to use. They often moved long distances for a chance to escape service and unskilled labor. Ernest L. Washington, a porter in the New York District, had three years of college and taught night classes in painting in the public schools. He moved to St. Louis to take the skilled position of paint mixer at Pullman's repair shop.[4]

When they looked for new employees, managers considered not only race but skill in a new way. They welcomed workers without previous training in the crafts, "common, ordinary, strong men" whom the foremen could train to do one of the craft specialties designed before the war. Some white and even a few black craftsmen were hired as mechanics at Pullman shops in the year after the strike, but most workers, white or black, entered the shops in helper-level jobs.[5] Yet the company was not planning to exploit these men by keeping them at helper's wages while they did craftsmen's work but to create a force of nonunion mechanics who would accept Pullman's version of scientific management. The company classified the new men as helper-apprentices, a position that the U.S. Railroad Administration developed to alleviate the wartime shortage of mechanics. As helper-apprentices, workers learned a craft in stages, with promotion through prescribed levels at increased pay, so that by the end of five years they were mechanics. During the war Pullman shops had shown little interest in using this position: in November 1919, for instance, the shops employed 554 helpers and 73 apprentices but only 13 helper-apprentices. But now this government innovation could be used to create mechanics as defined by management rather than the craft unions.[6]

The company's determination to rebuild a nonunion shop force made it willing to pay the price for employing so many new, half-trained work-

Table 3. Percentage of Men Hired Who Were Black

Repair Shop	Pre-1922 Strike	Sept. 1922– Dec. 1923	1924–26	1927–29
Calumet	1.3	51.1	17.4	7.1
Richmond	0.0	5.6	14.9	28.0
Wilmington	2.5	34.6	33.3	26.1

Source: Derived from samples described in the appendix.

ers; at first, cars were in poor repair and customers complained. Within a year, however, the condition of the equipment improved as the new workers learned their jobs. As an employee representative explained about one specialty, "You know as well as I do that it doesn't take any great amount of knowledge to learn to paint pipes. . . . You can pick up a laborer and in a very short time teach him that particular end of it."[7]

Perhaps because of the company's long experience of pitting black and white workers against each other as porters and conductors, management chose to offer new job opportunities primarily to black men. Pullman shops did not reach out to hire other racial minorities, although many corporations believed it necessary to hire more widely in order to undercut unions. At its plants near the Calumet Repair Shop, U.S. Steel employed relatively equal numbers of black and Mexican workers for this purpose. Yet Pullman did not use its Mexican operations to recruit workers, although some Mexicans labored at its repair shops in the United States. Luis Lopez, one of the few Mexicans hired at the Calumet shop, presented a letter of recommendation from a brother who worked for the company in Mexico City, but Pullman officials did not actively encourage Mexican workers to come north. The company's focus on using black men also meant that the Richmond repair shop did not hire Asians or Asian Americans, although it could have recruited among the Japanese car cleaners employed at Pullman's yards in California. Many railroad repair shops in that state already hired Asians to counter the shopcraft unions, which denied them membership.[8]

As Pullman managers created biracial shop forces, they maintained the traditional gender division of labor; they offered no new opportunities to women, either white or black.[9] This policy reflected the gender ideology of top management, who dictated that women could do men's jobs only in extraordinary circumstances, even if the work was unskilled. The supervisor of industrial relations insisted on the gender division for car cleaning, for instance, except "on the Pacific Coast, where the demand for labor is such that it is extremely difficult to retain male help of the proper class." He ordered that "it is satisfactory to employ women cleaners to a limited extent, and only to the extent that it is necessary to properly clean the cars."[10] Because of top management's gender ideology, women comprised only 11 percent of company employees in the 1920s. Although Pullman innovated in its use of black men, its limited use of women workers mirrored the situation in the railroad industry and heavy manufacturing, where women made inroads only in clerical work, and even there remained a minority, in the 1920s.

In its repair shops the Pullman Company embarked on a policy that was a step beyond those pursued by most U.S. corporations. Many employers hired more black men in the 1920s both as a bulwark against the AFL unions and because the new immigration laws cut off the supply of European labor. But few industries or companies followed Pullman and provided black men with opportunities for skilled work. Rather, most created a color line that consigned African Americans to unskilled and semiskilled jobs. The only widely available opportunities for black men to rise to skilled and foreman positions were in the hard and grueling work of foundries. Pullman followed these practices in its manufacturing facilities, where black men found no other opportunities for skilled work. Pullman's policy in the repair shops and yards was distinctive in its use of the helper-apprentice position to create skilled black workers. In the steel industry, which had pioneered the creation of job ladders to allow men to progress from laborer to semiskilled to skilled work, black men were hired only for jobs that did not lead upward. Black workers often found greater opportunity in industries like meatpacking, which had no internal labor markets defined by established rules.[11]

All Pullman repair shops followed the same hiring and training policy at the same time, and this suggests that the central office conceived and dictated this initiative. F. L. Simmons, the supervisor of industrial relations, monitored the hiring of black men at the repair shops from August through November 1922 by requiring shop managers to make weekly reports. The social scientists Sterling Spero and Abram Harris, who studied the Pullman Company in the 1920s, asserted that the corporation displaced the manager of the Calumet shop, who had not attempted to reopen during the strike and reportedly objected to hiring black workers. Yet documentation of the development of a racial policy by the Department of Industrial Relations does not exist, so we must infer who was responsible for devising this policy and their reasoning.[12]

The policy undermined the shopcraft unions and it was tailored to that end. The sleeping-car service did not adopt an equal opportunity employment policy in general, and it did not open the better positions as conductors, supervisors, or office clerks to black men. Furthermore, Pullman managers did not provide new opportunities in the repair shops to black women, none of whom became seamstresses, although black men were upholsterers. Black men found positions as shopcraft workers as long as they remained nonunion and thus helped keep System Federation #122 out of Pullman repair shops. Spero and Harris reported that Pullman executives told them that "in spite of the fact that it [the company] finds this labor perfectly satisfactory, they would continue to use Negro labor only as long as it was unorganized."[13] While other railroads fought the shopcraft unions too, none followed Pullman's lead in systematically integrating the skilled crafts. By 1929 only 2 percent of skilled workers in U.S. car and railroad shops were black, and a large number of them worked for Pullman. The Pullman Company had long been among the most antiunion companies in the industry and had been willing to pay any price to maintain an open shop. Other companies that refused to compromise with the unions, like the Pennsylvania Railroad, did not require such an unusual policy because their repair and yard workers had not been as committed to unionism and strikes as Pullman workers.[14]

That top officials were intent on giving black men new opportunities only where necessary to impose management control was manifested too in the integration of the freight-car-building plant that Pullman acquired in 1922 when it took over the Haskell and Barker Company of Michigan City, Indiana. In early 1923 the Department of Industrial Relations established several boardinghouses to shelter black men recruited to move to that city and work in the factory. According to white workers, black workers accepted the lower pay that the company offered them as part of its strategy to cut wage rates. Haskell and Barker's president, Edward F. Carry, had become president of the Pullman Company in 1922, the first president from a manufacturing, not a railroad, background.[15] Under his leadership the company fought the railroad shopmen's strike and proceeded to integrate the repair shops and the Michigan City plant. Yet whether he initiated the new racial strategies is unclear from the documents.

Integrating the shop forces marginalized System Federation #122, because the unity of the federation during the strike had been built on a policy of segregation and hierarchy. Black workers were unskilled car cleaners or laborers in their own federal labor unions or in segregated lodges of the Brotherhood of Railway Carmen (BRCA). In contrast, the locals of Pullman's Employee Representation Plan (ERP) in the repair shops were integrated, and black men became elected representatives on par with white men. In other industries such as meatpacking, integrated ERPs attracted solid support from black workers because they were so much more egalitarian than AFL unions.[16]

The Pullman Company could expect that black shop workers would support the ERP, because the shopcraft unions did not change their racial policies. Rather, the officials of System Federation #122 reacted immediately and negatively when the company began to train large numbers of black men for skilled jobs. General Chairman John Nelson wrote to President Carry to protest that most of the newly employed "colored people . . . will never become efficient or loyal employees."[17] Furthermore, the unions sought to organize Pullman's white workers by capitalizing on any signs of hostility to the new black workers. They found their first opportunity when one thousand white workers walked out of the Michigan City plant to protest the hiring of African Americans. The leaders of System Federation #122 proposed sending an organizer to help with the walkout in order to attract these manufacturing workers to the carmen's union. Perhaps because the unions made no headway with the strike, Pullman management did not proceed to hire large numbers of black workers at the Michigan City plant. By the end of 1923 Pullman employed only forty-five black men. Thereafter, a small number of black workers remained on the payroll, perhaps to remind white workers of what could happen if they defied management. The system federation did not reassess its policies on race, however, but continued to appeal only to white shop workers. The AFL shopcraft unions refused to open equal membership to black mechanics and went no further than arranging to have the International Brotherhood of Firemen and Oilers organize black helpers so that they could not be used as strikebreakers.[18]

Applying National Policy Locally

Directives from the Department of Industrial Relations about wages, hours, and job classifications and the terms on which to rehire strikers limited the discretion that managers had in running their shops and shaped the choices that they made as they reconstituted their workforces. But local customs and the composition of local labor markets also influenced their decisions, especially about opening new opportunities to black men. Each shop manager faced somewhat different problems and possibilities, which produced workforces that were distinct in their racial and ethnic composition.

The Calumet Repair Shop in Chicago, where the Pullman Company faced the most militant of its shop workers, made extensive use of the new racial policy and job structure as it rehired many strikers. Forty-four percent of the strikers came back to work on the company's terms in the fall of 1922, but others waited. Their resolve weakened when the shopcraft unions settled the strike at the Illinois Central's Burnside repair shop in November 1922 and the Pullman Company began to transfer repair work to the Car Works. As they saw their neighbors going back to work or worse—taking their jobs—more men and women returned to the shop. Some were veterans like the upholsterer Friedrich Steinle and the seamstress Helen Elbring, who had also taken part in the 1894 strike and came back to the jobs that had provided their livelihood for decades. Eventually, 71 percent of the strikers were again Calumet employees. To discipline these former union members, however, management played on local racial antipathies. Half the workers newly hired in the first fifteen months after the strike were black, although the percentage of black men hired previously had been minuscule (see table 3), and many local factories remained all white.[19]

Calumet management created an integrated shop force by using the new job structure to its fullest extent; upward mobility was the norm, not the exception, at the shop in the 1920s. Foremen in every department created new mechanics, black and white, by training helper-apprentices and promoting them quickly; 89 percent of white helper-apprentices and 90 percent of black ones became mechanics, on average in two years. Helpers also advanced, albeit at a slower rate than helper-apprentices. It took them five years on average to become mechanics. Only among the helpers did white men seem to be advantaged—92 percent of them but only 61 percent of black helpers were upwardly mobile. Management's use of the new job structure transformed the shop force, as table 4 reveals. By 1926, black men comprised 10 percent of mechanics, 36 percent of helpers, and 27 percent of laborers. The percentage of black mechanics increased slowly in the next few years as more helper-apprentices were promoted.[20]

At the Calumet Repair Shop white men had to be willing to work as equals with black men, something that many white Americans were reluctant to do. The opportunities for advancement to mechanic status may have helped some to overcome their hesitancy, but whether they were less prejudiced or had fewer opportunities for skilled jobs, two-thirds of the white men who came to work at the shop in the 1920s were European immigrants. Many were members of those groups of Europeans most disdained during this high point of nativism: 41 percent were eastern Europeans, and 27 percent were Italian. Polish-born John Gagatek and Italian-born Carlo De Antoni exemplify the immigrants hired as helper-apprentices in 1923. Both were young men in their twenties who lived in the Pullman area, and both became mechanics well before the end of

Table 4. Percentage of Male Shop Workers Who were Black, by Skill Level

	Calumet		Richmond		Wilmington	
	1926	1929	1926	1929	1926	1929
Mechanic	10.2	12.0	0.7	1.2	0.0	2.4
Helper	36.3	29.3	7.0	12.5	38.4	41.0
Unskilled	27.1	22.2	29.4	52.2	80.0	68.4
Total	18.1	15.3	5.1	7.4	19.2	19.4

Source: Derived from samples described in the appendix.

the decade. They made careers at the Calumet shop, and Gagatek retired only in 1969 when the shop closed. Some new immigrant workers could not qualify for jobs that required English literacy, but they could succeed as repair shop workers as long as a bilingual fellow employee was available to translate the foreman's orders. These men found that a job in the Calumet Repair Shop was among the best paying to which they could aspire, even though a mechanic could maintain only a marginal standard of living if he was the sole support of his family.[21]

The new black workers at the shop were predominantly southerners who had moved to Chicago's black ghetto, six miles north of Pullman, as part of the "Great Migration" during World War I and the 1920s. Like Gagatek and De Antoni, they also were usually young men and followed the same career path of upward mobility to a craft job at which they then remained for decades. Georgia-born Edward Heard was twenty-three when he became a helper-apprentice in the paint department. He was promoted to mechanic status only eleven months later, and he remained at the shop until his retirement in 1968. Gagatek, De Antoni, Heard, and hundreds of other men worked together without incident, although a tense racial situation persisted in Chicago after the 1919 race riot. The Ku Klux Klan even organized in the Calumet area as the repair shop hired large numbers of black men for the first time. African Americans could take jobs at the shop, and others could continue to labor at the Car Works because they commuted by train directly to the plants. They did not have to walk through white neighborhoods where they might be attacked by those who were unwilling to work together as equals.[22]

Although they worked together peacefully, Calumet's black and white shop workers lived in different neighborhoods as part of antagonistic communities. The South Side of Chicago was a patchwork of white ethnic and class-based neighborhoods resisting the expansion of the black ghetto. Ethnic consciousness remained strong despite the mix of nationalities in most of the poorer white neighborhoods. Some ethnic enclaves remained—61 percent of Poles and 50 percent of Italians still lived in neighborhoods where they predominated. The concept of a hierarchy of races among those of European origin continued to shape perceptions, and when they tried to move into neighborhoods like Roseland, eastern and southern European immigrants and their children faced hostility from Americans of northern and western European ancestry. Ethnic identity structured both community institutions and informal social relations, and immigrant parents made a conscious effort to build cultural and social institutions to limit the influence of U.S. culture on their children. Their success and the ubiquity of ethnic identification is visible among those who came to work at the Calumet shop in the 1920s; 91 percent of the immigrants and 43 percent of U.S.-born white workers identified their "race" as a European nationality.[23]

If they were divided among themselves, the European immigrants and their children united against the new black migrants to Chicago. In the context of competition for jobs and housing, white residents from twenty-six ethnic groups and three religions—Catholics, Protestants, and Jews—put racial covenants on virtually every piece of property in the Pullman area. Although local political and business leaders encouraged the movement to solidify racial boundaries, Pullman workers who were homeowners joined the neighborhood protective associations that initiated and implemented the campaign. In the early 1920s Frank Lowden, George Pullman's son-in-law and the governor of Illinois during the 1919 race riot, headed a coalition of Chicago business leaders who saw the answer to the city's racial tensions in de facto segregation. Lowden's group proposed to improve facilities and residences within the existing black ghetto so that African Americans would not want to move to other neighborhoods. Their plan came to naught, but it encouraged white resistance to integration, which spread to all areas of neighborhood life. When twenty-five black girls attempted to transfer into Roseland's Fenger High School in 1928, white students walked out en masse and the local chamber of commerce supported their strike. The superintendent of schools caved in to this pressure, and the girls returned to their old high school. At other places where people of different races might have come together, like movie theaters, segregation ruled, although it was illegal under Illinois law.[24]

The defensiveness in Chicago's white working-class neighborhoods contrasted sharply with the elan and optimism of "Bronzeville," the ghetto where Pullman's black shop workers lived. Black migrants from the South saw Chicago was "a land of hope," and Bronzeville, though crowded and poverty stricken, was the scene of great entrepreneurial and cultural creativity. King Oliver, Jelly Roll Morton, and Louis Armstrong revolutionized jazz, Jesse Binga founded one of the first black-owned banks, and black workers brought home wages that made a better life possible for themselves and their families. Black pride and racial consciousness blossomed. Building and enjoying their own community and improving their economic situation, black workers did not look for leadership from white workers nor necessarily for any interaction with them, because insults and attacks often resulted from interracial contacts.[25]

Pullman's black workers shared in the optimism of Bronzeville in the 1920s. The four thousand porters who lived there comprised much of the community's stable middle class, and Pullman's skilled black shop workers also were relatively advantaged compared to their neighbors. Half of all black men in Chicago earned less than $1,200 per year in the mid-1920s, but a Pullman mechanic who earned only the minimum wage of seventy cents per hour brought home $1,500 per year even if he was laid off for six weeks. Between the porters and car cleaners, the Calumet shop workers, and the laborers and foundrymen at the Car Works, the Pullman Company was among the largest, if not the largest, employer of black men in Chicago. The company continued to offer financial support to a wide range of institutions in the black community, and public opinion toward the company was positive.[26]

The contrasting community experiences and expectations of black and white workers helped to maintain acquiescence to management control at the Calumet Repair Shop because they counterbalanced common experiences on the shop floor. For black workers the wages, hours, and benefits that the shop provided were part of the promise of a better life in the North. For white workers they were the best around, especially if one were an immigrant, but they paled in comparison to what unionized Pullman workers had achieved previously.

Acquiescence to management control also rested, however, on the incentive pay plan that the company established in June 1923 in an attempt to regain some benefits of piece rates. Executives did not dare to reimpose piece rates in the repair shops and yards, but incentive pay plans that individualized wage rates and hence workers' experiences were common in U.S. industry in 1920s. C. W. Pflager, the mechanical superintendent in the central office, designed the plan by ranking the specialties in each craft into three levels of difficulty and assigning each level different rates of pay. A-level jobs paid the Railway Labor Board minimum mechanics' rate, seventy cents per hour, but B- and C-level jobs could pay more. Foremen decided what rate workers received within the appropriate range, seventy to seventy-three cents per hour for B-level jobs and seventy to seventy-five cents for C-level ones. Pflager expected this system to "provide an incentive for men to develop skill in their work and speed in production," while it enhanced the power of foremen. Creating a hierarchy of craft tasks that could bring higher wages also encouraged workers to stay with the company because it extended the internal labor market within the repair shops. Now workers could climb a ladder of opportunity below the supervisory level, from laborer to helper-apprentice, mechanic A, mechanic B, mechanic C, and then three rungs on the supervisory level—leader, assistant foreman, and foreman. But the incentive pay system also revealed the different perspectives of managers and union workers on what constituted a just wage. Pflager believed that incentive rates were "more just than the present method of paying the same rate to all mechanics, regardless of their qualifications."[27]

Vacancies in the supervisory positions occurred only rarely, but many men rose through the craft ranks, and only a few were ever demoted. Half of those who were classified as A-level mechanics before the end of 1926 rose to a higher level by the end of the decade, on average in two years. B-level mechanics were not as likely to reach the C-level, but 39 percent also were promoted on average in two years. The new rules about seniority might have made mobility risky, because workers no longer had seniority in their craft but only in their specialty. When workers moved up, they went down to the bottom of a seniority roster and were most at risk during layoffs. But during the prosperous 1920s, when layoffs beyond the normal seasonal ones were few, workers took their chances. The new structure of opportunity encouraged them to remain with Pullman, and on average men hired in the 1920s stayed with the shop for twenty-five years.[28]

By the mid-1920s management seems to have decided that the racial balance at Calumet was optimal for maintaining control of the shop floor, and the percentage of new workers who were black declined precipitously thereafter (see table 3). Only 7 percent of the men hired in the last three years of the decade were black. Indeed, black employees complained to the central office that supervisors were no longer even hiring black men to replace those who quit. Although the percentage of shop workers who were black declined slightly in the late 1920s (see table 4), the central office did not interfere. The Calumet Repair Shop had been restructured as the company desired and now seemed safely nonunion.[29]

Pullman's St. Louis repair shop, where workers also struck in 1894 and 1922, hired and promoted black men much as the Calumet shop did. Black men comprised almost half the shop force at St. Louis by the end of the 1920s, and many were mechanics.[30] But not every Pullman repair shop used black workers in this manner, because local conditions could warrant different applications of the policy of integration. The Wilmington repair shop, the only other Pullman shop in a border state, hired large numbers of black men but confined almost all to helper-level jobs. In Wilmington, unlike St. Louis, the combination of a slumping industrial sector, a moribund labor movement, and southern racial mores meant that giving black workers only somewhat better opportunities was enough to return white workers to nonunion ways.

In Wilmington management's determination to stamp out support for System Federation #122 led supervisors to take a hard line with returning strikers. Only 39 percent of the Wilmington strikers returned to work in the fall of 1922, and supervisors refused to rehire those who asked to come back later. C. W. Wilcox, leader of the Wilmington local of System Federation #122, sought reinstatement for strikers at the end of 1923 by appealing to F. L. Simmons, the supervisor of industrial relations. Simmons informed him that Pullman had no national policy against rehiring strikers but that the decision was in the hands of local management. In Wilmington the strike had been an unprecedented challenge to management control, while at Calumet it was one more contest in a long struggle. Wilmington supervisors decided not to be forgiving, and many strikers were forced to find work in other cities.[31]

As well as taking a harder line with those who had been most committed to the strike, Wilmington management implemented the new policy of racial integration despite having access to a large pool of unemployed skilled white workers. Local shipyards and railcar plants laid off thousands of workers after World War I. As the city's manufacturing sector slumped throughout the 1920s, white men took any job that they could find and often replaced black men in service jobs like chauffeur and waiter, which the whites had previously disdained. Despite high white unemployment, black men comprised one-third of those hired at the Wilmington repair shop in the first four years after the strike (see table 3). Indeed, the shop hired black men at a rate three times their representation in the local population, and it offered the vast majority of them jobs at the helper level in defiance of local racial norms that consigned black men to unskilled labor. This challenge to the local social order reflected management's determination to eliminate the union threat by playing on the most potent local division—race.[32]

Supervisors implemented this policy in the context of heightened racial antagonism in the city. A proposal to change the school code that would have benefited black as well as white schools set off years of political wrangling and a white backlash against African Americans. Because of the tense racial situation the new opportunities that Pullman provided for black men could be expected to elicit opposition. Wilmington management had to be vigilant if racial hostility were not to threaten the cooperation necessary for efficient production. Thus in 1925 the shop manager fired a young white helper-apprentice in the upholstery department for disrupting harmony; his discharge noted that he was "an agitator, tried on several benches, stirs up trouble between white & colored."[33] This man's father had long been employed in the same department, but family ties did not protect him. White workers lasted only if they followed company racial policy, regardless of their own feelings.

George Pullman's racial strategy: white conductor, black porter, 1915 (Chicago Historical Society, ICHi-26271)

The model factory on Lake Vista: the Pullman Car Works, administration building, and erecting sheds, ca. 1880s–1890s (Chicago Historical Society, ICHi-23065)

An environment for producing nonunionized skilled workers: street scene in the
company town of Pullman, 1892 (Chicago Historical Society, ICHi-21815)

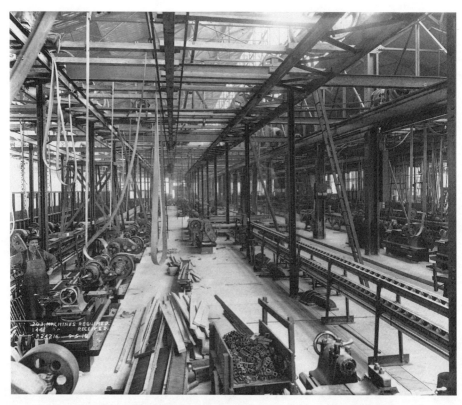

New technology: interior of the Pullman Car Works, 1918 (Chicago Historical Society, #24216)

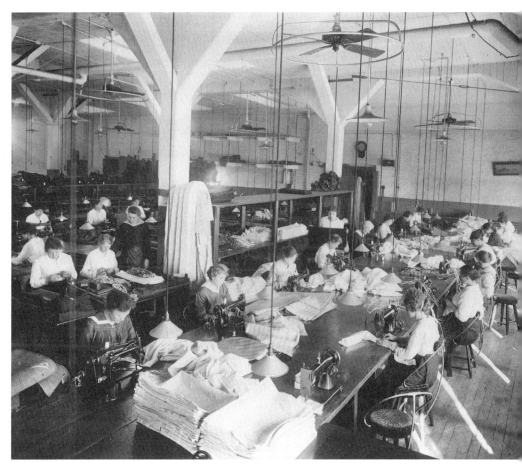

Women in their sphere: sewing room, Pullman Car Works, ca. 1917–18 (Chicago Historical Society, ICHi-19682)

New jobs for women during World War I: women clerical workers, administration building, Pullman Car Works, 1918 (Chicago Historical Society, #24244)

Racial integration at the Pullman Car Works during World War I: one black worker out of ten (second from left at rear of car), riveting, 1917 (Chicago Historical Society, ICHi-34563)

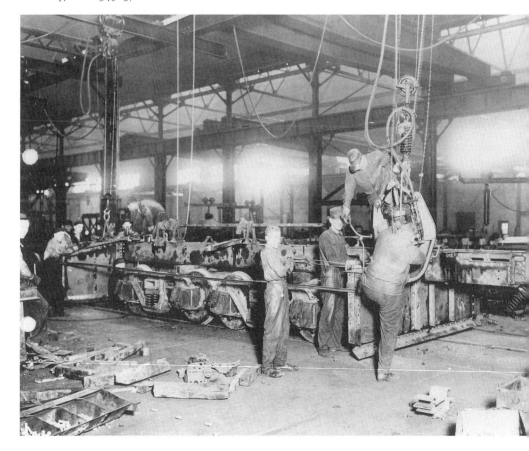

A racially integrated and aging workforce: two black men and three white men packing in the storeroom of the Calumet Repair Shop, 1954 (Pullman Company Archives, The Newberry Library, Chicago)

Although Wilmington supervisors hired large numbers of black men, unlike their counterparts at Calumet and St. Louis they did not use the new job structure to create many black or white mechanics. Most men entered the Wilmington repair shop as helpers, not helper-apprentices, and even those helpers who eventually became mechanics took a long time to do so, on average about a decade. In 1926, 40 percent of Wilmington shop workers held helper-level jobs, but only 20 percent of the Richmond shop force and 29 percent of Calumet workers did. This practice held down labor costs at Wilmington, because helpers did tasks done by mechanics elsewhere. Other shops did not follow this course, because it violated the contract for repair shop workers that the Department of Industrial Relations had signed in December 1923 with their ERP. This was a national contract that codified job descriptions, wages, and grievance procedures, and with modifications it remained in force until 1934. The company committed itself to contractual agreements on wages and working conditions only with those workers whom it feared might join railroad unions, and through 1923 only the shopcraft workers and the conductors had warranted such a commitment.[34]

Some new Wilmington workers, like Louis Johnson, left the shop when they realized that they were being exploited rather than accorded the opportunity for advancement available elsewhere. Johnson had had three years of mechanical training at Tuskegee Institute before being hired as a helper-apprentice in 1923. By 1926, with no promotion in sight, he transferred to Pullman's New York District to become a porter. Although the base pay of porters was much lower than the weekly earnings of helper-apprentices, tip income could produce take-home pay well beyond what a Pullman employee could earn from an hourly wage.[35] Black men continued to be attracted to the position of Pullman porter in the prosperous twenties when tips were plentiful. But most Wilmington shop workers, white and black, did not protest contract violations, and they stayed with the shop. The majority had been born in the area, and a job at Pullman allowed them to remain close to family and friends.

Pullman management violated Wilmington's racial hierarchy by allowing black men to become helpers, but it did not go much further. Sixty-eight percent of white helpers eventually became mechanics, but only 21 percent of black helpers did. Indeed, more black helpers fell to the unskilled level than rose to the skilled one. Thus in the mid- to late 1920s virtually all the skilled workers at the Wilmington shop were white, but they worked with many black helpers who could be upgraded immediately to take their place if conditions warranted it (see table 4).

This was a common pattern at many southern workplaces and at northern railroad repair shops, like the Illinois Central's Burnside shop, where management struggled to keep unions at bay.[36]

Black workers experienced a mixture of new opportunities and old inequities at the Wilmington shop, a situation that reflected the complexity of race relations in the city itself. The Ku Klux Klan flourished there in the 1920s, but black voters held the balance of power in local elections. Restaurants, theaters, and schools were segregated but not public transportation. African Americans supported two branches of the National Association for the Advancement of Colored People, but they could not serve on juries or practice law. These contradictions developed from the interaction of a long-settled biracial population. Black community life was vibrant and separate, with its own churches, theaters, clubs, and celebrations, but unlike Chicago's, Wilmington's black population was not growing rapidly and searching for space. Yet Wilmington's white residents showed the same interest in distancing themselves from African Americans that Chicago's did. In the 1920s many white families moved out of Wilmington to new suburbs protected by racial covenants, but most of Pullman's white workers could not afford to join them. The Pullman shop force, white and black, continued to live in close if not happy proximity within the city limits.[37]

When the Pullman Company and the Pennsylvania Railroad broke the shopcraft unions in Wilmington, the local labor movement lapsed into insignificance. The probusiness, antiunion sentiment long dominant in the city reigned supreme, now focused on the fear of foreign radicals, especially communists. The few AFL unions that survived stressed their respectability and antiradical role. John C. Saylor, head of the Wilmington Central Labor Union, boasted that this alliance of craft unions took "the right position on public issues" and that it helped acculturate workers to a U.S. political and economic philosophy. Saylor acknowledged that most Wilmington workers lacked interest in unions and that the more innovative organizations held dances to attract members: "People today seem to want to enjoy themselves more than ever. They want to be entertained—not preached at. And the labor organization that has social features to it is looked upon with a more friendly attitude."[38]

The Wilmington shop was not the only one that applied the new policies differently than Calumet and St. Louis. Although only 43 percent of strikers returned to the Richmond repair shop in the fall of 1922, fewer than 6 percent of those hired to replace them were black (see table 3). The Richmond shop found it much easier than the Calumet and Wilmington shops to secure skilled white workers who were strangers to the shopcraft unions and who had no neighborly ties to the strikers. Migration to the West boomed in the 1920s as people from all over the nation and immigrants from many countries searched for their California dream. As in the past, Richmond supervisors hired men who lived throughout the East Bay area and showed no particular preference toward any European nationality nor toward U.S.-born rather than foreign-born men. Although the black population of Richmond was small, many African Americans lived in nearby Oakland. A large number of them were Pullman porters, car cleaners, and laundry workers. Had the Richmond shop manager felt the need to hire more black men, he could have done so easily.[39]

In the 1920s the Richmond shop force reflected a racial hierarchy, but it was that of the East Bay area, not that of Wilmington or Chicago. Although black people experienced discrimination in jobs and housing in Richmond, Asians and Asian Americans were the primary focus of white racism in California. Hiring patterns at the Pullman shop reflected local conditions; the shop hired some African Americans and Mexicans, but it excluded Asians and Asian Americans entirely. At the same time the racial and ethnic identities that produced both tight-knit communities and divisiveness in Chicago and Wilmington seemed to have less force among the rapidly changing and highly decentralized population of the East Bay. Some black residents of Richmond even remembered the 1920s as a time when poor Italians, African Americans, Asians, and Mexicans lived and often socialized together.[40]

At the Richmond repair shop, unlike at Calumet or Wilmington, opportunities for black men actually increased throughout the 1920s (see tables 3 and 4). By the end of the decade black men comprised 28 percent of those being hired at Richmond, a higher percentage than at either Calumet or Wilmington. Black men also were entering helper-level and mechanic positions in greater numbers. The low unemployment rate for white men in the East Bay area may well have created these new opportunities for black men, but so too did the local racial hierarchy. In California, when hiring white men became difficult, hiring black men was preferable to hiring Asians.

Because of the low unemployment rate for white men, the Richmond shop also continued to welcome back those strikers who would renounce the unions. Sixty-three percent of the strikers eventually returned to the shop, including three former union activists who had been named in the injunction that the company secured to stop the picketing of the shop and the visiting of workers' homes. Richmond management could rehire strikers without feeling the need to create large numbers of black mechanics to hold them in check because the shopcraft unions posed much less threat in the East Bay area than they did in Chicago, where union power had been diminished but not vanquished. The shopcraft unions still had contracts with many repair shops in Chicago, including the Illinois Central's Burnside shop. The Santa Fe Railroad and the Pullman Company had broken the shopcraft unions in Richmond, and organized labor lost much of its clout locally, just as it did in Wilmington. Realtors and the city's largest employer—Standard Oil—once more dominated Richmond government. Civic rhetoric paid lip service to labor, but Richmond saw no strikes during the 1920s.[41]

Although local conditions warranted diverse applications of the new racial policy, Pullman officials remained committed to it throughout the 1920s. When they established a new repair shop at Atlanta, Georgia, in 1927 to handle the growing tourist travel to Florida, top management did not hesitate to violate the racial hierarchy of the Deep South by applying this policy. The Pullman Company located the repair shop on the east side of Atlanta in Kirkwood, an undeveloped suburb that was predominantly white until the 1960s. Yet the newly appointed shop manager hired large numbers of black men, and 44 percent of the shop force was black in 1929. Just as in 1922–23, the company recruited black workers partially from current employees like porters and car cleaners. Moreover, like management at Calumet and St. Louis, supervisors in Atlanta used the new job structure to create black mechanics.[42]

Pullman's Atlanta repair shop challenged the local social order by violating many basic tenets of white supremacy. In Atlanta, Jim Crow and segregation reigned supreme, African Americans had been effectively disenfranchised, and black people who were not publicly subservient to white people found it healthier to leave town. The unions of white railroad workers had succeeded in displacing most skilled black workers from the railroad industry. Yet although a few jobs in the Pullman shop were segregated (watchmen were white and laborers were black), many jobs and departments were racially integrated. Black men held skilled and helper positions, and they received the same wage rates as white men in their job classifications.

In a striking challenge to the southern racial hierarchy, some white helpers worked in departments with black mechanics who took home much larger paychecks than they did. Furthermore, the Atlanta shop challenged southern taboos about race and gender as black upholsterers and white seamstresses worked together in the upholstery department. This resulted, as it did in other Pullman shops, from the confluence of racial policy and gender stereotyping, which limited employment for black women to janitorial work. The only compromise that corporate officials made with Atlanta's racial norms was to establish segregated locals for the shop's employee representation plan. All the other Pullman repair shops had integrated ERPs, but the supervisor of industrial relations determined that two separate but equal locals were preferable in the Deep South.[43]

By the mid-1920s the company had created a seemingly stable, non-union workforce in its repair shops. Each shop was racially integrated, and workers were fairly evenly divided between former strikers and newcomers. Although the return of more white strikers and the hiring of more white men diminished the black presence at some shops, black workers comprised a significant proportion but not a majority of each shop force. They held 15 to 20 percent of the jobs at Buffalo, Calumet, and Wilmington and 40 to 50 percent at Atlanta and St. Louis but only 7 percent at Richmond. Because of Pullman's racial strategy for defeating System Federation #122, black men comprised a higher percentage of the Pullman shop force than they did of the local adult male population in all these localities.[44]

At this point the company began to relax some sanctions against the strikers who had spurned the unions and returned to work. In 1926, when workers at the Calumet Repair Shop elected the machinist Sidney G. Day, a returned striker, to represent them in the ERP, management did not interfere, and Day served as their representative for seven years. Moreover, in 1929, when the company again responded to wage increases at unionized railroad repair shops and raised mechanics' wages, top management specified that the favoritism toward those who helped break the 1922 strike should end. Strikebreakers would no longer receive higher wages than returned strikers did.[45] Pullman officials had made their peace with the strike of 1922, and now they could afford to be generous.

Race in the Bureaucratically Structured Workplace

As it developed a new racial strategy for the repair shops, the Pullman Company also elaborated its system of personnel management by adding benefits and programs designed to tie workers to the corporation. Like other large employers that made "welfare capitalism" central to their labor management strategies, Pullman tried to create a strong relationship with individual workers by offering such benefits as free life insurance and by adding new facilities like cafeterias and dispensaries. In 1926 the company again offered workers a stock purchase plan, but it was among the most limited offered by major corporations. The idea that stock ownership gave workers a stake in the fruits of increased productivity induced many corporations to make their shares available on an ongoing basis. The Pullman Company, however, offered only a limited number of shares, which quickly sold out, and only a small minority of employees actually bought stock.[46]

Rather than giving workers an economic stake in the company, management promoted the concept of the corporation as a family, a tactic that many companies used to encourage both teamwork and respect for authority. This image dominated the *Pullman News,* the magazine for employees that the Department of Industrial Relations inaugurated in May 1922, just before the railroad shopmen's strike and shortly after Edward Carry became company president. Noting that Pullman workers were separated by great distances and that many traveled or transferred to other areas of the country, the magazine attempted to bring the "Pullman family" together through news of the activities of groups and individuals in each locale. Carry saw no inherent contradiction in his vision for the corporation as "a happy family and an efficient organization."[47] Articles in the *Pullman News* expounded this vision, which presumed that what benefited the company would, like the prosperity of the ideal family, accrue to all. In this model corporate family all members could discuss problems, but only the male head of the household, the executive, could make decisions. As Carry told a group of the elected employee representatives, "If we do have a difference now and then, come in and talk it over and hear our side of the matter. . . . I know your problems and I want to help solve them."[48]

As the Department of Industrial Relations fostered personal ties between workers, it did so in a way that divided them by race, class, and gender. Sports teams in the districts, shops, and plants grew as never before, adding bowling to the ever-popular baseball and soccer but also the first baseball teams for "colored" men and "Pullman laundry girls." Tennis and golf became the avocations of the groups formed by supervisory personnel. Social clubs proliferated, most also segregated by race, class, or gender, such as the Calumet Social Club established in 1926 for black men who worked at the Calumet Repair Shop. Women clerks at the Chicago headquarters formed a division of the Railway Business Women's Association, while male supervisors belonged to the Pullman Circle. The company continued to form musical groups among its African American workers, and by the mid-twenties it sponsored black singing groups or bands in several repair shops as well as those comprised of porters.[49] Company activities and programs bound all workers to the firm, but as they reified racial and sexual differences, they helped to maintain the different perspectives of white and black workers.

Handling black workers became a central concern for management in the sleeping-car service, because black workers comprised 60 percent of all employees by 1929. The bureaucratic rules, policies, and benefits capped by the employee representation plan governed black and white workers alike, but the company treated black workers separately in several important ways. Other companies were using black "welfare workers" to help incorporate black workers into previously white workplaces, and the Pullman Company proceeded to hire them too, not only in the repair shops but also to supervise the porters. Pullman officials accorded these men the supervisory titles and pay that it had denied Julius Avendorph before his death in 1923. While Avendorph had functioned as a labor contractor, the welfare workers were personnel professionals, the only black supervisors in the company, and a key factor in reconciling the bureaucratically ordered workplace with the legacy of white racism.[50]

Pullman welfare workers organized the racially segregated social groups formed throughout the sleeping-car service. They also established new locals of the Pullman Porters Benefit Association of America (PPBAA), which offered members insurance benefits. Black shop workers joined in large numbers because the company's free life insurance policy was for whites only. With the new membership of black shop and yard workers, the PPBAA had ninety-three hundred members by the late 1920s. Ironically, its broad array of benefits was so popular that Pullman's white workers became dissatisfied with the simple life insurance that the company provided for them. In 1929 the company responded by establishing a contributory group insurance plan comparable to the PPBAA's; it provided compensation for death, disability, and sickness.[51]

Welfare workers also helped black workers resolve grievances, and consequently they competed with the ERP representatives to "service" black workers in the repair shops. As the ERP for the shops developed, employee representatives objected to the role of the welfare workers, and the company phased out the positions as men left or retired. But in the 1920s welfare workers provided important services for the company, like negotiating the exceptions to equal treatment. For black shop workers the most glaring exception involved the free passes that the Pullman Company had long provided to all white shop workers who wanted to travel. Most black shop workers had been born in the South and wanted to visit family they had left behind. But racial segregation of Pullman sleeping cars in the South, coupled with the small number of cars for African Americans, made extending this practice to black shop workers problematic. Off-duty porters could don uniforms while sleeping in white-only cars and pass unnoticed by white patrons. But had black shop work-

ers used the passes, they would have openly challenged Jim Crow practices. The job of welfare workers included making sure that black shop
workers accepted having to pay for transportation that was free for their
white shop mates and having to travel in segregated cars.[52]

Yet for black shop workers in the 1920s the deviations from equal
treatment were less startling than the experience of equality. In a bureaucratically regulated workplace rules, not people and their prejudices,
determined a worker's experience. African Americans new to industrial
workplaces often expected, and were encouraged to expect, to be treated
as individuals. In the South their employment relations with white bosses
usually were personal ones, and in northern strikebreaking situations
supervisors often patronized black workers while exploiting them. Some
new black shop workers had such expectations initially, and several at
the Calumet Repair Shop requested personal favors from management.
The helper Sam Harden asked the company to loan him $50 to help his
parents in Mississippi. He did not want to sell his company stock, and
his foreman supported the request, noting that Harden was a good employee and worthy of the loan.[53]

Requests that conflicted with bureaucratic procedures could not be
granted, and their denial educated workers, like Texas-born Terrence P.
Hines, to a new reality. Hines asked not to be laid off only four months
after he was hired as a helper-apprentice. He wrote to his supervisor: "I
am in a financial strain at present. . . . I bought a building in the spring
and have gotten $350 behind in my payments. . . . My wife is just getting
up from confinement. . . . My only means to meet the bills is my labor. . . .
I am willing to accept a cut if it is necessary in my rate. . . . Please do this
for me and I pledge the company my faithful support."[54] Managers could
not cut one individual's rate when a contract was in force. Neither could
they interfere with the seniority system governing layoffs that had to
operate according to rules if it was to meet workers' expectations. Hines
was laid off, but he was also recalled. Like most other helper-apprentices
at Calumet, he was promoted to the mechanic level within a few years,
and he continued to work at the shop until 1941. The value of seniority
rules faithfully applied became evident quickly as black workers in Pullman repair shops were recalled in turn after layoffs, while at many other
workplaces they were not. In consequence the average length of service
of Pullman's black shop workers was similar to that of white men hired
in the 1920s.[55] Over time the perspective of black workers changed; they
no longer asked for personal favors but relied on and attempted to shape
the rules of the bureaucratic workplace.

Black workers' experiences in the integrated shops not only altered their perspective but could also draw them into alliances with white workers. Such a situation arose in 1925 at the Calumet Repair Shop when some new white workers petitioned the ERP to change the structure of the workweek. They wanted to replace the six 8–hour days with five days of 8 hours and 45 minutes, plus a half-day on Saturday. This created more of a weekend without shortening the forty-eight-hour week. Black workers objected because this schedule necessitated an exceptionally early starting time, and, unlike white workers, they had to commute long distances. Calumet's black welfare workers reported to the supervisor of industrial relations that black workers were now listening to the arguments of the returned strikers, whom they characterized as "pretty red." These former union members rejected the proposed work hours because they saw it as a first step toward returning to prewar conditions that had been banished in the railroad industry. They objected to working more than eight hours per day without overtime pay, and they saw changing the structure of the workweek as a precursor to bringing back piece rates. Because management wanted the new schedule, the ERP eventually approved it.[56] Yet such experiences eroded the barriers between black and white workers.

The Fruits of George Pullman's Racial Strategy

At the very time that hiring black workers in the repair shops and extending the benefits of welfare capitalism seemed to have stymied the shopcraft unions, the Pullman Company found itself with another significant union challenge—from the porters. Management had had little trouble squashing the efforts of small groups of porters to organize in the past, but in the decade of the "New Negro," porters were more ready to unify against the conditions that they had long decried. Porters lived in the growing urban communities where African Americans expected to create a better life for themselves and their families, but Pullman management continued to thwart their expectations by forcing them to rely on tips for a decent living, with the subservience that tips necessitated. Providing for their families was a constant concern when that base pay was $810 per year, although an urban family needed $2,088 for a decent level of living. In the 1920s, as black workers found new jobs in industry, including in the Pullman Company, porters increasingly became dissatisfied with their low base pay, extremely long hours, and lack of opportunities for advancement. The job of Pullman porter still had great prestige among the black working class, but industrial jobs now had attractions too, like hours and wages equal to those of white workers and sometimes the promise of upward mobility.[57]

Although paying the porters as little as possible made economic sense to Pullman executives, their policy also reflected the racism that had shaped white perspectives toward black Americans since the era of slavery. The *Pullman News* provided a glimpse into this mind-set in 1922 when it explained why the company hired Major N. Clark Smith, a well-known black musician, to instruct porters in singing folk songs: "The Pullman Company has a two-fold object in backing this musical enterprise. In the first place it believes musical education will be good for the men. They are of a singing race and music adds to their cheerfulness and contentment. In the second place a real service will be performed in developing and preserving the melodies of the American Negro."[58] The image of the happy slave singing in the fields was alive and well in the minds of Pullman executives. It was an image that urban black men, and the porters in particular, had left behind.

The porters' growing interest in unionizing resulted not only from the ideas current in their communities but also from their experiences at work. The porters' ERP did not address any of their larger concerns, because the company had not seen it as a necessary bulwark against unionization. Moreover, many porters were afraid to use its grievance procedures to appeal discharges, suspensions, or other disciplinary actions because decisions usually went against them. At the same time porters saw that Pullman conductors had vastly improved their conditions by boycotting the ERP altogether and supporting their own union.[59]

Pullman porters put real pressure on the company for the first time by coming together around one model of unionization—a black craft union. The Railway Men's International Benevolent Industrial Association had continued to organize among the porters in the early 1920s, but most porters were not attracted to the industrial union. In 1925 a group of porters decided to establish a craft union, and they invited the socialist editor A. Philip Randolph to lead their Brotherhood of Sleeping Car Porters (BSCP). These porters had pride in their job and the skills that it required, and they created a union that was similar in many respects to the white-dominated railroad craft unions. "Brotherhood" meant that the fraternal aspects of the union were central to its character, and the emphasis in BSCP literature on "manhood" and "self-respect" reflected not only issues for black men but also the traditional self-presentation of U.S. craftsmen. Although the BSCP included the few black women who worked on Pullman cars as maids, it was decidedly an organization of and for men.[60]

If porters rejected the Railway Men's International Benevolent Industrial Association, they accepted its premise that black workers had to organize themselves and could not rely on white unions. The BSCP's racial and class-conscious stance, as well as its vision for the greater role that it could play as a vanguard struggling for all black workers, was exemplified in the name of its newspaper—the *Black Worker*. In the 1920s, when many African Americans preferred the term *Negro* and color consciousness privileged lighter skin, adopting the term *black* was a way to reach out to the poorest workers and those of the lowest social status.[61]

As the BSCP attracted porters in virtually every Pullman district, the company responded by using many strategies that it had deployed against the shopcraft unions. The supervisor of industrial relations had already begun to build up the porters' division of the ERP in response to demands from the Railway Men's International Benevolent Industrial Association. In 1924 the company "negotiated" an 8 percent wage increase for porters and maids with the ERP and signed the first contract with the porters' representatives. Two more negotiating sessions followed in the 1920s at critical junctures. Right after the formation of the BSCP the company made an agreement with the porters' and maids' representatives that provided another 8 percent wage increase and new rules on working conditions, such as crediting time for layovers and delays. In 1929, when the BSCP faced serious internal difficulties, the company offered another wage increase and more improvement of working conditions in a bid to sink the union entirely. Behind the carrot, however, was always the stick. Supervisors punished porters who joined the BSCP or refused to vote in ERP elections with dismissal or denial of the positions that afforded more lucrative tips. The company also sought to undermine support for the BSCP in black communities by using Pullman philanthropy to maintain the allegiance of key community leaders and institutions. It tried to smear Randolph as a communist and irreligious to provoke distrust among the black clergy and among black people in general, few of whom voted for Socialists or communists in the 1920s.[62]

To undermine the union drive the Pullman Company also used the weapon that it had found so useful in the repair shops—encouraging racial competition for jobs. Within two months of the founding of the BSCP, the company began to hire Filipinos in the Commissary Department as attendants, cooks, and busboys. This violated the seniority rules that governed access to these jobs, rules that in effect had reserved these jobs for black men. Management expected this action to undercut enthusiasm for organizing, just as threats to replace black porters with white men had done in the past.[63]

The company now needed to use all these tactics because the passage of the Railway Labor Act in 1926 made the BSCP threat credible. The act abolished the Railroad Labor Board and its power to set wages, but it affirmed government's role in mediation and encouraged the growth of unions in the industry. It banned yellow-dog contracts and allowed company unions only where workers had not been intimidated or coerced into joining them. The BSCP sought to use the provisions of the Railway Labor Act to force the Pullman Company to recognize it, and not the ERP, as the representative of the porters and maids, and the union kept the company before government boards throughout the late 1920s. Because it relied on voluntary mediation, however, the Railway Labor Act, like prewar legislation, could not force any company to do anything, and Pullman, as it always had, refused to accept mediation.[64]

When it found the government to be unhelpful, the BSCP continued its struggle on another front and in 1927 sought an international charter from the AFL. Jurisdictional claims from white-dominated unions blocked this request, and the BSCP found no support from the AFL railroad unions when it threatened to strike in 1928. But AFL president William Green opened the door to the BSCP by arranging for its locals to become federal labor unions, just as the locals of Pullman car cleaners once had been. The AFL granted charters to nine federal labor unions of porters initially, and several more locals organized in the next few years. Yet in 1929 the Pullman Company seemed to be winning its fight against the BSCP just as it had against the shopcraft unions. BSCP membership declined precipitously after the union leadership pulled back from the strike threat, and the company used its panoply of rewards and punishments to pacify the porters themselves.[65]

Two Roads to the Open Shop in the 1920s

The company re-established the open shop in the sleeping-car service by expanding bureaucratic forms of labor management and by a new use of race—integrating the repair shops and the Commissary Department. Maintaining the open shop in the manufacturing division was not as difficult because there had been no period of union contracts to give workers higher aspirations and no major changes in shop-floor procedures to disrupt routines. Factors that had formerly impeded factory-wide unity at the Car Works, such as the variety of products, continued to create divisions among workers. The plant actually began to produce a line of automobile bodies in addition to railroad passenger cars, freight cars, and streetcars. The size of the workforce still fluctuated widely from a core of about eight thousand to more than twenty thousand, and many workers had only a tangential relationship to the company, taking a job at the Car Works only when lacking employment elsewhere. As in the past the sheer number of workers who could be called for any job, and the absence of a seniority system governing layoffs and recalls, increased the competition among workers and hampered unity. The Brotherhood of Railway Carmen (BRCA) presented no serious challenge at the Car Works or the Michigan City plant, nor had the steel industry seen any resurgence of organizing in the 1920s that might have attracted Pullman manufacturing workers.[66]

With little to fear from unions in its manufacturing plants, the company had no need to compromise with production workers in the manner that it did with repair shop workers. Consequently, labor management policies in the two divisions of the company diverged further in the 1920s. Shop workers earned hourly wages, while manufacturing workers earned piece rates that changed with every contract. The company signed a contract covering repair shop and yard mechanics but not manufacturing workers. This violated the structure of the ERP, which grouped repair shop and manufacturing workers together, but Pullman executives deemed this part of the price of warding off any resurgence of System Federation #122. In the mid-1920s, when Pullman officials became concerned about turnover at the manufacturing plants, they established a training course for foremen to make them more "diplomatic." Among other tips, the training manual instructed foremen to get evidence before they fired someone.[67] This was as far as the company felt it needed to go in transforming the nature of supervision.

In contrast, repair shop workers had much more security, even though the seniority system again allowed some management discretion. Where many workers had similar lengths of service, foremen could use efficiency as a criterion for whom to keep during a mass layoff, and they did not have to rehire those who quit, were sickly, or "not much good." Nor could seniority protect one from discipline if one's behavior displeased a foreman. Workers found themselves suspended for actions such as "petty quarrels which . . . interfered with efficient cooperation."[68] Yet the grievance procedure functioned to some extent, and workers won as well as lost appeals about discharges and violations of seniority rights. Even a seniority system with discretion created the core of long-term workers, despite the seasonal layoffs that caused the shops to employ 40 percent more workers in the spring rush season than in the summer slack season. Because of the seniority system the average cumulative service of men hired at the Calumet Repair Shop during the 1920s was twenty-five years.[69]

Dissatisfaction at the Car Works was still expressed as it had been since the 1880s, through small strikes over discrete issues. Decades-old problems, like inefficient working conditions and poor tools that hampered earnings from piece rates, continued to create discontent. But workers found that lodging complaints through the ERP brought no improvements and only strikes forced pressure from above to rectify conditions. Foremen were still supposed to "sell" the new piece rates to workers at the beginning of a contract, and their failure also produced walkouts. The company expected such actions and allowed them within limits that preserved management control. Workers could return from a walkout without penalty so long as they did so within one week. Management also issued passes to workers who refused new wage rates to get them out of the plant quickly to avoid any spread of the job action beyond the small group or department level.[70]

The weakness of this "system" for producing real gains for workers was apparent in the largest strike of the era, a walkout in 1924 by fifteen hundred car builders who rejected a cut in piece rates. When the car builders refused to return after one week, the company imported strikebreakers, threatened loss of pension rights, and used armed guards and plainclothesmen to intimidate pickets. Because of the scale and length of the job action the BRCA sent in organizers to help coordinate the strike. The U.S. Department of Labor also sent in a conciliator, but as usual the company proved unresponsive to mediation. Although the strikers held out for five weeks and turned away thousands of potential strikebreakers, they finally accepted the wage cut to avoid a blacklist.[71] The car builders could have won this strike only if other workers had supported them. But Pullman manufacturing workers had not united in a strike for two decades, and the BRCA could not bring them together.

Labor management policies for the two divisions of the corporation—manufacturing and sleeping-car service—diverged even more after 1924 when Pullman's board of directors established them as separate companies. The sleeping-car service was still known as the Pullman Company, while the manufacturing division evolved a new identity. In 1927 the board formed a holding company, Pullman Inc., to oversee both and then moved to fulfill George Pullman's unrealized dream of creating a monopoly in car building through mergers. In 1929 the manufacturing company absorbed the Bessemer, Alabama, car-building plant of the Tennessee Coal, Iron, and Railroad Company. The next year it bought the Osgood Bradley Car Company and the Standard Steel Car Company, acquiring thereby plants in Butler, Pennsylvania; Hammond, Indiana; and Worcester, Massachusetts. Now named Pullman Standard, the manufacturing company became the world's largest builder of passenger and freight cars. Pullman Standard became an increasingly important source of profits for Pullman Inc. because dividing the company insulated manufacturing workers from government oversight, regulations, and labor laws aimed at the railroads and thus from railroad labor unions too.[72]

Although the holding company kept some employee benefits like the pension plan uniform for both companies, increasingly labor relations in the Pullman Company and in Pullman Standard diverged. The repair shop workers and the manufacturing workers were divided again, because each company now had its own employee representation plan. The ERP in the sleeping-car service became more democratic in 1926 with passage of the Railway Labor Act because the latter required that each level of a grievance system had to have equal numbers of worker and management representatives. Previously, only management had staffed the highest levels at Pullman, a condition that remained in the grievance system at Pullman Standard.[73]

By 1929 Pullman executives could look with pride on their success in fending off unions in both the manufacturing company and the sleeping-car service through the development of separate and complex labor management strategies. As had been true in the past, however, the company's victory over unions was more apparent than real. Like other U.S. workers in the 1920s, Pullman employees might have been pacified, but they were not necessarily satisfied. Outside forces were about to weaken management's hand again and demonstrate that welfare capitalism and racial integration could not be relied on to maintain a nonunion workforce. The Great Depression of the 1930s wiped out the relatively steady employment that underlay many workers' acquiescence to management control in the 1920s, and it eroded the financial strength that allowed corporations to survive costly strikes. When the federal government once more entered the field of labor-management relations on the side of workers, the policies of the 1920s would be severely tested, and the Pullman Company's manipulation of race would prove to be a two-edged sword.

5 A New Deal for Pullman Workers?

The Great Depression of the 1930s was an unprecedented economic catastrophe that called into question Americans' faith in unfettered capitalism and business leadership. Even the companies most committed to welfare capitalism could not protect their employees from suffering. Workers did not accept impoverishment passively but used the state and unions to help themselves. On the basis of the votes of workers and farmers the Democratic Party gained control of Congress, and Franklin D. Roosevelt assumed the presidency. Through Roosevelt's New Deal the federal government once more became a positive force in the lives of workers by providing basic social welfare benefits such as old age pensions and unemployment insurance as well as by supporting workers' right to unionize. The Wagner Act of 1935 allowed workers to choose their representatives in secret elections overseen by the National Labor Relations Board. It enumerated unfair labor practices by employers and compelled companies to bargain with the representatives chosen by their workers.

Workers sought more security for themselves and their families not only through New Deal social welfare programs but also through a renewed commitment to union organizing. They built more than new unions; they created a new labor movement. On most railroads and in many large manufacturing corporations, workers organized successfully, obtained recognition of their representatives, and negotiated union contracts. Yet Pullman Inc. successfully resisted its workers' attempts to unionize. It had only one "failure"—being forced to recognize and bargain with the Brotherhood of Sleeping Car Porters (BSCP). The Brotherhood's triumph signaled a new stage in the development of the U.S.

labor movement as black workers successfully challenged not only anti-union employers but also racist unions.

Mass Unemployment and the Compromise of the 1920s

The depression of the 1930s weakened even the largest companies and devastated workers. Prosperity seemed to turn to depression overnight. With the economic collapse orders for new railcars disappeared, while Pullman's sleeping-car service experienced its last good year in 1928. Except for brief increases in the volume of travel for special events such as Chicago's Century of Progress Fair in 1933, the trend in usage of sleeping cars was almost steadily downward. The Pullman Company, which had never missed paying a dividend, ran at a loss for three years during the depression.

As the downturn threw more and more Americans out of work and cut the demand for railroad travel, Pullman workers by the thousand faced the challenge of earning a living. The corporation began laying off workers in 1930, and by the end of that year sixteen hundred employees of the sleeping-car service were idled. During the next decade thousands of porters and conductors experienced layoffs, and two-thirds of the repair shop workers were furloughed at least once. Pullman manufacturing workers suffered more and longer unemployment than did workers in the sleeping-car service because contracts for new railcars virtually disappeared, while trains continued to operate, albeit on reduced schedules. In January 1933, at the depth of the depression, half of Pullman Inc.'s 31,147 employees were out of work. The Car Works was building but two cars and employing only 600 people on a part-time basis, a far cry from the 7,000 to 8,000 who labored there in normal times. A year later employment had risen only to 1,500, as some car builders who had not worked in two years returned to their jobs. As late as 1935 employment at the Car Works had climbed only to 4,000, and 3,000 to 4,000 workers who were employed in normal periods were still on the streets.[1]

As profits disappeared, many corporations decided they could not afford welfare capitalism and even jettisoned their pension plans. But Pullman Inc. continued virtually all its programs, although officials scaled some back. Along with other companies that remained committed to welfare capitalism, Pullman actually expanded its efforts to give relief to its own employees who were laid off. As in the past, officials seemed most solicitous of workers in the sleeping-car service, and in November 1930 the board of directors authorized the expenditure of $15,000 per month in unemployment relief to aid the most destitute among them. The company continued this program until federal relief programs began in 1933. Such measures increased worker loyalty to Pullman, especially among those who lived in cities and states that did little to aid the unemployed.[2] Perhaps the corporation did less for its manufacturing workers because the cost would have been enormous, given the number of workers that it had laid off and the length of their unemployment.

By themselves, however, welfare benefits could not address the problem of widespread and long-term unemployment. The equilibrium of the 1920s disappeared as workers began to rethink the compromises that they had made with management. Furloughs aroused more than just fear of poverty. They brought to the fore the issue of how to define and ensure fairness in layoffs and recalls. In Pullman's sleeping-car service, seniority, the method that railroad workers considered fair, continued to govern staffing decisions. All workers did not suffer equally, though, because managers could defer certain work, and some departments experienced more layoffs than others did. Thus Nathan Carter, a black Mississippian who was hired as a helper in the cabinet department of the Calumet Repair Shop in 1929, never experienced a furlough during the depression. But Italian-born Serafino Panozzo, who was hired as a helper at the same time but in the tin department, was laid off six times by 1933. Moreover, mechanics often experienced more furloughs than helpers in the early years of the depression, as some repair shop managers sought to decrease costs by laying off proportionately more high-wage workers. As long as they furloughed workers within each occupational category in order of seniority, managers stayed within the rules of the contract with the employee representation plan (ERP). Even though the vast majority of mechanics and helpers at Pullman repair shops experienced at least one layoff during the depression, virtually all returned to the shops, because management continued to respect the seniority system. Those with little seniority often faced repeated and long bouts of unemployment, but co-workers tried to help by creating relief committees to distribute milk, clothes, coal, and groceries to those on extended layoffs.[3]

At companies that did not have seniority systems, management often instituted work sharing—cutting hours for everyone rather than laying off some and allowing others to work full time. Pullman's central office staff opted for work sharing, agreeing to take what employees referred to as "Hoover days"—one day per week or month off without pay—in an attempt to avoid having anyone laid off.[4] The office staff was more imbued with the concept of the "Pullman family" than were other groups of employees, and white-collar workers had had no experience with relying on seniority to govern layoffs.

Besides maintaining benefit programs and the seniority system, Pullman's sleeping-car service upheld its commitment to black repair shop workers. Unlike many companies, including some railroads, which laid off black workers first and rehired them last, Pullman repair shops administered the seniority system equitably. In Wilmington race-based layoffs became common as the depression deepened and white workers replaced black workers in many fields. But, as table 5 shows, there were no statistically significant differences in the average seniority of white and black helpers who were laid off at Pullman's Wilmington repair shop between 1930 and 1935. Nor, as table 6 shows, were there any large or consistent differences in the percentages of white and black workers who returned from furloughs. In the Chicago area discriminatory layoffs also were common: U.S. Steel, International Harvester, and some meatpacking plants all laid off black and Mexican workers before white workers. But at the

Table 5. Analysis of Variance of Average Seniority of Men Laid Off Each Year, by Race

	Calumet						Wilmington		
	Mechanics			Helpers			Helpers		
	F	Sig.	Eta^2	F	Sig.	Eta^2	F	Sig.	Eta^2
1930	3.178	0.078	0.034	0.339	0.563	0.007	4.239	0.046	0.090
1931	1.079	0.301	0.007	3.865	0.054	0.062	1.110	0.296	0.016
1932	0.050	0.823	0.000	0.093	0.761	0.001	2.229	0.142	0.043
1933	0.085	0.771	0.001	1.791	0.185	0.026	1.148	0.289	0.022
1934	8.692	0.004	0.056	5.464	0.023	0.058	1.021	0.321	0.035
1935	5.888	0.016	0.017	8.233	0.005	0.075	3.934	0.055	0.089

Source: Analysis of variance derived from samples described in the appendix.
Key: F = F-ratio; Sig. = observed significance level; Eta^2 = proportion of total variability in seniority accounted for by race

Table 6. Percentage of Men Who Returned from Layoff, by Race

	Calumet		Wilmington	
	White	Black	White	Black
1930	99.0	94.0	100.0	100.0
1931	99.4	98.3	94.1	88.9
1932	99.0	95.0	88.5	91.7
1933	99.1	98.1	99.1	96.2
1934	98.6	98.1	94.8	91.7
1935	100.0	98.0	93.5	95.8

Source: Derived from samples described in the appendix.

Calumet Repair Shop black mechanics and helpers were laid off and re-called without prejudice. Only in 1934 and 1935 were there statistically significant differences in the average seniority of black and white work-ers who were furloughed. Yet it is unlikely that this reflected systematic discrimination against black workers. Race accounted for only a small fraction of the variability in the seniority of those laid off, and virtually all the furloughed workers, black and white, were recalled to the shop.[5]

If the company did not discriminate in layoffs, it did join other em-ployers in giving preference to white men when filling the few new po-sitions that became available during the depression.[6] The company's commitment to its current black employees did not extend to African Americans in general, who found fewer opportunities for jobs at Pullman than they had in the 1920s. At the repair shops in Wilmington and Rich-mond, where black men comprised more than a quarter of new workers in the late 1920s, the decline in hiring African Americans was marked, as table 7 shows. The Calumet shop, on the other hand, had hired new workers primarily from its immediate, all-white neighborhood since the late 1920s, and therefore the proportion of new workers who were black remained steady at about 6 percent. Black men were never entirely shut out of new employment at Pullman repair shops in the 1930s, but they no longer found the broad welcome that made the company a magnet for African Americans in the 1920s.

Throughout U.S. industry employers gave as much work as possible to white male breadwinners rather than to women or minority men. The depression created a crisis in working-class homes as husbands and fa-thers could no longer provide for their families. Discriminatory layoffs and recalls and preferential hiring that favored white men resulted in part from this concern. The crisis of male breadwinners also reinforced older attitudes toward women's employment. In the sleeping-car service this return to tradition affected primarily its largest group of women—those who worked in its offices.

The only significant growth in women's employment at Pullman in the 1920s had been in clerical work, and to attract women the company

Table 7. Percentage of Men Hired from 1927 to 1942 Who Were Black

Repair Shop	1927–29	1930–33	1934–36	1937–42
Calumet	7.1	6.1	4.7	6.7
Richmond	28.0	0.0	2.7	6.8
Wilmington	26.1	27.3	6.7	15.9

Source: Derived from samples described in the appendix.

adopted a more modern demeanor. In response to young women who wanted to remain on the job and often kept their marriages secret until they became pregnant, management first ignored, then dropped, its rule forcing women to quit office jobs when they married.[7] In 1929 the *Pullman News* even ran an article approving of the ways in which "working wives change old style conceptions of marriage obligations." The article suggested that more wives would work in the future and urged a restructuring of marital obligations: "If a wife works as long and as hard in the business world every day as her husband does, she should not in fairness be expected to be responsible for all the woman's job in the home. . . . The old feeling that man should be the head of the family is at war with the newer philosophy that every individual has a right to freedom and full self-expression."[8]

As the depression undermined the position of male breadwinners, attitudes shifted, and company policy reflected the older belief that married women should be working outside the home only if they were the sole support of their families. The 1929 contract for Pullman's black maids first differentiated between two groups of women—those who supported others and those who did not. It required that layoffs be governed not only by seniority and fitness but also by whether a woman had dependents. This contract, signed before the downturn, reflected the greater likelihood that a black woman would be supporting a family. In the mid-1930s management extended this policy to white women clerical workers, noting that "a woman whose husband is regularly employed shall not be considered a bona fide head of a family."[9]

Men never recognized such familial obligations in constructing the rules governing their own employment, but they found such distinctions appropriate for women. So did many women who wanted to be full-time homemakers when they had children and who looked forward to leaving their paid jobs for motherhood. When economic crisis struck and their husbands could not support the family, these women, even if the mothers of small children, returned to the workforce but only to help out until their husbands could find jobs. One comptometer operator in Pullman's central office happily quit in 1931 when she became pregnant, but by the time her daughter was six months old, her husband, father, and two brothers were all unemployed. Leaving her daughter in her mother's care, she returned to her old job, and she supported her extended family for several years until the men were re-employed.[10]

The depression reinforced the gendering of Pullman work as a primarily male activity because management targeted women when cutting staff. As the number of travelers using the sleeping-car service declined in the late 1930s, managers abolished more women's jobs in offices and consolidated their work into jobs for men. When workers challenged these actions through the grievance system, Pullman officials restated their long-held views about appropriate work for women. They contended that the new jobs were not suitable for women because they involved night work or movement outside offices into the realms of blue-collar workers like the yards. In another economy move the Calumet Repair Shop eliminated the one supervisory position for a woman, forewoman of the seamstresses. When the incumbent retired, the shop manager gave the job to one of the male leaders. The company's long history of limiting employment opportunities for women was reinforced as it participated in the nationwide movement to bolster the white male breadwinner during the Great Depression.[11]

Workers Take Action

As the depression deepened and corporate welfare proved inadequate to address its effects, workers took action. The specter of unemployment aroused intense fears from the earliest days of the downturn and motivated Pullman workers to look for other ways to bolster job security. Their first responses were defensive. The Brotherhood of Sleeping Car Porters, for instance, appealed to the security concerns of porters and maids by opposing immigration. This issue surfaced in early 1930 at a meeting of the National Negro Labor Conference, the union's forum for encouraging all black workers to join the labor movement. Oscar De Priest, Chicago's black member of Congress, found a ready audience when he urged a group of workers not only to join the American Federation of Labor (AFL) but also to work for additional curbs on immigration. He singled out Mexicans, who had not been barred by the draconian immigration bill of 1924, as unfair competition for U.S. workers. The BSCP continued to make an issue of immigration, and in 1933 union president A. Philip Randolph testified in support of Sen. Clarence Dill's legislation to require railroads to employ only U.S. citizens in service positions in interstate commerce. This bill appealed to porters not only because thousands were laid off but also because it countered the Pullman Company's use of Filipinos to undermine the BSCP.[12]

Pullman repair shop workers also responded defensively to unemployment. They demanded a stabilization plan to even out production and provide year-round employment to a core group of workers. The railroad shopcraft unions, including System Federation #122, had demanded such a plan during World War I. By the late 1920s a few railroads had developed stabilization plans in concert with unions, and Pullman shop workers revived the demand for year-round employment through their employee representation plan. F. L. Simmons, the supervisor of industrial relations, recommended a plan that involved reducing the workday during the two normal seasons (fall and winter) and the slow summer season while maintaining the nine-hour day only during the spring rush. Company executives ignored his recommendation, however, claiming that they could not plan because they could not gauge the railroads' demand for cars.[13]

Mass unemployment first galvanized workers in the sleeping-car service to make new demands, but wage cuts once more focused their attention on unions as an answer to their problems. Although layoffs threatened workers from the beginning of the depression, like most large corporations Pullman did not immediately cut wages. And in 1931, when deficits loomed for the sleeping-car service, management did not follow the path that George Pullman took in 1893 when he placed the entire burden of wage cuts on workers. The development of a bureaucratic structure of labor relations and fear of unions had created a norm of fairness unknown to Pullman himself. In the 1930s salaried employees in the sleeping-car service were the first to experience reductions in pay, while office workers, who as yet had no contract through their employee representation plan, followed. When deeper cuts seemed necessary, management targeted the company's largest group of workers, the porters. Officials violated the contract that they had signed with the porters' ERP and cut porters' and maids' base pay by $5 per month. Pullman officials felt secure in ignoring the porters' elected representatives because they no longer feared the Brotherhood of Sleeping Car Porters. Mass unemployment among porters, combined with company favoritism toward those who were not union members, had cut membership in the union to fewer than one thousand by 1932.[14] Pullman repair shop workers, however, would exert more control over wage cuts, because of the resurgence of the railroad shopcraft unions.

As individual corporations demanded wage reductions in 1931, the railroad unions regrouped and insisted on a national conference to develop a uniform policy. In 1932 the unions and the major railroads negotiated the first national agreements since 1919. The shopcraft unions insisted that their wage rates remain unchanged but accepted a schedule of temporary reductions. The initial reduction of 10 percent would be phased out in stages on a set timetable so that when business improved, workers did not have to fight to return to what they considered a just wage while companies got windfall profits. Because of the length of the depression the unions and the railroads negotiated two extensions of the reductions, and full earnings returned only in April 1935. Pullman repair shop workers would agree only to this plan.[15] Simmons counseled corporate officials not to ignore the wishes of the shop workers for fear that they would bolt the employee representation plan. If the company pressed the employee representatives for a different agreement, "our employes would probably decline to make an agreement for fear that they might injure the prospects of the railroad employes . . . and thus boomerang their own interests."[16] A decade after banishing System Federation #122 from its repair shops, Pullman management found the unions right outside the door again. Pullman workers kept abreast of what railroad repair shop workers did, and they would remain nonunion only so long as the company followed industry-wide wage patterns.

Union Resurgence

Workers in the sleeping-car service looked to the railroad unions because the latter took an aggressive stance from the earliest days of the depression. The railroad unions had lost many members after World War I, but they remained among the strongest of U.S. unions and so were ready to take advantage of the downturn. Beyond their actions to protect wage rates, the AFL railroad unions responded to workers' concerns about security, and they were instrumental in extending the role of the federal government toward the provision of social welfare. Because seniority systems had governed railroad employment for decades, railroad workers as a group were older than workers in most other industries. When railroads began to renege on their pension plans and layoffs threatened this benefit for others, the unions took action. In 1932 they demanded a government-run retirement program for railroad workers. Once Franklin D. Roosevelt set out to give Americans a New Deal, the unions were poised to make real gains for themselves and for railroad workers.

Roosevelt's policies attempted to revive the economy while aiding those in greatest distress and setting new standards for equity in labor relations. The Emergency Transportation Act of 1933, designed to counter the precarious financial condition of many railroads by eliminating duplication of service, also reflected railroad workers' concern for security and fairness through maintaining employment levels and workers' earnings. The act also outlawed yellow-dog contracts and forbade railroads from using their funds to support company unions. The AFL shopcraft unions immediately challenged company unions on the railroads and began to recoup the losses that they had suffered in 1922. The Brotherhood of Sleeping Car Porters also set out to use the new legislation to kill Pullman's employee representation plan and revitalize its membership. But the Brotherhood found that the legislation did not specifically apply to the Pullman Company, which was deemed a common carrier, not a railroad. Unlike the Railway Labor Act of 1926, the emergency legislation, passed in the bustle of the famous "Hundred Days," had not been carefully drafted to include Pullman. Thus the BSCP campaigned to revise the Railway Labor Act to include the stronger prolabor provisions of the new bill.[17]

In 1934 Congress responded to the demands of the railroad unions and the BSCP by amending the Railway Labor Act and passing the Railroad Retirement Act. The latter created the first government pension system for nongovernment workers. It superseded all private pension plans, regardless of their adequacy, and was an important first step in countering management efforts to use welfare benefits to build nonunion workforces. Government pensions undercut loyalty to any one company by allowing workers to count their total employment on the railroads toward their pensions and hence to leave one railroad for another with impunity. Although Pullman and the railroads challenged the constitutionality of the retirement plan, a rewritten version passed court challenge in 1935. Congress also established unemployment compensation for railroad workers in 1938, including disability coverage in case of accident or sickness. Congress responded more quickly and more broadly to the security concerns of railroad workers than it did to those of other workers in part because of the long history of federal oversight of the railroads and in part because of the strength of the railroad unions.[18]

The revised Railway Labor Act also extended government regulation of labor relations by creating enforcement mechanisms that weakened company unions. It undercut financial support for company unions by prohibiting employers from paying employee representatives for their time or defraying their expenses for union activities. This made management control of employee representatives more difficult. Most important, the act established the National Mediation Board with the power to hold elections where two or more organizations claimed the same membership. Companies could no longer ignore the outcome of mediation, and they were required to bargain with the union representing the majority of their workers. The act also established national boards of adjustment, comparable in scope to those in existence during World War I, to settle disputes arising from interpretations of contracts.[19]

The New Deal had at last provided Pullman porters with support to unionize, and they took full advantage of it. In the process they revealed that black workers were no longer either reliably antiunion or grateful to employers for the mere opportunity to work. The Pullman Company lost the loyalty of the vast majority of porters and maids in part because the wage cuts of the early 1930s treated them yet again as second-class citizens. The company unilaterally cut their wages at the same time that it negotiated with the repair shop workers. Officials misjudged, perhaps because they were still blinded by the racism that had shaped the treatment of porters since George Pullman first defined the job as suitable for black men. Moreover, a main counterweight to the BSCP, the Pullman Porters Benefit Association of America, was weakened in the 1930s when it lost thousands of members who were laid off and had to cut benefit levels. A substantial change in the reputation of unions in African American communities also aided the Brotherhood's organizing campaign. Black workers began to organize in many industries, and movements of the unemployed swept African American neighborhoods. Middle-class community leaders either became pro-union or found themselves ignored. Now, seemingly, the entire black community approved of porters' unionizing.[20]

With the enforcement machinery of the National Mediation Board behind it, the Brotherhood of Sleeping Car Porters signed up more than 51 percent of Pullman porters and maids and petitioned the government for recognition as their bargaining agent. The 1935 election between the BSCP and the company union was the first held under the amended Railway Labor Act, and the BSCP became the first union to win representation status with the Pullman Company. Porters and maids voted overwhelming for the BSCP; it received 4 votes to every 1 for the company union. The porters' and maids' renewed interest in the union reflected the explosive potential of discriminating against a racially homogeneous group of workers.

Despite the union's victory, porters and maids experienced no immediate gains because the company refused to negotiate. Under the leadership of David A. Crawford, who had replaced Edward Carry as president of Pullman Inc. in 1929, the company responded in a superficially more conciliatory fashion to unions. Polite letters went back and forth, but neither the new president nor the new supervisor of industrial relations, H. R. Lary, was more willing to share power than Pullman officials had been in the past. Crawford and Lary had worked for the company for many years, and they had, after all, seen federal support for labor organizations wax and wane. How long the new pro-union policies would last was unclear, and Pullman officials remained determined to resist unions.[21]

Limiting Union Gains

While Pullman workers, black and white, questioned the compromises that they had made with management in the 1920s, they did not struggle together but in fragments defined by occupation and race. Pullman executives remained adamantly opposed to outside unions, and their complex labor relations' policies helped them to prevail—except over the porters—despite the activism of their workers, union organizing drives, and the new labor laws. Indeed, only Pullman and the Pennsylvania Railroad succeeded in resisting the railroad unions.

The AFL shopcraft unions began organizing again at Pullman repair shops and yards in 1934, and the Brotherhood of Railway Carmen (BRCA) had active locals of both white mechanics and black coach cleaners at every Pullman yard in Chicago within a short time.[22] The sleeping-car service first responded to the new union offensive as many railroads did, by orchestrating the conversion of the divisions of its employee representation plan into "independent" unions. The company promoted the fiction that these were a spontaneous creation of the workers themselves. In reality management asked the leaders of the employee representation plan to secure petitions signed by a majority of workers in their divisions, and in violation of the law they solicited for membership on company time. The Department of Industrial Relations posted instructions on "workers' rights" that were designed to channel workers into the company-approved unions. Most important, supervisors used coercion where necessary to force workers into the unions. Pullman managers laid off mechanics and car cleaners who supported the shopcraft unions, and as fear became widespread, the International Brotherhood of Electrical Workers had to reassure Pullman electricians that their membership in the AFL union would be kept secret. Yet coercion was not always necessary because company unions had attractive features too, such as low dues. This meant, of course, that they could provide no benefits or support a strike, but the "independent" unions had already forsworn strikes.[23]

Management's first success in establishing company unions came with the formation of the Pullman Car Employes Association of the Repair Shops (PCEARS) in November 1934, and soon thereafter the yard workers, including the predominantly black car cleaners and the mostly white mechanics, formed the Independent Pullman Workers Federation. Just as the employee representation plan had, the company unions for the repair shops and yards split the constituency that System Federation #122 claimed. The railroads and manufacturers that succeeded in keeping the

AFL unions at bay during the depression had been those, like Pullman, that were most strongly committed to welfare capitalism. More than other Pullman employees, the repair shop and yard workers had received real benefits from their ERPs, and thus the company found it easiest to create "independent unions" in the shops and yards.[24]

Although the supervisor of industrial relations kept close watch over the company unions by providing secretaries to type up their minutes, as "independent" labor organizations these unions had to have contracts. Even the union for Pullman clerks, whose ERP had not been so endowed, now had a written agreement with the company. The unions for the repair shops and yards signed the old contract that management had made with the employee representation plan, but they were able to eliminate some of the most egregious violations of that contract, "proving" their superiority to the old ERPs. In the repair shops, for instance, the establishment of PCEARS coincided with a crackdown on the use of helpers to replace mechanics. At the Wilmington repair shop, which had used this inexpensive labor strategy more than any other Pullman shop, the percentage of the workforce in helper-level jobs declined by 40 percent. The new unions also forced managers to maintain the prescribed ratio of helpers to mechanics during furloughs rather than to lay off more of the higher-priced workers. Furthermore, in 1934 and 1935 the shops reclassified most of the helper-apprentices who should have been promoted earlier. As table 8 demonstrates, promotions slowed in the early 1930s, and at every shop some helper-apprentices were actually demoted by being reclassified as helpers. With the new company union in place, the vast majority of those who had been helper-apprentices since the 1920s became mechanics at last.[25]

Although the porters and maids rejected the company union, other Pullman workers responded to the combination of coercion and improvement as the new company unions attempted to address their needs. The

Table 8. Reclassification of 1929 Helper-Apprentices during the Great Depression

	1930–33		1934–35	
	Reclassified	Became Mechanics	Reclassified	Became Mechanics
Calumet	43.6%	40.0%	50.0%	78.6%
Richmond	14.2	50.0	78.6	90.9
Wilmington	7.8	20.0	82.8	73.6

Source: Derived from samples described in the appendix.
Note: Percentage reclassified does not total 100 because a small number at each shop remained helper-apprentices throughout the period.

leaders of the Pullman Car Employes Association of the Repair Shops responded to the concern for security among the relatively elderly shop force, whose average age was forty-one, by renewing the demand for a plan to stabilize employment. Company representatives refused this demand but found other ways to respond to concerns about security. Retirees could now continue their insurance if they paid the premiums, and instead of firing older workers, managers could shift them to easier jobs if they could no longer perform. The company also addressed the threat of worker obsolescence from technological changes, such as the introduction of spray painting, by allowing workers to shift jobs. As in so many instances where Pullman management wanted to maintain its flexibility, officials would agree to policies in principle but refuse to write them into a contract.[26]

Negotiations between PCEARS and company representatives revealed not only shop workers' concerns for job security but also their determination to maintain their standard of living. Older workers were family men with responsibilities, and severe layoffs at Pullman repair shops in 1938 and 1939 kept this issue alive. Workers had more and more difficulty paying the bills that they accumulated during furloughs and fell deeply in debt. Managers thought workers were profligate, as one memo revealed in stating that "we do not feel that jewelry and automobiles are essential."[27] In contrast, workers believed they should enjoy an American standard of living that included owning a home and a car. J. W. McDowell, a representative from the Atlanta shop, described the life that mechanics believed was their right: "Labor is entitled to their part of the fruits of their industry, not only in fair wages, but enough to have a little left over, and have some of the comforts and enjoyments that an upright citizen should have."[28] Pullman shop workers resented what they saw as the continuous grind of working to pay back debts accumulated during one layoff before facing another. The new government program of unemployment compensation could not maintain the standard of living to which these older workers were accustomed.[29]

Threats to workers' standard of living also led to continual sparring with management about a plan to stabilize employment. Several shop managers converted to the workers' position, having found the truth in what PCEARS leaders warned: "A man that is laid off for four months or three months yearly has no incentive whatever to take any pride in that job."[30] But employee representatives continued to charge that getting production out ahead of schedule—working as fast as possible—remained company policy.[31]

Pullman executives wanted company unions to focus on issues such as safety that did not threaten management control. Since the Progressive era, the company had a financial stake in safety, and it continued to promote and spread the best standards from its facilities in states that mandated tough regulations to those in states that did not. Yet workers themselves saw things somewhat differently. Although employees sometimes quit because of health problems caused or exacerbated by conditions at work, many would accept higher pay as a trade-off for hazard. PCEARS leaders, for instance, fought to designate sandblasting as a mechanic's job rather than a helper's job (the usual designation in the railroad industry) because of "the risk on a man's health."[32]

The company unions often played the role that Pullman officials desired, however, that of mediator between employees and managers rather than champion of workers. Most PCEARS leaders and Pullman managers had worked together for many years, and their negotiations had the quality of conversations between old acquaintances. Some PCEARS leaders were inspectors and a few later became supervisors themselves. They often saw things from management's perspective. As the Calumet representative W. C. Mechling said, "Well, the men come to us almost every day and they want this and they want that. You know there are ninety percent of them that are unreasonable and we have to tell them the same thing, how damn lucky they are to be working."[33]

Yet if worker representatives felt a community of interest with lower-level managers, they distrusted the motives of top company officials. Another Calumet representative, Esque A. Iles, expressed this sentiment during a discussion of layoffs: "There is no need for the employees of the Pullman Company to kid themselves that the Pullman Company is handing them a lot of cream back on a silver platter. Whenever revenue gets to the place where it is not coming in heavy enough to satisfy Wall Street and the majority of those financiers getting their dividends on their outlay, there is going to be a shortage of work in some way. We are the poor fellows that have to pay for it."[34] Even some managers seem not to have trusted the solicitude of the heads of the "Pullman family." One management representative, in response to a comment that it was easy for the company to replace skilled workers, said, "If we all dropped dead right now, the company could still go on. It wouldn't make a bit of difference to anybody. Our immediate families would miss us and that is all there would be to it."[35]

The sympathy between worker and management representatives broke only on occasion, when issues arose that highlighted differences in working-class and middle-class cultures. When PCEARS demanded more cleanup time for paint sprayers so that they would not have to shower in front of hundreds of other men, a management representative seemed surprised that this would bother them. The men he knew did not mind walking around in "their birthday clothes" at golf clubs. The PCEARS negotiator responded somewhat acerbically that not many painters belonged to golf clubs.[36]

A New Deal for Manufacturing Workers

The creation of company unions in the shops and yards and the refusal to bargain in good faith with the Brotherhood of Sleeping Car Porters did not end Pullman Inc.'s problems with unions in 1934 and 1935. The manufacturing workers also began to organize on a scale not seen since 1904. They posed a real threat because for the first time Congress enacted legislation supporting the right of all workers, not just railroad workers, to form unions. The National Industrial Recovery Act of 1933, which sought to stabilize production and employment through codes of fair competition, promised workers the right to form unions and bargain with their employers. As in the past, Pullman executives were willing to go along with minimum wages and maximum hours provisions and to participate in writing the code for the railroad car–building industry, but they balked at union recognition.[37] Emboldened by government support, workers at Pullman Standard's Bessemer, Alabama, plant approached the Brotherhood of Railway Carmen of America for representation. At this point, however, BRCA leaders hesitated, questioning whether the union's jurisdiction extended to a manufacturing company that the Railway Labor Act did not include in its purview. Pullman Inc. was an indeterminate case, part "railroad" and part manufacturer.[38]

When the National Industrial Recovery Act was declared unconstitutional, Congress incorporated its support for workers' right to organize in the Wagner Act. Through the National Labor Relations Board this legislation provided the machinery for manufacturing workers to choose their representatives, just as railroad workers did under the aegis of the National Mediation Board. In response, many manufacturers tried to create independent unions from their employee representation plans, taking the same path that the railroads and Pullman's sleeping-car service had after the passage of the amended Railway Labor Act. In 1936 Pullman Standard signed its first contract with the ERP for the manufacturing workers, now rechristened as the Pullman Employes Union. Among other provisions, the contract granted manufacturing workers the type of seniority system that the company had previously allowed workers in the sleeping-car service.[39] Pullman Standard accepted a stronger company union because for the first time since the 1890s the labor movement offered an industrial union that might attract its disparate manufacturing workers.

By 1934 workers in mass-production industries were uniting on a factory-wide basis, striking, and trying to form unions. They objected to the AFL policy of placing them in weak federal labor unions and then attempting to parcel them out into separate craft unions. Some AFL union leaders also favored organizing on an industry-wide basis, and in 1935 John L. Lewis of the United Mine Workers led them in forming the Committee on Industrial Organization. The next year these unions left the AFL and became a rival labor organization, the Congress of Industrial Organizations (CIO). Its Steel Workers Organizing Committee (SWOC) targeted not only steel producers but also steel users like Pullman Standard.

SWOC organized on a geographical basis: the Pullman Car Works, for instance, was part of the union's Roseland–Harvey–Chicago Heights subdistrict, which had organizing drives in twenty to twenty-five plants. The working-class ethos that had long supported unions and radicals in that area survived the era of corporate dominance and provided fertile ground for union organizing in the 1930s. Communists now outnumbered anarchists or socialists among local radicals, but as in the past their ties to the community assured them support. They had taken a prominent role in the early 1930s in movements of the unemployed for more adequate relief, and their demonstrations became political street battles, with the American Legion and the Chicago police "Industrial Squad" (or "Red Squad") arrayed against "the people." This public visibility as champions of the victims of the depression set the stage for worker acceptance of those SWOC organizers, like Mario Manzardo, who were communists. Manzardo began work in 1927 at the Pullman Car Works where, as he said, he "found out what it was to be a worker." He was fired as a "malcontent" but remained in the greater Pullman area to fight for the unemployed and build the steelworkers' union.[40]

The railcar builders' interest in the new union was not difficult to understand. They had suffered with the piece-rate system and despotic foremen for decades, and now they had been out of work for years, not just months. The new company union was too little too late, as was the corporation's attempt to alleviate some unemployment among employees of the Pullman Car Works. In order to compete with the airlines and automobiles, Pullman executives decided to air condition every railcar in the Pullman fleet, and they centered the work at the Calumet Repair Shop in order to employ those laid off from the Car Works. In 1936 and 1937 the Calumet shop ran three shifts per day and hired more than one thousand new workers, most of whom were Pullman railcar builders.[41]

As an industrial rather than a craft union, SWOC fit the reality of railcar building as the AFL's Brotherhood of Railway Carmen did not. After years of scientific management and reorganization for mass production, the type of craft identity that remained in railroad repair shops, where each department housed a different trade, had long disappeared in railcar manufacturing. The Calumet Repair Shop, where mass-production methods had made the greatest inroads in Pullman repair work, was not immune to the SWOC drive, either. The influx of men from the Car Works during the air-conditioning project provided the core of SWOC's support at the shop. But Calumet workers had always led organizing among Pullman shop workers, and they had always been ready to join whatever union movement was on the rise in the neighborhood. According to a company report, 175 workers attended the initial organizing meeting for the repair shop's Lodge #1721 in April 1937. The five officers elected at that meeting were all men hired at the shop after the 1922 strike, not new transplants from the Car Works. SWOC made real progress at the repair shop, and even PCEARS representatives acknowledged privately that they doubted that as many as 55 percent of the Calumet workers supported the company union.[42]

Pullman Inc. mobilized all its resources to defeat the CIO challenge. The supervisor of industrial relations received almost daily spy reports on CIO activities around the country between April and December 1937. SWOC was a real threat at the Car Works and the Calumet Repair Shop, and workers at Pullman's Bessemer, Alabama, plant also were looking to the CIO because the AFL had turned them away two years earlier. The CIO was even organizing Pullman yard workers in New York. The spy reports also reveal the company's concern about communists in the CIO and the Brotherhood of Sleeping Car Porters. Brotherhood leadership worked with the CIO to help other black workers organize, and C. L. Dellums, head of the porters' local in Oakland, California, was long suspected of being a communist. Although the BSCP remained in the AFL to fight racism in that organization, the porters refused to encourage black workers to join AFL unions that denied them equity and so became involved in CIO organizing drives.[43]

SWOC, like all CIO unions, could appeal to black workers because it was avowedly interracial. Unlike the AFL, the CIO welcomed all and committed itself to racial equity. SWOC sent organizers into Chicago's Bronzeville to bring in the black workers who lived far from the steel mills or the Pullman plants at which they labored, and BSCP members aided this effort. SWOC organizers worked through local ethnic and racial associations, but at the same time the union tried to build a "culture of unity" to draw workers out of ethnic and racial particularism and into a broader movement. The leadership of the union local at the Calumet Repair Shop reflected the CIO's commitment to diversity: one of the five officers, the secretary, was a black worker, Jim Mason. Men named Sullivan, Nelson, Wonder, and Galkowski, who reflected the ethnic diversity of Pullman's workforce, filled the other positions.[44]

Mason did not represent the majority of Calumet's black shop workers, however. Only 4 percent of the known SWOC members at the Calumet Repair Shop were black, many fewer than would be expected from their percentage of the shop force, and company spies reported that most black shop workers remained loyal to PCEARS. When black men in Chicago were almost twice as likely to be unemployed as white men, many of Calumet's black shop workers stood by a company that treated them fairly in layoffs, recalls, and promotions. Some black men had even become C-level mechanics at Calumet, and they may have been loath to jeopardize that achievement. Furthermore, the racism that had closed the Pullman area to black residence had not abated, and black and white repair shop workers still socialized separately.[45] Bringing them together to challenge the company would not be an easy task. The racial strategy that the company perfected to marginalize the AFL worked against the CIO too.

If SWOC's neighborhood organizing strategy did not mitigate racial divisions, it could help steelworkers to counter cooperation among employers who continued to work together to overcome union challenges. Pullman Inc. helped Republic Steel to house strikebreakers at its plant near the Car Works. According to Ray Sarocco, a SWOC organizer, the "Calumet shop were triked [*sic*] into conditioning Pullmans for the Republic scabs."[46] In its fight against the CIO, Pullman Inc. aligned itself with the companies known as "Little Steel," the smaller steel companies that resisted SWOC after the giant in the industry, U.S. Steel, capitulated.

Little Steel waged a brutal and violent war against SWOC in the south Chicago–northwest Indiana region. It culminated in the Memorial Day Massacre at Republic Steel in 1937 when the Chicago Red Squad killed ten people and wounded scores of others. Strikers and their families, not realizing the lengths to which the company and its allies would go to stop them, used the holiday to stage a protest march. Although business spokesmen and their media supporters tried to blame the carnage on the workers, a congressional inquiry revealed the determination of the Little Steel companies to win at any price. Despite the New Deal's support for labor organizing, the strong ties of Chicago's Democratic Party to both the AFL and the Little Steel companies led it to deploy the Red Squad against the CIO.[47]

The fight at the Car Works and the Calumet shop had less tragic results but also was violent. As the supervisor of industrial relations, H. R. Lary, later reminisced: "I recall out in Calumet Shops one day when the CiO [*sic*] . . . got a little tough and I got just as g d tough and said this is the way its [*sic*] going to be and that's the way it was. Well we had things in those days pretty much in our own hands."[48] But the key to Pullman's defeat of SWOC at the Calumet Repair Shop was not violence alone but the aid of the company union. While SWOC attempted to capture such unions from within, it had only limited success with this initiative outside the U.S. Steel Corp.[49] PCEARS leaders remained loyal to the company, threatening workers with loss of their jobs if they joined SWOC and using violence to intimidate them when necessary. As one leader said, explaining how to stop workers from switching to outside unions after they had finished their probationary period and had seniority: "I don't see but one thing to do and that is drop something on his head, if it is after the thirty day period."[50] The national chairman of PCEARS, Robert Sharpe, advised Calumet leaders to use less violence: "Don't go to him and say, 'If you don't join up here, I am going to pin your ears back. We are going to spoil your work. We are going to steal your tools.'"[51] Sharpe recommended a more subtle approach: have PCEARS members isolate the offender, refusing to talk to the worker except when absolutely necessary. This made people feel like outcasts, and they would join the company union for companionship.

The company union triumphed at the Calumet Repair Shop, and the CIO drive at the Pullman Car Works also came to naught. Though SWOC organizers reported slow but steady growth in membership at the Car Works through June 1937, they had little success thereafter. Severe layoffs in 1938 and 1939 again put much of the workforce on the streets. SWOC membership throughout the Pullman area declined as the recession of late 1937 caused widespread unemployment.[52] Little Steel and Pullman Standard defeated their workers, the CIO, and the good intentions of the New Deal too.

Although the federal government now supported workers' attempts to organize, actually building new unions proved difficult. Even the railroad shopcraft unions, with long-standing support from the state, found it hard to beat the most savvy antiunion employers. Pullman officials stopped the shopcraft unions and SWOC through a combination of positive incentives, manipulation of racial divisions among workers, and intimidation. As in the past, those who dropped their support for the outside unions were allowed to remain in Pullman employment.[53] Such forgiveness was not necessarily a foolish move on the company's part. It left the Calumet Repair Shop divided at least three ways—between CIO supporters, PCEARS supporters, and older workers who had residual loyalty to the AFL.

The New Compromise at the Repair Shops

Despite its loss, SWOC had an immediate effect on Pullman repair shops; it made PCEARS into a union that could force some real changes from the company. Although management viewed PCEARS as a continuation of the old employee representation plan, workers did not. They signaled this as early as 1935 by electing primarily new men, who had not been ERP representatives, to leadership positions. PCEARS leaders helped to defeat SWOC, but they expected a reward for their role in stopping the CIO—a new contract. In January 1937 the company followed its long-standing policy of raising wages whenever the AFL shopcraft unions achieved higher rates, but Pullman repair shop workers wanted more. They demanded what SWOC organizers had promised: an end to the incentive wage system of variable rates and three skill grades for mechanics, and a two-week paid vacation.[54] Ben Lewis, system chairman of PCEARS, told company officials that if they ignored workers' demands, the representatives from Calumet "would be afraid to go to work the day that the men in their shop heard of this agreement. They spoke of the activity of the C.I.O. in their shops, and said that the men were very much upset with the manner in which the Association had been handled in the past and expressed fear that they would not be able to hold them in line much longer."[55]

PCEARS leaders used the threat posed by SWOC to force a contract that more closely approximated those of the AFL shop craft unions. When PCEARS and company representatives met in August 1937, Chairman Lewis set the tone of the negotiations in an opening speech:

> We have all read and heard of the upheaval and terrorism inflicted by the leaders of the C.I.O., and while the sympathies of workingmen are generally with the employee, rather than the employer, I believe that I am voicing the opinion of the members of this Association in general, when I say that we are not in sympathy with some of the radical and Communistic ideas of these leaders. We believe in the old saying, 'You can catch more flies with sugar than with vinegar.' . . . Therefore, it is the feeling of this delegation that we should be given credit for having kept this Association intact as it was organized and were able to keep out these radical outside influences.[56]

In an intense eleven-day bargaining session, PCEARS representatives forced the company to provide the credit and completely rewrite the contract. The result was a compromise, the first contract since the 1922 strike to reflect mechanics' views about the organization of the shop floor.

Negotiations focused on the power of foremen, and the charges that PCEARS leaders made were strikingly similar to those that Pullman workers had voiced since the 1880s. Union leaders alleged that some foremen played favorites in hiring, layoffs, and recalls even in this time of widespread suffering, and they objected to foremen's power to fire workers because the seniority system allowed "discretion." In the years to come PCEARS further attacked foremen for undermining workers' initiative.[57] In the absence of union rules Pullman workers had been resisting arbitrary and tyrannical foremen, just as they had since the nineteenth century, by slowing down the pace of production through informal agreement. Because PCEARS leaders were themselves skilled workers, they saw this as the natural response to foremen who "start out practically as drivers. Naturally, the men do not want to cooperate and production goes down."[58] They believed that leadership ability rested on craft skill and long-term knowledge of one's co-workers and that productivity emanated from cooperation, not coercion and control. Union leaders insisted that eliminating the variable rates that gave foremen the power to drive workers was an absolute precondition for holding the allegiance of the repair shop workers.[59]

PCEARS leaders also wanted seniority alone to govern elevation to supervisory positions. The company refused this demand outright, insisting not only on its right to manage but also on the requirement that leaders be able to do the paperwork necessary for monitoring worker output. Because many older Pullman workers lacked literacy skills, at least in English, supervisors were often younger men with less seniority. Pullman executives still clung to a scientific management perspective, while the leaders of the company union maintained a mechanic's vision of production as cooperative endeavor.[60] As the Calumet representative Esque A. Iles said: "I wouldn't hold it right down to reading and writing, but there are some men that I really believe have been deprived of leader's jobs who are more cooperative with their men. I believe they would have gotten better service for the management and had less squabbles and fusses in their departments than some of those that have been appointed."[61]

While the company eliminated the variable rates that augmented foremen's power, it refused PCEARS's demand to scrap the three levels of craft tasks themselves. So PCEARS leaders demanded reclassification of some tasks to better reflect changes in the content of jobs or the rules of the AFL shopcraft unions. Beginning in 1937, some specialties were upgraded from lower to higher levels, but none was downgraded. Thus some workers received higher wages because of reclassification as well as the general rate increase. In another compromise workers would now have seniority by job level rather than by specialty. Workers aimed to reinstate the job structure with the department-wide seniority that they had under System Federation #122 before the 1922 strike. The compromise on seniority helped undermine specialization because it forced foremen to give workers a variety of experiences; when layoffs were severe, the foremen would need workers who could cover several jobs.[62]

In the new contract PCEARS also sought to rein in management's use of helpers, apprentices, or helper-apprentices as inexpensive labor. Worker representatives had complained about the managers who did this for years, but only with the threat of SWOC could they get the central office to consistently police shop managers. The 1937 contract specified the range of training required for each position and the time period after which promotion was mandatory. The new contract also made the forty-hour week standard, and workers received time and a half for overtime. While PCEARS adopted the SWOC demand for a paid vacation, the company resisted this because it was not yet the industry norm for railroad workers.[63]

That the contract for which PCEARS leaders fought looked very much like those of the AFL shopcraft unions was not surprising, although they used the threat of the CIO to attain it. A core of workers who had been members of System Federation #122 remained in each repair shop in 1937. At the Calumet, Wilmington, and Richmond repair shops about one-fifth of mechanics had participated in the 1922 strike, as had about one-tenth of their supervisors, men who had been promoted from the ranks in the intervening years. The resurgence of the shopcraft unions on the railroads heartened them and provided a model for younger repair shop workers. If company officials had any illusions about the attitude of PCEARS leaders toward System Federation #122, they lost them during the 1937 negotiating session, as the employee representatives referred critically to workers who had broken the 1922 strike.[64]

PCEARS members were not necessarily apathetic or antiunion; some were in fact members of AFL or CIO unions. When Robert Sharpe was chairman of the national board of PCEARS, he reflected on this situation: "When I am out to get members, I don't care whether a man belongs to the A.F. of L. or the C.I.O. or what. . . . I really appreciate a man who is union minded."[65] Given the hostility of the Pullman Company to dealing with outside unions, he told workers that they could belong to any union as long as they joined PCEARS too. Sharpe likened the company and the workers to a husband and wife who had to live in the same building: each had to do his part if they were to get along or otherwise it was hell.[66] Although Sharpe used domestic imagery, his version of the Pullman family differed significantly from that propagated in the pages of the *Pullman News,* where wise managers, like good patriarchs, made all decisions. From Sharpe's perspective, workers and managers, like husband and wife, were equal partners who had to cooperate.

Besides attempting to reinstate the standards set by the AFL shopcraft unions, the company union gained support by addressing workers' concern for security. Like the porters, Pullman repair shop workers saw immigrants as unfair competitors and demanded action. In 1937 the company instituted a rule that all new repair shop workers had to be citizens. Shop managers went even further: the Wilmington shop had never hired many foreign born, but now other Pullman repair shops hired primarily native-born Americans too. The leaders of PCEARS demanded that the company fire all aliens, but officials refused, pointing out that it was illegal for them to fire people who had not become citizens only for that reason and that the number of aliens among the shop workers, 138, was not large.[67]

Yet fear of immigrant competitors remained and surfaced again in 1940 when PCEARS demanded a two-cent per hour increase for laborers at the Richmond repair shop. Management initially refused because Pullman already exceeded the rate paid for laborers by railroads in California. Homer Black, a white painter from the Richmond repair shop, explained why the increase was justified in terms of the role of Mexican labor in undercutting wage rates in the West: "I will tell you frankly I don't compare our people. The Pullman Company employes are mostly colored men, Italians, and a few Portuguese on the laboring gangs. On the railroads, it is 99 per cent Mexicans. I don't think they can be compared. You go down and look at the mode of living of those men on the railroads, the quarters they live in—they have no standard of living. It is below that."[68] This equation of black Americans and southern Europeans as the worthy workers and the stigmatizing of Mexicans was peculiar to the social hierarchy of the Southwest before World War II, but the fear of immigrant competition in some form was widespread.

PCEARS continued to function as an advocate for workers in the years that followed. Demands that all six repair shops backed enthusiastically and that the company had no pressing counterinterest in were the easiest for PCEARS to accomplish. Because of union pressure the company eliminated almost all night work by 1939, for instance.[69] Where management remained adamant, as on the issue of equal pay for women, PCEARS's no-strike policy and the end of the CIO threat meant that it could accomplish little. During the 1937 contract negotiations, almost two decades after the period of government control when seamstresses had enjoyed one year of equal pay with upholsterers, PCEARS demanded that seamstresses again be paid the mechanic's rate. Some women who experienced the year of equal pay under federal administration still worked at Pullman repair shops, and they wanted a return to the conditions that System Federation #122 had provided. Each year beginning in 1937 PCEARS demanded equity for the seamstresses and also for women leaders, who were paid less than male leaders. In the 1930s most U.S. unions showed little concern for gender equity. Even CIO unions that were formally committed to equity for men and women did little to narrow wage differentials for comparable work. PCEARS's leaders were more responsive to women's demands, but they were not more successful in meeting them.[70]

Company representatives responded to demands for equal pay for women as negatively as they had in the past. Management representatives contended that "the market" set a separate, lower wage structure for women than for men, and they derided the idea that women could be as skilled as men. In contrast, the men who led PCEARS described women as equal to men in their abilities and worthy of equal opportunities. On this basis they protested management's decision to replace the retired forewoman of the Calumet seamstresses with a part-time male leader rather than with the woman who had substituted for her previously.[71] Without the power of the federal government behind it, however, the union could not budge the company on this issue.

PCEARS could help those few women who were doing jobs traditionally held by men because the gender-neutral contract defined jobs and set their pay rates in terms of skill level. The Wilmington shop manager had hired a widow in 1934 in the electric department, giving her the job title "girl"—meaning "gofer"—with commensurate low pay. She did helper's work and under the 1937 contract was reclassified as such with the appropriate pay scale.[72] The problem for most women who worked at Pullman was that they held either traditional women's jobs or clerical jobs whose wage rates had been set on the basis of their gender. Indeed, the new company union for clerks—which included the largest number of white women working for Pullman—had signed a contract that accommodated two pay scales based on gender.

While the 1937 contract that PCEARS representatives achieved was only minimally acceptable to the workers at the Calumet Repair Shop, where SWOC still had supporters, it stabilized the company union elsewhere. In the smaller repair shops almost all workers belonged to PCEARS, while at Calumet membership rose to 75 percent by 1938. In succeeding years a more militant stance toward achieving better standards and enforcing the contract continued to distinguish the Calumet local from those at the other shops. Company officials were aware of this split and tried to deepen it by encouraging competition for work between the shops.[73] Tensions between Calumet and the smaller shops also continued over the relative merits of the AFL shopcraft unions and the CIO's SWOC. Jeremiah Kelleher, who headed the Wilmington repair shop workers, equated the CIO with communism as he railed against "Bolsheviks" among the Calumet shop workers and touted the investigations of the House Un-American Activities Committee. Kelleher had been a member of System Federation #122 and a striker in 1922, and his hostility to the CIO may have resulted from a residual attachment to the AFL.[74] Competing perspectives on unionization as well as competition between the shops for work weakened PCEARS and worked to management's advantage.

The Challenge of Black Workers

The Pullman Company's labor policies had only one conspicuous failure in the 1930s: the company had been unable to defeat the Brotherhood of Sleeping Car Porters. Although Pullman resisted signing a contract with the BSCP for two years, it surrendered in 1937 after the Supreme Court upheld the constitutionality of the amended Railway Labor Act. When Pullman officials did make peace with the BSCP, they feared the possibility of a national rail strike that would involve the porters if the latter had no contract. They were also still fighting SWOC at this point. The company no longer had the financial strength to face long strikes or lockouts with equanimity, and the board of directors had even begun to contemplate permanent contraction in the sleeping-car service.[75] The combined pressure of the federal government, the AFL, and the CIO helped bring the company to the bargaining table. In its first contract the BSCP secured a significant raise in wage rates for porters and maids, established overtime rates, and reduced the standard work month. Porters would still welcome tips in the future, but the union had forced the Pullman Company to pay them a living wage at last.[76]

The porters' victory heartened other black Americans to continue their own struggles. The BSCP had shown that black unity, a refusal to surrender, and an understanding of how to make the most of government support for labor organizing could overcome even the most recalcitrant employer. The Brotherhood encouraged all black workers to unionize, but it also demanded equity within the labor movement by attacking racism in other AFL unions. The porters' example spread through the Pullman Company too, as black repair shop workers began to demand equity from

PCEARS and from management. By 1938 black workers at the Calumet Repair Shop were refusing to come to union meetings, although they had been loyal to PCEARS in the fight against the CIO. The white majority at Calumet insisted on holding meetings in the Pullman area where they lived; black workers who lived miles to the north could not get home to dinner and back to a meeting easily. They had put up with such impositions in the past but now refused to submit to inequities imposed by white co-workers.[77]

A breach within the company union between white and black workers at the St. Louis repair shop also opened but with different results. Initially, the chairmanship of the St. Louis local rotated between a white man and a black man, representing the numerical equality of black and white workers in the shop force. After the first two years white workers decided they did not want to have a black chairman again and suggested establishing two separate locals on the model of the Atlanta shop, which had had segregated ERP locals too. The incoming black chairman, David Knox, protested vigorously to the supervisor of industrial relations. Knox was committed to the policy of racial equity and integration that the company had encouraged and that he, unlike most southern black men, had experienced. Joining the St. Louis shop as a helper-apprentice in 1922, Knox became a cabinetmaker after two years. Like other black shop workers, he had not suffered discriminatory layoffs, and with other leaders of the employee representation plan he created PCEARS.[78]

Yet the supervisor of industrial relations refused to intervene, because under the new federal regulations he could not unilaterally decide on such issues for an "independent" union. The white workers got segregated locals but only because some of their black co-workers agreed. They preferred separation because they felt that "it would promote better feeling if each group could run its own business without interference."[79] For decades black workers had been torn about whether to organize separately, and in the 1930s many still doubted that their voices would be heard and that their needs would be met in integrated settings. But the majority of black shop workers at St. Louis shared Knox's perspective, and they elected him now as leader of their segregated local.

Knox used that position to challenge race-based company policies. Because they had separate locals, black shop workers at Atlanta and St. Louis had direct representation on the national board of PCEARS. One of the three Calumet representatives to the national board, Esque A. Iles, also was African American, and together these men tried to use PCEARS to promote racial equity. Knox began that process at the 1937 bargaining session by asking that black shop workers get the same free transportation benefit as white workers outside the South, where no Jim Crow laws made their travel difficult for the company. The company refused this request, but black shop workers had only begun to demand changes at Pullman.[80]

As the nation prepared to enter another world war, black workers, even those like Pullman's, who considered themselves relatively fortunate, found their voice and demanded equity. The success of the BSCP was only the most prominent example of the rise of black labor in the 1930s when African Americans refused to be exploited and manipulated as they had been in the past. Like white workers, they used the state and unions to achieve their goals. Although New Deal legislation did not obviate the need for workers to struggle in order to unionize, it opened the possibility for success. American workers would use wartime conditions to build unions and propel the U.S. labor movement to its greatest strength. But the black militancy that surfaced in the 1930s would shape the course of unionization too, forcing white workers to choose between the ideal of worker unity and the claim of white supremacy.

6   The War at Home

During World War II U.S. workers sought to achieve the goal that they had set but not attained in the preceding decade: secure, high-wage jobs under union control. As in World War I, the state intervened more aggressively in labor-management relations to avoid strikes and keep production high. The National War Labor Board forced recalcitrant employers to allow honest representation elections and to engage in collective bargaining. Total mobilization also eradicated unemployment and opened new opportunities for women and racial minorities that challenged the monopoly that white men held over the better jobs in industry. Furthermore, in contrast to its posture during the first world war, the state now validated rather than denied the claims of racial minorities for respect and equality. While the campaign for "One Hundred Percent Americanism," with its ugly ethnic and racial biases, dominated the home front during the first war, the ideal of pluralism and the condemnation of Nazi racism issued from every official source during the second.

African Americans played an unprecedented role in establishing state support for racial equity by demanding a "Double V"—victory over racism at home and abroad—and Pullman's black workers were in the forefront of this movement. The Brotherhood of Sleeping Car Porters (BSCP) formed the basis for the March on Washington Movement that forced President Roosevelt to ban discrimination in defense industries. Yet the war effort did not call into question all forms of hierarchy. The first step toward establishing racial equality was not matched by any comparable movement for gender equity. Re-establishing man's role as breadwinner remained a central concern for both men and women, and women's war work was constructed as a temporary phenomenon.

Despite government condemnations of prejudice, the war against racism at home generated significant resistance among white workers. This not only limited the gains that racial minorities made in employment but also shaped the course of unionization. The Congress of Industrial Organizations (CIO) and the American Federation of Labor (AFL) fought each other as hard as they fought employers, and race became a major factor in their contests. Both tried to organize Pullman workers, and the contest between them reveals how racism played a critical role in shaping and limiting the U.S. labor movement during the 1940s.

Race Radicals and the Sleeping-Car Service

The extent of black activism during World War II would not have surprised any close observer of the militancy of black workers, especially Pullman workers, in the late 1930s. Rather than rest when they achieved their contract with the Pullman Company in 1937, the leaders of the Brotherhood of Sleeping Car Porters immediately set out to organize buffet car, parlor car, and coach porters on the railroads. The AFL granted the BSCP jurisdiction over all train porters, and by 1939 the Brotherhood had defeated company unions on many railroads in elections overseen by the National Mediation Board. The BSCP also helped the red caps, porters who carried luggage at railroad stations, to form a federal labor union within the AFL.[1]

While the porters sought to organize other black service workers in the railroad industry, Pullman's black shop workers demanded more equity in employment opportunities and benefit policies within the company. Like the porters, the black shop workers were no longer grateful to Pullman for their employment, and they forcefully rejected the compromises of the past. In 1940 the upholsterer Tillman Davis took action and accused his foreman of discrimination against black workers in assigning overtime. Davis, who had been hired as a helper-apprentice at the Calumet Repair Shop after the 1922 strike, experienced the best that Pullman repair shops had to offer black men. He was promoted quickly and by 1940 was a C-level upholsterer, but he was not satisfied with less than complete equality. The shop manager threatened Davis with a thirty-day suspension for insubordination unless he retracted the charge and apologized for the language he used. Davis readily apologized for the way he had made his charge but refused to retract its substance. He accepted the thirty-day suspension and returned to the shop, a symbol of black assertion but also a reminder of management's power in the absence of a real union.[2] The willingness to stand up against discrimination and to demand equal access to all opportunities characterized black activism during the war and shaped both federal policies and union contracts.

As the U.S. government strengthened national defense, a host of situations arose that revealed racial discrimination. African Americans now used the rhetoric of the war as a tool to demand their rights. For Pullman workers the military buildup in 1941 highlighted the old inequity in travel benefits, which black shop workers had first protested in 1937 through their company union, PCEARS. Porters now felt the effects of the company's reluctance to challenge segregation too. Because many sleeping cars that transported troops to southern bases returned north virtually empty, off-duty porters could no longer pass unnoticed by white passengers simply by staying in uniform. On many cars returning north, porters outnumbered passengers. To avoid open challenges to Jim Crow laws and sentiments, the company forced off-duty porters, like black shop workers, to sit up all night in segregated coaches rather than to share the sleeping cars with the few white customers.[3]

Black shop workers, led by David Knox, the representative from St. Louis, wanted Pullman to take "Americanism" seriously and stop discriminating. Knox insisted that "now is the time to go into it." Pullman's white repair shop workers supported their black co-workers, and Stanley Meyer, a white employee representative from Buffalo, argued: "There are men there that have boys in the service whom they would like to visit. They wonder if they do visit a son in camp, and they are told they have to stay in the day coach all night because they are denied the privilege of riding in the Pullman car, how the son who is in service will feel toward the country he is being trained to defend."[4] In many companies white workers supported black protests against racial discrimination so long as the issues raised were articulated as this one was, as a workplace grievance that did not challenge white prerogatives more broadly.

Although H. R. Lary, the supervisor of industrial relations, insisted that Pullman could not move faster than public opinion and that demanding integration of railcars in the South was explosive, Knox warned, "You say we are dealing with dynamite there. We probably feel that you are dealing with dynamite."[5] PCEARS leaders argued that change in race relations was coming. They kept abreast of legal challenges to overturn segregation statutes and used new court decisions to try to influence company officials to change policy. As they had in 1937, PCEARS leaders also brandished the threat of the CIO and the Communist Party, whose egalitarian policies were well known to black workers.

Finding employers like Pullman unwilling to change, black Americans increasingly looked to the state for action. Beginning in the 1930s, the National Association for the Advancement of Colored People brought a wide range of challenges to segregation and discrimination in the courts. Now BSCP president A. Philip Randolph and the leaders of other civil rights organizations demanded that the executive branch act not only to desegregate the armed forces but also to mandate equal access to defense jobs. Randolph set out to organize a march on Washington by black Americans to press for these goals. He used Brotherhood locals as a base for the movement, and by the spring of 1941 he claimed that 100,000 African Americans would join the protest. Fearing the consequences of such a public attack on the reality of racism in the United States, President Roosevelt responded in June 1941 and issued the first executive order mandating that federal contractors hire without discrimination. Roosevelt also established the Committee on Fair Employment Practice (known as the FEPC) to monitor implementation and investigate complaints, and he appointed Milton P. Webster, president of the Brotherhood's Chicago local, to the committee.[6] Although many black Americans worked together to achieve this step forward, Randolph and the BSCP played the central role in forcing change through mass mobilization. George Pullman's original racial strategy had borne some strange fruit indeed.

The militancy of black workers destroyed any lingering faith that Pullman management might have had about hiring them to create a more tractable, nonunion workforce. Although some Pullman officials still averred that "the Negro race" had "excellent adaptability" to the servant role, the victory of the BSCP led the company to try to remold the porters by specifying attributes that management believed would lead to hiring less assertive men. In 1941 a new directive on qualifications for porters barred West Indians, perhaps because several BSCP leaders were from the West Indies. It also decreed that "men who have attended colleges or universities are not considered the most desirable material to act as servants," and supervisors were directed, "do not employ a light complexioned man."[7] By drawing the color line more sharply and ensuring that porters did not have the educational credentials to demand promotion, officials hoped to create a more pliable set of employees. The extent to which supervisors implemented this directive is unclear, and the BSCP, as well as Pullman's other black workers, continued to both challenge the company and demand equity in U.S. society.

New Opportunities for Women and Minorities

Even before the United States entered World War II, the conflict stimulat-
ed industrial production. The stubbornly high unemployment rate began
to fall, especially in localities where shipyards and heavy industry were
clustered. Some cities, like Richmond, California, became veritable boom-
towns: its population soared from 24,000 to 100,000 in the year after the
Kaiser-Bechtel shipyards opened. The war buildup brought prosperity back
to Pullman manufacturing plants too as they converted to defense production. Aside from retrofitting railcars for troop transport, Pullman Standard
stopped production of railcars and turned out armaments, from shells to
tanks to aircraft wings. To manufacture landing craft and patrol boats, the
company reopened the Calumet Shipyard just south of the Pullman neighborhood in Chicago. It had been idle since World War I.

The boom in armaments production encouraged workers to desert
jobs in sectors of the economy that did not respond to the upturn quickly. Pullman's sleeping-car service and the railroads remained in a depression until the massive troop movements of 1942. Layoffs were common
and wages stagnated. Repair shop workers, who had skills that easily
transferred to defense work, left Pullman and the railroads to take advantage of these new opportunities. In 1940 and 1941 Pullman's Richmond
repair shop lost more than 9 percent of its workers, including many older, experienced men. Turnover worried every shop manager.[8]

Initially, the defense buildup benefited white men rather than women
or minorities. Companies recalled those they had laid off in the dark years
of the depression, but they also hired white men preferentially for new
jobs. Ensuring that white men could support their families continued to
be a priority for white employers and workers. The unemployment rate
for white men plummeted, while that for black men remained virtually
unchanged through the middle of 1941. From its inception the Committee on Fair Employment Practice received numerous complaints of racial
discrimination, and it found that even those localities, like Chicago, that
had ordinances against discrimination did not enforce them. Pullman
manufacturing plants followed the policy of white preference too and
generated a number of complaints to the FEPC. Sidney Fieldon, a Pullman car cleaner, took a welding course so that he could qualify for a defense job, but he was denied employment at the Pullman Car Works in
1941. Other black men who were denied jobs there found that managers
hired white men, regardless of qualifications. Pullman and other companies also continued to discriminate against Asians. William Kunhing, a
legal Chinese national who had taken an aircraft course, was denied work

at Pullman Standard in November 1942. This doctoral candidate at the University of Chicago told the FEPC that he wanted to go into war work to defeat the Axis and to break down racial barriers.[9] But those barriers would be breached only with total mobilization.

In 1943, when the demand for war workers peaked and virtually all white men were either employed or in the armed forces, employers finally turned to racial minorities and women. Then new opportunities seemed to herald a new order. The number of black men who were skilled workers doubled, as did the number in semiskilled positions. By the end of 1943 women comprised one-third of the nation's ammunitions workers, one-tenth of steelworkers, and two-fifths of those in aircraft production. Although the FEPC helped open some workplaces to women and racial minorities, its lack of enforcement power limited its role in the process. Labor scarcity was the key to change. Thus when Pullman Standard had to create a workforce of eight thousand at the Calumet Shipyard virtually overnight, women and minorities found opportunities that they had previously been denied at Pullman manufacturing plants. By October 1943, 1,402 of the shipyard workers were women and 794 were not white, including some Chinese and Filipino nationals as well as black Americans.[10]

Despite the relative scarcity of white men, many employers were reluctant to hire racial minorities or women, as policies in different units of Pullman Inc. reveal. Pullman's sleeping-car service first required large numbers of new workers in 1942, and by the end of 1943 the company's workforce had climbed from twenty-four thousand to thirty-one thousand. Yet Pullman repair shop managers did not hire large numbers of black men as they had in the 1920s, even though jobs at Pullman shops would have been attractive to the many black men still working in poorly paid and insecure unskilled and service jobs. Rather, shop managers opened opportunities to white men whom they had ignored previously, the old and the young, and to white women. The company dropped its bar on hiring employees older than forty-five, and for the first time the repair shops hired sixteen- and seventeen-year-old boys. While overall the number of black shop workers rose from 885 in 1941 to 1,097 in 1946, black men made much greater gains at Pullman repair shops in the 1920s. Although company officials stated that black workers produced equally as well as white workers, supervisors did not hire them as frequently now that they were no longer a bulwark against unionism.[11]

The FEPC found much more resistance to equal opportunity hiring in some areas of the country than in others. Not surprisingly, the extent to which a Pullman repair shop hired black men in 1943 and 1944 varied, as it had in the past, in terms of its local labor market and social hierarchy. Yet at none of the shops did black men constitute as much as one-fifth of new workers. As table 9 shows, more than three-quarters of Wilmington's new workers were white men, many of whom were outside the normal age range for newly hired workers. Although the Wilmington shop had violated local racial ideology in the 1920s, it retreated to the discriminatory pattern that was common in the city. Barely one-tenth of workers hired during World War II were black men. Nor did the shop hire as many women as other Pullman repair shops did. Like other local industries, the Wilmington repair shop gave preference to men and hired women sparingly during the emergency.[12]

Pullman's Richmond repair shop also hired few black men, even though African Americans had replaced Asian Americans as the largest racial minority locally. The great migration to California of white and black workers from the old southwestern states—Texas, Oklahoma, Arkansas, Missouri, Louisiana, and Mississippi—changed the social structure of Richmond and much of the state. As African Americans became more numerous, they also experienced more prejudice. Residential segregation now forced them to live either in North Richmond or in public housing projects near the Pullman repair shop. Although Richmond's black population exploded, only 5 percent of those hired at the repair shop in 1943–44 were black men, whereas 61 percent were white youths younger than eighteen. The labor shortage in the East Bay region was so severe that its communities pioneered work programs for high school students, and the Pullman shop took full advantage of this effort to maintain a predominantly white workforce. Boys who had been born in California, lived in Richmond, and had never worked before were hired as laborers and then given the opportunity to become helpers. Most, however, stayed less than a year at Pullman before leaving for better-paying jobs at the shipyards.[13]

Nationwide, large numbers of white women found openings in defense work at the height of the war boom, and in some places they were hired

Table 9. Percentage of Shop Workers Hired in 1943–44, by Race, Sex, and Age

Repair Shop	Black Men	White Women	White Men		
			Under 18	18–44	Over 45
Calumet	17.2	46.4	10.3	15.8	10.3
Richmond	5.0	25.0	60.7	5.7	3.6
Wilmington	9.5	9.5	9.5	52.5	19.0

Source: Derived from samples described in the appendix.
Note: The sample for the Calumet shop contains no black women; those for Richmond and Wilmington contain one each.

instead of minority men. White men might prefer white women as co-workers, because they expected women to be temporary employees, unlike minority men who would accumulate seniority and become permanent members of the workforce. Government, companies, and unions sought to maintain the customary roles of men and women in the labor market, and thus women had access only for the duration of the war to the blue-collar jobs that previously had been reserved for men. Women had to sign away their rights to accumulate seniority and hence to claim future employment.[14] Gender could still be the basis for inequitable policies in the workplace, but because of the ban on racial discrimination in defense industries, race could not. Any man hired during the war was a regular employee, governed by whatever employment rules currently obtained.

The Pullman Company also hired women at the height of the war boom as "emergency employees" whose seniority counted only until the end of the war. When insufficient numbers of current employees responded to a trainee program to create mechanics quickly, Pullman opened the program to women. For the first time since World War I, Pullman repair shops and yards hired white women in positions other than sewing, car cleaning, or clerical work. Most women began work in the shops and yards as laborers and then became helpers in a wide range of crafts—machinist, steamfitter, painter, and electrician, among others. Fewer women actually became mechanics because older employees had been given the first opportunities for upgrading. At the Calumet Repair Shop white women comprised almost half of those hired in 1943 and 1944, while only 17 percent of new employees were black men and none were black women. Women like Myrtle Hedlund, a middle-aged married woman who had been born in Illinois and lived in the area, took the new opportunities at the Calumet shop. Hedlund was hired as a laborer in November 1943 and was promoted to helper in the brass department less than a month later. She worked at the shop for almost three years before being discharged.[15]

White women always had access to much better jobs than did minority women, and the war did little to change this. Black women's participation in industrial occupations tripled during the war, but they found only the lowest-paying work. At Pullman black women replaced black men as car cleaners, janitors, and train "porterettes." Black women also were temporary employees because the Brotherhood of Sleeping Car Porters, no less than the representatives of white men, insisted that women could take men's jobs only for the duration.[16]

Men sought not only to block long-term competition for jobs from women but also to ensure that women did not undermine pay rates by working for lower wages. When some companies converted to armament production, managers found that they could pay women lower wages as long as they classified the jobs for women as requiring less skill than those that employed only men. In this way women could be paid less without undercutting men's wage rates and alarming union leaders. In the sleeping-car service women took jobs for which wage rates and classifications had long been set by contract, and thus they did not have to fight to attain equal pay.[17]

The willingness to hire women did not reflect any widespread belief in their ability to perform skilled tasks. As the memo announcing the trainee program at Pullman repair shops stated: "We cannot expect Trainees to turn out the same quantity or quality of work as a mechanic of long experience. This is especially true of women, outside of certain jobs which require dexterity."[18] In the view of Pullman officials women had nimble fingers and therefore could sew or type, but managers doubted their ability to master anything else. This perception of women's abilities as centered on their small motor skills was pervasive, despite the government's propaganda effort to change beliefs about women's capabilities.[19]

Pullman managers also viewed women workers as qualitatively different from men and treated them accordingly. Many people believed that working in a male occupation damaged a woman's reputation and that in a male-dominated workplace she faced "moral hazards." Thus Pullman supervisors were much more likely to police the deportment of women than of men, such as warning them about the use of profanity. Like most employers, Pullman executives also believed that women would need special attention from supervisors, and they instituted what they saw as "an increasingly progressive handling of relations with women employes" by appointing two women to the new jobs of women's counselor and women's consultant.[20] These positions were analogous to the black welfare workers hired in the 1920s when the company first brought black men into the repair shops and still regarded them as needing significantly different supervision than white men. Similarly, many corporations expanded their counseling services to help women adjust to the workplace.[21]

Despite viewing women as needing different treatment than men, neither employers nor the government did much to alleviate women's greatest difficulty—the weight of their double burden. When women took paid employment, they remained responsible for housekeeping and child care. Pullman shop managers expected greater absenteeism from women because their new women workers, like most women who took men's jobs during the war, were primarily middle-aged married mothers. Some women shop workers asked for leaves of absence because of problems

with child care, and compared with men they also requested a dispropor-
tionate number of leaves to care for sick family members. Yet beyond
granting these leaves of absence, the Pullman Company did no more than
most U.S. corporations. Virtually none provided child care, and the government's program to create child-care centers proved modest. Because
of union policies in the railroad industry, however, the sleeping-car service did grant six-week paid maternity leaves.[22]

The men who worked in Pullman repair shops, like men in other
industries, were at best ambivalent toward their new co-workers. They
continued to support the seamstresses in their demand for the higher
mechanics' wage rate that the company denied them, but there was widespread discomfort over what were seen as threats to masculinity when
women did men's jobs. Thus PCEARS asked that, at those repair shops
where women were now employed as helpers, "regular" laborers be paid
the maximum helper's rate for the duration of the war. Otherwise, older
men who had remained laborers and refused the trainee program in order to safeguard their seniority would be working alongside women helpers who earned more than they did. That this demand contravened decades of worker insistence on a hierarchy of wages by skill level did not
faze men eager to preserve traditional gender roles.[23]

Segregation, Discrimination, and the Maintenance of Inequality

The war boom opened new opportunities for women and racial minorities, but many jobs remained off limits. Both management and labor contributed to discriminatory practices and the maintenance of job segregation. Managers continued to view women and minority employees
through a lens compounded of various prejudices as well as calculations
about the usefulness of diversity in weakening labor unity. But the
strength of labor unions now meant that workers, primarily white men,
had the ability to structure opportunities too. Whether they helped or
hindered women and minority men often depended on how fearful white
men were about their own futures.[24]

In general, the new opportunities for women and minorities were
limited to temporary work or jobs that had the least appeal to white men.
Few women or minority men became supervisors, for instance, except
over all-female or all-minority work groups. Only at Pullman's Buffalo
and St. Louis repair shops did a few black men attain even the lowest level
of supervisory positions, as leaders. At St. Louis, where the majority of
blue-collar workers were black, only 12 percent of supervisors were Af-

rican American. Racial discrimination also blocked minority access to most clerical jobs, except in the federal government, where the FEPC had greater influence. At Pullman black men found new clerical opportunities in the storerooms of Pullman repair shops as packers, stock keepers, and shipping clerks, but by 1946 African Americans held only 4 percent of the total clerical positions in the shops.[25]

Although the company allowed black men into its storerooms, management continued to deny members of racial minorities access to clerical jobs in its offices. In 1943 a Pullman employment agent referred Emilio Evangelista, a Filipino immigrant who applied to be a clerk in the central office accounting department, to the Commissary Department, the company's Filipino ghetto, even though the company needed "male clerks." In his complaint to the FEPC Evangelista charged that the employment agent who told him that he would be happier with his "clan" was "a German and his shadowy belief in democracy is pretty well seasoned with ugly racial discrimination."[26] The agent hired other men who had lesser qualifications than Evangelista but not brown skin. An internal company memo on this case suggests the validity of the charge of discrimination: "I think it rather dangerous to say that Evangelista did not possess the necessary qualifications, particularly in view of his educational background. His application states that he is a graduate of Loyola University."[27] Even when the FEPC intervened, management could find ways around compliance with federal policies. The Pullman Company finally rejected Evangelista on a technicality—high blood pressure. As he wrote to the committee's director of enforcement, if he were perfectly healthy, he would have been on the battlefield.[28]

The maintenance of racial barriers in the office also denied opportunities to minority women, and, as was true for men, education did not help them breach those barriers. Another complaint to the FEPC in 1943 involved Florie Wellington and Reuben Young, who answered a newspaper advertisement for jobs as checkers (a clerical position) in Pullman's Commissary Department. The employment agent informed them that the company did not hire Negroes in those positions, and he referred them to jobs as car washers.[29] Internal company memos also support their charge of discrimination. Executive Vice President Champ Carry wrote, "It is a fact that we have had applications from colored girls for checkers, and there is no question that they are qualified as far as education is concerned."[30]

Carry went on to explain the underlying causes for Pullman's refusal to hire racial minorities in most office jobs: "Personally, I have no great feeling about whether we should hire colored commissary checkers, but the difficulty comes in the fact that once we do hire them they immediately acquire seniority in the clerks' organization, and there is no telling where they will eventually end up in the organization . . . so we might as well face the fact squarely that they could appear in almost any office in the Company."[31] Pullman would hire racial minorities if it could keep them in low-level, dead-end jobs, such as porter or maid. But the company had developed a structure of internal promotion in the office decades earlier, and now it was codified by a contract with a company union. A complete color barrier was the only way to keep minority men or women from rising in the clerical ranks and thereby to protect top management or white customers from having to interact with minority employees in nonmenial positions. In most companies the combination of management preference and concern for the feelings of white customers kept the color barriers up.

Pullman executives intended to resist federal policy on fair employment practices, but they were beginning to understand that because of "the war against racism," they would have to be more discreet. The FEPC raised public consciousness that racial discrimination in employment was unfair, because the most qualified job applicants were not necessarily white people. Yet white privilege was still a priority to most white Americans, and companies found more subtle ways to maintain it. As Pullman president David Crawford wrote: "I still feel that [X] was pretty weak in letting a couple of colored girls pester him into saying something that he had been told not to say. This is a serious business. . . . I still think that some broad statement that fitness and ability govern our employment decisions, without regard to race, creed, etc., should enable any hiring agent to dispose of people seeking to make trouble in connection with these employment practices."[32]

Because of their economic importance the railroad corporations could resist Roosevelt's order banning discrimination, and the white-dominated AFL railroad unions did the same. The FEPC had, consequently, little effect on the industry. The Pullman Company could also evade the president's directive, however, because the FEPC focused its effort on firms that had at most a few minority employees, not those like the sleeping-car service that had a black majority. Pullman officials told FEPC staffers in Chicago that, given the company's reputation for hiring African Americans in large numbers, they resented having to check into individual complaints. Pullman executives stonewalled, insisting, for instance, that the two women who had applied to be checkers were not qualified and that their attitude was a problem. Officials in Washington encouraged local staffers to investigate all complaints and to tell the Pullman Company that its lack of response to a complaint would be taken to mean that the charge was valid. But the FEPC's caseload was so great that staffers could not keep up with complaints and so were forced to focus on the worst offenders.[33] Chicago staffers noted that "we regret, of course, that we had to close these cases without an adjustment, but the problem is a very difficult one. We know, of course, that the Pullman Company does not operate completely free of discrimination, but since it does have 51 per cent of its workers who are colored and they are believed to be scattered over a wide range of occupations, we were reluctant to make an issue of these complaints."[34] Company officials resisted fair employment practices, but increasingly they did so circumspectly. They feared not only the FEPC but also the porters' "walking off the job in these times when we cannot replace them."[35]

The reluctance of companies to breach the color line in the office opened new opportunities for white women because all employers experienced a wholesale loss of white male clerical workers to the draft. Although the federal government exempted skilled workers in defense industries from conscription, it deemed male clerical workers replaceable. The war made clerical work a predominantly female occupation in the United States. In the sleeping-car service women took clerical jobs in the storerooms of repair shops for the first time as well as positions that had been men's work in every office. Companies were happy to expand women's role in the clerical ranks because they could pay women less than men. Most clerical workers had no union contract to proscribe such practices. The Pullman Company could pay women clerical workers less because its contract with their company union recognized two pay scales based on gender. Even though women obtained new clerical jobs during the war, they did not have access to the best positions in the office, those in management.[36]

The FEPC gave racial and religious minorities an avenue to fight discrimination, but U.S. workers did not share equally in the opportunities presented by the war boom. Whether because of extraordinary demand for labor or FEPC investigations and public hearings, minority men and women found entry to more workplaces and better jobs. But progress stopped well short of equal opportunity. The lack of strong feminist pressure meant that the gains that white women made depended on the needs of white men: to take industrial jobs during the war but to vacate them thereafter and to keep the office a white preserve.

A Victory Fifty Years in the Making

The war boom produced prosperity and opportunity, but workers remained committed to their collective concern for more power in the workplace.

Union organizing surged the minute the economy improved in 1940, as workers who had not been able to overcome their employers' resistance in the late 1930s went on the offensive. This union drive reflected not only workers' enduring concerns for just wages, security, and fairness but also new issues raised by the war. Because of the gains that women and racial minorities made in the workplace, race and gender assumed a critical role in union organizing. Since many AFL unions discriminated racially while CIO unions were committed to racial equality, the bitter battle between them to organize the unorganized often hinged on the issue of race.[37] This was true both where unions were successful in organizing and where they failed, as the experience of Pullman workers reveals.

In 1940, when the CIO's Steel Workers Organizing Committee (SWOC) revived its stalled campaign in the steel industry, it opened organizing drives at all six Pullman manufacturing plants. SWOC still faced competition from the company union and the AFL's Brotherhood of Railway Carmen (BRCA), and the CIO union found organizing Pullman plants extremely difficult. Indeed, the BRCA scored the first success, winning the Michigan City, Indiana, freight car plant, where 90 percent of the workers signed up with the AFL union in February 1941. SWOC then narrowly lost a representation election at the Pullman Car Works later that year. Workers charged that management used a range of unfair practices to defeat SWOC, from intimidation of individual workers to threatening the credit of a local store owner whom the union asked for space for its headquarters. Pullman Standard sweetened its antiunion stance by offering a pay raise, but workers later charged that they received only half of what was promised if SWOC lost the election.[38]

The success of the BRCA at Michigan City was a warning to SWOC organizers regarding the nature of their task. The AFL union's appeal did not rest solely on its support for traditional craft identity and work rules but was grounded in its policy of racial segregation. Only a handful, thirty-two, of the two thousand Michigan City workers were black, and they were concentrated in the foundry and wheel and axle departments, where black men had first been hired in 1923. According to one complaint to the FEPC, the manager at Michigan City refused to hire black men in other departments because of concern that white workers would object. The BRCA had sided with white workers at Michigan City in their 1923 hate strike when plant management first hired black men, and white workers remembered that support.[39]

SWOC also found white racism an impediment to organizing at Pullman's Bessemer, Alabama, plant. White machinists there walked off the job when a black man was put on a boring machine, a previously "white" job. AFL unions worked with Bessemer employers to keep CIO unions out of local plants by charging that CIO organizers were agents of race mixing and radicalism. SWOC appealed to black workers at the Pullman plant, but two AFL shopcraft unions won certification in its all-white craft departments. Because black workers were numerous at this Pullman manufacturing plant, however, SWOC succeeded in organizing the majority of workers.[40]

Unions attempting to organize Pullman manufacturing plants faced a quite different racial situation than those organizing in the sleeping-car service. Except at Bessemer, black workers were a decided minority, and management reserved most skilled jobs for white men. The United Steelworkers of America (USWA)—the product of SWOC's organizing—found its chances of winning a majority at Pullman manufacturing plants improved as the number of minority and women workers increased. The union became an advocate for these new workers, protesting, for instance, when Pullman management in Hammond, Indiana, discriminated against "colored" workers in seniority. The United Steelworkers also appealed to women by promising them wages equal to men's. The National War Labor Board did not mandate equal pay for women but merely permitted employers to raise women's wages to equalize them with men's if they so desired. Few employers, including Pullman Standard, did so, and nationally the gap between men's and women's wages actually rose during the war. The United Steelworkers would force Pullman Standard to pay equal wages in its first contract, although the union negotiator testified that this was one of two demands (the other involved posting job notices and control of bulletin boards) that the company resisted most strongly.[41]

Supporting women and minority workers bore fruit when the United Steelworkers had its first victory in Pullman Standard's Chicago-area plants at Hammond in November 1942. The union won a majority at the Calumet Shipyard shortly thereafter. The Pullman Car Works was the union's toughest test, but in January 1944, half a century after the Pullman strike, it won an election with two-thirds of the vote. The United Steelworkers' newspaper at the shipyard exulted that workers had finally overcome the company's strategy: "For years this company had utilized every known and conceivable method to defeat any attempt of the workers to organize—they had pitted nationality against nationality—race against race—divide and rule, that was it! As long as they could maintain disunity and racial strife, they could continue to print the rules and regulations governing employment in their plants."[42] Naming their local for Eugene Debs, the men and women of the Car Works had at last come together in an industrial union. If the memory of the great strike remained part of local lore, the Pullman Car Works was now a bastion of steelworkers rather than railroad workers.

The CIO's United Steelworkers could build on the new diversity among Pullman manufacturing workers more easily than could the AFL shopcraft unions but only by containing the prejudices and fears of older white men. The USWA leadership recognized that countering racism and sexism was vital and sponsored an educational program to that end. In a radio broadcast that the union aimed at Pullman workers just before the 1944 election at the Car Works, one of the new women workers, Esther Holt, described the reaction when women first took men's jobs at the plant: "We know a lot of old-timers shook their heads. They thought we'd be a danger to their working conditions, that we'd take their jobs away from them, and work for less money."[43] Holt tried to assuage the men's fears by arguing that with the union's help, all would benefit.

Yet even the most egalitarian of CIO unions, like the United Packinghouse Workers of America, found that black militancy strained the coalition of white and black workers that had formed in the 1930s. The difficulty of the CIO's task in countering racism was made clear in the hate strikes that erupted in 1943 and 1944 in many northern factories where CIO unions had contracts. The Calumet Shipyard experienced a hate strike less than a year after its union newspaper crowed that Pullman workers had overcome racism in the election at the Car Works.[44]

The hate strike at the Calumet Shipyard in 1944 reflected the wartime contest for jobs and housing in the south Chicago–northwest Indiana industrial area. Previously all-white workplaces like International Harvester's West Pullman and Wisconsin Steel plants hired black men for the first time. But when African Americans sought to move closer to those jobs, they found the racial covenants that had blanketed the greater Pullman area in the 1920s still barred them from the neighborhoods. In 1943 white residents of Roseland staged protests because of the construction of new housing for African Americans, and residents of the greater Pullman area rioted in 1947 when the Chicago Housing Authority announced that it would build a racially integrated public housing project. The racial tensions that erupted in 1947, when more than one thousand police struggled for two weeks to contain the violence of white mobs, had begun to build during the war.[45] They surfaced in the weeklong hate strike at the shipyard.

As was true in many hate strikes, the flash point at the shipyard was not the hiring of minority men per se but promotion. Black men made concerted efforts to break down barriers to their advancement in a wide range of industries, from the railroads to shipbuilding, and they used a variety of tactics.[46] In order to obtain positions as work-group leaders at the Calumet Shipyard, black workers had complained to the FEPC and staged wildcat strikes. Both black and white workers wanted leaders of their own race, and in 1944, when the company began to appoint black men to these positions in racially mixed departments, tensions rose. Some white men were too threatened to listen to union leaders counseling tolerance. On December 5, 1944, when a black pipe fitter became the leader of a racially mixed group of seven workers, 166 of 301 pipe fitters walked out of the shipyard. The next day more than 600 of the 2,400 workers on the day shift joined them. At its height about 900 workers took part in the wildcat strike that lasted eight days and threatened to provoke racial clashes in the surrounding neighborhoods. Shipyard management called in Chicago police to keep the peace. Elmer Henderson, head of the local office of the FEPC, reported that "a great deal of the credit [for peace] should go to the Negro workers of this yard who in the face of the most provocative circumstances did not lose their heads or attempt retaliation against the strikers."[47]

The majority of shipyard workers did not strike, but ending the walkout was not easy. At a mass meeting the strikers booed USWA officials who urged them to return to their jobs. The president of the union local insisted that most workers were tolerant but that there was an "aggressive pressure group" among black workers and an "anti-Negro pressure group" among white workers. Although a newspaper reporter who attended the meeting noted the role of white southern migrants in the strike, they were not the only source of racial prejudice. An FEPC investigator reported that the naval commander in charge of the Pullman shipyard also believed that black Americans should not demand better jobs, especially supervisory positions. The United Steelworkers local at the shipyard insisted that Pullman management also exacerbated racial tensions by not having a consistent policy, that the company discriminated in some departments and not others. Union leaders charged that Pullman managers did this purposely to weaken their organization.[48]

While the United Steelworkers of America struggled to contain the volatile racial situation in its organizing drives at Pullman manufacturing plants, in the end it succeeded in winning representation status at five of the six plants. The company unions in the manufacturing plants were not a serious hindrance because they had never been especially strong or popular. The AFL shopcraft unions were more of an obstacle, but there was no "golden age" of AFL union contracts during World War I for Pullman manufacturing workers to look back on. Indeed, many manufacturing workers were suspicious of the AFL, and some charged that the BRCA organizer at the Car Works was on the company payroll and that he gave management the names of CIO members.[49] Yet it is not clear that the United Steelworkers would have been successful without the intervention of the federal government. Pullman Standard continued to use every weapon to defeat the union, which attained its victories only with the aid of National War Labor Board hearings and direct oversight of elections.

Nor did a union's status as workers' representative change the perspective of Pullman Standard officials toward collective bargaining. The company continued to resist negotiating, and unions again needed help from the government. But overloaded agencies charged with keeping labor peace in wartime found it difficult to implement federal law. The BRCA local at the Michigan City plant struck three times in eight months before the National Mediation Board entered the dispute and forced the company to negotiate a contract. The board intervened at that point only because Michigan City workers ignored both pleas not to disrupt war work and the threat that the plant would lose its priority rating and close. Pullman Standard also delayed and refused information to the National War Labor Board so that the United Steelworkers' local at the Hammond plant still had no contract in 1944, although it had won representation status in 1942. Hammond management so intimidated workers by discharging people for union activity that the local refused to submit membership lists to the company for dues checkoff. The wartime no-strike pledge hampered all unions when they sought to force companies to the bargaining table. Pullman workers often took things into their own hands, and the company charged the Calumet Shipyard had suffered twenty-three wildcat strikes in the first eighteen months after the union won the representation election. The intervention of federal boards and arbitrators proved decisive in bringing contracts to Pullman manufacturing workers, but only their own willingness to take action elicited that aid.[50]

The War at Home between the AFL and the CIO

Workers in the sleeping-car service also sought to take advantage of wartime conditions to unionize. By the early 1940s Pullman conductors earned substantially less than railroad conductors, because the independent union that Pullman conductors established during World War I, the Order of Sleeping Car Conductors, had been defunct since the mid-1930s. They saw the porters make real advances through their AFL union, and in 1942 the conductors voted to join the AFL's Order of Railway Conductors in an election monitored by the National Mediation Board. Pullman's racial division of porters and conductors fit perfectly with the established order in the AFL; porters had formed their own black craft union, and conductors joined the all-white union for their trade. But not all workers in the sleeping-car service would find the AFL unions such an easy fit when they sought to unionize.[51]

Pullman repair shop and yard workers were also restive, because the company unions were unable to pressure management to agree to the wages and standards that AFL and CIO unions could promise. They were ready to demand improvements in their current jobs rather than attempt to leave Pullman for better jobs elsewhere. Security had long been the major concern of these workers, and in taking a new job a man forfeited seniority and pension benefits. Many Americans questioned how long the war, and thus the new jobs, would last, and some expected the depression to return when the war ended.[52] For an older man with a family the new opportunities were problematic. On the one hand, they promised wages that would enable him to support his family in the style that seemed appropriate for U.S. mechanics. After the experience of the depression, when they had failed to provide for their families, many men welcomed the chance. On the other hand, forfeiting seniority and pension risked a man's long-term ability to be the family breadwinner.

During contract negotiations in 1942 the PCEARS leader Stanley Meyer explained to management the quandary of many older workers. They were attracted to other industries by high wages but also because they were still experiencing layoffs that undermined the gender roles that they wished to preserve. "In a lot of cases the wives of some of our men have been forced to go to work in order to keep up the household and in many cases it has disrupted the harmonious relationship in the family. Where there are children it necessitates getting some-body else to take care of them."[53] At the same time wives also sought to preserve traditional gender roles and used the rhetoric of the war to encourage husbands to take new jobs: "The wives are calling their husbands slackers because they haven't got guts enough to go out and get other work." Yet the concern for security made many cautious, and Meyer averred that the men "say they have so many years of service, pensions, and all that, but some of the women can't see it."

At workplaces like Pullman repair shops that did not have plantwide seniority systems, even new opportunities in the shop could be problematic. To move up to skilled jobs workers had to give up seniority at the unskilled or helper level. Thus when Pullman instituted a trainee program in 1943 to produce new mechanics and offered the positions to current employees, fewer than half took advantage of the opportunity to upgrade. While the percentage that became trainees varied from shop to shop, no more than one-quarter to one-half of helpers and laborers did so. Caution was as common for black men as for white men, because they shared the concern for being stable breadwinners.[54] Their concern for security ensured that Pullman repair shop workers could not rely on the individual solution to low wages—taking another job at Pullman or elsewhere. They would have to find a collective solution if the company union could not achieve their goals.

Although workers were losing faith in the company unions, the AFL shopcraft unions found organizing Pullman repair shops and yards difficult because their workforces were racially integrated. The shopcraft unions still discriminated, and most went no further than allowing non-white workers into segregated lodges represented by white leaders. Some unions still prohibited the promotion of black helpers to mechanic status. Even after 1944, when the Supreme Court decreed in *Steele v. Louisville and Nashville Railroad* that unions had to fairly represent all workers in a bargaining unit, AFL railroad unions resisted. Thus even if white repair shop and yard workers were attracted to the AFL unions for their trades, black shop and yard workers were not. Instead, they found two possibilities for unionizing, the integrated unions of the CIO and the Brotherhood of Sleeping Car Porters.[55]

With fifteen thousand members the Brotherhood stood at the height of its power during World War II. Claiming to lead all black workers, it pursued organizing drives that set it in opposition to both AFL and CIO unions. When the AFL railroad unions refused to end their racist practices, the BSCP expanded its jurisdiction and began organizing all black railroad workers, including craft workers like firemen, switchmen, and brakemen. BSCP leaders waged a series of battles with other AFL railroad unions, incorporating service workers directly but establishing a separate organization for "colored locomotive firemen" that was open to black workers in any railroad craft. The actions of the BSCP also brought it into conflict with other black unions, such as the Association of Colored Railway Trainmen and Locomotive Firemen, which had been first in the field to organize black firemen.[56]

The Brotherhood's claim to speak for all black workers was hotly contested. The National Negro Congress, racially integrated CIO unions, and the Communist Party all made claims to leadership but on a different basis than the BSCP or other black unions. They insisted that achieving equality required multiracial organizing. The BSCP was drawn into the bitter fight between the AFL and CIO, although the BSCP and the CIO worked together on such civil rights issues as desegregating the armed forces. A. Philip Randolph joined AFL president William Green in demanding that communists be barred from union membership and in calling on CIO unions to return to the AFL.[57]

Ironically, the CIO union that battled white-dominated AFL unions and the BSCP for the allegiance of railroad workers was one that A. Philip Randolph had helped to establish in the 1930s—the International Brotherhood of Red Caps. From the outset this union had been biracial because, unlike Pullman porters, not all red caps were African Americans. When the AFL's white-only Brotherhood of Railway Clerks claimed jurisdiction over red caps, the Red Caps' president Willard Townsend led the membership out of the AFL to form an independent union. But he and Randolph remained allies until 1942 when the Red Caps joined the CIO. Renamed the United Transport Service Employees of America (UTSEA), the union claimed jurisdiction over all railroad service workers, including those employed by Pullman. Willard Townsend assumed the leadership of the CIO's Civil Rights Commission, potentially becoming a voice with a stature equal to Randolph's. Although the BSCP and UTSEA shared a similar goal, a United States where blacks and whites could work and live together as equals, they differed on how to attain it. Randolph and the BSCP believed that black self-organization and government action held the key. Townsend and UTSEA members believed that they could accomplish this only through multiracial organizing, even though many of the white red caps broke away and returned to the AFL.[58] UTSEA became the CIO's wedge to fight the AFL in the railroad industry, and in 1942 it claimed that it was "the only labor organization operating under the Railway Labor Act . . . which is in compliance with President's Order 8802 forbidding racial discrimination, thereby extending to Negroes and whites alike full and complete membership."[59]

Because its membership was almost entirely black, UTSEA began by targeting areas of minority employment in the railroad industry. The Brotherhood of Dining Car Employees, the black craft union formed during World War I, joined UTSEA after the AFL's white-dominated Hotel and Restaurant Workers assumed jurisdiction over the craft. Then UTSEA sought to organize black locomotive firemen in the South, though it quickly withdrew in favor of the BSCP and other groups that had begun their efforts earlier. At this point BSCP leaders described Townsend's activities only as "not . . . very complimentary."[60] In 1943, however, the competition between the unions intensified as UTSEA began organizing train porters claimed by the BSCP, and the Brotherhood began to organize dining car employees claimed by the CIO union. The unions raided each other's membership as much as they organized the unorganized, and the bitterness between them escalated, reaching its peak after the war when UTSEA tried to organize Pullman porters.[61] The BSCP responded with a campaign of vilification, including a flyer that played on every trope of racial and labor struggle: "Watch out for the stool pigeon Communist Pullman Porters National (Dis) Organizing Committee for C.I.O., a union-wrecking-disruptionist . . . One Big Union of all railroad workers—Dream . . . [it] will bring back Company Union slavery and make an Uncle Tom and Clown of every Porter."[62]

UTSEA made its first foray into the Pullman Company in 1943 to organize service workers whom the BSCP had ignored—those in the laundries. Some black women laundry workers had already asked the BSCP to help them organize, but the Brotherhood referred them to the AFL's white-dominated Laundry Workers Union. Although the porters' union was in the forefront of the fight against racism and willing to raid the jurisdiction of other AFL unions in support of black men, BSCP leaders shared the gender biases of many men in the United States. They believed that women belonged in the home, supported by male breadwinners. Accordingly, they focused their organizing on men, and even consigned the Pullman maids, with whom they had been joined in the company union, to second-class status in the BSCP.[63]

UTSEA recognized that Pullman laundries fit its jurisdiction perfectly—the laundry workers were a multiracial group of service workers—and stepped in. Strategically, Pullman laundry workers were ideal too because the majority now was black. That majority also was female, but UTSEA leaders did not see this a problem. As the union's newspaper, *Bags and Baggage*, reported: "An interesting angle of the drive from the UTSEA-CIO point of view is that this section of the industry is composed largely of women. . . . These women 'have plenty on the ball' and from all appearance will set a new union pace for many of the UTSEA locals of dining car employees and red caps composed of men."[64] Women at Pullman's Oakland and Buffalo laundries joined UTSEA first, but organizing went quickly at all nine plants. Within a few months the union called for a representation election among the nearly one thousand workers, which it won handily with more than 70 percent of the vote.[65] Pullman management now had three "outside" unions to bargain with for its sleeping-car service, the porters' and conductors' unions in the AFL, and UTSEA in the CIO.

UTSEA did not rest with the laundry workers but expanded its purview to include Pullman repair shop workers, building on previous CIO organizing at the Calumet Repair Shop. The United Steelworkers now renounced interest in railroad shop workers, and UTSEA claimed three hundred members at the Calumet shop in the first ten days of its organizing drive. The union appealed to Calumet workers' history, saying that they had "recaptured that same militant spirit that was characteristic of Pullman workers years ago."[66] The leaders of UTSEA Local #80 at the Calumet shop were white, black, and Hispanic, and they attempted to build a union that reflected their diversity. One of their first activities was handling a grievance for a white painter who believed that he had been laid off outside his seniority because, as a Jehovah's Witness, he had refused to buy war bonds.[67]

Calumet's black workers flocked to UTSEA. They had been withdrawing from active participation in the company union since 1938 when their white co-workers ignored their concern about meetings being held only in the Pullman area, far from their homes. Like Tillman Davis, who had protested discrimination in overtime, they were no longer satisfied merely with skilled jobs. They wanted complete equality with white workers, but PCEARS could not force the company to provide it. Ensley L. Moseley and Robert E. Mason, who were leaders of the UTSEA local, had careers at Pullman similar to Davis's. They had been hired in the wake of the 1922 strike as helper-apprentices and promoted to C-level mechanics. Like him, they would remain shop workers into the 1960s, but they were ready to organize for their rights during World War II.[68]

UTSEA expanded its organizing drive to other Pullman repair shops and found many workers eager to join because they were so disillusioned with the company union. PCEARS could not induce management to abolish the division of crafts and the incentive wage system, only to modify them. Favoritism in the assignment of overtime continued, and UTSEA exposed the "vacation racket" in which workers received their one-week vacation only if they were paid-up members of PCEARS. By the middle years of the war the record of the company union looked shabby, and it made no headway on the shop workers' greatest concern, guaranteed year-round employment.[69]

More workers began to look to UTSEA when they considered the implications of the antitrust suit filed in 1940 against Pullman Inc. In 1937 the Roosevelt administration began to use antitrust legislation to discipline big business, focusing on pricing policies and the role of monopolies in holding new processes off the market. Pullman Inc. was vulnerable on both grounds. The railroads sought to free themselves from Pullman service contracts, and they accused the corporation of using its monopoly to inhibit technological innovation, especially the introduction of lightweight passenger railcars. The federal coordinator of transportation charged that the Pullman monopoly inflated overhead costs and hence prices. All recommended eliminating Pullman's monopoly in favor of letting each railroad own and operate sleeping cars. The Justice Department's suit demanded that Pullman Inc. divest itself of either its manufacturing business—Pullman Standard—or the sleeping-car service—the Pullman Company. While the suit dragged on throughout the war as the corporation fought it up to the Supreme Court, workers feared for their jobs and the possibility that they would lose seniority and group insurance in any sale.[70]

During this period Pullman officials refused even to contemplate future shutdowns, much less to make any commitments to workers. In 1942 management reduced use of maids on trains but denied dismissal allowances to the small number of women with twenty years or more of service. Doing so would have set a precedent that would have been costly if applied to other workers. The following year, management rejected PCEARS's first demand for a plan of severance pay if at any time in the future the company decided to abandon the shops. The company also rejected the union's demand for guaranteed year-round employment when the war was over for those who had stayed with Pullman when they could have gotten higher wages in defense work.[71] Because company executives refused to discuss the future or plan for it, UTSEA invited Calumet Repair Shop workers to attend a meeting about how "to take action to safeguard your seniority and other benefits under any transfer of Pullman properties."[72]

But despite the threat to workers' security and discontent with the company union, UTSEA had difficulty building a majority at the repair shops. While black shop workers, who were disappointed by PCEARS's inability to make progress on their demands for racial equity, flocked to UTSEA, white shop workers proved more hesitant. The officers of UTSEA locals at the repair shops reflected the racial diversity to which the union aspired, but the union's international officers all were black, as were the vast majority of its members. UTSEA leaders knew that this hindered organizing in workplaces, like the Pullman repair shops, where white workers were in the majority. Although Pullman's white and black shop workers had cooperated in the company union and management reported that there were no serious problems of race relations, not all of Pullman's white workers believed in racial equality and integration, and many were not ready to join a union with a black majority. In the first representation election held in Pullman repair shops in March 1944, UTSEA received 42 percent of the vote against the company union. Because no more than 25 percent of Pullman repair shop workers were black, UTSEA attracted significant, but not sufficient, support from white workers.[73]

The results might have been different had the election been held a few months later, after Pullman Inc. announced that it would sell the sleeping-car service. That the corporation would shed the historic heart of the business shocked the old staff, but it did not surprise those who watched the bottom line. Manufacturing railcars was now much more profitable than operating sleeping cars. Moreover, Pullman executives looked to the future, and the future was not in railroads. In 1944, as they decided to sell the sleeping-car service, they acquired M. W. Kellogg Company, which designed and constructed petroleum-refining and chemical-processing plants.[74]

Perhaps because of UTSEA's aggressive organizing, other unions began to show interest in Pullman workers. In 1943 the Brotherhood of Sleeping Car Porters started organizing the predominantly black car cleaners, who were still claimed by the AFL's Brotherhood of Railway Carmen. Many car cleaners in the Chicago yards, especially women, joined the BSCP. As the BSCP and UTSEA continued their organizing campaigns throughout 1944, the AFL shopcraft unions became concerned. Townsend and Randolph now seemed to be cooperating both on national issues, like desegregating the armed forces, and on raiding the jurisdiction of the shopcraft unions, with UTSEA focusing on Pullman repair shop workers and the BSCP on the yard workers. In April 1945 the AFL shopcraft unions began a formal campaign to revive System Federation #122 "in order to prevent A. Philip Randolph from getting in and getting a toe-hold, and also in order to prevent the CIO from getting in."[75] At the same time the shopcraft unions demanded that the AFL leadership stop the BSCP from raiding their jurisdiction. AFL leaders remonstrated with Randolph, but they were afraid to actually punish the porters' union with suspension. Because of the AFL's poor record on racial equality, punishing the BSCP might have led to a wholesale defection of black workers from AFL unions.[76]

The ensuing contest at Pullman repair shops and yards modified the racial practices of the AFL shopcraft unions. AFL organizers made detailed studies of the racial breakdown of every class and craft of worker at every Pullman repair shop and yard and found that the majority of mechanics were white and the majority of car cleaners black. But at most shops and yards at least a few jobs were integrated, and at some facilities many were, so that separating black and white workers into segregated locals would not be easy. Eventually, the shopcraft unions stopped insisting on segregated locals, and the organizing committee even produced flyers with quotations on unionism by "Wendell Phillips, Emancipator and Orator," in an effort to attract black workers.[77] Racial diversity at Pullman yards also forced a change in the Brotherhood of Sleeping Car Porters. By 1945 the BSCP was appealing to the yard forces by insisting that the union "includes WHITES, FILIPINOS, MEXICANS and other workers on a basis of ABSOLUTE EQUALITY."[78]

Although the reasons for their racially exclusive pasts differed, neither the AFL shopcraft unions nor the BSCP would find it easy to appeal to Pullman workers across racial lines. Black shop workers' preference for UTSEA revealed the limits of the Brotherhood's appeal in any multiracial workplace. Both UTSEA and the BSCP were composed primarily of service workers, and therefore neither had much to offer mechanics from a strictly craft perspective. As a multiracial union, however, UTSEA spoke to the experience of Pullman's black shop workers in integrated workplaces in a manner that the BSCP's focus on self-organization for black workers did not. The company's two different racial strategies—creating a segregated job as porter for some black men and providing other black men with opportunities through integration—encouraged different perspectives in porters and repair shop workers.

During 1945 the competing organizing drives at the shops and yards created what one union leader described as "one of the most ridiculous situations I have ever been confronted with."[79] The AFL shopcraft unions, the company unions for the shops and yards, UTSEA, the BSCP, and even the United Mine Workers District #50 solicited support from Pullman workers. Furthermore, organizing Pullman repair shop and yard workers was extremely difficult, because it required a massive number of organizers to reach the six repair shops and the more than one hundred yards. The shopcraft unions faced an additional problem in that Pullman mechanics were not classified according to AFL craft lines, and thus it was not clear which union should claim which workers.[80]

Despite the threat to the very existence of their jobs, Pullman repair shop and yard workers did not share a common perspective in 1945. Race divided them, but so did their allegiances to different models of worker organization. Some black workers looked to the BSCP for its leadership in the fight against racism, but others joined UTSEA and the multiracial CIO. The company unions also continued to appeal to black workers, arguing that they should vote for their company union, "If you want to continue to be treated as an EQUAL by your UNION and by your FELLOW WORKERS."[81] The Independent Pullman Workers Federation further appealed to black car cleaners by questioning what the porters knew about yard maintenance work and hence whether the BSCP could adequately represent them. White workers also were divided. Some believed that the company unions had worked well at Pullman; some wanted craft unions in a revived System Federation #122; and others saw the CIO, with its industry-wide organizing, as the wave of the future. Despite the new federal structures that supported union organization, Pullman repair shop and yard workers remained outside either the AFL or the CIO because they were so divided.[82]

Throughout 1945 the unions battled inconclusively. The AFL shopcraft unions found themselves virtually shut out of Chicago, between support for UTSEA at the Calumet Repair Shop and allegiance to the BSCP in the Chicago yards. The Richmond repair shop also seemed to be leaning toward UTSEA, and the shopcraft unions failed to sign up any workers at the St. Louis shop, where a majority of mechanics were black.[83] Interest in the CIO waned at Wilmington after the lost election in 1944, however, and UTSEA organizers reported that the company union men there started a whispering campaign to raise the "color question." Racial prejudice also seemed to be at work in Buffalo and Atlanta, where the entrance of the AFL shopcraft unions broke the organizing down along racial lines. In some places the company unions actively contested the outside unions, and workers were afraid to talk to organizers. At other points company union leaders organized surreptitiously for the shopcraft unions.[84]

System Federation #122 changed the terrain of struggle when it appealed to the National Mediation Board to recognize the repair shops and yards as a single unit for the purpose of union representation. The system federation argued that it had represented both shop and yard workers at Pullman during World War I and that this combination was the customary bargaining unit on the railroads. The Pullman Company had specifically created separate company unions for the shops and yards to counter the system federation. Leaders of the AFL shopcraft unions believed that combining the repair shops and yards would lessen the threat of UTSEA and the BSCP, each of which organized in only one sector. They also thought that the porters' union found support primarily among the predominantly black car cleaners in the yards, whose votes would be outnumbered by those of white workers if the repair shops and yards were combined.[85]

In a rare display of unity the BSCP, UTSEA, and both company unions urged the National Mediation Board to maintain the separation of Pullman repair shops and yards. Although UTSEA and the BSCP still fought each other for other railroad workers, the unions cooperated here because they targeted different parts of the Pullman workforce. In their appeals to the board all four unions cited the second-class status of black workers in the AFL shopcraft unions as a major reason to reject the combination. In the words of the brief filed by PCEARS, black workers had enjoyed "equal seniority rights, rates of pay, and equal representation and promotional privileges that would be a matter of question" under System Federation #122.[86]

The National Mediation Board rejected this plea and followed its previous precedents and the wishes of the AFL shopcraft unions, which now represented virtually all railroad repair shop and yard workers. In this, as in many cases, the National Mediation Board ignored the needs of black workers and the decision of the Supreme Court that unions must fairly represent all workers in the bargaining unit. Because it did not reject exclusionary unions or the craft jurisdictions designed by the AFL, the National Mediation Board undercut UTSEA, the BSCP, and other black challengers time after time and failed to protect black workers in the railroad industry.[87]

Pullman executives were less concerned about the combination of repair shop and yard forces into one representation unit than they were about the second part of the board's ruling, which divided Pullman workers into the six standard AFL shopcraft classifications plus storeroom nonclerical workers.[88] Officials expected that AFL or CIO unions might win a majority among several groups of shop and yard workers, but they knew that "a more serious development for the Company will be the almost certain increase in cost following the establishment of craft lines on a strict basis in Pullman work with resultant inflexibility and higher labor costs."[89] Because of this threat to its ability to keep profits up through applying mass-production methods to repair work, the company continued to resist the union drive. Local supervisors kept up surveillance of union meetings to pinpoint workers who were straying from the company unions. At the same time Pullman executives recognized that some of their old tactics would lead to government censure and that "in a representation dispute, management must pursue a strictly neutral, 'hands off,' policy."[90] While that did not stop at least one foreman from trying to influence workers' votes, the election held in the shops and yards in December 1946 under National Mediation Board supervision generally reflected the views of the 91 percent of eligible workers who voted.[91]

The results of that election left most of Pullman repair shop and yard workers in company unions, as table 10 shows. The system federation failed to win representation status overall, and only one shopcraft union, the International Brotherhood of Electrical Workers, won a majority of the workers in its craft. The Brotherhood of Sleeping Car Porters won a majority among the storeroom nonclerical workers, because during the war black men and women had come to predominate in positions such as linen checkers in the yards.[92] PCEARS, the company union for the repair shops, retained the loyalty of a majority of the blacksmiths, machinists, sheet metal workers, and mechanics in power, heat, and light. In these crafts the CIO's UTSEA, not the AFL shopcraft unions, was the

Table 10. Results of 1946 Representation Election at Pullman Repair Shops and Yards

		Percentage of Votes Cast					
	Workers Eligible	Company Unions		AFL	CIO	AFL	
Craft	to Vote	IPWF	PCEARS	Shop Craft	UTSEA	BSCP	Void
Carmen	8,233	14.1	18.7	27.6	7.2	30.1	2.2
Blacksmiths	89	5.7	58.6	3.4	28.7	1.1	2.3
Electricians	1,683	25.5	10.9	53.1	3.0	6.9	0.6
Machinists	238	3.0	51.1	17.3	25.5	1.3	1.7
Power, heat, and light	244	3.7	59.7	6.9	23.6	2.3	3.7
Sheet metal	335	0.9	54.8	19.4	24.2	0.6	
Storeroom	766	7.6	10.2	20.7	6.2	52.7	2.3
	11,588	14.5	20.0	30.0	7.9	25.6	2.0

Source: H. R. Lary, memo to superintendents et al., 20 Dec. 1946, 06/01/03, Box 15a, File 328a, PANL.

Key: IPWF = Independent Pullman Workers Federation; PCEARS = Pullman Car Employes Association of the Repair Shops; UTSEA = United Transport Service Employees of America, CIO; BSCP = Brotherhood of Sleeping Car Porters.

second most popular choice, as it retained some support that it had garnered in the 1944 election.

No union won a majority among the largest group of Pullman shop and yard workers, the carmen. Through its popularity with black car cleaners the BSCP was the top vote getter among them, but no union had anywhere near a majority. About one-third of the carmen voted for the company unions, and slightly fewer voted for the AFL's Brotherhood of Railway Carmen. UTSEA had not contested the yards, and therefore it received a much smaller proportion of the total vote among the carmen. Because of the mixed results of this election, the company unions remained the bargaining agents for most Pullman repair shop and yard workers.

The difficulty that workers had in transforming their discontent into a cohesive union movement lay not only in the racial division between them but also in the choices presented by the U.S. labor movement. A truly egalitarian system federation might have won a majority by appealing simultaneously to the heritage of racial equity in the company unions and the desire for jobs that met the standards set by the AFL shopcraft unions. The Brotherhood of Sleeping Car Porters was too firmly associated with the aspirations of one race and one occupation to appeal to all shop and yard workers. On the other hand, the strength of the AFL unions in the railroad industry minimized the appeal of the CIO's UTSEA. Belonging to the CIO would cut Pullman workers off from other railroad workers and the possibility of their support, which had been vital in the strikes of 1894 and 1922.

The warfare between the AFL and the CIO took a deep toll on U.S. workers, especially black workers. It bankrupted UTSEA, which had borrowed large sums from the CIO in order to organize Pullman repair shops. The labor federation continued to bankroll UTSEA, but the union never expanded its membership significantly. The BSCP also expended much effort and money to no result. It never managed to attract black skilled workers, nor did it appeal across racial lines to white, Mexican, or Filipino service workers. Moreover, because the warfare between the AFL and the CIO continued, the BSCP and UTSEA contested elections for porters and dining car employees into 1948. This bitter fight weakened both unions and did nothing to advance the interests of black workers.[93]

During the war the issue of racial equity assumed a new salience in no small part because of the activism of Pullman's black workers, but ironically their own gains were limited. White resistance to racial equality kept barriers to black advancement up and shaped the course of unionization. As a result the black majority in the sleeping-car service made little headway into the better jobs in the repair shops or offices. Because of the war between the AFL and the CIO, porters and laundry workers found their unions weakened and less able to pressure the company to meet their demands. Furthermore, many black repair shop and yard workers, along with white co-workers, remained in ineffective company unions. Pullman manufacturing workers all were unionized, but the gains that black workers had made at Pullman Standard were tied to defense production that was ending. Nor did the white racism that surfaced in the shipyard hate strike portend well for the future of black workers during a union era in Pullman manufacturing plants.

After the war Pullman workers who were represented by AFL or CIO unions seemed poised to move ahead in achieving better wages and working conditions. Those in company unions would continue the struggle to overcome their racial divisions and unionize too. Yet the major challenges for AFL and CIO unions would not be those that they were best equipped to handle—controlling wages and conditions on the shop floor. Rather, they would struggle to be racially egalitarian and to cope with the precipitous decline of the railroad industry.

7   *The Last Pullman Workers*

In the immediate postwar years Pullman workers' struggle to unionize ended in victory. By 1950 every blue-collar worker at Pullman Standard and the Pullman Company, plus the latter's clerical staff, belonged to a union affiliated with the American Federation of Labor (AFL) or the Congress of Industrial Organizations (CIO). All had contracts that embodied the best standards demanded by those unions, and the union period brought real improvements in wages, working conditions, and protection from arbitrary supervision. It did not bring much progress on racial equity at the workplace, however. When a conservative majority in Congress ended the federal government's attempt to end discrimination in employment, unions did not take up the fight. Rather, most became at least passive supporters of white privilege.

Yet white workers did not have long to savor victory, either, because the unions did not develop as a strong counterweight to employer power. In the AFL only the shopcraft unions cooperated to make joint demands on companies, and the AFL and CIO continued their jurisdictional battles in the late 1940s. The labor movement pulled back from broad challenges to capitalist leadership in economic and social policy as domestic anticommunism burgeoned during the Cold War and as a conservative Congress began to limit union power with the Taft-Hartley Act of 1947.

Unions that did not work together or address larger economic and social issues would prove of only limited value, as Pullman and railroad workers were the first to learn. In the postwar era the automobile, truck, and airplane reigned supreme, and passenger railroads began their steep decline to virtual oblivion. Pullman union locals would have relatively little time to enjoy a collective bargaining process focused on how to reshape jobs to workers' standards. Their test would be how to protect workers in the face of industry-wide decline. The unions' inability to address that catastrophe adequately or to work together in the movement for racial justice reveals the limits of a century of workers' struggle.

Reconversion

Reconversion to a peacetime economy was a painful process for all corporations that produced armaments. When defense contracts ended in 1945, Pullman Standard once more closed the Calumet Shipyard and laid off thousands of workers at its other plants. As was true everywhere, minority workers and women, who had been the last hired, took the brunt of the layoffs.[1] The new union contracts guaranteeing that seniority governed layoffs precluded any "affirmative-action" exceptions, had anyone argued for them. Layoffs reinforced the minority status of black workers in all Pullman manufacturing facilities, except the plant in Bessemer, Alabama. By the end of 1945 the percentage of black workers at the Pullman Car Works was no higher than it had been before the war. Yet more than just the seniority system may have contributed to this result. Black workers were committed to the Double V, and they intended to keep their jobs or obtain better ones. The assistant manager of the Car Works told staffers for the Committee on Fair Employment Practice that foremen found black workers more difficult to fit into the postwar organization: they resisted fill-in assignments and downgrading more aggressively than white workers did.[2] Whether that was the case or not, black workers lost their wartime gains at Pullman Standard and in many other companies too.

Where dislocation was minor or the return to expanded civilian production was relatively quick, however, black men often retained the gains that they made during the war. The full effect of reconversion did not hit the sleeping-car service until 1947, because extensive military demand for railroad transport during demobilization kept trains rolling and employment relatively high. In July 1945 Pullman repair shops even experienced a labor shortage and advertised for new workers. This ensured that many black shop workers remained in the skilled jobs and storeroom clerical positions to which they had upgraded during the war. Indeed, few men whose initial employment at the repair shops predated 1946 experienced any layoffs before 1949. Most could build on their seniority so that they were not forced to move down to less-skilled positions, even in the 1950s when contraction began in earnest. Furthermore, men who had become helpers at Pullman repair shops during World War II, both black and white, continued to move up to skilled jobs in the late 1940s and early 1950s. Black workers made real gains in the railroad industry as a whole during the war, and they maintained these until the severe decline in passenger traffic in the 1950s.[3]

Although some black men made permanent gains from their wartime employment, only one group of women—white clerical workers—was as fortunate. Across the country companies pushed women out of "men's" blue-collar jobs, sometimes with the acquiescence of male unionists, sometimes without. Women disappeared from the shop floor in Pullman manufacturing plants, except in their traditional space in the upholstery departments. Even as the Pullman Company actively recruited new workers for its repair shops, supervisors let go most women hired as "emergency employees." The president of the Brotherhood of Railway Carmen noted that "female employees are being laid off wherever the company can employ males to take their places."[4] Only 10 percent of the women who held "men's jobs" as laborers or helpers at the Calumet Repair Shop remained at their posts after military demand for Pullman trains declined. Thereafter, most women mechanics and helpers in the repair shops were, once again, seamstresses. Yet Pullman managers continued to hire women for clerical jobs in the stores departments of the repair shops and yards—jobs that had been male bastions before the war—even as they refused to hire them for blue-collar jobs that had traditionally gone to men.[5]

The expulsion of women from "men's jobs" did not necessarily reflect their desires. While women clerical workers and those in unskilled jobs at Pullman repair shops often quit work voluntarily after the war, more wartime women mechanics and helpers left their jobs involuntarily through layoffs and disciplinary actions. Across the nation women were especially loath to give up jobs that paid "men's wages." Black women, who had many fewer opportunities than white women, also clung to their new jobs.[6] Maggie Hudson, one of Pullman's train "porterettes," told her union newspaper that "she feels that this avenue of employment should remain open not only on the basis of sex, but on the basis of the ability to do the job."[7] Although the Brotherhood of Sleeping Car Porters was in the forefront of the movement for racial equality, it had always defined portering as a man's job, and it did not support the porterettes like Hudson, whom the company phased out quickly.

After the war few women, white or black, were hired for "men's jobs" outside the clerical sector, and the exceptions reveal the continuation of the prejudices of the past about work that was appropriate for women. For the Pullman Company to hire a woman in a "man's job," she had to be an outstanding worker and to be sponsored by a male union representative or supervisor. In 1947 the Calumet Repair Shop rehired one woman war worker whom the shop committeeman for the company union recommended because she had done an exceptional job. He asked this, noting that "we understand the management attitude toward hiring women for mechanical work."[8] In another case in the early 1950s the manager of the Wilmington repair shop promoted one woman from helper to electrician, noting that this particular woman "can produce as much work as a man."[9] In general, women did not find that type of support.

The few extraordinary women who filled "men's jobs" did not change management's preference for men in mechanical tasks. Nor did the war experience change the company's policy toward paying women less than men wherever possible. In 1946 Pullman repair shops had difficulty securing enough seamstresses, but the company refused to raise their wage rate. Instead, it allowed managers to ignore the general policy of age discrimination and hire women older than forty-five, because older women were more likely than younger ones to accept the lower pay.[10]

The wartime assault on discrimination in employment opened some permanent opportunities in industry for black men, if not for women, but it faltered thereafter. By 1946 a conservative backlash against President Roosevelt's policies was in full swing, with northern Republicans and white southern Democrats in Congress ready to roll back the movement toward racial equity as well as the power of organized labor. These members of Congress began by refusing to reauthorize the Committee for Fair Employment Practice, which had always been anathema to U.S. businessmen. The AFL also refused to endorse reauthorization of the agency in order to protect its unions that discriminated, revealing how little progress the war on racism had actually made among many white workers. The organization's stance also signaled how little the AFL unions would do for their black members in the postwar years. Some large industrial states, such as Wisconsin, Massachusetts, and New York, and some cities such as Chicago adopted fair employment statutes and established commissions to monitor their enforcement. But businesses fought such movements and defeated them in other important states like California. Black workers once more found their opportunities shrinking, because enforcement of equal opportunity legislation was spotty.[11]

While increasing numbers of black men entered industrial employment in the United States in the late 1940s and 1950s, the national averages hide great local variation and the continued effects of discrimination. In Pullman's sleeping-car service the seniority system protected black workers already on the job in 1945, but its egalitarian operation did not necessarily influence hiring policies thereafter. When the Pullman Company needed new workers for its repair shops just as thousands of Americans lost their jobs from defense production cutbacks, managers could afford to discriminate, and some did. Black men found their best opportunities at the Calumet Repair Shop, as demonstrated in table 11. There they comprised 48 percent of all men hired after the war, and they entered jobs at all skill levels. Yet even at Calumet, white men were more likely to be hired as mechanics, and black men were more likely to be hired for unskilled jobs.

At the Wilmington and Richmond repair shops racial discrimination returned in force. Black men continued to find work at the Wilmington shop but only as unskilled laborers. Shop management had not practiced such extreme discrimination since before the 1922 strike. Black men were certainly available, had management wished to hire them—Wilmington's black ghetto was forming around the repair shop, and by 1950 the local unemployment rate for black men was two and one half times that for white men. But as the city experienced another postwar economic decline, the Pullman repair shop reverted to the city's most traditional racial practices. White preference also guided hiring at Pullman's Richmond repair shop after 1945, when local shipyards and other defense industries laid off thousands of workers. Although the black population of Richmond and the surrounding area continued to grow, and black men were more likely than white men to be unemployed, the Pullman repair shop hired few African Americans after the war. Moreover, management hired them primarily as unskilled laborers, while it hired only white men directly into mechanic positions. The California dream for black workers, like the wartime promise of equal opportunity, was brief indeed.[12]

Table 11. Percentage of Men Hired in Pullman Repair Shops after 1945 by Skill Level and Race

	Calumet		Richmond		Wilmington	
	White	Black	White	Black	White	Black
1946–1948						
Mechanic	50.0	50.0	100.0	0.0	100.0	0.0
Helper	63.2	36.8	95.0	5.0	100.0	0.0
Unskilled	23.1	76.9	73.3	26.7	0.0	100.0
1949–closing						
Mechanic	69.8	30.2	100.0	0.0	100.0	0.0
Helper	25.0	75.0	90.0	10.0	100.0	0.0
Unskilled	13.6	86.4	66.7	33.3	0.0	100.0

Source: Derived from samples described in the appendix.

Pullman's Wilmington repair shop could discriminate against black workers after the war because it was subject to no fair employment statute. Elsewhere, such laws often had little effect because of inadequate enforcement mechanisms. Richmond, California, passed fair employment legislation in 1949, but it had no enforcement provisions and no effect on Pullman's repair shop. All but the strongest state agencies, like that in New York, found it difficult to make national corporations and national unions conform to local law. Nor is it clear that opportunities for black men at the Calumet Repair Shop resulted from the Chicago legislation, which seemed to have no effect at the Pullman Company's headquarters, where management enforced the color line. Of the 1,493 employees at Pullman headquarters in 1953, none were nonwhite women and only eight were nonwhite men. When faced with inquiries from state fair employment commissions about the company's hiring practices, Pullman executives tried to turn them away with an old tactic. They pointed out that enforcement of equal opportunity legislation threatened the black monopoly of porters' jobs and therefore could harm the very people it was supposed to help.[13]

Organizing Pullman Shop and Yard Workers

In the charged racial climate after the war, national unions continued to attempt to organize Pullman workers. The failure of the 1946 election to produce union representation for most of the repair shop and yard workers was no sign that they were happy with the status quo, only that they were divided, in part, by race. Unions saw a possibility for success as many workers expressed their discontent in a traditional way, through withholding their effort. Disciplinary problems burgeoned at the Calumet Repair Shop in 1946 and 1947: workers roamed around, used the telephone, ate, smoked, socialized, and engaged in horseplay when they were supposed to be on the job. One day supervisors caught one-tenth of the shop force trying to leave work early.[14] At the 1947 negotiating session between management and the company union, none of the worker representatives disagreed when Mechanical Superintendent John Cannon charged that "there has been a general let-down on the part of the employes in their daily output."[15]

After the 1946 election Pullman repair shop and yard workers had fewer unions to choose from, because the now-penniless United Transport Service Employees of America (UTSEA) ended its organizing drive in the shops. The option of a multiracial industrial union disappeared as the CIO drew back from unsuccessful challenges to the AFL. Yet the racial divide still produced bitter union rivalry within the AFL, as the Brotherhood of Sleeping Car Porters (BSCP) stepped up its drive among Pullman car cleaners. Even though not all the yard workers who attended its organizing meetings were black, the BSCP's appeal remained heavily racial and strongly focused on black carmen.[16] One example of this racial appeal was an open letter from Benjamin F. McLaurin, the BSCP international field organizer, to Pullman's New York Division carmen, warning them against an organizer for the Brotherhood of Railway Carmen (BRCA). McLaurin told them, "Don't be fooled by Car Cleaner, Thomas Mason, young Uncle Tom, who poses as your friend but who is being used by the white Carmen to betray you. Remember, the white man has always found some weak-minded Negro to do his dirty work." McLaurin charged that BRCA members believed that the white man was superior to the black man and that black men were content with second-class status. He challenged the Pullman car cleaners to "have the 'guts' to stand on your own feet."[17] Although the shopcraft unions had alienated black workers and the BSCP appealed primarily to African Americans, the U.S. labor movement provided no other choices for Pullman workers.

The showdown between the shopcraft unions and the Brotherhood came once the company unions disintegrated. Leaders of the Pullman Car Employes Association of the Repair Shops and the Independent Pullman Workers Federation found it difficult to make any headway in negotiations with management in 1947, because company officials refused every demand that increased costs. Pullman Inc. was on the verge of selling the sleeping-car service to a consortium of fifty-four railroads in order to settle the 1940 antitrust suit, and pressure to make the service as attractive as possible to the buyers was intense. Thus the company granted the latest wage increases set by the AFL shopcraft unions but neutralized the effect by cutting working hours from forty-eight to forty per week. Worker representatives were dispirited, knowing they had nothing to show for their efforts.[18] Because the organizations were ineffective, fewer and fewer workers paid their dues. By May 1948 the leaders of the company unions decided to call it quits and refused to contest the next representation election, slated for July.

The comparative appeal of System Federation #122 and the Brotherhood of Sleeping Car Porters was not the only factor determining the election results in July, however. In 1947 the sleeping-car service first felt the full effects of declining military demand for transport and laid off large numbers of yard workers. The number of carmen declined 24 percent between the 1946 and 1948 elections. Under the rules of the company union in the yards, mechanics with more seniority (mainly white) could bump car cleaners with less seniority (mainly black) rather than accept a layoff, so that black workers suffered disproportionately from the layoffs.[19] This undercut support for the BSCP, which polled only 17 percent of the carmen in 1948 (see table 12), rather than the 30 percent that it had won in 1946. System Federation #122 won the votes of two-thirds of the workers in each group contested, and twenty-six years after its defeat in the Railroad Shopmen's Strike, it again became the bargaining agent for Pullman shop and yard workers.

Yet lack of enthusiasm for the system federation among a significant minority of Pullman workers was clear from the election results. Turnout was down in every craft; the overall percentage voting dropped from 91 percent in 1946 to 85 percent in 1948. Furthermore, 14 percent of the ballots were voided, a much larger proportion than the 2 percent voided in the 1946 election. Many of these may have been the ballots of CIO supporters, who were attracted neither to the BSCP nor to the shopcraft unions, as a comparison of election results for the machinists, sheet metal workers, and blacksmiths reveals. The number of workers in these crafts had changed little since 1946, and the percentage of votes in 1946 for the CIO's UTSEA was virtually identical to the percentage of voided ballots in 1948. The continued resistance of black craftsmen to the shopcraft unions also can be seen in the slightly increased percentage of votes for the BSCP in those crafts. Yet if black workers and white CIO supporters resisted the shopcraft unions, most white shop workers voted for the system federation. Even some company union leaders went over, and several, like Stanley Meyer, the representative from the Buffalo repair shop, later became officers of the shopcraft locals and System Federation #122.[20]

Table 12. Results of 1948 Representation Election at Pullman Repair Shops and Yards

	Workers Eligible to Vote	Percentage of Votes Cast			
		IPWF and PCEARS	AFL Shop Craft	BSCP	Void
Carmen	6,264	2.7	67.4	17.1	12.7
Blacksmiths	89	1.3	67.5	3.6	27.5
Machinists	260	7.9	66.9	3.3	21.9
Sheet Metal	364	4.0	67.7	3.4	24.8
	6,977	2.8	67.5	15.7	14.0

Source: Report of Elections Results, National Mediation Board Case R-2020, 27 July 1948, 06/01/03, Box 15a, File 328c, PANL.

Key: IPWF = Independent Pullman Workers Federation; PCEARS = Pullman Car Employes Association of the Repair Shops; BSCP = Brotherhood of Sleeping Car Porters.

After the system federation's victory, the sleeping-car service ceased to oppose unionization of its employees. When the International Brotherhood of Firemen and Oilers, Roundhouse and Railway Shop Laborers organized laborers in the repair shops in December 1948, the company accepted the authorization cards without even demanding a vote. By 1950 every Pullman worker, including the predominantly female clerks, was represented by the appropriate union for railway workers. Except for the laundry workers, who remained in UTSEA, all belonged to AFL railroad unions.[21] Now management faced what George Pullman could never have imagined, a totally unionized workforce.

The Union Era in the Sleeping-Car Service

If the AFL railroad unions brought industry-wide standards to the Pullman Company, they did not treat white and black workers equally. After 1948 the only resorts for black workers who experienced discrimination were the state and local equal opportunity commissions, where they existed. In 1953, for instance, George C. Greenidge, a black car cleaner, complained to the Massachusetts Commission Against Discrimination that his yard foreman had promoted a white man to the position of carman helper-apprentice on which Greenidge had bid and for which he had more experience, schooling, and seniority. The new rules on posting jobs that System Federation #122 fought for were supposed to counter the old-style favoritism, but Greenidge's union local did not protest the foreman's discrimination through the grievance system. When the state commission intervened, the company agreed to conciliation and upgraded him. Management cooperated with the government commission for fear of wider attacks on its practices, especially the rule that only white men could be conductors.[22]

Black workers who experienced discrimination turned to the government for help, but a weakened BSCP seemed to retreat from its earlier advocacy for all black workers. The Brotherhood's fight against the AFL railroad unions had not increased its membership nor induced the white-dominated unions to embrace racial equity. Moreover, as Pullman business declined, so did BSCP membership, further weakening the union's ability to do more than represent the porters. The Brotherhood was also caught in the difficult position of advocating fair employment practices while being a black union based on a racially defined occupation. Perhaps because of this situation, the union maintained a low profile on discrimination within the Pullman Company itself. According to one Pullman official, company executives threatened BSCP president A. Philip Randolph with hiring white men as porters after he requested that the company open conductor and other positions to black men. The BSCP seemed to turn inward, and it declined the AFL's request that it organize airline flight attendants. In occupational terms this was an appropriate task for the BSCP and would have brought in sorely needed members from a growing industry, but flight attendants were all white women and the union had defined itself as black and male.[23]

The federal legislation that would be effective in enforcing equal opportunity, the Civil Rights Act of 1964, came too late to help black workers in the sleeping-car service. The BSCP called for its immediate implementation at Pullman, and in 1966 the company announced that it would finally open conductor positions to porters, but no porters ever became conductors. By the mid-1960s so many Pullman conductors had been laid off and were willing to relocate to fill vacancies that porters had no chance to move up. But the porters did not let old wrongs go unpunished, and they filed a class-action suit under the Civil Rights Act, charging the Pullman Company with discrimination against the porters and those who as porters-in-charge had done conductors' work for lower pay. Court action was slow despite the clear evidence of a century of discrimination. The porters won the case only in 1979.[24]

The AFL railroad unions played a more positive role for white women workers in the sleeping-car service than they did for black women or men. The unionization of Pullman clerical workers helped white women because the new contract with the Brotherhood of Railway and Steamship Clerks outlawed practices that had allowed supervisors to discriminate against them in the past. All job openings now had to be posted so that workers could bid on them, and men and women were combined on the same seniority roster. Previously, with job openings secret and with men and women on separate rosters, department heads could easily advance a man with less seniority over a woman with more. Not coincidentally, women first became supervisors in the central office after the union contract went into effect. The shopcraft unions also helped white women by insisting on gender-neutral language in their contracts. Seamstresses in the repair shops and yards finally received the mechanics' rate when the 1951 contract reclassified them as upholsterers.[25]

Yet just as the Brotherhood of Railway Carmen did not aid black men who experienced discrimination, it did not protect black women car cleaners during downsizing. The union agreed to a separate listing of male and female jobs for car cleaners, even though women had done every job during World War II. In the late 1950s and early 1960s the company proceeded to cut the force of car cleaners by allowing men to do "women's jobs." Martha Dennis, who became a Pullman car cleaner in 1943, was laid off, and men with less seniority were assigned to her work. She charged that the company was attempting to eliminate women cleaners entirely. Her union local gave Dennis no support, and she too had to appeal to a state fair employment commission for redress. (The outcome of the case is not clear in the extant records.)[26]

If the AFL unions were much less than fully supportive of minority workers, they did bring the standards that white men had long desired. Most important in the repair shops and yards, the new contracts eliminated the craft specialties with their different rates of pay. Reclassification was difficult because Pullman jobs had been defined so differently from the standard crafts, and only a special mediation board could redraw the classifications and sort out jurisdictional disputes between the shopcraft unions. Once the board's work was complete, Pullman's attempt to import mass-production methods into the repair shops ended, and the number of specific job titles at Pullman repair shops reached an all-time low.[27]

The Limits of Union Power

Ironically, the strict application of union work rules complicated the biggest problem for Pullman workers in the 1950s—the threat of job loss. The Pullman Company's profit margin depended primarily on lowering labor costs through introducing mass-production methods in repair and through creating low-wage jobs specifically for women and minorities in the clerical and service areas. Now unions stood in the way of both those strategies, and by 1953 the company spent 75 percent of its earnings on wages and benefits. Under a new president, Carroll R. Harding, efficiency drives and staff cutbacks became the order of the day. Between 1947 and 1953 the workforce shrank by one-fourth.[28]

With a squeeze on profits Pullman's board of directors approved only limited capital improvements and decided to focus them at particular facilities. Among the repair shops, officials favored Calumet and St. Louis, choosing them to service the new lightweight cars. This decision sealed the fate of the other shops. To cut costs the company needed to close shops entirely rather than to decrease employment across the board, because repair shops have high overhead and run efficiently only with a full workforce. In 1951 Harding recommended closing the Atlanta repair shop, which was the least strategically located, but the company did not do so for another three years. Then its financial situation was so bad that officials also temporarily closed the other five repair shops for one month, beginning at Christmas. Similar one- to two-month closings occurred in 1956, 1957, and 1958, and even the most senior workers, who had not experienced layoffs since the Great Depression, were idled.[29]

By the mid-1950s not only the decline of railroad passenger traffic but also the terms of the settlement of the antitrust suit threatened the existence of the sleeping-car service. Pullman Inc. had agreed that members could withdraw from the consortium of railroads that had bought the service and could handle their own sleeping-car operations. Despite management's attempts at economy, some railroads believed that they could run sleeping cars less expensively if they did not have to pay for the superstructure of the Pullman Company. Pullman managers, ticket agents, conductors, and repair shop workers duplicated the work of railroad managers, agents, conductors, and shop workers. Ironically, only the porters were indispensable because the railroads had no directly comparable workers. In 1956 the first railroads withdrew from the consortium, and more followed their lead each year. With fewer and fewer cars to run or service, the Pullman Company laid off thousands of workers and closed the Wilmington and Buffalo repair shops in 1958 and the Richmond shop in 1960.[30]

If unions could do little about decisions made by the railroads or about the overall decline in passenger traffic, the closings and layoffs challenged them to protect Pullman workers until they could find other employment. In the 1950s, when railroads took over their sleeping-car service, they usually hired the Pullman porters who had worked those trains too. To protect its members the Brotherhood of Sleeping Car Porters had only to ensure that the railroads adopted its contract with the Pullman Company. None of the other Pullman workers found ready employment when their work was transferred to the railroads, and their unions had to ease the transition to unemployment. A precedent existed in the railroad industry to help them, the 1936 Washington Agreement. In the midst of the depression the AFL railroad unions had negotiated with the major railroads to protect workers in cases of coordination of service or consolidation. Under the agreement, during a protective period of five years, displaced workers received allowances based on length of service. Those with more than fifteen years of service received as much as 60 percent of their average monthly wage. If workers shifted to lower-paid jobs on the railroads, they received their current higher wage rates for the five years too. In 1942 this agreement was extended to workers faced with the railroad equivalent of a plant closing—abandonment of service. Now these workers too would receive dismissal allowances or reimbursement of moving expenses if they found jobs at other railroad facilities.[31]

Unfortunately for its workers, the Pullman Company had not been a signatory to the pact because it had no contracts with railroad unions in 1936. Throughout the 1940s company officials resisted becoming party to the agreement, and in 1948 they specifically refused to follow its provisions for white conductors and clerks displaced by coordination of Pullman and railroad ticket services in Atlanta, Georgia.[32] Once all Pullman workers belonged to unions, the company's position seemed to soften, and in 1952 at the unions' request the company asked to be made a party to the agreement. This would not help porters or laundry workers in any case, because neither the BSCP nor the UTSEA was party to the original agreement.

Yet despite what seemed like greater concern for workers' futures, Pullman officials narrowly construed the grounds for implementing the agreement. When they closed the Atlanta repair shop in 1954, they refused to give dismissal allowances or moving expenses to the workers. The best that they offered workers was their pick of vacancies at other repair shops and yards. The Atlanta shop workers would have to pay their moving expenses to start over in jobs for which none of their previous seniority would count. Under the provisions of the Washington Agreement, one-quarter of the Atlanta shop workers qualified for the maximum dismissal allowances, and another half would have received significant amounts. System Federation #122 asked for negotiation, demanding implementation of the provisions of the agreement, but the company refused.[33]

The system federation then appealed to the National Mediation Board but here too failed to achieve its goal. During the first months of mediation the company compromised on the issue of transfer of seniority and moving expenses but continued to resist dismissal allowances for those who could not be placed or for the continuation of benefits during the five-year protective period. At this impasse the company rejected arbitration, and the unions were left with the alternative of striking or admitting defeat. System Federation #122, like the shopcraft unions in general, represented a group of relatively elderly workers; their average age was about fifty. Most of these workers had never been on strike, and they may well have hoped merely to hang on long enough to collect their pensions. They were not willing to sacrifice for the Atlanta workers. The system federation did not call for a strike vote but continued to press for implementation of the Washington Agreement in contract negotiations. The company remained adamant and denied that this was an appropriate issue for collective bargaining.[34]

More Pullman workers faced unemployment in 1958 when the company closed the Wilmington and Buffalo repair shops. Most Pullman shop workers wanted dismissal allowances, because they did not want to move hundreds of miles from their homes for jobs at other facilities. Their age certainly made the prospect of uprooting more difficult. Wilmington shop workers, most of whom had been born in the area and had strong community ties, found moving particularly unattractive. Only five of fourteen Wilmington machinists who were offered jobs at the Calumet and St. Louis repair shops with their seniority intact agreed to go, and one later changed his mind, taking a job with Westinghouse Electric in nearby Lester, Pennsylvania. The Wilmington and Buffalo shop workers, like those in Atlanta, were left to fend for themselves. Wilmington shop workers filed a lawsuit challenging the company's refusal to continue their group insurance plan during the protective period, but the court dismissed their action. Under continued union pressure, however, the Pullman Company finally gave dismissal allowances of $1,000 each to qualifying workers when it closed the Richmond repair shop in 1960. Yet many would have received much more under the terms of the Washington Agreement.[35]

The early 1960s saw a lull in railroad takeovers of Pullman service, but passenger traffic continued to decline, threatening even the future of the porters. The porters' and conductors' unions now pressed the Pullman Company to adhere to the Washington Agreement too, but they had no more success than the system federation. At this point System Federation #122 changed tactics and negotiated directly with the railroads to ensure that when railroads took over sleeping-car service, those yard workers who maintained the cars could carry their seniority with them to the railroad and bump any railroad workers in their craft with less seniority. The BSCP also negotiated similar agreements directly with the railroads, because with passenger traffic declining, railroads did not necessarily need all the porters who had serviced their sleeping cars but who could replace other train porters. Only the last Pullman Company workers actually received the full benefit of the Washington Agreement, and as in the past only the intervention of the federal government achieved this result. In the mid-1960s the National Mediation Board began to heed the pleas of the railroad unions and broadened the application of the Washington Agreement, because declining passenger traffic had produced massive layoffs in the industry. By the time the Pullman Company went out of business in 1969, management had to implement the provisions of the agreement and give separation allowances to all workers who did not find jobs on the railroads. At the Calumet Repair Shop, the last shop to close, most of those workers who did not take jobs on other railroads had sufficient seniority to receive dismissal allowances of more than $10,000 apiece, the equivalent of eighteen months' full-time pay for a mechanic.[36]

The Last Pullman Workers

When the sleeping-car service closed after 102 years of operation, the other half of George Pullman's empire, manufacturing, continued. Pullman Standard was the world's largest builder of railcars in the 1940s and 1950s, and its employees rode the crest of postwar prosperity for industrial workers. Once workers at all six plants voted for union representation, company officials began to accommodate themselves to the idea of collective bargaining. In 1946 they signed the first union contract without forcing workers to strike or appeal to government boards for intervention. Workers won major wage increases and finally enjoyed union-controlled seniority and grievance systems. Unlike Pullman repair shop workers who declined to strike for their rights, Pullman Standard workers who belonged to the United Steelworkers of America (USWA) struck for three months in 1951 to obtain a master contract for all plants. They settled for common contracts at that point but achieved their goal in 1953. Thereafter, Pullman Standard was tied to pattern bargaining in the steel industry. When the USWA negotiated a contract with major steel producers, it expected Pullman Standard to match its provisions. Thus Pullman workers benefited from the combined power of U.S. steelworkers.[37]

Yet the decline of the railroads could not help but affect the manufacturing company and its workers negatively. The demand for passenger cars decreased along with passenger traffic, and by the mid-1950s the increase in trucking cut demand for freight cars too. Pullman Standard became increasingly dependent on international orders for railcars as the domestic market declined. Officials of Pullman Inc. continued to diversify, and in 1951 the holding company bought Trailmobile, the country's second-largest maker of highway truck trailers, the very product undermining demand for freight cars.[38] Pullman Standard also tried to adapt to the new era by refocusing on an old product—mass transit. The Pullman Car Works had produced thousands of streetcars in the late nineteenth and early twentieth centuries; now it manufactured subway trains for major urban transportation systems as well as passenger railcars.

When downsizing became necessary, Pullman Standard acted as the Pullman Company had: it closed obsolete facilities first and increasingly centralized operations in Chicago. In 1957 the corporation closed the obsolete Pullman Car Works and replaced it with a state-of-the-art plant on the outskirts of the Pullman neighborhood. While car builders in

Chicago found their jobs secured, those who worked at the Worcester, Massachusetts, plant were not as fortunate. Demand for passenger rail-cars declined so severely that contracts for subway cars could not make up the difference. Pullman Standard closed the Worcester plant in 1958 and formally shut it down after a two-year layoff. As demand for freight cars declined, the company also shuttered aging freight car facilities, beginning with the Hammond plant in 1961. At that point, the workers, who had no hope for future employment at Pullman Standard, found that their Steelworkers' contract made no clear provision for severance pay. The USWA began to recognize the need for such provisions only as employment in the steel industry decreased after the mid-1950s. Yet the lack of severance pay was not necessarily critical for laid-off manufacturing workers, because many found alternative employment as U.S. industry continued to prosper.[39]

Although it was unprepared for plant closings, the USWA provided Pullman Standard workers with high wages and good benefits throughout the 1950s. But the CIO union did no more for minority workers than the AFL railroad unions did, even though their votes had been crucial to USWA victories. After the war, concern for building a culture of unity gave way, many white workers remained wedded to white privilege, and the cause of black equality suffered. A few CIO unions continued to make racial equity a priority, but the USWA, like most others, did little to respond to charges of discrimination. This forced workers to go to management or government for redress. Nor did the unions fight to expand opportunities for minority workers by attacking segregated seniority rosters. Indeed, by the time the CIO merged with the AFL in 1955, it did not even protest the inclusion of blatantly discriminatory railroad unions in the new organization.[40]

Although USWA files contain no complaints of discrimination from black workers at Pullman Standard's northern plants, both traditional employment practices and the racism of white workers stood in the way of expanded hiring of black workers. Management recruited new workers through references from current employees, and workers alerted friends and family as soon as jobs were posted. Because white workers predominated in the northern plants and few had black friends, white men and women had the best opportunity to get jobs at these Pullman plants. Even as Chicago's black ghetto expanded southward toward the Pullman Car Works in the 1950s, the percentage of African Americans in the workforce did not increase substantially. The racial balance at International Harvester's West Pullman and Wisconsin Steel plants remained relatively stable too. Some Pullman-area residents—primarily the children of European immigrants—expressed disdain for African Americans and a sense of white superiority. They believed that European immigrants had created U.S. prosperity by working hard to get ahead, and they saw black Americans as inferior and lazy. In order to halt the expansion of the black ghetto, they met African Americans who moved into the area with verbal and physical threats. These culminated in a full-scale race riot in 1953 in which white mobs attacked blacks. Not surprisingly, white workers at Pullman Standard and International Harvester plants were unlikely to encourage the hiring of more black workers, who might wish to live near their place of employment.[41]

The white racism that worked through informal mechanisms in northern Pullman Standard plants was enshrined in institutional arrangements in the South. Pullman's freight car–building plant in Bessemer, Alabama—the Pittsburgh of the South and such a bastion of white supremacy that the 1963 civil rights demonstrations made barely a dent in racial segregation and discrimination—had segregated bathhouses, toilets, time clocks, and jobs. Riveters, for instance, were all white at Bessemer, while the buckers who helped them were black. To maintain that distinction white riveters insisted that buckers never touch a rivet gun, although this would have facilitated putting in the four rivets that were driven from the inside out in each corner cap of a box car. At Pullman Standard plants in the North, the riveter, who stood on the outside of the car, simply handed the gun to the bucker, who stood on the inside and drove in these rivets. At Bessemer the riveter had to climb into the car and the bucker out, so that only a white man drove rivets. The company allowed this inefficiency and maintained segregated physical facilities in deference to the prejudices of its white workers.[42]

Almost half the Bessemer workers were black, but white workers controlled the union local and kept black workers from exercising their seniority rights to gain access to the better jobs that white workers wanted. Indeed, as white workers gained power through unionization in the 1940s, they may well have increased the extent of discrimination and job segregation at the plant. By the early 1960s the grievance committee was not even processing black workers' complaints, and the USWA district representative did nothing to rectify the situation. As the civil rights movement gained momentum, black workers at Bessemer wrote to USWA president David McDonald, threatening to sue the union for unfair labor practices.[43]

Black workers found, as they had since World War II, that only the federal government could help them. When implementation of the 1964 Civil Rights Act began, the Office of Federal Contract Compliance tar-

geted plants like Pullman Standard's Bessemer. In 1967 the agency insisted that segregation of both jobs and physical facilities had to end. The
plant had sixteen classes of jobs, but few black workers held positions in
the top classes, and none could be found in the top two. Opening new
jobs to black men proved difficult because the union stood in the way.
Management found few black workers who already had skills like tool
and pattern making, but the USWA local resisted instituting "super-
seniority" to allow black workers with less seniority to skip over white
workers with more and train for the better jobs.[44]

Pullman Standard officials found integrating physical facilities somewhat easier to accomplish, but white workers resisted these changes too,
and managers feared a race riot if they did not proceed carefully. To end
segregation at the eight lines for time clocks, they did more than simply
assign people to mixed lines. Because the time-clock area was cramped,
management feared the men would fight if inadvertent pushing occurred.
Rearranging the space solved that problem, and only a few minor incidents
occurred. Nevertheless, white workers did not accommodate changes easily. When the company eliminated separate toilet facilities, the USWA
local petitioned to have venereal disease tests given weekly, because
white workers believed that black workers carried disease. Management
refused and sought to educate white workers by circulating government
pamphlets that explained that venereal diseases could not be acquired from
toilet seats. Then, when the company built new bathhouses and assigned
workers to them at random, white workers refused to use the facilities,
preferring to go home sweaty and dirty rather than clean up alongside
black workers. Bessemer's white workers continued their boycott of the
bathhouses for years.[45]

Ironically, in the 1960s Pullman Standard's black workers found more
support in their fight for upgrading at the Michigan City plant, from their
local of the AFL's Brotherhood of Railway Carmen (BRCA). The union's
long adherence to white supremacy had ended only in 1966 when it added a nondiscrimination clause to its contract, but local conditions produced greater support for black workers than the union's racist history
might have predicted. By the mid-1960s almost 40 percent of the plant's
workers were black, and they included men who were active in local civil
rights organizations and in the black power movement. They protested
inequities and found support from the white leader of their BRCA local,
James Kintzele. He promised, for instance, to honor a picket line at the
plant that a branch of the National Association for the Advancement of
Colored People threatened to establish to help one black worker fight his
claim to upgrading. The next year the union local grieved the discharge

of a black power advocate and had his punishment reduced to a five-day suspension. Managers charged that Kintzele was supporting black workers "as part of his rebellion against the firm posture which we have taken in our dealings with him."[46] Whether this was the case or not, the irony of an AFL union's being more supportive of black workers than a CIO union reveals the decline of the CIO's commitment to racial equity.

The final test for the USWA, like that for the AFL's railroad unions, was plant closings. The virtual demise of U.S. passenger rail service by the early 1970s destroyed the market for passenger railcars in the United States. Producers in countries that had extensive rail service met world demand. Although the federal government provided increased subsidies for mass transit after the oil crisis of 1973, neither Pullman Standard nor other U.S. car builders benefited sufficiently to survive. Aerospace manufacturers acquired some of the contracts, but even more detrimental was that each transit system demanded individually designed cars. Pullman Standard produced its profits by making cars of its own design with only slight modifications for individual buyers. Without this basic standardization, profit margins were small or nonexistent. When demand for freight cars declined too, Pullman Standard closed its remaining plants in 1981, and Pullman Inc. abandoned railcar building entirely.[47]

When Pullman Standard workers faced plant closings, they looked to the Steelworkers' union for help but found less support than the sleeping-car workers received from AFL railroad unions. Perhaps because the railroad unions faced the issue of downsizing so much earlier, they had instituted a plan, the Washington Agreement, to cushion change for workers. It no doubt helped that they negotiated this agreement during the New Deal, when concern for workers and unemployment stood at an all-time high. The USWA developed its contracts during the post–World War II period of unprecedented prosperity and as a consequence had not focused on permanent job loss. In the late 1950s, when union leaders began to recognize that threat, public opinion had shifted radically. Few Americans seemed to believe that "Big Labor" needed any help, and Congress devoted itself to reining in and punishing unions. Although the USWA contract promised some Pullman workers severance pay, benefits did not compare to those mandated by the Washington Agreement. Under the USWA plan workers with at least three years of service received four to eight weeks' pay. Even so, when the Chicago plant closed, only seven hundred of its two thousand workers actually qualified for severance pay. Production had been at such a low level and so sporadic for at least a decade that many workers found jobs at Pullman only intermittently and never accumulated three years of service. Like earlier generations of car builders, they had to find work at other plants in the area to survive. Although the benefit level was low, Pullman Standard resisted paying its workers anything. The USWA had to pursue the company through the National Labor Relations Board and the courts to obtain severance pay for those who qualified.[48]

The closing of the manufacturing plants in 1981 proved especially devastating for the last Pullman workers. Unlike those who suffered from plant closings in the 1950s, these workers found few job opportunities that required their skills or would pay them even half of what they had been earning. In the 1970s the basic industries of the United States collapsed and layoffs soared. In the southeast Chicago–northwest Indiana manufacturing area, the unemployment rate hit 14 to 16 percent. Workers at Pullman Standard's plant in Chicago did not accept their lot meekly but launched a "save-our-jobs" campaign through their union local. As Ray Robles, secretary of the Eugene Debs Local, stated: "If they think the membership is gonna just sit there and lay down and die and give up virtually everything the labor struggle has always done they gotta be crazy."[49]

Pullman workers tried to interest other companies in buying the plant and resuming production. They also worked with other steelworkers to back plant-closing legislation designed to limit the power of U.S. corporations to close or move plants without considering the future of their workers or local communities. As John Bowman, president of the Pullman local, asked state legislators who were considering the plan, "Can we just tell the country and the communities to go to hell and just close it down and make a ghost town out of it?"[50] The answer for politicians was yes, but USWA national and regional leaders were not much more supportive of this grassroots initiative. Union officials declined to make any demand that boldly challenged the power of U.S. capitalists and that the latter were sure to fight with every weapon they had. To pass plant-closing legislation would have necessitated more positive political action and a huge investment in community organizing. The USWA hierarchy seemed to see their role as stewards, protecting the money in the union pension fund and limiting expenditures for "lost causes." Pullman workers ended up fighting the USWA itself, when the district leadership took over the administration of Local 1834 in order to stop its expenditures on the campaign.

In the closing decades of the twentieth century, Pullman workers found, as they had in the past, that trade unions, though useful, were not adequate to the task of ensuring economic justice. Pullman manufacturing workers, white and black, male and female, stood together in the "save-our-jobs" campaign, but they could not defeat either mobile capital or an ossified union bureaucracy. Pullman workers had never acqui-esced to either corporate or national union leaders, but they had not dis-covered a way to translate their militancy into a wider movement that could reshape the U.S. economic system in accordance with their stan-dards of fairness. Since the late nineteenth century, only the state had ever ensured workers' jobs or even their voice on the shop floor, but dur-ing the presidency of Ronald Reagan neither Pullman workers nor the labor movement as a whole found any effective way to exert influence in the political process.

Pullman workers, like other U.S. workers, had failed to realize what the 1894 Pullman strike had taught Eugene Debs: that they needed po-litical power. With no workers' party to bring issues like plant closings into the political arena or even a Democratic Party strongly committed to labor, workers were unable to protect themselves during the deindus-trialization of the United States. When that process began in the 1950s with the railroad industry, the regulatory bodies and the union-industry agreements created in the 1930s helped cushion the blow for workers in Pullman's sleeping-car service. But as deindustrialization hit its peak in the 1980s and the last Pullman workers faced plant closings, business set the terms of any discussion of economic matters among both Republi-cans and Democrats. The New Deal era was over.

Workers' ineffective political voice was a product of the same divi-sions that wracked their unions. From the 1880s on, Pullman's men and women, like most Americans, had never struggled together across craft, industry, and racial lines. Over the years they joined many different or-ganizations that seemed to provide vehicles for their struggle against the company, but all were characterized by their relatively narrow focus. Such unions, even when united in the AFL-CIO, were not suitable vehicles for realizing racial, gender, or economic justice in the late twentieth centu-ry. In the postwar era U.S. capitalists expanded their control over gov-ernment policy and popular consciousness, in part, because unions did not embrace such tasks. By 1981 racial and gender prejudices and stereo-types showed signs of diminishing, and, if there had been a future, Pull-man workers might have built a more inclusive union. Their struggle against one particular employer was over, although the issues of work-place democracy and racial and gender equity remain for U.S. workers.

Conclusion

What, then, can we conclude from a century of labor struggle at Pullman? First, of course, there was not *one* struggle but many. The Pullman strike of 1894 did not involve all Pullman workers, nor did any other movement embrace the entire workforce. The lack of unity reflected the origins of workers' struggles. Workers first responded to exploitation through self-organization, as individuals joining together to decide among themselves on a course of action. They only secondarily reached out to national organizations or joined larger movements. The local, democratic character of their response meant that Pullman workers first coalesced in groups defined by the criteria that the corporation had for hiring them: possession of a particular skill, willingness to work for low wages, race, and gender. In the end a divided workforce produced unions that were relatively narrow in scope too. They could deliver decent jobs but not power or economic justice. Even at their height in the late 1940s and 1950s, U.S. unions lacked a common vision, and the American Federation of Labor (AFL) and the Congress of Industrial Organizations (CIO) were locked in bitter combat. They could not meet challenges, like protecting workers adequately from economic decline, that required a broader perspective.

Pullman workers affected more than their own lives through their century of activism; they played an important role in the development of the U.S. labor movement. The corporation's national scope and its pivotal position at the intersection of the railroad industry and heavy manufacturing created the possibility for its workers' struggles to have wider significance. Pullman workers were everywhere, and their diversity ensured that some would be attracted to and participate in almost any labor union or movement. Their rejection of George Pullman's two innovations for creating inexpensive and docile workers—building a model town and defining the job of porter by race and gender—had ramifications far beyond the company itself. The former produced the 1894 Pullman strike, whose failure weakened the union movement as a whole, and industrial unions in particular, for decades. The latter created the seedbed of the movement for black economic equality that transformed the federal government into an adversary of racism and challenged the labor movement to do the same.

Because different groups of Pullman workers struggled separately, their histories were distinctive. By the 1890s most white craftsmen were no longer artisans but skilled workers enmeshed in large-scale industries like Pullman. Although ethnically diverse, they shared a craft perspective and a commitment to an ideal of independence that they expressed by asserting their standards for just labor and seeking to control their work. Pullman car builders and repair shop workers struck in 1894 as a consequence of that ideal, and they used the American Railway Union (ARU) as a vehicle for their struggle. The ARU was an industrial union, but within it workers grouped together by craft. Thus when the ARU was destroyed, it is not surprising that Pullman and railroad craftsmen looked to craft unions. Over the decades Pullman repair shop workers continued to identify themselves by craft, and they struggled until they attained the goal of nineteenth-century railroad workers—a system federation of craft unions. But by the time they were victorious, their demand for job control had been divorced from an ideal of independence. Security within the company was their primary concern, and their unions reflected that in refusing to risk a strike, even when the company denied standard benefits to displaced workers. The proud strikers of the 1890s had given way to the older, cautious men of the 1950s.

Changing technology redirected the focus of Pullman manufacturing workers from the railroad industry to the steel industry, and eventually they joined another industrial union—the United Steelworkers of America. But craft, skill, and ethnic divisions ensured that building unity again would take decades. The appeal of industrial unions like the Steelworkers reflected the spread of a new method of labor control and recruitment, internal labor markets. Young men with no craft skills were incorporated into industrial America through job structures that allowed them to move from unskilled to skilled positions. Throughout the United States men learned "skills" on the job. Pullman instituted internal labor markets in the context of an extreme division of labor that undercut the crafts. In the 1930s, when men whose skills had been developed outside the factory were reduced to a small minority of the workforce, an industrial union could once more appeal to Pullman manufacturing workers, promising them the job security that they desired but had never found as Pullman employees.

If the trajectory of white men's struggles at Pullman was from militant assertion of independence to security consciousness, black men had a quite different experience. George Pullman was the first major northern employer to hire large numbers of black men, and initially they were grateful to be employed. In the 1920s the company gave black men a more unusual opportunity, to become skilled railroad repair shop workers. But by the mid-twentieth century black men were the corporation's most militant workers. They had learned that exploitation and discrimination were products not only of the personal employment relations of the South but also of bureaucratic structures that otherwise promised "fairness." They forced both U.S. unions and the federal government to confront institutionalized racism. During World War II Pullman porters led the movement that produced the first federal intervention against discrimination in employment. Less well known is the influence of Pullman's black workers on U.S. unions. During World War I Pullman's car cleaners forced the Brotherhood of Railway Carmen to admit black members, if only in segregated locals. In the 1930s and 1940s the Brotherhood of Sleeping Car Porters continued the attack on institutionalized racism in AFL railroad unions with a series of organizing drives among black workers that challenged the control of those white-dominated unions.

But if working for Pullman made black workers activists, it did not lead them all to choose the same vehicles for struggle. By racially integrating some jobs but not others, the corporation created a new division between black workers in the twentieth century. Those like the porters, who worked in segregated jobs, found black unions the appropriate form for organizing. But those like the repair shop workers, who labored in racially integrated jobs, had to find a way to build integrated unions. This division led to a bitter battle among black workers during the 1940s in which Pullman workers played a key role. This battle undercut the struggle for black equality and was an important component of the debilitating war between the AFL and the CIO.

Unlike the opportunities offered to black men, those that women found at Pullman were not exceptional but followed a common pattern in railroading and heavy industry. Throughout the industrial period the primacy of women's domestic role shaped their paid employment. In general, neither black men nor white men welcomed women into their workplaces or their unions. They shared with management a belief that woman's place was in the home and that only certain jobs were appropriate for women. In a "male" sphere like railroading this meant that initially women could do little except sew and clean. With the widespread feminization of office work in the twentieth century, Pullman and the railroads began to hire more women for clerical work. If women's jobs at Pullman were not exceptional, neither were their struggles. Like most U.S. women who worked in male-dominated settings, they unionized but always in concert with and subordinate to their male co-workers. Furthermore, race divided Pullman women as well as its men, because employers always considered race and gender simultaneously when they defined criteria for hiring. The new opportunities for white women in the office were simultaneously a denial of access to both black women and men.

Pullman workers' struggles originated in their reactions to policies that were common in U.S. businesses. The corporation's primary goal was increased profit and pleasing stockholders, and officials insisted that they could attain their profit goals only if they had a free hand to manage labor without "interference" from either unions or government. Pullman retained that freedom for many decades, because it pursued a labor management policy that was flexible and complex, tailored to each fragment of its workers. Management followed no single method but rather constantly reshuffled and mixed strategies as seemed useful in response to workers' activism. Yet the experience of the Pullman Company in the 1920s highlights how difficult it was for even the most savvy employer to re-establish control if workers had experienced even a short period of union contracts. Only by adding a new racial strategy—integrating repair shop workforces—to its mix of bureaucratic structures and antiunion tactics and by tailoring that strategy to regional differences was the company successful.

The possibilities presented by racial diversity were always an important part of management calculations for controlling the workplace and keeping wages low. In the nineteenth century this took the form of simultaneously segregating and segmenting jobs. Although the prejudice that African Americans made good servants continued to shape company policy, labor scarcity and militancy in the World War I era encouraged deviations from past practice. The corporation now integrated some jobs, while it maintained the hierarchy of races by discriminating in its offices as well as in skilled jobs in its manufacturing plants.

The struggles of Pullman workers also reveal how important the state was to the success or failure of unions. In comparison with European nations the central government of the United States was weak, but its influence was not negligible. In the late nineteenth and early twentieth centuries, the federal government more often supported employers than workers. The use of federal troops and an injunction to smash the 1894 Pullman strike was only the most extreme manifestation of what government could do when under the sway of big business. But the absence of any legislation to address the consequences of plant closings when the United States deindustrialized also demonstrates the importance of what the state does not do. Federal efforts to ensure racial or gender equity during the two world wars further underline the influence of even a "weak" state. During World War I the government was more supportive of gender equity than racial equity, while the reverse was true in the second war. In both instances the combination of action and inaction shaped the opportunities open to women and minorities and had a lasting effect on the composition of the workforce.

The federal government found itself involved in labor relations during wartime as a consequence of its determination to promote efficient production of war materiel. Workers could make gains in this situation because they could not be replaced easily. Yet the degree of federal involvement in labor relations varied considerably, and so did the results for workers. When the U.S. Railroad Administration controlled the railroads during World War I, many workers in the sleeping-car service unionized, and all made significant gains. In contrast, Pullman manufacturing workers neither unionized nor made much headway against the company, because they were not subject to government control. Furthermore, state action could encourage a shift in workers' perspective from the local to the national level. The experience of working under national contracts for several years transformed the allegiance of railroad repair shop workers from their local communities to their national unions.

Yet in wartime the state was less prolabor than it was concerned to keep workers happy on the job. The only time that the federal government could be called prolabor was during the New Deal, but its support for unionization did not bring instantaneous results. Union victories came slowly as the AFL and the CIO fought each other for members, and especially as race became a major factor in their contests. The extent of racism among white workers meant that even the most well-intentioned unions had difficulty maintaining a commitment to racial equity. When the federal government began a war on racism in World War II, the inability of most unions to live up to the mandate of nondiscrimination highlighted their narrowness and lack of vision. In the 1960s, when the federal government committed itself to ensuring fairness for all individuals, regardless of race or gender, most old unions could not embrace these goals and became increasingly irrelevant.

A century of struggle by Pullman workers produced a unionized workforce but not a powerful one because it was so divided. Now the struggle for Pullman workers is over, not because they reached their goals but because their jobs disappeared. The question for U.S. workers remains how to build a movement for economic and social justice.

Appendix: The Pullman
Repair Shop Databases

Included in the Pullman Company Archive at the Newberry Library are thousands of employee service records with detailed job histories. Most of these records belong to workers hired after 1904, when the company established a centralized personnel department with standardized procedures. With the assistance of grants from the National Endowment for the Humanities and the National Science Foundation, Janice Reiff and I created databases of job histories and demographic information from these service records for workers at three Pullman repair shops—Calumet, Richmond, and Wilmington.

Because the employee service records are not complete, we began constructing samples of workers in each repair shop from the microfilmed payroll records that are also in the Pullman Archive and that we presumed to include the entire workforce. To ensure that we included workers from as much of the twentieth century as possible, we chose one payroll date at random from each five-year period from 1904 to 1969. This provided us with twelve complete payrolls for the Calumet Repair Shop, ten for the Wilmington shop, and nine for the Richmond shop. The payrolls chosen are for the years 1906, 1911, 1917, 1921, 1926, 1931, 1936, 1943, 1948, 1952, 1958, and 1965. Wilmington does not have 1958 or 1965 payrolls, because it was closed; similarly, Richmond does not have 1906, 1958, or 1965 payrolls. The databases created from the payrolls include all information given, the most important of which are job titles, wage rates or earnings, and hours worked. The data are not strictly comparable across time, but each payroll provides much the same information. I used these databases for the cross-sectional analysis of the structure of jobs at each repair shop.

The payrolls chosen became the basis for creating the databases of individuals' job histories. The records for Calumet shop workers are in the form of complete packets, including employee service cards with demographic information and job histories, medical records, letters and memos, and a wide variety of other material. Our strategy for constructing the Calumet database was to select names randomly from each payroll until we amassed the packets of two hundred people. Because records from the earliest years are the least complete, we found many fewer than we wanted for those years. Because those who remained at the shop for many years would show up on more than one payroll, long-term employees had a better chance to be in the samples. We also realized that in order to have samples of black and women workers that were large enough for meaningful analysis, we would have to oversample black men and all women. The analyses in this book are based on a Calumet sample that includes 2,063 individual workers, of whom 465 women and 208 black men come from oversampling.

Creating the Wilmington and Richmond databases involved a somewhat different process. The Newberry collection does not include the complete employee packets for these shops. Job histories are available, however, in the form of the employee service record cards for each shop. The Pullman Archive also includes another set of "general file cards," which include names, some demographic data, and job histories for individual workers. These cards were generated by the central office and do not include records for precisely the same workers as the collections of employee service records from each shop. The archive also has social security application forms for Pullman workers that provide detailed demographic data. The database for Wilmington was constructed from the combined resources of the employee service record cards, the general file cards, and the social security application forms for workers identified from the payrolls. The Wilmington sample includes 986 workers for whom there is both demographic data and job histories. We followed the same process for the Richmond shop, where the existence of the general file cards was critical to the construction of the sample, because employee service record cards were extant only for those with names beginning with the letters F through Z. The Richmond sample contains 747 workers for whom we found both demographic data and job histories.

The relative accuracy of the samples in reflecting the underlying structure of employment at the repair shops is good, especially after 1921. I tested the accuracy of the samples by comparing the attributes of workers employed in a shop during a specific year with those listed on the payroll for that year. In the case of the Calumet shop, the comparison uses those in the initial sample only, not oversampled black men or women. Not all the workers in the group for any year would have been on the specific payroll chosen for that year, but they had started at the shop before or during that year and left during or after that year. Their skill level for the year in question was derived from their job histories. Some workers appear on multiple payrolls and in multiple year-based samples.

As the ratios in table A1 show, by 1921 the number of workers in the Calumet sample for any year is a significant proportion (between one-third and three-quarters) of the total number of employees on the sample payroll. This

Table A1. Calumet Sample at Payroll Years

	Length of Cumulative Service				Sample	Payroll	
Year	Mean	Median	Min.	Max.	Size	Size	Ratio
1906	28.0	28.9	5.7	54.7	113	1,005	11.2
1911	27.0	27.5	5.6	54.7	208	1,263	16.5
1917	26.3	27.8	0.1	54.7	332	1,219	27.2
1921	26.1	28.0	0.1	54.7	377	1,005	37.5
1926	27.6	29.5	0.1	55.2	586	1,323	44.3
1931	28.4	29.9	0.4	55.2	660	1,021	64.6
1936	25.2	27.6	0.1	55.2	810	2,244	36.1
1943	28.7	29.5	0.1	54.7	655	1,072	61.1
1948	28.5	29.5	0.1	54.7	614	942	65.2
1952	27.7	29.1	0.1	54.7	569	1,014	56.1
1958	28.7	29.1	5.5	53.2	416	207	201.0
1965	25.5	25.9	0.1	51.9	320	438	73.1

is not the case for the earliest years, and thus conclusions must be most tentative before World War I. The ratio generally increases over time, as we would expect more recent employees' records to be extant. Furthermore, anomalies also occur in expected directions. The 1936 air-conditioning project produced fewer records and workers with shorter periods of cumulative service. The 1958 payroll from a layoff period was only one-half the size of the sample, and the sample includes only long-term employees, who would have had the seniority to be kept on during a period of extensive layoffs. By 1965 the ratio is highest, but cumulative service is again decreasing with the coming closing of the shop. The sample includes employees who worked as little as a few days and as long as fifty-five years. Before 1917 no short-term employees are included in the sample, again suggesting caution in drawing conclusions. Otherwise, the median of cumulative service is close to the mean, so that the sample has a normal distribution in terms of length of service.

Table A2 compares the distribution of workers in jobs of different skill and wage levels on each payroll to that of the workers in the Calumet sample for that year. At every year until 1965 the sample overrepresents skilled workers. Although the closest fit between sample and payroll skill distributions occurs in 1965, as we would expect from the ratio (table A1), all are reasonably close. Helpers are underrepresented in the samples in 1906, 1911, and 1921 to a level that may significantly affect conclusions drawn about helpers in those years. The same is true for the unskilled in 1911, 1917, and 1921. Thus I am careful about drawing conclusions about helpers or the unskilled at Calumet before 1926. On the other hand, the number of skilled workers is sufficient to draw conclusions from the sample with the caveat that these were primarily the mechanics who survived the seniority system, which was not union controlled.

Table A2 suggests the general accuracy of the Calumet sample in other ways. Supervisory employees are consistently underrepresented in the sam-

Table A2. Percentage of Calumet Shop Workers in Jobs with Different Skill and Wage Levels

	Skilled	Helper	Unskilled	Apprentice	"Women"	Supervisor	Clerical
1906							
Sample	77.7	9.7	5.8	1.9	1.9	2.9	0.0
Payroll	69.9	14.5	5.3	1.9	1.7	4.7	1.9
1911							
Sample	82.2	9.4	2.6	0.0	3.1	2.1	0.5
Payroll	74.6	15.7	4.4	0.2	1.7	3.3	0.1
1917							
Sample	73.2	13.9	7.4	0.6	1.6	1.9	1.3
Payroll	60.9	16.9	12.5	0.0	1.5	5.1	3.1
1921							
Sample	76.7	9.8	5.3	0.3	1.7	4.2	2.0
Payroll	61.4	13.1	12.1	1.1	1.7	7.0	3.4
1926							
Sample	59.2	24.0	8.4	0.9	1.6	2.8	3.2
Payroll	53.4	26.0	8.1	0.5	1.1	5.5	5.2
1931							
Sample	64.3	19.2	7.6	0.8	1.4	2.8	4.0
Payroll	57.8	18.3	7.7	1.2	1.3	8.3	5.3
1936							
Sample	64.8	17.0	8.7	1.0	1.5	2.2	4.8
Payroll	58.5	22.7	6.8	2.1	0.8	5.2	3.9
1943							
Sample	66.7	14.9	6.9	0.5	1.6	2.7	6.8
Payroll	61.2	13.1	8.4	0.5	1.2	8.8	6.8
1948							
Sample	70.0	9.4	6.0	0.7	1.7	4.4	7.9
Payroll	63.2	11.6	8.2	0.6	1.1	9.7	5.6
1952							
Sample	71.1	7.6	6.9	0.9	1.4	4.3	7.8
Payroll	66.2	10.1	7.7	0.7	1.0	6.6	7.9
1958							
Sample	70.0	7.4	5.7	0.5	1.2	5.7	9.4
Payroll[a]							
1965							
Sample	69.6	7.0	5.4	0.3	0.6	6.1	11.8
Payroll	71.1	4.6	6.4	0.0	0.7	6.9	10.3

a. The payroll database for 1958 includes names and pay amounts but no occupational designations.

ple because the service records of upper management were not included with the shop records. The numbers of apprentices and women in "women's jobs" were always small, as reflected in the sample. The number of clerical workers in the repair shop increased steadily across time; the sample reflects this and is quite accurate in percentage terms by 1931.

A similar analysis of the Richmond sample also suggests that it is generally representative of the structure of the shop over time (tables A3 and A4),

Table A3. Richmond Sample at Payroll Years

Year	Length of Cumulative Service				Sample Size	Payroll Size	Ratio
	Mean	Median	Min.	Max.			
1911	17.8	12.5	0.3	47.0	81	640	12.7
1917	16.1	11.2	0.1	47.0	145	450	32.2
1921	19.2	19.5	0.7	47.0	165	341	48.4
1926	21.0	20.1	0.1	47.0	294	407	72.2
1931	22.3	21.5	0.4	47.0	295	418	70.6
1936	19.8	20.0	0.2	47.0	329	641	51.3
1943	22.3	21.7	0.1	47.0	269	355	75.8
1948	19.7	16.5	0.1	47.0	303	443	68.4
1952	19.3	14.2	0.1	47.0	269	448	60.0

Table A4. Percentage of Richmond Shop Workers in Jobs with Different Skill and Wage Levels

	Skilled	Helper	Unskilled	Apprentice	"Women"	Supervisor	Clerical
1911							
Sample	65.8	13.9	5.1	3.8	1.3	6.3	3.8
Payroll	68.2	9.4	13.1	0.3	2.4	4.9	1.6
1917							
Sample	58.3	23.6	6.3	2.8	1.4	5.6	2.1
Payroll	57.4	18.5	9.2	1.1	1.8	7.7	4.3
1921							
Sample	59.5	16.0	7.4	4.3	3.1	6.1	3.7
Payroll	64.1	9.2	8.6	2.1	2.1	11.0	3.0
1926							
Sample	51.4	19.5	11.6	3.4	2.4	4.1	7.5
Payroll	53.3	16.2	7.9	2.9	1.5	10.3	7.9
1931							
Sample	54.3	18.8	9.6	2.4	3.1	5.8	6.1
Payroll	52.4	22.1	5.5	3.1	1.7	10.6	4.6
1936							
Sample	50.3	24.1	13.1	1.2	2.7	4.6	4.0
Payroll	51.6	30.6	6.7	0.0	0.6	7.3	3.1
1943							
Sample	45.7	16.0	20.8	1.5	3.0	6.3	6.7
Payroll	55.8	14.2	10.5	0.0	2.3	11.6	5.7
1948							
Sample	39.6	25.4	19.8	1.3	2.3	5.9	5.6
Payroll	58.6	16.3	9.1	0.0	1.8	8.6	5.7
1952							
Sample	65.4	14.1	7.4	0.0	2.2	6.7	4.1
Payroll	65.2	14.4	6.3	0.0	2.0	8.3	4.0

although some areas are of concern. First, the number of unskilled workers in 1911 is so small that no conclusions about them should be drawn from the sample. Second, the proportion of skilled workers is smaller than expected in 1943 and 1948. This may reflect the tight labor market in Richmond, where skilled workers left the shop rapidly for better opportunities elsewhere. The skilled would be underrepresented because the records of short-term workers were less likely to be kept than those of long-term employees. The Wilmington sample provides the best fit in comparison with payrolls for helpers and skilled workers, but unskilled workers are consistently underrepresented (tables A5 and A6). Their numbers are small enough to make analyses before 1926 problematic.

Table A5. Wilmington Sample at Payroll Years

	Length of Cumulative Service				Sample Size	Payroll Size	Ratio
Year	Mean	Median	Min.	Max.			
1906	27.9	29.1	1.9	53.6	210	882	23.8
1911	24.4	24.1	0.5	53.6	289	1,098	26.3
1917	21.3	19.3	0.1	53.6	393	819	48.0
1921	19.8	16.5	0.1	53.6	473	539	87.8
1926	23.2	24.6	0.3	53.6	486	637	76.3
1931	24.1	25.1	0.2	53.6	473	541	87.4
1936	25.2	25.8	0.2	53.6	409	444	92.1
1943	23.9	24.5	0.1	53.6	400	463	86.4
1948	22.9	24.2	0.3	52.1	370	494	74.9
1952	23.5	25.3	0.4	51.3	286	417	68.6

Table A6. Percentage of Wilmington Shop Workers in Jobs with Different Skill and Wage Levels

	Skilled	Helper	Unskilled	Apprentice	"Women"	Supervisor	Clerical
1906							
Sample	68.1	11.0	4.3	3.8	0.0	8.1	4.8
Payroll	63.0	14.0	7.5	4.2	1.1	6.4	3.8
1911							
Sample	71.9	12.5	3.1	1.7	0.3	6.6	3.8
Payroll	64.1	17.3	6.1	3.0	1.0	5.6	2.9
1917							
Sample	77.4	10.0	3.1	0.5	0.8	4.1	4.1
Payroll	64.4	18.1	5.3	0.1	1.7	7.5	2.9
1921							
Sample	67.1	14.0	3.8	2.3	0.8	4.5	7.4
Payroll	57.1	16.0	5.1	3.2	1.5	11.1	6.0

Table A6. (continued)

	Skilled	Helper	Unskilled	Apprentice	"Women"	Supervisor	Clerical
1926							
Sample	43.3	38.3	4.1	1.7	0.4	4.3	7.9
Payroll	39.0	33.6	8.4	2.4	0.3	8.5	7.7
1931							
Sample	43.6	36.2	5.3	1.9	0.4	5.1	7.4
Payroll	38.3	38.5	6.3	2.4	0.6	8.0	5.9
1936							
Sample	54.3	25.9	6.9	2.2	0.5	4.7	5.4
Payroll	53.6	24.2	7.9	1.8	0.7	6.8	5.0
1943							
Sample	56.3	22.9	6.5	0.8	2.0	4.8	6.8
Payroll	52.1	23.4	7.6	0.9	1.7	8.0	6.3
1948							
Sample	57.9	21.3	7.9	0.0	2.2	5.7	4.9
Payroll	49.9	24.4	9.4	0.2	1.6	9.0	5.5
1952							
Sample	60.1	20.6	7.3	0.3	1.7	5.2	4.5
Payroll	57.6	20.6	8.2	0.7	1.5	6.8	4.6

NOTES

Abbreviations

AFLRED   American Federation of Labor–Railroad Employes Department, Records 1917–1970, Cornell University

BSCP   Brotherhood of Sleeping Car Porters Collection, Chicago Historical Society

FEPC   Fair Employment Practices Committee, Closed Cases, National Archives, Region VI, Chicago, RG 228-70

UTSE   Papers of the United Transport Service Employees of America in Congress of Industrial Organizations, Secretary/Treasurer's Collection, Archives of Labor and Urban Affairs, Reuther Library, Wayne State University, Detroit

PANL   Pullman Company Archive, Newberry Library, Chicago

PP   Pullman Company Payrolls, microfilm, PANL

PS   Pullman Scrapbooks, microfilm, PANL

USRA   U.S. Railroad Administration, Records of the Division of Labor, National Archives, College Park, Md., RG 14

USWA   United Steelworkers of America Collection, Chicago Historical Society

The numbers assigned to documents in the Pullman Company Archive, such as 03/03/01, refer to record group, subgroup, and series. The company kept four series of scrapbooks of newspaper clippings: one on the town of Pullman ("Town"); one on the 1894 strike ("Strike"); and two of miscellaneous clippings ("A," kept by the secretary's office, and "B," kept by the vice president's). In the notes, a clipping designated as PS A26 is in the twenty-sixth scrapbook of the A series.

Introduction

1. Descriptions of the Pullman strike and boycott abound in everything from textbooks to monographs. The most detailed overview is Almont Lindsey, *The Pullman Strike* (Chicago: University of Chicago Press, 1942), but Lindsey does not place the strike in the larger history of Pullman workers and their attempts at unionization. Stanley Buder, *Pullman: An Experiment in Industrial Order and Community Planning, 1880–1930* (New York: Ox-

ford University Press, 1967), places the strike in the context of the model town but does not examine the railroad industry or its workers. Two important and much-republished contemporary sources are William H. Carwardine, *The Pullman Strike,* 4th ed. (Chicago: Charles H. Kerr, 1971), and the U.S. Strike Commission, *Report on the Chicago Strike of June–July 1894* (Washington, D.C.: Government Printing Office, 1895).

2. For interpretations of the 1890s as a turning point, see works as diverse as David Brody, *Workers in Industrial America: Essays on the Twentieth Century Struggle,* 2d ed. (New York: Oxford University Press, 1993); David Gordon, Richard Edwards, and Michael Reich, *Segmented Work, Divided Workers: The Historical Transformation of Labor in the United States* (New York: Cambridge University Press, 1982); and David Montgomery, *The Fall of the House of Labor: The Workplace, the State, and American Labor Activism, 1865–1925* (New York: Cambridge University Press, 1987). The essays in Richard Schneirov, Shelton Stromquist, and Nick Salvatore, eds., *The Pullman Strike and the Crisis of the 1890s: Essays on Labor and Politics* (Urbana: University of Illinois Press, 1999), approach the Pullman strike and the 1890s as a turning point from a variety of perspectives.

3. William H. Harris, *Keeping the Faith: A. Philip Randolph, Milton P. Webster, and the Brotherhood of Sleeping Car Porters, 1925–1937* (Urbana: University of Illinois Press, 1977), details the porters' struggle to organize but does not relate it to the struggles of other Pullman workers. Randolph's role in the labor movement and the civil rights movement are ably recounted in Jervis Anderson, *A. Philip Randolph: A Biographical Portrait* (New York: Harcourt Brace Jovanovich, 1972), and Paula Pfeffer, *A. Philip Randolph, Pioneer of the Civil Rights Movement* (Baton Rouge: Louisiana State University Press, 1990). For the role of Randolph and the union in the March on Washington Movement, see Herbert Garfinkel, *When Negroes March: The March on Washington Movement in the Organizational Politics for FEPC* (Glencoe, Ill.: Free Press, 1959), and Merl E. Reed, *Seedtime for the Modern Civil Rights Movement: The President's Committee on Fair Employment Practice, 1941–1946* (Baton Rouge: Louisiana State University Press, 1991).

4. Stuart Brandes, *American Welfare Capitalism, 1880–1940* (Chicago: University of Chicago Press, 1970); Harry Braverman, *Labor and Monopoly Capital* (New York: Monthly Review Press, 1974); Richard Edwards, *Contested Terrain: The Transformation of the Workplace in the Twentieth Century* (New York: Basic Books, 1979); Sanford M. Jacoby, *Employing Bureaucracy: Managers, Unions, and the Transformation of Work in American Industry, 1900–1945* (New York: Columbia University Press, 1985); Stephen Meyer, *The Five Dollar Day: Labor Management and Social Control in the Ford Motor Company, 1908–1921* (Albany: State University of New York Press, 1981); Daniel Nelson, *Managers and Workers: Origins of the New Factory System in the United States, 1880–1920* (Madison: University of Wisconsin Press, 1975); Robert Ozanne, *A Century of Labor-Management Relations at McCormick and International Harvester* (Madison: University of Wisconsin Press, 1967).

5. James R. Barrett, *Work and Community in the Jungle: Chicago's Pack-*

inghouse Workers, 1894–1922 (Urbana: University of Illinois Press, 1987); David Brody, *Steelworkers in America: The Nonunion Era* (New York: Harper and Row, 1960); Patricia Cooper, *Once a Cigar Maker: Men, Women, and Work Culture in American Cigar Factories, 1900–1919* (Urbana: University of Illinois Press, 1992); Rick Halpern, *Down on the Killing Floor: Black and White Workers in Chicago's Packinghouses, 1904–1954* (Urbana: University of Illinois Press, 1997).

6. Irving Bernstein, *Turbulent Years: A History of the American Worker, 1933–1941* (Boston: Houghton Mifflin, 1970); Brody, *Workers in Industrial America*, 135–56; Lizabeth Cohen, *Making a New Deal: Industrial Workers in Chicago, 1919–1939* (New York: Cambridge University Press, 1990); Walter Galenson, *The CIO Challenge to the AFL: A History of the American Labor Movement, 1935–1941* (Cambridge, Mass.: Harvard University Press, 1960); Gary Gerstle, *Working-Class Americanism: The Politics of Labor in a Textile City, 1914–1960* (New York: Cambridge University Press, 1989); Nelson Lichtenstein, *Labor's War at Home: The CIO in World War II* (New York: Cambridge University Press, 1982); Montgomery, *The Fall of the House of Labor*, chaps. 1–4; Shelton Stromquist, *A Generation of Boomers: The Pattern of Railroad Labor Conflict in Nineteenth-Century America* (Urbana: University of Illinois Press, 1987); Christopher Tomlins, "AFL Unions in the 1930s: Their Performance in Historical Perspective," *Journal of American History* 65 (1979): 1021–42.

7. William Forbath, *Law and the Shaping of the American Labor Movement* (Cambridge, Mass.: Harvard University Press, 1991); Victoria Hattam, *Labor Visions and State Power: The Origins of Business Unionism in the United States* (Princeton, N.J.: Princeton University Press, 1993); Jeffrey Haydu, *Making American Industry Safe for Democracy: Comparative Perspectives on the State and Employee Representation in the Era of World War I* (Urbana: University of Illinois Press, 1997); Joseph A. McCartin, *Labor's Great War: The Struggle for Industrial Democracy and the Origins of Modern American Labor Relations, 1912–1921* (Chapel Hill: University of North Carolina Press, 1997); Karen Orren, *Belated Feudalism: Labor, the Law, and Liberal Development in the United States* (New York: Cambridge University Press, 1991); Christopher L. Tomlins, *The State and the Unions: Labor Relations, Law, and the Organized Labor Movement in America, 1880–1960* (New York: Cambridge University Press, 1985).

8. Josef J. Barton, *Peasants and Strangers* (Cambridge, Mass.: Harvard University Press, 1975); John Bodnar, Roger Simon, and Michael Weber, *Lives of Their Own* (Urbana: University of Illinois Press, 1982); Brody, *Steelworkers in America*; Carolyn Golab, *Immigrant Destinations* (Philadelphia: Temple University Press, 1977); Susan Hirsch and Janice Reiff, "Job Segregation and the Replication of Local Social Hierarchies," in *Essays from the Lowell Conference on Industrial History, 1982 and 1983*, ed. Robert Weible (North Andover, Mass.: Museum of American Textile History, 1985); Stephen Thernstrom, *The Other Bostonians* (Cambridge, Mass.: Harvard University Press, 1973).

9. Karen Anderson, *Wartime Women: Sex Roles, Family Relations, and the*

Status of Women during World War II (Westport, Conn.: Greenwood Press, 1981); Harold M. Baron, "Racial Domination in Advanced Capitalism: A Theory of Nationalism and Divisions in the Labor Market," in *Labor Market Segmentation,* ed. Richard Edwards, Michael Reich, and David Gordon (Lexington, Mass: D. C. Heath, 1973); Val Burris and Amy Wharton, "Sex Segregation in the U.S. Labor Force," *Review of Radical Political Economy* 14 (1982): 43–56; Maurine Greenwald, *Women, War, and Work: The Impact of World War I on Women Workers in the United States* (Westport, Conn.: Greenwood Press, 1980); Susan E. Hirsch, "Rethinking the Sexual Division of Labor: Pullman Repair Shops, 1900–1969," *Radical History Review* 35 (1986): 26–48; Angel Kwolek-Folland, *Engendering Business: Men and Women in the Corporate Office, 1870–1930* (Baltimore, Md.: Johns Hopkins University Press, 1994); Ruth Milkman, *Gender at Work: The Dynamics of Job Segregation by Sex during World War II* (Urbana: University of Illinois Press, 1987); John Modell, *The Economics and Politics of Racial Accommodation* (Urbana: University of Illinois Press, 1977); John Modell and Edna Bonacich, *The Economic Basis of Ethnic Solidarity* (Berkeley: University of California Press, 1980); Elyce J. Rotella, *From Home to Office: U.S. Women at Work, 1870–1930* (Ann Arbor, Mich.: UMI Research Press, 1981); Sharon Hartman Strom, *Beyond the Typewriter* (Urbana: University of Illinois Press, 1992); William A. Sundstrom, "The Color Line: Racial Norms and Discrimination in Urban Labor Markets, 1910–1950," *Journal of Economic History* 54 (1994): 382–98; George von Furstenberg, Bennett Harrison, and Ann Horowitz, eds., *Patterns of Racial Discrimination* (Lexington, Mass.: D. C. Heath, 1974).

10. Edwards, Reich, and Gordon, *Labor Market Segmentation,* and Gordon, Edwards, and Reich, *Segmented Work, Divided Workers,* provide applications of the concept of labor market segmentation to historical research.

11. William A. Sundstrom links the racial division of labor in the railroad industry to the development of aspects of labor market segmentation in "Half a Career: Discrimination and Railroad Internal Labor Markets," *Industrial Relations* 29 (1990): 423–40.

12. James N. Baron and William T. Bielby, "Bringing the Firm Back in: Stratification, Segmentation and the Organization of Work," *American Sociological Review* 45 (1980): 737–65.

13. David Roediger, *The Wages of Whiteness: Race and the Making of the American Working Class* (New York: Verso, 1991), examines the role of white racism in the development of working-class consciousness in the nineteenth century. Several older works document the racial practices of U.S. unions: John H. Bracey, August Meier, and Elliott Rudwick, eds., *Black Workers and Organized Labor* (Belmont, Calif.: Wadsworth, 1971); Horace Cayton and George Mitchell, *Black Workers and the New Unions* (Chapel Hill: University of North Carolina Press, 1939); and Sterling Spero and Abram Harris, *The Black Worker: The Negro and the Labor Movement* (New York: Columbia University Press, 1931). On the railroad industry specifically, Eric Arnesen, "'Like Banquo's Ghost, It Will Not Down': The Race Question and the American Railroad Brotherhoods, 1880–1920," *American Historical Review* 99

(1994): 1601–33, examines the unsuccessful challenge to segregation in the railroad operating unions. Alice Kessler-Harris, *Out to Work: A History of Wage-Earning Women in the United States* (New York: Oxford University Press, 1982), provides an overview of women and the labor movement. Mary H. Blewett, *Men, Women, and Work: Class, Gender, and Protest in the New England Shoe Industry, 1780–1910* (Urbana: University of Illinois Press, 1988), and Elizabeth Faue, *Community of Suffering and Struggle: Women, Men, and the Labor Movement in Minneapolis, 1915–1945* (Chapel Hill: University of North Carolina Press, 1991), analyze the role of gender in the social division of labor and labor protest in specific industries and locales. Melinda Chateauvert, *Marching Together: Women of the Brotherhood of Sleeping Car Porters* (Urbana: University of Illinois Press, 1998), explores the gender dynamics within that union. Paul M. Taillon, "Culture, Politics, and the Making of Railroad Brotherhoods, 1863–1916" (Ph.D. diss., University of Wisconsin, 1997), opens the discussion of both gender and race in one sector of the railroad industry.

Chapter 1: Working for a Monopoly in Formation

1. The history of the company, Pullman's financial dealings, and the drive for monopoly are ably recounted in Stanley Buder, *Pullman: An Experiment in Industrial Order and Community Planning, 1880–1930* (New York: Oxford University Press, 1967), pt. 1; Greg LeRoy, "First Class Profits and Performances upon the Public: Pullman Porters, 1867–1912" (paper presented at the Third Annual Illinois State History Symposium, Springfield, 1982), 2–8; and Liston E. Leyendecker, *Palace Car Prince: A Biography of George Mortimer Pullman* (Niwot: University Press of Colorado, 1992). Leyendecker provides the best account of Pullman's irascible personality. For big businessmen as a group see Sanford M. Jacoby, "American Exceptionalism Revisited: The Importance of Management," in *Masters to Managers: Historical and Comparative Perspectives on American Employers*, ed. Sanford M. Jacoby (New York: Columbia University Press, 1991), chap. 8.

2. Even after the Pullman monopoly was secure, railroads were interested in recapturing their own service ("Six Railways to Use Own Sleeping Cars," *Chicago Examiner*, 29 Mar. 1909, PS A29).

3. Janice Reiff and Susan Hirsch, "Pullman and Its Public: Image and Aim in Making and Interpreting History," *Public Historian* 11 (1989): 100–101.

4. Pullman Palace Car Company, *Annual Statements, 1887–96*, in *Reports of Railroad Companies, 1881–1960*, Newberry Library; Almont Lindsey, *The Pullman Strike* (Chicago: University of Chicago Press, 1942), 27.

5. The best general discussion of the history of labor market segmentation is David Gordon, Richard Edwards, and Michael Reich, *Segmented Work, Divided Workers: The Historical Transformation of Labor in the United States* (New York: Cambridge University Press, 1982), chap. 5, 206–10. My analysis differs from theirs in identifying an instance of segmentation that

originated much before the 1920s and in arguing that, rather than channeling racial segregation, segmentation could be a consequence of it.

6. Management defended this company policy, sometimes described as "an ancient and honorable custom," for decades. See Chicago Commission on Race Relations, *The Negro in Chicago* (Chicago: University of Chicago Press, 1922), 391; LeRoy, "First Class Profits," 7–9, 31; William A. Sundstrom, "Half a Career: Discrimination and Railroad Internal Labor Markets," *Industrial Relations* 29 (1990): 424–27.

7. Walter Licht, *Working for the Railroad: The Organization of Work in the Nineteenth Century* (Princeton, N.J.: Princeton University Press, 1983), 21, 42, 65–69, 88–89, 223–25; Leon F. Litwack, *North of Slavery: The Negro in the Free States, 1790–1860* (Chicago: University of Chicago Press, 1961); David Roediger, *The Wages of Whiteness: Race and the Making of the American Working Class* (New York: Verso, 1991), pt. 2; Sterling Spero and Abram Harris, *The Black Worker: The Negro and the Labor Movement* (New York: Columbia University Press, 1931), 284–94; Robert S. Starobin, *Industrial Slavery in the Old South* (New York: Oxford University Press, 1970).

8. William H. Harris, *Keeping the Faith: A. Philip Randolph, Milton P. Webster, and the Brotherhood of Sleeping Car Porters, 1925–1937* (Urbana: University of Illinois Press, 1977), chap. 1.

9. Buder, *Pullman*, 191; LeRoy, "First Class Profits," 32–33; Reiff and Hirsch, "Pullman and Its Public," 102; Allan Spear, *Black Chicago: The Making of a Negro Ghetto, 1890–1920* (Chicago: University of Chicago Press, 1967), 98.

10. At first the company met the need for laundry services by contracting with commercial laundries, but over time it developed its own facilities in a half-dozen locations. As late as World War I the ethnic and racial variation in car cleaners and laundry workers held. Reports by investigators from the Women's Service Section of the U.S. Railroad Administration detail the racial, ethnic, and gender variation among Pullman yard workers (Box 97, Files 196–98 and 202, Women's Service Section, USRA), as do weekly reports of organizers for Pullman System Federation #122 (5478, Box 8, AFLRED). For regional differences in the ethnicity and race of service and unskilled workers, see David M. Katzman, *Seven Days a Week: Women and Domestic Service in Industrializing America* (New York: Oxford University Press, 1978), chap. 2; David Montgomery, *The Fall of the House of Labor: The Workplace, the State, and American Labor Activism, 1865–1925* (New York: Cambridge University Press, 1987), 74–81.

11. During the 1894 strike one newspaper reported that only two black families were living in the model town of Pullman, and the men were teamsters, not car builders ("Pullman Laid Bare," *Chicago Inter-Ocean*, 22 July 1894, PS Strike 6). None of the craftsmen hired before the 1920s at Pullman's Chicago (Calumet), Wilmington, or Richmond repair shops was black. See the appendix for discussion of the samples on which this and other conclusions about the shop workers are based.

12. Of shop workers hired before the 1894 strike, 82 percent of the skilled

workers at Wilmington were American born, whereas 72 percent of those in Chicago had been born abroad (Mrs. Duane Doty, *The Town of Pullman: Its Growth with Brief Accounts of Its Industries* [Pullman, Ill.: T. P. Struhsacker, 1893], 35). See Bruce C. Nelson, *Beyond the Martyrs: A Social History of Chicago's Anarchists, 1870–1900* (New Brunswick, N.J.: Rutgers University Press, 1988), chap. 1, for the composition of Chicago's workforce in the late nineteenth century. In 1890, 65 percent of men aged twenty-one and older in Wilmington were native-born whites, while 60 percent of men twenty-one and older in Chicago were foreign born. These figures are derived from U.S. Census Office, *Compendium of the Eleventh Census: 1890, Population*, pt. 1 (Washington, D.C.: Government Printing Office, 1892), 765.

13. Doty, *The Town of Pullman*, 57, 90, 111, 116, 130–31, 150; Susan E. Hirsch, "Rethinking the Sexual Division of Labor: Pullman Repair Shops, 1900–1969," *Radical History Review* 35 (1986): 34–36, 39–40; Douglas P. Hoover, "Women in Nineteenth-Century Pullman" (master's thesis, University of Arizona, 1988), 24. For analyses of the effect of gender roles on employment and wages in the Victorian era, see esp. Mary H. Blewett, *Men, Women, and Work: Class, Gender, and Protest in the New England Shoe Industry, 1780–1910* (Urbana: University of Illinois Press, 1988), chaps. 4 and 6, and Claudia Goldin, *Understanding the Gender Gap: An Economic History of American Women* (New York: Oxford University Press, 1990), chap. 3.

14. The discussion of the origin of bureaucratic forms of labor-management relations that follows relies on Alfred D. Chandler, *The Visible Hand: The Managerial Revolution in American Business* (Cambridge, Mass.: Harvard University Press, 1977), 94–109; Licht, *Working for the Railroad*, 83–84, 125, 143–44, 157, and chap. 7; Shelton Stromquist, *A Generation of Boomers: The Pattern of Railroad Labor Conflict in Nineteenth-Century America* (Urbana: University of Illinois Press, 1987) 222, 230–31; and Sundstrom, "Half a Career," 423–34. On the gender and racial ideology of the unions, see Paul M. Taillon, "Culture, Politics, and the Making of Railroad Brotherhoods, 1863–1916" (Ph.D. diss., University of Wisconsin, 1997).

15. Joseph Husband, *The Story of the Pullman Car* (1917; rpt. Grand Rapids, Mich.: Black Letter Press, 1974), 48.

16. LeRoy, "First Class Profits," 21–24; Sundstrom, "Half a Career," 423–24, 427.

17. "Porters Won't Strike," *Chicago Herald*, 14 July 1890, PS A13. Rumors of replacing black porters with white ones surfaced even earlier. See "The Colored Porter Will Stay," *Chicago Times*, 26 June 1889, PS A12.

18. Margery Davies, *Woman's Place Is at the Typewriter* (Philadelphia: Temple University Press, 1983), chaps. 2–5; Angel Kwolek-Folland, *Engendering Business: Men and Women in the Corporate Office, 1870–1930* (Baltimore, Md.: Johns Hopkins University Press, 1994), introduction, chap. 2; Elyce J. Rotella, *From Home to Office: U.S. Women at Work, 1870–1930* (Ann Arbor, Mich.: UMI Research Press, 1981), 129.

19. Unidentified clipping, *Chicago Record-Herald*, 13 Feb. 1902, PS A26. A few women were hired in clerical positions at Pullman as early as 1889 (*Pull-*

man News, Jan. 1937, 87, PANL), but women were first hired for clerical jobs at the Chicago (Calumet), Wilmington, and Richmond repair shops in 1917.

20. "Thomas Henry Wickes," *St. Louis Railway Register,* 12 Jan. 1889, PS A12; "T. H. Wickes of Pullman Co.," *Boston Evening Transcript,* 28 Mar. 1905, PS A28; Buder, *Pullman,* 31, 155; LeRoy, "First Class Profits," 22–24.

21. *Pullman News,* October 1924, 184; memorandum, St. Louis Series 10 and 18, Box 97, File 198, Women's Service Section, USRA; Sanford Jacoby, "The Development of Internal Labor Markets in American Manufacturing Firms," in *Internal Labor Markets,* ed. Paul Osterman (Cambridge, Mass.: MIT Press, 1984), 23–29.

22. Licht, *Working for the Railroad,* 232; Mark Perlman, *The Machinists: A New Study of American Trade Unionism* (Cambridge, Mass.: Harvard University Press, 1961), 11.

23. "Pullman's Men on a Short Strike," datelined Wilmington, 6 Sept. 1886, PS Town 1; Buder, *Pullman,* 138; Carol E. Hoffecker, *Wilmington, Delaware: Portrait of an Industrial City, 1830–1910* (Charlottesville: University Press of Virginia, 1974), 125–35.

24. Pullman's motivations and influences are discussed in Buder, *Pullman,* chap. 4, and James B. Smithson, "The Incorporation of Community: An Analysis of the Model Town of Pullman, Illinois as a Social Experiment" (Ph.D. diss., Cornell University, 1988).

25. Doty, *The Town of Pullman,* app., 23.

26. Ibid., 34. See Buder, *Pullman,* chaps. 5–8, on the town and its residents.

27. See Doty, *The Town of Pullman,* for an extensive description of all departments of the Car Works as well as other Pullman industries. The production figures come from Buder, *Pullman,* 17, and James Dredge, *A Record of the Transportation Exhibits at the World's Columbian Exposition* (New York: John Wiley and Sons, 1894), 386.

28. Doty, *The Town of Pullman,* 34–35; Spear, *Black Chicago,* 12, 29–35. The vast majority of Scandinavians employed at Pullman were Swedes: 1,163 out of 1,422. According to the U.S. Census of 1890, 59.6 percent of Chicago men aged twenty-one or older were foreign-born white; 38.4 percent were native-born white; and 2.0 percent were nonwhite. The demographic profile was virtually identical for Ward 34, which included the model town (58.3 percent foreign-born white; 40.8 percent native-born white; 1.0 percent nonwhite).

29. John Higham, *Strangers in the Land: Patterns of American Nativism, 1860–1925,* 2d ed. (New York: Atheneum, 1965), chap. 6; Doty is quoted in Buder, *Pullman,* 80.

30. Hartmut Keil, "Chicago's German Working Class in 1900," in *German Workers in Industrial Chicago, 1850–1910: A Comparative Perspective,* ed. Hartmut Keil and John B. Jentz (DeKalb: Northern Illinois University Press, 1983), 19–36.

31. Buder, *Pullman,* 89; Doty, *The Town of Pullman,* 30, 33–34. David Brody, *Steelworkers in America: The Nonunion Era* (New York: Harper and Row, 1960), 96–100, analyzes a similar situation in steel towns.

32. Many commentators reported that women and children responded to the town more favorably than men did. See Buder, *Pullman*, 62–63, 95–98; William H. Carwardine, *The Pullman Strike*, 4th ed. (Chicago: Charles H. Kerr, 1971), 18; Commissioners of State Bureaus of Labor Statistics, *Report on Industrial, Social and Economic Conditions of Pullman, Illinois* (1884), 7, Chicago Historical Society; "The Model Suburb," *Chicago Sun*, 19 May 1886, PS Town 1.

33. Stuart Brandes, *American Welfare Capitalism, 1880–1940* (Chicago: University of Chicago Press, 1970), 78; Buder, *Pullman*, 124–25; Wilma J. Pesavento, "Sport and Recreation in the Pullman Experiment, 1880–1900," *Journal of Sport History* 9 (1982): 38–62; Wilma J. Pesavento and Lisa C. Raymond, "'Men Must Play; Men Will Play': Occupations of Pullman Athletes, 1880–1900," *Journal of Sport History* 12 (1985): 233–51; Steven S. Reiss, "Ethnic Sports," in *Ethnic Chicago: A Multicultural Portrait*, 4th ed., ed. Melvin G. Holli and Peter d'A. Jones (Grand Rapids, Mich.: William B. Eerdmans, 1995), 529–56.

34. "Religion, Etc. at Pullman," *Chicago Herald*, 5 Feb. 1886, and "Picture of Pullman," *Chicago Herald*, 7 Feb. 1886, both in PS Town 1; Buder, *Pullman*, 66–67; Doty, *The Town of Pullman*, 46–47; Edward Kantowisc, "The Ethnic Church," in *Ethnic Chicago*, ed. Holli and Jones, 574–603; Leyendecker, *Palace Car Prince*, chap. 1.

35. Unidentified clipping, *Chicago Railway Review*, 20 Sept. 1884, PS Town 1; "Chicago's Busy Suburb," *Chicago Tribune*, 18 Sept. 1888, PS Town 2; "Among the Railways," *Chicago Inter-Ocean*, 14 Oct. 1892, PS A15; Doty, *The Town of Pullman*, 35.

36. My analysis of job titles in Payroll, Pullman Car Works, First Half of May 1893, PP, shows that at most 68 percent of workers were skilled. See also Buder, *Pullman*, 150; Doty, *The Town of Pullman*, 72–74, 145–55, 168–76.

37. See testimony of Thomas Heathcoate, U.S. Strike Commission, *Report on the Chicago Strike of June–July 1894* (Washington, D.C.: Government Printing Office, 1895), 423.

38. "In Pullman's Kingdom," *Chicago Herald*, 17 Feb. 1883, "Contract or Piece-Work," *Chicago Journal of Commerce*, 11 Apr. 1883, "Annual Shake Up at Pullman," *Chicago Herald*, 5 June 1883, "Poor Pay at Pullman," *Chicago Herald*, 2 Oct. 1885, "At Pullman," *Chicago Tribune*, 3 Oct. 1885, "Pullman," *Chicago Times*, 6 Aug. 1886, "Men and Moneybags," *Chicago Herald*, 14 Aug. 1886, and "Pullman," *Chicago Tribune*, 29 Mar. 1887, all in PS Town 1; "News from the Suburban Towns," *Chicago Tribune*, 16 Nov. 1887, PS Town 2; Carwardine, *The Pullman Strike*, 91.

39. "A Strike at Pullman," *Chicago Daily News*, 30 Sept. 1885, "Threatening Trouble," *Chicago Inter-Ocean*, 30 Sept. 1885, "The Trouble at Pullman," *Chicago Daily News*, 2 Oct. 1885, "Struck Work," *Chicago Inter-Ocean*, 2 Oct. 1885, and "Strikes Are Increasing," *Chicago Herald*, 23 Feb. 1886, all in PS Town 1; Carwardine, *The Pullman Strike*, 37, 50.

40. "The Situation at Pullman," *Chicago Times*, 1 Oct. 1885, "The Pullman Workmen," *Chicago Tribune*, 1 Oct. 1885, "Quiet at Pullman," *Chica-*

go Daily News, 1 Oct. 1885, "At Pullman," *Chicago Tribune,* 3 Oct. 1885, and "Eight-Hour Movement at Pullman," *Chicago Tribune,* 16 Apr. 1886, all in PS Town 1; B. Nelson, *Beyond the Martyrs,* chap. 2.

41. "At Pullman," *Chicago Tribune,* 3 Oct. 1885, PS Town 1; Bruce Laurie, *Artisans into Workers: Labor in Nineteenth-Century America* (New York: Noonday Press, 1989), chap. 5; Montgomery, *Fall of the House of Labor,* 208–9; Stromquist, *A Generation of Boomers,* 49, 62, 95.

42. "Threatening Trouble," *Chicago Inter-Ocean,* 30 Sept. 1885, and "A Strike at Pullman," *Chicago Daily News,* 30 Sept. 1885, both in PS Town 1. See Michael Piore, *Birds of Passage: Migrant Labor and Industrial Societies* (New York: Cambridge University Press, 1979), chaps. 3 and 4 and pp. 150–52, on the attitudes and motivations of migrant workers. Piore notes that the Dillingham Commission found that in the early twentieth century more northern and western Europeans, not merely those from eastern and southern Europe, were returning to their homelands than had previously—in other words, that they were migrants rather than immigrants.

43. "Pullman," *Chicago Herald,* 30 Oct. 1887, and "Life in the Suburbs," *Chicago Herald,* 20 May 1888, both in PS Town 2; Commissioners of State Bureaus of Labor Statistics, *Report,* 13–14; Lindsey, *The Pullman Strike,* 73–74.

44. Buder, *Pullman,* 80, 97–104, 122–23; Janice L. Reiff, "'His Statements . . . Will Be Challenged': Ethnicity, Gender and Class in the Evolution of the Pullman/Roseland Area of Chicago, 1894–1917," *Mid-America* 74 (1992): 234–36.

45. Buder, *Pullman,* 81; Commissioners of State Bureaus of Labor Statistics, *Report,* 10.

46. "Pullman's Big Strike," *Chicago Mail,* 1 Oct. 1885, "Struck Work," *Chicago Inter-Ocean,* 2 Oct. 1885, "Complaints from Pullman," *Chicago Herald,* 25 Jan. 1986, "Great Strike at the Pullman Car Works," *Chicago Tribune,* 5 May 1886, "Demonstration at Pullman," *Chicago Herald,* 9 May 1886, "All Quiet at Pullman, Of Course," *Chicago Herald,* 10 May 1886, "Keeping Up Steam," *Chicago Times,* 10 May 1886, "Hunting Dynamite in Pullman," *Chicago Herald,* 12 May 1886, and "In the Southern Suburbs," *Chicago Herald,* 13 May 1886, all in PS Town 1; B. Nelson, *Beyond the Martyrs,* 178–84; Richard Schneirov, *Labor and Urban Politics: Class Conflict and the Origins of Modern Liberalism in Chicago, 1864–97* (Urbana: University of Illinois Press, 1998), 191–204.

47. "Hyde Park," *Chicago Daily Graphic,* 11 May 1886, "At Pullman and Cummings," *Chicago Tribune,* 17 May 1886, "Pullman: Strike Declared Off," *Chicago Inter-Ocean,* 18 May 1886, "No Compromise at Pullman," original source unknown, 18 May 1886, "Holiday Parade at Pullman," *Chicago Herald,* 7 Sept. 1886, and "Hard Times at Pullman," *Chicago Herald,* 22 Aug. 1887, all in PS Town 1; Lindsey, *The Pullman Strike,* 28.

48. Brody, *Steelworkers in America,* 9–14, 28–34, 44–47, 50–60; Gordon, Edwards, and Reich, *Segmented Work, Divided Workers,* chap. 4; Montgomery, *Fall of the House of Labor,* 22–44, 116–28, 321.

49. Payroll, Pullman Car Works, First Half of May 1893; Doty, *The Town of Pullman*, 145–50, 153–54; U.S. Strike Commission, *Report*, 88–90.

50. My analysis of job titles from the Car Works payroll suggests that, at most, two-thirds of all workers were skilled. Some workers, like those in woodworking, were already operatives, and Montgomery's estimate that only 60 percent were skilled is probably correct. Nineteen percent were definitely unskilled, and the rest were semiskilled (Payroll, Pullman Car Works, First Half of May 1893; Montgomery, *Fall of the House of Labor*, 129).

51. Payroll, Pullman Car Works, First Half of May 1893. In *Contested Terrain: The Transformation of the Workplace in the Twentieth Century* (New York: Basic Books, 1979), 16, Richard Edwards explains the importance of the nature of the product in the inability of the Car Works to move beyond hierarchical control by foremen to technological control through the pacing of machinery.

52. "A Pullman Strike," *Chicago Evening Journal*, 22 July 1887, "Hard Times at Pullman," *Chicago Herald*, 22 Aug. 1887, and "Pullman Makes a Concession," *Chicago Herald*, 2 Sept. 1887, all in PS Town 1; "Odd Strike at Pullman," *Chicago Tribune*, 6 Jan. 1888, "Claims of the Carvers," *Chicago Herald*, 9 Jan. 1888, and "They Leave Pullman," *Chicago Herald*, 24 Jan. 1888, all in PS Town 2; "It Was Easily Settled," *Chicago Tribune*, 29 Jan. 1891, and "Preferred to Walk Out," *Chicago Herald*, 24 May 1891, both in PS A13; "For a Living Wage," *Chicago Times*, 13 May 1894; Buder, *Pullman*, 142, 150; Carwardine, *The Pullman Strike*, 101; Doty, *The Town of Pullman*, 73–74; U.S. Strike Commission, *Report*, 90, 421, 423, 441.

53. See Heathcoate's testimony, U.S. Strike Commission, *Report*, 88–91.

54. Doty, *The Town of Pullman*, 117–20.

55. Ibid., 118; Richard Hofstadter, *Social Darwinism in American Thought*, rev. ed. (Boston: Beacon Press, 1955).

56. Payroll, Pullman Car Works, First Half of May 1893, lists fewer than one hundred apprentices or "boys." For yearly totals see Illinois Factory Inspectors, *First Annual Report of the Factory Inspectors of Illinois for the Year Ending December 15, 1893* (Springfield, Ill.: H. W. Rokker, 1894); *Second Annual Report of the Factory Inspectors of Illinois for the Year Ending December 15, 1894* (Springfield, Ill.: Edward F. Hartman, 1895); *Third Annual Report of the Factory Inspectors of Illinois for the Year Ending December 15, 1895* (Springfield, Ill.: Edward F. Hartman, 1896); *Fourth Annual Report of the Factory Inspectors of Illinois for the Year Ending December 15, 1896* (Springfield, Ill.: Phillips Bros., 1897); *Fifth Annual Report of the Factory Inspectors of Illinois for the Year Ending December 15, 1897* (Springfield, Ill.: Phillips Bros., 1898), all at Chicago Historical Society. Also see "Life in the Suburbs," *Chicago Herald*, 20 May 1888, PS Town 2; Doty, *The Town of Pullman*, 38, 111, 115–16, 180–84; Hoover, "Women in Nineteenth-Century Pullman," 24–30; Janice Reiff, "A Modern Lear and His Daughters: Gender in the Model Town of Pullman," in *The Pullman Strike and the Crisis of the 1890s: Essays on Labor and Politics*, ed. Richard Schneirov, Shelton Stromquist, and Nick Salvatore (Urbana: University of Illinois Press, 1999), 68–75.

57. "Pullman's Palace Car Co.: Annual Meeting," *Pullman Arcade Observer*, 22 Oct. 1887, PS Town 2. See Doty, *The Town of Pullman*, 21, 57, 87, 125–30, 150, 196, for jobs done by women, and U.S. Strike Commission, *Report*, 433, 454, 458. In the 1890s Pullman payrolls did not list full names, so it is impossible to verify from that source which jobs women held. However, in 1904, when the payrolls for the Car Works did use full names, no women appeared except in jobs identified by Doty as women's work.

58. Doty, *The Town of Pullman*, 30, 70.

59. Payrolls, Pullman Car Works, First Half of May 1893 and First Half of May 1894, PP; Buder, *Pullman*, 159–60.

60. The painter is quoted in "Preferred to Walk Out," *Chicago Herald*, 24 May 1891, PS A13. See also Mary H. Blewett, "Work, Gender and the Artisan Tradition in New England Shoemaking, 1780–1860," *Journal of Social History* 17 (1983): 221–48; Lawrence Glickman, "Inventing the 'American Standard of Living': Gender, Race, and Working-Class Identity, 1880–1928," *Labor History* 34 (1993): 221–35; Susan E. Hirsch, *Roots of the American Working Class: The Industrialization of Crafts in Newark, 1800–1860* (Philadelphia: University of Pennsylvania Press, 1978), chap. 4; Martha May, "Bread before Roses: American Workingmen, Labor Unions and the Family Wage," in *Women, Work and Protest: A Century of U.S. Women's Labor History*, ed. Ruth Milkman (Boston: Routledge and Kegan Paul, 1985), 1–21.

61. Carwardine, *The Pullman Strike*, 79.

62. U.S. Strike Commission, *Report*, 88.

63. Of 3,221 workers, 966, or 30 percent, had rent deducted from their paychecks (Payroll, Pullman Car Works, First Half of May 1894).

64. Laurie, *Artisans into Workers*, 192–99; Lindsey, *The Pullman Strike*, 118; Montgomery, *Fall of the House of Labor*, 200–201; Richard Schneirov, "Labor and the New Liberalism in the Wake of the Pullman Strike," in *The Pullman Strike and the Crisis of the 1890s*, ed. Schneirov, Stromquist, and Salvatore, 208–15; Stromquist, *A Generation of Boomers*, 49, 62, 75–84.

65. Curtis is quoted in U.S. Strike Commission, *Report*, 88. See also "More Pay or a Strike," *Chicago Times*, 7 May 1894, PS Strike 1; Reiff, "A Modern Lear," 75; U.S. Strike Commission, *Report*, 91, 418, 434.

66. "L" to Mr. Hoornbeck, 11 May 1894, 01/01/01, Box 7, File 97, PANL; Blewett, *Men, Women, and Work*, conclusion; Ileen DeVault, "'To Sit Among Men': Skill, Gender, and Craft Unionism in the Early American Federation of Labor," in *Labor Histories: Class, Politics, and the Working-Class Experience*, ed. Eric Arnesen, Julie Greene, and Bruce Laurie (Urbana: University of Illinois Press, 1998), 259–83; Alice Kessler-Harris, *Out to Work: A History of Wage-Earning Women in the United States* (New York: Oxford University Press, 1982), 82–86, 152–60.

67. A few surviving examples of spy reports are "L" to Mr. Hoornbeck, 11 May 1894, and an undated memo about a telephone call from Mr. Middleton in 01/01/01, Box 7, File 97, both in PANL; "Aid from St. Paul," *Chicago Times*, 14 May 1894; Buder, *Pullman*, 142; Carwardine, *The Pullman Strike*, 37, 50.

68. U.S. Strike Commission, *Report*, 442.

69. Heathcote is quoted in "For a Living Wage," *Chicago Times*, 13 May 1894. See also U.S. Strike Commission, *Report*, 6, 442; Stromquist, *A Generation of Boomers*, 60.

70. "Colored Men Take Places," *Chicago Daily News*, 29 June 1894; Eugene Debs, *The Negro Workers* (New York: Emancipation Publishing, 1923), 8; LeRoy, "First Class Profits," 27; Lindsey, *The Pullman Strike*, 261.

71. U.S. Strike Commission, *Report*, xxxviii; see also Carwardine, *The Pullman Strike*, 40–41.

72. Susan E. Hirsch and Robert I. Goler, *A City Comes of Age: Chicago in the 1890s* (Chicago: Chicago Historical Society, 1990), 79–80; Lindsey, *The Pullman Strike*, 317–18; Robert Ozanne, *Wages in Practice and Theory: McCormick and International Harvester, 1860–1960* (Madison: University of Wisconsin Press, 1968), 120–21; Schneirov, *Labor and Urban Politics*, 289–91, 340–43; U.S. Strike Commission, *Report*, 622.

73. "Pullman Men Out," *Chicago Times*, 12 May 1894; "Aid from St. Paul," *Chicago Times*, 14 May 1894; "They Cheer the Speaker," *Chicago Daily News*, 14 May 1894; "Money for Pullman Men," *Chicago Daily News*, 16 May 1894; "In Line to Strike," *Chicago Times*, 22 May 1894.

74. "K. of L. Offers Its Aid," *Chicago Daily News*, 27 June 1894; "Took Down the Gates," *Chicago Daily News*, 29 June 1894; "Kensington Mob Has Arms," *Chicago Daily News*, 6 July 1894; "The Railroad Strike," *(St. Louis, Mo.) Labor*, 7 July 1894; "Pullman Crisis Is Near," *Chicago Times*, 5 Aug. 1894, PS Strike 7; Harry Jebsen Jr., "The Role of Blue Island in the Pullman Strike of 1894," *Journal of the Illinois State Historical Society* 67 (1974): 275–93; Lindsey, *The Pullman Strike*, chap. 11; U.S. Strike Commission, *Report*, xl, 338, 589; Stromquist, *A Generation of Boomers*, chap. 4.

75. "Colored Men Take Places," *Chicago Daily News*, 29 June 1894, 10; Lindsey, *The Pullman Strike*, 139–40; Robert E. Weir, "Dress Rehearsal for Pullman: The Knights of Labor and the 1890 New York Central Strike," in *The Pullman Strike and the Crisis of the 1890s*, ed. Schneirov, Stromquist, and Salvatore, 36–37.

76. Henry Seidel Canby, *The Age of Confidence* (New York: Farrar and Rinehart, 1934), 25–26; Susan E. Hirsch, "The Search for Unity Among Railroad Workers: The Pullman Strike in Perspective," in *The Pullman Strike and the Crisis of the 1890s*, ed. Schneirov, Stromquist, and Salvatore, 43–64; Hoffecker, *Wilmington*, 59, 123.

77. The worker is quoted in "Pullman Workman," *(Wilmington, Del.) Every Evening*, 10 July 1894. See also "Massmeeting of Laborers," *Every Evening*, 28 May 1894, p. 1; "Massmeeting of Laborers," *Every Evening*, 29 May 1894; "No Prospect of Any Strike Here," *Every Evening*, 9 July 1894; U.S. Strike Commission, *Report*, 554, 571, 589.

78. Hoffecker, *Wilmington*, 115–36. The *(Wilmington) Every Evening and Commercial* covered labor issues extensively during 1886. Throughout April and May articles detailed the Knights' attempts and failures at organizing leather workers, construction workers, and machinists.

79. "No Prospect of Any Strike Here," *Every Evening,* 9 July 1894.

80. In 1900 the Irish comprised 37 percent of the foreign born in Wilmington (U.S. Census Office, *Twelfth Census of the United States, 1900, Population,* pt. 1 [Washington, D.C.: U.S. Census Office, 1901], 132). See also Edward Bubnys, "Chicago, 1870 and 1900: Wealth, Occupation and Education" (Ph.D. diss., University of Illinois, 1978), 72; Canby, *Age of Confidence,* 28–29; Hoffecker, *Wilmington,* 116–17.

81. Hoffecker, *Wilmington,* 117–18; Carol Hoffecker, *Delaware: A Bicentennial History* (New York: W. W. Norton, 1977), 108–9, 185–86, 189; Yda Schreuder, "The Impact of Labor Segmentation on the Ethnic Division of Labor and the Immigrant Residential Community: Polish Leather Workers in Wilmington, Delaware in the Early-Twentieth Century," *Journal of Historical Geography* 16 (1990): 409–10. In the sample of Wilmington shop workers, only seven black men were hired before 1918, all as laborers.

82. James R. Barrett, *Work and Community in the Jungle: Chicago's Packinghouse Workers, 1894–1922* (Urbana: University of Illinois Press, 1987), 127–30; Schneirov, *Labor and Urban Politics,* 340; William M. Tuttle Jr., *Race Riot: Chicago in the Red Summer of 1919* (New York: Atheneum, 1970), 112–13.

83. "Seek Work at Pullman," *Chicago Daily News,* 20 July 1894; "Are Sick of Their Jobs," *Chicago Daily News,* 24 July 1894; "Some Shops to Open," *Chicago Herald,* 23 July 1894, PS Strike 6; "Women Aid the Fight," *Chicago Record,* 1 Aug. 1894, "Pullman Starts Up," *Chicago Tribune,* 3 Aug. 1894, "Desert the Strike," *Chicago Evening Post,* 4 Aug. 1894, "Send Workmen Home," *Chicago Record,* 4 Aug. 1894, "War on Deb's Friends," *Chicago Herald,* 4 Aug. 1894, and "Pullman Crisis Is Near," *Chicago Times,* 5 Aug. 1894, all in PS Strike 7; Buder, *Pullman,* 194, 196; U.S. Strike Commission, *Report,* 591.

84. Montgomery, *Fall of the House of Labor,* 209; U.S. Strike Commission, *Report,* 589.

85. Buder, *Pullman,* 201, 206–7; Stromquist, *Generation of Boomers,* 93–97. Even his Illinois business friends found Pullman an embarrassment when they sought the support of or accommodation with labor (Ferdinand W. Peck to George M. Pullman, 5 Apr. 1897, Pullman Archives, South Holland Historical Society, South Holland, Illinois). Gov. John Altgeld worked hard at the 1896 Democratic convention to break President Cleveland's control over the party and helped engineer the nomination of William Jennings Bryan (Harry Barnard, *Eagle Forgotten: The Life of John Peter Altgeld* [Secaucus, N.J.: Lyle Stuart, 1973], 280–373).

Chapter 2: Two Roads to the Open Shop

1. Pullman's brothers, Albert and Charles, had worked for the company, but neither remained by 1900. Pullman never trusted his twin sons—playboys who died young—in his business, nor did his daughters' husbands make their careers with the corporation. See "George M. Pullman Dies Suddenly," *Chicago Times Herald,* 20 Oct. 1897; *Pullman News,* August 1929, 111; Liston

E. Leyendecker, *Palace Car Prince: A Biography of George Mortimer Pullman* (Niwot: University Press of Colorado, 1992), 123–24, 206, 214–15, 246, 251–52, 259–61.

2. As part of the reorganization, the company's name was changed from the Pullman Palace Car Company to the Pullman Company. See Annual statements, Pullman Company, 1897–1900, in *Reports of Railroad Companies, 1881–1960*, Newberry Library; "Pullman in Good Shape," *Chicago Tribune*, 14 Oct. 1904, PS A27.

3. "The Census Man Abroad in the Land," *Calumet Index*, 23 Apr. 1910; "A Bird's Eye View of the Calumet Shops Where Teamwork Is the Key Word," *Pullman News*, Jan. 1946, 111; Stanley Buder, *Pullman: An Experiment in Industrial Order and Community Planning, 1880–1930* (New York: Oxford University Press, 1967), 201, 206–7, 212–15.

4. Payrolls, Pullman Car Works, First Half of May 1893 and First Half of May 1904, PP; "Peril to Health in Sleeping Cars," *Chicago Tribune*, 28 Oct. 1903, "Blow, Kill, Burn and Brush the Germs Away These Days in Pullmans," *Denver Post*, 24 Apr. 1904, untitled clipping, *Chicago Inter-Ocean*, 27 May 1904, and "Pullman in Good Shape," *Chicago Tribune*, 14 Oct. 1904, all in PS A27; Buder, *Pullman*, 219.

5. William Thomas and Florian Znaniecki, *The Polish Peasant in Europe and America*, ed. and abr. by Eli Zaretsky (Urbana: University of Illinois Press, 1984), 128.

6. Between the 1894 strike and the end of 1904, 19 percent of skilled workers and 43 percent of semiskilled workers hired at the Calumet shop were born in southern or eastern European countries. According to one employee, a Scots foreman in the paint department of the Car Works hired only Scotsmen (employee W001, interview by author, 26 Jan. 1981, Chicago. She was a clerical worker at Pullman's central office beginning in 1921, and her father was a painter at the Car Works). See also Leyendecker, *Palace Car Prince*, chap. 7; Rudolph J. Vecoli, "Chicago's Italians prior to World War I: A Study of Their Social and Economic Adjustment" (Ph.D. diss., University of Wisconsin, 1963), 196, 199.

7. Because Payroll, Pullman Car Works, First Half of May 1904, gives complete names for virtually all workers, we are able to ascertain the occupations of women. In 1900 state factory inspectors reported that the Car Works had 6,000 employees, of whom 5,924 were males older than sixteen. The inspectors found that the company employed only 50 women older than sixteen, 26 boys younger than seventeen, and no young girls (see *Eighth Annual Report of the Factory Inspectors of Illinois for the Year Ending December 15, 1900* [Springfield, Ill.: Phillips Bros., 1901], 122, Chicago Historical Society).

8. In 1910 only 0.2 percent of the men aged twenty-one and older in Ward 33 (which included the Pullman area) were nonwhite. This figure is derived from statistics in U.S. Bureau of the Census, *Thirteenth Census of the United States, 1910: Population* (Washington, D.C.: Government Printing Office, 1913–14), 2:514. See also Rick Halpern, *Down on the Killing Floor: Black and White Workers in Chicago's Packinghouses, 1904–1954* (Urbana: Universi-

ty of Illinois Press, 1997), 23, 36–38; Allan Spear, *Black Chicago: The Making of a Negro Ghetto, 1890–1920* (Chicago: University of Chicago Press, 1967), chap. 1.

9. Payroll, Pullman Car Works, First Half of May 1904; "Pullman Car Builders on Strike," *Chicago American*, 3 Aug. 1902, PS A26; 1937 Conference Proceedings, 213, 06/01/04, Box 25, File 677, PANL.

10. "Rebuff, Then a Bullet," *Chicago Evening Post*, 8 Aug. 1901, PS A25.

11. "Foreman Shot by Former Workman," *Chicago Inter-Ocean*, 9 Aug. 1901, PS A25.

12. Brian Gratton, "'A Triumph of Modern Philanthropy': Age Criteria in Labor Management at the Pennsylvania Railroad, 1875–1930," *Business History Review* 64 (1990): 632, 640.

13. "Car Builders Go on Strike," *Chicago American*, 7 Sept. 1901, PS A25; untitled clipping, *Chicago American*, 30 Jan. 1902, "Pullman Car Builders on Strike," *Chicago American*, 3 Aug. 1902, "Pullman Strikers Expect to Win in Few Days," *Chicago American*, 4 Aug. 1902, and "Strikers Win at Pullman," *Chicago American*, 15 Aug. 1902, all in PS A26; James R. Barrett, *Work and Community in the Jungle: Chicago's Packinghouse Workers, 1894–1922* (Urbana: University of Illinois Press, 1987), chap. 4; David Brody, *Workers in Industrial America: Essays on the Twentieth Century Struggle*, 2d ed. (New York: Oxford University Press, 1993), 24–25; David Montgomery, *The Fall of the House of Labor: The Workplace, the State, and American Labor Activism, 1865–1925* (New York: Cambridge University Press, 1987), 212, 259–69.

14. *(Chicago) Workers Call*, 1902, passim; *Chicago Socialist*, 1903–5, passim; Montgomery, *Fall of the House of Labor*, 269; Graham R. Taylor, "Satellite Cities—II. Pullman," *Survey* 29 (2 Nov. 1912): 130; Vecoli, "Chicago's Italians," 197.

15. Barrett, *Work and Community*, 131–35, 138–42. An untitled clipping, *Chicago Record-Herald*, 28 Sept. 1902, PS A26. *The Lakeside Directory* (Chicago: Chicago Directory Co., 1904), 66–71, lists locals of the following unions with offices in the Pullman area: Amalgamated Woodworkers; the International Brotherhood of Blacksmiths and Helpers; the Brotherhood of Painters, Decorators and Paperhangers; the Metal Polishers, Buffers, Platers, Brass Molders, and Brass and Silver Workers International; the United Brotherhood of Carpenters and Joiners; International Association of Car Workers; and the United Metalworkers International.

16. "Pullman Laundry Girls Strike," *Chicago Tribune*, 24 Apr. 1903, untitled clipping, *Chicago Examiner*, 27 Apr. 1903, and "Girls Face Lockout," *Chicago Record-Herald*, n.d., all in PS A26; Payroll, Pullman Car Works, First Half of May 1904.

17. "Public Travels in Unkempt Sleepers," *Chicago Inter-Ocean*, 18 June 1902, "Cleaners Strike: Cars Are Grimy," *Chicago Tribune*, 18 June 1902, untitled clipping, *Chicago Daily News*, 19 June 1902, and "More Pay for Pullman Men," *Chicago Chronicle*, 13 July 1902, all in PS A26.

18. "Pullman Trades Ask Sunday Off," *Chicago Tribune*, 16 Dec. 1902, and "Pullman Car Men Gain Great Victory," *Chicago American*, 1 Feb. 1903, both in PS A26.

19. "Pullman Co. Works Lay Off 2,000 Men," *Chicago Examiner*, 12 Dec. 1903, "Will Be Idle at Pullman," *Chicago Tribune*, 12 Dec. 1903, untitled clipping, *Chicago Evening Journal*, 12 Dec. 1903, "No Work for 14,000," *Chicago Tribune*, 24 Dec. 1903, and "Big Strikes Impend," *Chicago Evening Post*, 26 Feb. 1904, all in PS A27.

20. Reinhard Bendix, *Work and Authority in Industry* (New York: John Wiley and Sons, 1956), 274–78; Montgomery, *Fall of the House of Labor*, 269–75.

21. The notice is quoted in "Pullman Shut Down," *Chicago Tribune*, 15 Sept. 1904, PS A27. See also "Hundreds to Lose Employment at Pullman," *Chicago Examiner*, 2 July 1904, "Force Cut at Pullman," *Chicago Evening Post*, 2 July 1904, "Pullman Shops to be Closed Down," *Chicago Evening Journal*, 1 Aug. 1904, "Plan Fight on Unions," *Chicago Daily News*, 30 Aug. 1904, "Fear Shutdown at Pullman," *Chicago Tribune*, 31 Aug. 1904, "Expect Cut at Pullman," *Chicago Evening Journal*, 31 Aug. 1904, "See Blow at Labor Unions in Shut Down," *Chicago American*, 15 Sept. 1904, "26,000 Dinner Pails Are now Empty in Chicago," *Chicago Examiner*, 16 Sept. 1904, and "$1,700,000,000 Capital War on Unions," *Chicago Examiner*, 28 Sept. 1904, all in PS A27; "Pullman Gates Shut," *Chicago Daily News*, 15 Sept. 1904.

22. Barrett, *Work and Community*, 172–80; Halpern, *Down on the Killing Floor*, 23, 36–38; Montgomery, *Fall of the House of Labor*, 269–75.

23. "Pullman Shut Down," *Chicago Tribune*, 15 Sept. 1904, "Pullman Gates Shut," *Chicago Daily News*, 15 Sept. 1904, "Big Shops Start, Ignoring Unions," *Chicago Tribune*, 26 Sept. 1904, "Idle Army Goes to Work in Joy," *Chicago Journal*, 3 Oct. 1904, and "Pullman Rules Laid Down by Wickes," *Chicago American*, 3 Oct. 1904, all in PS A27.

24. Wickes is quoted in "Work Resumed at Great Plants," *Chicago Tribune*, 27 Sept. 1904, PS A27. See also "500 Men Are Given Employment by Pullman Co.," *Chicago Examiner*, 4 Oct. 1904, and "Pullman Earnings To Be Big," *Chicago Inter-Ocean*, 29 Dec. 1904, both in PS A27.

25. "Car Shops Close Till December," *Chicago Tribune*, 16 Sept. 1904, "12,000 Men Will Be Given Work Today," *Chicago Examiner*, 26 Sept. 1904, and "Workmen by the Thousand Submit to Lower Wages," *Chicago Daily Journal*, 26 Sept. 1904, all in PS A27.

26. U.S. Strike Commission, *Report on the Chicago Strike of June–July 1894* (Washington, D.C.: Government Printing Office, 1895), xlvi–liv; Shelton Stromquist, *A Generation of Boomers: The Pattern of Railroad Labor Conflict in Nineteenth-Century America* (Urbana: University of Illinois Press, 1987), 265; Laurence S. Zakson, "Railway Labor Legislation, 1888 to 1930: A Legal History of Congressional Railway Labor Relations Policy," *Rutgers Law Journal* 20, no. 2 (1989): 320, 329.

27. Zakson, "Railway Labor Legislation," 329–32.

28. Minute Book 1, Executive Committee, Board of Directors, Pullman Co., meeting of 17 June 1902, 02/01/02, vol. 15, PANL; "More Pay for Pullman Men," *Chicago Chronicle*, 13 July 1902, PS A26; Greg LeRoy, "First Class Profits and Performances upon the Public: Pullman Porters, 1867–1912" (paper presented at the Third Annual Illinois State History Symposium, Springfield, 1982), 28.

29. Except on the Pacific coast, where the black population was small, the company had no difficulty recruiting porters and at any one time had as many as six hundred men on a waiting list for employment. See U.S. Commission on Industrial Relations, *Final Report and Testimony*, 64th Cong., 1st sess., S. Doc. 415 (Washington, D.C.: Government Printing Office, 1916), 10:9553–54; U.S. Department of Labor, *Wage Chronology: Railroads—Nonoperating Employees, 1920–62*, B.L.S. Report #208 (Washington, D.C.: Government Printing Office, 1963), 1.

30. The company's hostility to rate regulation surfaced in repeated rumors that Pullman might abandon the business of operating sleeping cars and concentrate on manufacturing them. See "Pullman Submits to Cut in Rates," *Chicago American*, 17 Dec. 1909, PS A29; Buder, *Pullman*, 217; Zakson, "Railway Labor Legislation," 320, 329–37.

31. "Pullman Employees Seek Increase," *Chicago Evening Post*, 24 Nov. 1906, PS A28; "Biggest Pullman Tip Yet," *Chicago Tribune*, 4 Feb. 1908, PS A29; "Plea of the Pullman Porters," *Chicago Defender*, 31 Dec. 1910; LeRoy, "First Class Profits," 28–29.

32. Robert T. Lincoln, president, to Bruce Haldeman, chairman, Citizens' Committee, YMCA, Louisville, Ky., 13 Dec. 1910, Robert Todd Lincoln Papers, 7, Chicago Historical Society; Minute Book 1, executive committee meetings, 3 Feb. 1900, 4 June 1900, 18 Apr. 1913, and 4 December 1913; "R.R. Porters Should Be Pensioned After 25 Years' Service," *Chicago Defender*, 9 May 1914; "Pullman Co. to Pension Its Faithful Porters," *Chicago Defender*, 18 July 1914; U.S. Department of Labor, *Pension Funds for Municipal Employees and Railroad Pension Systems in the United States*, 61st Cong., 62d sess., S. Doc. 427 (Washington, D.C.: Government Printing Office, 1910), 88–89; F. Emerson Andrews, *Corporation Giving* (New York: Russell Sage Foundation, 1952), 23–26; Beth T. Bates, *Pullman Porters and the Rise of Protest Politics in Black America, 1925–1945* (Chapel Hill: University of North Carolina Press, 2001), 41–47; Lizabeth Cohen, *Making a New Deal: Industrial Workers in Chicago, 1919–1939* (New York: Cambridge University Press, 1990), 179–83; Stromquist, *A Generation of Boomers*, 247–48.

33. "R.R. Porters Should Be Pensioned," *Chicago Defender*, 9 May 1914; "Pullman Company to Better Service; Lectures Porters," *Chicago Defender*, 15 Aug. 1914; "Pay for Shining Shoes Is Not a Tip Says Porter," *Chicago Defender*, 29 Aug. 1914; Commission on Industrial Relations, *Final Report*, 9547–48, 9550–54, 9562–63, 9567, 9595, 9610.

34. Questionnaire from National Industrial Conference Board re Employee Stock Purchase Plans, March 1930, 06/01/01, Box 3, File 64, PANL; "Pullman Company Refuses Porters Higher Wages," *Chicago Defender*, 21 Aug. 1915; "Pullman Porters Meet in Convention," *Chicago Defender*, 6 Nov. 1915; Joseph Husband, *The Story of the Pullman Car* (1917; rpt. Grand Rapids, Mich.: Black Letter Press, 1974), 155–56.

35. "Pullman Car Conductor Refused to Jim Crow Mrs. Booker T. Washington," *Chicago Defender*, 22 Apr. 1911; "Negro Fellowship League: Address by Pullman Conductor Bell," *Chicago Defender*, 24 Apr. 1915.

36. Husband, *The Story of the Pullman Car,* 124. See also "New Mills for Pullman," *Chicago Tribune,* 29 Jan. 1905, and "Pullman Co. Will Make Steel Cars," *Chicago Tribune,* 2 Jan. 1906, both in PS A28; "$3,000,000 for Pullman Buildings," *Chicago Journal,* 15 May 1909, and "Pullman Co. Spends $3,000,000 on Plant," *Chicago Record Herald,* 15 May 1909, both in PS A29; "Steel Freight Car Plant of the Pullman Co., Pullman, Ill.," *Railway and Engineering Review* 50 (11 June 1910): 544–47.

37. In 1912 only one thousand of the ten thousand workers in the combined workforce of the Car Works and Calumet Repair Shop had twenty years or more of service with the company. See table 1. See also statement of C. W. Pflager, mechanical superintendent, 1941–42 Conference with Company Representatives, 153, 06/01/04, Box 26, File 695, PANL; "The Census Man Abroad in the Land," *Calumet Index,* 23 Apr. 1910; Edward Greer, *Big Steel: Black Politics and Corporate Power in Gary, Indiana* (New York: Monthly Review Press, 1979), 73–75; Michael Piore, *Birds of Passage: Migrant Labor and Industrial Societies* (New York: Cambridge University Press, 1979), 149–54; G. Taylor, "Satellite Cities—II. Pullman," 122–23; Vecoli, "Chicago's Italians," 196, 199, 279, 338–44.

38. G. Taylor, "Satellite Cities—II. Pullman," 122.

39. Venturelli's employee service record is part of the Calumet database (see appendix).

40. G. Taylor, "Satellite Cities—II. Pullman," 122.

41. David Brody, *Steelworkers in America: The Nonunion Era* (New York: Harper and Row, 1960), chap. 5; David Gordon, Richard Edwards, and Michael Reich, *Segmented Work, Divided Workers: The Historical Transformation of Labor in the United States* (New York: Cambridge University Press, 1982), 141–43; John Higham, *Strangers in the Land: Patterns of American Nativism, 1860–1925,* 2d ed. (New York: Atheneum, 1965), 51–184.

42. John S. Runnells and Joseph Husband, "What a New System of Management Did for Us," *System* 29 (1916): 117, 121. This article ran in five monthly installments from February through June 1916.

43. Minute Book 1, executive committee meeting, 18 Dec. 1911; *Pullman Car Works Standard,* Aug. 1917, 3, Chicago Historical Society; Runnells and Husband, "What a New System . . . Did," 115–16, 121; Montgomery, *Fall of the House of Labor,* 214–33; Daniel Nelson, *Managers and Workers: Origins of the New Factory System in the United States, 1880–1920* (Madison: University of Wisconsin Press, 1975), 70–71.

44. Runnells and Husband, "What a New System . . . Did," 117, 121, 396, 503–4. The new numbered jobs with different pay rates and the "move men" appear in 1917 payrolls for the Car Works.

45. The supervisor and superintendent are quoted in Runnells and Husband, "What a New System . . . Did," 625. See also Minute Book 1, executive committee meeting, 11 May 1915.

46. See Kathleen D. McCarthy, *Noblesse Oblige: Charity and Cultural Philanthropy in Chicago, 1849–1929* (Chicago: University of Chicago Press, 1982), chap. 5, on the role of Louise deKoven Bowen and Hull House in the Progres-

sive movement. For Alice Hamilton's life and work see "Alice Hamilton," *Notable American Women: The Modern Period,* ed. Barbara Sicherman and Carol Hurd Green, with Ilene Kantrov and Harriette Walker (Cambridge, Mass.: Harvard University Press, 1980), 303–6. Bowen played a similar role in organizing stockholders, including women of the McCormick family, to pressure International Harvester to end night work for women (Robert Ozanne, *A Century of Labor-Management Relations at McCormick and International Harvester* [Madison: University of Wisconsin Press, 1967], 99–100).

47. Alice Hamilton, "What One Stockholder Did," *Survey* 28 (1 June 1912): 387–88; Illinois Bureau of Labor Statistics, *First Report on Industrial Accidents in Illinois for the Six Months Ending December 31, 1907* (Springfield, Ill.: Phillips Bros., 1908), 46–47, 116–17; *Second Report on Industrial Accidents in Illinois for Twelve Months Ending December 31, 1908,* in *Fifteenth Biennial Report of Bureau of Labor Statistics, 1908* (Springfield: Illinois State Journal Company, 1910), 350–53; Gordon, Edwards, and Reich, *Segmented Work, Divided Workers,* 148.

48. Minute Book 1, executive committee meeting, 11 May 1915; "Lead Poisoning, 1908–1963," 06/05/01, Box 1, File 2, PANL; Hamilton, "What One Stockholder Did," 388–89.

49. The editor was writing in *Pullman Car Works Standard,* May 1917, 2. See also *Pullman Car Works Standard,* June 1917, 4–5, 11, and Aug. 1917, 3; G. Taylor, "Satellite Cities—II. Pullman," 127, 129.

50. *Pullman Car Works Standard,* Jan. 1917, 10; Feb. 1917, 12; June 1917, 13; Aug. 1917, 10; Sept. 1917, 10; Dec. 1917, 11; and Jan. 1918, 11.

51. The article quoted appears in *Pullman Car Works Standard,* June 1917, 3. See also *Pullman Car Works Standard,* July 1916, 14; Herbert G. Gutman, "Work, Culture and Society in Industrializing America, 1815–1919," *American Historical Review* 78 (1973): 544–45, 558–60; Edward P. Thompson, "Time, Work-Discipline, and Industrial Capitalism," *Past and Present* 38 (1967): 56–97.

52. "Pullman Repair Shop Is Opened," *Chicago Evening Journal,* 17 Sept. 1900, PS A25; Minute Book B, Board of Directors, Pullman Company, meeting of 17 Oct. 1901, 02/01/02, vol. 2, PANL.

53. Payrolls, Calumet and Wilmington repair shops, Second Half of April 1906, Second Half of March 1911, Second Half of October 1917, PP; Mark Perlman, *The Machinists: A New Study of American Trade Unionism* (Cambridge, Mass.: Harvard University Press, 1961), 92; G. Meredith Rountree, *The Railway Worker: A Study of the Employment and Unemployment Problems of the Canadian Railways* (Toronto, Canada: Oxford University Press, 1936), 144–45.

54. Minute Book 1, executive committee meeting, 5 Apr. 1911; Payroll, Richmond Repair Shop, Second Half of March 1911, PP; Robert E. L. Knight, *Industrial Relations in the San Francisco Bay Area, 1900–1918* (Berkeley: University of California Press, 1960), 260–61, 264–65, 387; Joseph Whitnah, *A History of Richmond, California* (Richmond, Calif.: Chamber of Commerce, 1944), 26–27, 55, 60, 100–101.

55. Hiring figures are derived from the Calumet sample. Ippolito's employee service record is part of the Calumet database (see appendix).

56. For instance, at Calumet a body builder 1 earned $0.415 per hour, whereas a body builder 2 earned $0.358; a blacksmith 1 earned $0.431 per hour, and a blacksmith 2 earned $0.401 (Payrolls, Calumet, Wilmington, and Richmond Shops, Second Half of October 1917, PP).

57. In 1911 blacksmiths earned $0.356 per hour at Calumet, $0.351 at Richmond, and $0.336 at Wilmington. Body builders earned $0.35 at Calumet and $0.343 at the other shops. Varnishers earned $0.373 at Calumet, $0.369 at Richmond, and $0.353 at Wilmington (Payrolls, Calumet, Wilmington, and Richmond Repair Shops, Second Half of March 1911 and Second Half of October 1917).

58. The minimum tenure for this group of workers was 0.1 year and the maximum 46.6 years. Skilled workers at Richmond and Wilmington also had long tenures; the average for those in the samples who were hired between 1911 and 1917 was 10.5 and 14.7 years, respectively. See John B. Payne, director general of the railroad, letter re Pullman Car Lines Decision #25, 27 July 1920, in employment packet of employee C001, Calumet Shop, 06/02/03, PANL; Harry D. Wolf, *The Railroad Labor Board* (Chicago: University of Chicago Press, 1927), 128–29.

59. *Pullman Car Works Standard*, Feb. 1917, 10; David Fairris, "From Exit to Voice in Shopfloor Governance: The Case of Company Unions," *Business History Review* 69 (1995): 497–501.

60. "Through Line Via 93rd Street to Pullman," *Daily Calumet*, 10 Apr. 1910; "New Line a Success," *Daily Calumet*, 9 July 1910; G. Taylor, "Satellite Cities—II. Pullman," 123.

61. The spelling "employe" was the customary form in the railroad industry until the mid-twentieth century. This spelling will be used instead of "employee" wherever it was so used in the documents.

62. The six unions were the International Association of Machinists, the International Brotherhood of Boilermakers, the International Brotherhood of Blacksmiths, the Brotherhood of Railway Carmen, the Sheet Metal Workers' International Alliance, and the International Brotherhood of Electrical Workers. See Payroll, Calumet Repair Shop, Second Half of October, 1917; Colin J. Davis, *Power at Odds: The 1922 National Railroad Shopmen's Strike* (Urbana: University of Illinois Press, 1997), 15–20; Perlman, *The Machinists*, 92; G. Taylor, "Satellite Cities—II. Pullman," 122.

63. Davis, *Power at Odds*, 27–31; Knight, *Industrial Relations*, 252–53; Montgomery, *Fall of the House of Labor*, 246–48; Selig Perlman and Philip Taft, *History of Labor in the United States, 1896–1932* (New York: MacMillan, 1935), 368–73.

64. In 1910 barely 2 percent of skilled repair shop workers were African American, and they labored for southern railroads. See "Economic Practice at Burnside: Co-operative Methods and Saving Affected at the Main Shops of the Illinois Central," *Railway Master Mechanic* 39 (June 1915): 192; Horace Cayton and George Mitchell, *Black Workers and the New Unions* (Chapel

Hill: University of North Carolina Press, 1939), chap. 15; Davis, *Power at Odds*, 22; Montgomery, *Fall of the House of Labor*, 85–86; Sterling Spero and Abram Harris, *The Black Worker: The Negro and the Labor Movement* (New York: Columbia University Press, 1931), 308; William A. Sundstrom, "Half a Career: Discrimination and Railroad Internal Labor Markets," *Industrial Relations* 29 (1990): 427; Warren C. Whatley, "African-American Strikebreaking from the Civil War to the New Deal," *Social Science History* 17 (1993): 525–58.

65. Davis, *Power at Odds*, 31–36; Jeffrey Haydu, *Making American Industry Safe for Democracy: Comparative Perspectives on the State and Employee Representation in the Era of World War I* (Urbana: University of Illinois Press, 1997), 94; Joseph A. McCartin, *Labor's Great War: The Struggle for Industrial Democracy and the Origins of Modern American Labor Relations, 1912–1921* (Chapel Hill: University of North Carolina Press, 1997), 40–45.

66. Melvyn Dubofsky, *We Shall Be All: A History of the IWW* (Chicago: Quadrangle Books, 1969); G. Taylor, "Satellite Cities—II. Pullman," 130.

67. Johnson became the neighborhood's second Socialist alderman in 1917 but only by winning a three-way race with 35 percent of the vote. The Socialist Party continued to poll 12 to 18 percent of the vote in presidential elections in the Pullman area. Election results are from the yearly *Chicago Daily News Almanac*, Chicago Public Library. See also "One Big Union In and Around Chicago," *Industrial Solidarity*, 8 Apr. 1916, 1, 4; *Pullman Car Works Standard*, May 1917, 3.

68. "One Big Union," *Industrial Solidarity*, 8 Apr. 1916, 1, 4.

69. From the *Calumet Index:* "Entertainment for Benefit of Red Cross Society by Local Germans," 22 Jan. 1915, "The Poles Pledge Allegiance to America," 13 July 1917, and "Garibaldi Club Gives Farewell Party for Soldier Boys," 28 Sept. 1917; *Pullman Car Works Standard*, Jan. 1917, 6, and May 1917, 2; Brody, *Workers in Industrial America*, 35–38; Cohen, *Making a New Deal*, 21–26; Janice L. Reiff, "'His Statements . . . Will Be Challenged'; Ethnicity, Gender and Class in the Evolution of the Pullman/Roseland Area of Chicago, 1894–1917," *Mid-America* 74 (1992): 237, 239–52; G. Taylor, "Satellite Cities—II. Pullman," 124–25.

70. When the federal government took over the sleeping-car service and increased wages in 1918 (see chap. 3), some former employees wrote to ask whether they could claim retroactive increases. See letters from the summer of 1918 in E-38-3, General File 1918–22, USRA. See also Emil Frankel, "Labor Turnover in Chicago," *Monthly Labor Review* 9, no. 3 (Sept. 1919): 49–50.

71. Barrett, *Work and Community*, chap. 6; James Grossman, *Land of Hope: Chicago, Black Southerners, and the Great Migration* (Chicago: University of Chicago Press, 1989), chaps. 7, 8; Chicago Commission on Race Relations, *The Negro in Chicago* (Chicago: University of Chicago Press, 1922), 361, 431; Montgomery, *Fall of the House of Labor*, chap. 7; Spear, *Black Chicago*, chaps. 7, 8; Spero and Harris, *The Black Worker*, 151–61, 174–81.

72. Management is quoted in *Pullman Car Works Standard*, Feb. 1917, 10. Only 0.5 percent of the population of Ward 9, which included the Pullman

area, was nonwhite in 1920. See also *Pullman Car Works Standard,* July 1916, 10; July 1917, 16; and Oct. 1917, 12; "Pullman Porters' Evil Influence," *Chicago Defender,* 2 Feb. 1918, recounts "uncouth conduct" by the newly hired southern men. From the *Calumet Index:* "The Negro From the Southern View," 27 Nov. 1909; "Pullman Men's Society in Campaign for Members," 26 Mar. 1910; "Dave Harris' Old Time Black Face Men Coming," 19 Jan. 1917; "Feast of Fun at Minstrel of Country Club," 9 Mar. 1917; and "City to Make I.C. Better Housing of Its Negroes," 13 July 1917. The Car Works had two hundred "colored" workers on March 31, 1921, according to F. L. Simmons to Phil H. Brown, commissioner of conciliation, Dept. of Labor, 5 Apr. 1922, 06/01/01, Box 1, File 23, PANL. International Harvester hired many black men at its plant near the black ghetto even as it barred them from West Pullman. See Robert Ozanne, *Wages in Practice and Theory: McCormick and International Harvester, 1860–1960* (Madison: University of Wisconsin Press, 1968), 48; Thomas Lee Philpott, *The Slum and the Ghetto: Immigrants, Blacks, and Reformers in Chicago, 1880–1930* (Belmont, Calif.: Wadsworth, 1991), 140, 183–84; Arvarh E. Strickland, *History of the Chicago Urban League* (Urbana: University of Illinois Press, 1966), 33–34.

73. The manager is quoted in the 1940 Conference Proceedings, 20–23 Aug., 169, 06/01/04, Box 26, File 690, PANL. In 1911, 10 percent of Richmond workers held helper-level jobs; in 1917, 21 percent did.

74. At Wilmington only 6 percent of those hired for skilled positions before 1910 had been born in southern or eastern Europe, but 31 percent of skilled workers hired between 1910 and 1917 were born there. Only 3 percent of all workers hired between 1910 and 1917 at the Wilmington shop were black, and these were hired as laborers. No black or Asian men were at the Calumet shop before 1917 or at the Richmond shop before the 1922 railroad shopmen's strike. See Lawrence Crouchett, Lonnie Bunch III, and Martha Winnacker, *Visions toward Tomorrow: History of the East Bay Afro-American Community, 1852–1977* (Oakland, Calif.: Northern California Center for Afro-American History and Life, 1989), 9, 16; Walker D. Hines, *War History of American Railroads* (New Haven, Conn.: Yale University Press, 1928), 18–19; Carol Hoffecker, *Corporate Capital: Wilmington in the Twentieth Century* (Philadelphia: Temple University Press, 1983), 27–29, 63–69, 94; Knight, *Industrial Relations,* 99, 213–14; Yda Schreuder, "The Impact of Labor Segmentation on the Ethnic Division of Labor and the Immigrant Residential Community: Polish Leather Workers in Wilmington, Delaware in the Early-twentieth Century," *Journal of Historical Geography* 16 (1990): 410.

75. Payrolls, Calumet, Richmond, and Wilmington Shops, Second Half of October 1917. Through 1917 the skilled seamstresses in Pullman repair shops earned only 55 percent of what the male upholsterers did. Richmond hired women only as seamstresses or typists before 1922. In Wilmington women were hired only as seamstresses, clerks, or stenographers before 1922. See Maurine Greenwald, *Women, War and Work: The Impact of World War I on Women Workers in the United States* (Westport, Conn.: Greenwood Press, 1980), chap. 1.

76. Untitled articles on Pullman clerical workers in *Chicago American,* 12 Feb. 1902, *Chicago Chronicle,* 12 Fcb. 1902, *Chicago Inter-Ocean,* 12 Feb. 1902, and *Chicago Record Herald,* 13 Feb. 1902, all in PS A26; "Lots of News Found in Car Shops Magazine," *Calumet Index,* 6 July 1917; "Pullman Co. Engages Woman Ticket Seller," *Chicago Examiner,* 19 July 1917, PS A33; *Pullman Car Works Standard,* Feb. 1917, 12, Mar. 1917, 8, 14, May 1917, 14, 15, June 1917, 15, July 1917, 15, and Feb. 1918, 15. The first women clerical workers appear on the payrolls of the Calumet, Richmond, and Wilmington shops in 1917. According to these payrolls, the position of comptometer operator (female) commanded less pay than that of a traditional clerk (male), while women timekeepers were paid lower wages than men timekeepers. The effect of the marriage ban for clerical women but not blue-collar women can be seen in their average length of service. Women clerical workers hired at the Calumet shop between 1918 and 1922 averaged 9.0 years of employment, only one-third as long as men clerical workers hired in that period and also less than seamstresses hired during that period (10.8 years), even though many seamstresses had truncated careers because of the 1922 strike. Information on the marriage ban comes from my interview of employee W001. See also Samuel Cohn, *The Process of Occupational Sex-Typing: The Feminization of Clerical Labor in Great Britain, 1870–1936* (Philadelphia: Temple University Press, 1986), 40–41, 96–97, 198–99; Elyce J. Rotella, *From Home to Office: U.S. Women at Work, 1870–1930* (Ann Arbor, Mich.: UMI Research Press, 1981), 119–23, 129; Sharon Hartman Strom, *Beyond the Typewriter* (Urbana: University of Illinois Press, 1992), chaps. 1, 2.

77. All women in the Calumet sample who were hired as clerical workers from 1918 to 1922 were born in the United States. They ranged in age from seventeen to twenty-seven; 8 in 10 lived in Roseland or Kensington. Manson's employee service record is part of the Calumet database. See employee W001, interview by author, 19 Mar. 1981, Chicago; *Pullman Car Works Standard,* May 1917, 14; Ileen A. DeVault, *Sons and Daughters of Labor: Class and Clerical Work in Turn-of-the-Century Pittsburgh* (Ithaca, N.Y.: Cornell University Press, 1990); Rotella, *From Home to Office,* 114–15; Spear, *Black Chicago,* 155; Strom, *Beyond the Typewriter,* 297–301.

78. Complaint #81, Pullman Company—West Philadelphia Car Yards, 1, Box 97, File 201, Women's Service Section, USRA.

79. See Edith Hall, memorandum on 4th and T St. Yards, Box 97, File 200; Inspection Report, Columbia, S.C., 16 Feb. 1920, Box 97, File 196; Inspection of St. Louis Yards, Box 97, File 198; and other ethnic and racial statistics in various inspection reports in Box 97, File 196–202, all in Women's Service Section, USRA; Garret Rice, president, Local 16351 Car and Coach Cleaners, Chicago, to Mr. Carter, 1 Feb. 1919, and Ms. Clifford Thomas, Atlanta, Ga., to Walker D. Hines, director general, 17 Dec. 1919, both in E-38-3, General File 1918–22, USRA; *Black Worker* 8, no. 15 (Mar. 1947): 6; Chicago Commission, *Negro in Chicago,* 431. There were 1,950 "colored" car cleaners in 1921, according to F. L. Simmons to Phil H. Brown, 5 Apr. 1922, and the company had more than four thousand car cleaners in 1916, according to Husband (*Story of the Pullman Car,* 154).

Chapter 3: The State and Pullman Workers

1. Jeffrey Haydu, *Making American Industry Safe for Democracy: Comparative Perspectives on the State and Employee Representation in the Era of World War I* (Urbana: University of Illinois Press, 1997), 3–4, 6–10, chap. 2; Joseph A. McCartin, *Labor's Great War: The Struggle for Industrial Democracy and the Origins of Modern American Labor Relations, 1912–1921* (Chapel Hill: University of North Carolina Press, 1997), 2, 4, 78–80.

2. Employees of Pullman Company, Kansas City, Missouri to the director general, USRA, 29 May 1918, E-38-3, General File 1918–22, USRA. Box 39 contains many such letters from different Pullman facilities, including two from Charles A. Fisher, who claimed to represent several thousand workers at the Pullman Car Works.

3. McAdoo first seized the sleeping-car service on a temporary basis but made a final decision to keep it in May 1918. Until then Pullman officials acted as if they were not under government control. See "U.S. takes over Pullman Service," *Chicago Tribune*, 24 May 1918, and "U.S. takes over Passenger Cars of Pullman Co.," *Chicago Herald Examiner*, 24 May 1918, both in PS A33; Colin J. Davis, *Power at Odds: The 1922 National Railroad Shopmen's Strike* (Urbana: University of Illinois Press, 1997), 36–39.

4. Walker D. Hines, *War History of American Railroads* (New Haven, Conn.: Yale University Press, 1928), 7–8; 18, 162–65, 167–68, 177–78; Ruth O'Brien, *Workers' Paradox: The Republican Origins of New Deal Labor Policy, 1886–1935* (Chapel Hill: University of North Carolina Press, 1998), 73; Laurence S. Zakson, "Railway Labor Legislation, 1888 to 1930: A Legal History of Congressional Railway Labor Relations Policy," *Rutgers Law Journal* 20, no. 2 (1989): 320, 332–37, 341–44.

5. J. J. McDermott, Pullman conductor, Washington, D.C., to Director General McAdoo, 11 June 1918; "Two Pullman Employees," Chicago, Ill., to the director general, 3 June 1918; Elmer Haberk, secretary, Ludlow Lodge #819, Brotherhood of Railway Carmen (BRCA), telegram to the director general, 17 May 1918; Ernest Cecil, president, BRCA, Bromley, Ky., and C. M. Densferd, vice president, Sheet Metal Workers, telegram to A. O. Wharton, 17 May 1918; R. T. McQuillen, telegram to W. S. Carter, 2 Jan. 1919, all in E-38-3, General File 1918–22, USRA, among others.

6. Even in industries like meatpacking, where workers attempted to build a biracial union movement during World War I, white racism and black suspicion of white motives hampered organizing, and only a minority of black workers actually joined the movement. See E. W. Parlee, Hotel and Restaurant Employees International Alliance, to W. S. Carter, 18 Oct. 1918, E. W. Stokien, Brotherhood of Sleeping Car Porters' Protective Union, New York City, to Walker D. Hines, director general, 1 Oct. 1919, and Harry Leland, financial secretary, Dining and Sleeping Car Employees Local #282, AFL, Omaha, to Mr. Franklin, 3 Feb. 1920, all in E-38-3, General File 1918–22, USRA; Eric Arnesen, "Charting an Independent Course: African-American Railroad Workers in the World War I Era," in *Labor Histories: Class, Politics, and the Working-Class Experience*, ed. Eric Arnesen, Julie Greene, and Bruce

Laurie (Urbana: University of Illinois Press, 1998), 286–91; James R. Barrett, *Work and Community in the Jungle: Chicago's Packinghouse Workers, 1894 1922* (Urbana: University of Illinois Press, 1987), 203–19; Chicago Commission on Race Relations, *The Negro in Chicago* (Chicago: University of Chicago Press, 1922), 405–7, 418; Rick Halpern, *Down on the Killing Floor: Black and White Workers in Chicago's Packinghouses, 1904–1954* (Urbana: University of Illinois Press, 1997), 51–54; William H. Harris, *Keeping the Faith: A. Philip Randolph, Milton P. Webster, and the Brotherhood of Sleeping Car Porters, 1925–1937* (Urbana: University of Illinois Press, 1977), 14; Ira De A. Reid, *Negro Membership in American Labor Unions* (1930; rpt., New York: Negro Universities Press, 1969), 124–26; Sterling Spero and Abram Harris, *The Black Worker: The Negro and the Labor Movement* (New York: Columbia University Press, 1931), 58–64, chap. 7.

7. F. L. Simmons, memo to Clive Runnells, 1 Dec. 1920, 06/01/01, Box 2, File 49, PANL.

8. Although many historians have stressed the hostility of the on-train railroad unions to the new immigrants from southern and eastern Europe, by 1910 significant numbers of shop workers in northern cities were southern or eastern European immigrants and the shopcraft unions welcomed their participation. See F. L. Simmons to Frank McManamy, 1 Oct. 1919, 06/01/ 01, Box 3, File 58, PANL; Harry Smith et al., to director general of the railroads, 22 July 1918, and flyer calling first meeting of Pullman System Federation #122, 15 Sept. 1919, Chicago, both in E-38-3, General File 1918–22, USRA; "Striking Shopmen Meet and Organize a Local Federation," *Daily Calumet*, 6 Aug. 1919; Davis, *Power at Odds*, 21–23; Robert E. L. Knight, *Industrial Relations in the San Francisco Bay Area, 1900–1918* (Berkeley: University of California Press, 1960), 299, 360; McCartin, *Labor's Great War*, 58–60; Michael Mulcaire, *The International Brotherhood of Electrical Workers: A Study in Trade Union Structure and Functions* (Washington, D.C.: Catholic University of America, 1923), 26.

9. David Brody, *Steelworkers in America: The Nonunion Era* (New York: Harper and Row, 1960), chap. 11; Haydu, *Making American Industry Safe*, chap. 2; McCartin, *Labor's Great War*, 104–11; Larry Peterson, "The Intellectual World of the IWW: An American Worker's Library in the First Half of the Twentieth Century," *History Workshop* 22 (1986): 159; in the *Daily Calumet*: "What Americanization Means," editorial, 28 June 1918, "Campaign for Unions in the Mills Opened," 5 Sept. 1918, and "Amalgamated Ass'n Iron, Steel and Tin Workers Launched," 20 Nov. 1918; in the *Calumet Index*: "Flag Raising at Pullman Shops: Workmen Cheer Old Glory," 25 May 1917, "The Poles Pledge Allegiance to America," 13 July 1917, "Our Italians," editorial, 16 July 1917, and "Alien Slackers Hotly Shamed by Draft Aid," 17 Aug. 1917.

10. John Scott, acting president, AFLRED, to Frank McManamy, assistant director, Division of Operations, USRA, 16 Sept. 1919, and F. L. Simmons, assistant federal auditor, confidential memo for C. S. Pflager, mechanical superintendent, 8 Dec. 1919, both in 06/01/01, Box 1, File 10, PANL; John B. Payne, director general of the railroad, letter re Pullman Car Lines Decision

#25, 27 July 1920, in employment packet of employee Coo1, Calumet shop, 06/02/03, PANL; R. T. McQuillen, Chicago, telegram to W. S. Carter, 2 Jan. 1919, J. A. Franklin, memo of 27 Jan. 1919, and Fred C. Bolam, general vice president, International Brotherhood of Blacksmiths and Helpers, to W. S. Carter, 6 Mar. 1919, all in E-38-3, General File 1918–22, USRA. Numerous cases of local supervisors' failing to implement USRA directives, as detailed by the investigators for the Women's Service Section, may be found in Box 97, File 198, Women's Service Section, USRA; Hines, *War History*, 26, 45–46.

11. At the Calumet shop the vote on piecework was 895 against maintaining piece rates, 23 for, and 10 void. In 1921 the number of job titles was 111 at Calumet, 113 at Wilmington, and 106 at Richmond. See Payrolls, Calumet, Richmond, and Wilmington repair shops, 15 Nov. 1921, PP; 1941–42 Conference with Company Representatives, 149, 06/01/04, Box 26, File 695, PANL; Spec. 72–74, Box 1, Board of Adjustment #2, USRA; Spec. 123, Spec. 156, Spec. 163, and Spec. 182, Box 2, Board of Adjustment #2, USRA; Spl. 209, Spl. 210, Spl. 256, and Spl. 269, Box 3, Board of Adjustment #2, USRA; and Spl. 324, Box 4, Board of Adjustment #2, USRA; E. J. Vail, president, Local Protective Board of BRCA, Richmond, to E. F. Potter, chairman, Railway Board of Adjustment #2, 22 Mar. 1919, E-38-3, General File 1918–22, USRA; Hines, *War History*, 162–63, 166, 177.

12. *Pullman News*, Aug. 1922, 125; Haydu, *Making American Industry Safe*, 55–59, 66, 98.

13. "One Hundred Thousand Quit When Rail Administration Continues to Quibble," *New Majority*, 9 Aug. 1919; "Shopmen's Strike Threatens Local Steel Industries," *Daily Calumet*, 4 Aug. 1919; "Striking Shopmen Meet and Organize a Local Federation," *Daily Calumet*, 6 Aug. 1919; "Railroad Shopmen Here Still Out on Strike," *Daily Calumet*, 11 Aug. 1919; Davis, *Power at Odds*, 44–45; Hines, *War History*, 171–75.

14. No women in the Calumet sample were hired for unskilled labor or helper-level positions outside the upholstery department until USRA oversight ended in 1920. See Nancy F. Cott, *The Grounding of Modern Feminism* (New Haven, Conn.: Yale University Press, 1987), chaps. 1, 2; Maurine Greenwald, *Women, War, and Work: The Impact of World War I on Women Workers in the United States* (Westport, Conn.: Greenwood Press, 1980), 20, 48, 60–69, 107, 116; Hines, *War History*, 168.

15. Report of Investigation of Conditions at Council Bluffs, Iowa, Pullman–Union Pacific Yard, 10 Feb.1920, Box 97, File 202, Women's Service Section, USRA.

16. Memorandum, St. Louis Series 29, 25 Aug. 1919, Box 97, File 198, Women's Service Section, USRA.

17. Ibid.; memorandum, St. Louis Series 2–8, 10, 11–16, 18, 46, and 47, Box 97, File 198; Index of Complaints by Name of Road and Digest, Pullman Company, #93, Box 97, File 291; memorandum to St. Paul Series 20, Box 97, File 199; and report from Florence Clark, Interview with Shop Committee from BRC Shop local re Seamstresses and the Case They Have up with the Division of Labor, 21 Aug. 1919, Box 97, File 198, all in Women's Service

Section, USRA; Spl. 208, 30 July 1919, Box 3, Board of Adjustment #2, USRA. Initially, the Calumet shop paid seamstresses 50 to 68 cents per hour; all seamstresses were paid the then-current mechanics' rate of 72 cents per hour by April 1920. See Payrolls for the Second Half of May 1919, the Second Half of July 1919, and the First Half of April 1920, Calumet Repair Shop, PP; Susan E. Hirsch, "Rethinking the Sexual Division of Labor: Pullman Repair Shops, 1900–1969," *Radical History Review* 35 (1986): 26–48.

18. The Calumet oversample for black workers includes eleven men, two of whom became helpers, hired from the beginning of government control to the 1922 strike. Black workers comprised 5 percent of those hired at the Wilmington shop during the same period. Company-wide, Pullman had eighteen "colored" skilled yard mechanics on Mar. 31, 1921, according to F. L. Simmons to Phil H. Brown, commissioner of conciliation, Dept. of Labor, 5 Apr. 1922, 06/01/01, Box 1, File 23, PANL. See also Brief, Pullman Car Employes Association of the Repair Shops, 2, 1946 Representation of Pullman Employees, National Mediation Board, R-1625, 06/01/05, Box 4a, PANL; Gail Bederman, *Manliness and Civilization: A Cultural History of Gender and Race in the United States, 1880–1917* (Chicago: University of Chicago Press, 1995), chap. 1; Philip S. Foner, *Organized Labor and the Black Worker, 1619–1981* (New York: International Publishers, 1981), 147–48; Hines, *War History,* 170; McCartin, *Labor's Great War,* 114–18; Spero and Harris, *The Black Worker,* 308.

19. In "Pullman Co. Officials Confer with Employes," 7 Sept. 1918, the *Chicago Defender* reported confidently on a meeting between porters and company officials at which Director General McAdoo was warmly praised and where "from both word and spirit of the conference it was gleaned that better days are ahead for the employes. Race men with education who enter the service in the future may confidently look for promotion to the very top . . . conductors." See also Payrolls, Chicago Southern District, June 1918 through Dec. 1919, PP; "Raise to Pullman Workers," *Chicago Evening Post,* 3 July 1918, PS A33; Chicago Commission, *The Negro in Chicago,* 391.

20. Untitled clipping, *(St. Paul, Minn.) Appeal,* 4 Dec. 1897; "Julius N. Avendorph, Who Is Doing Things for His Race," *Chicago Defender,* 10 Aug. 1918; "Julius Avendorph Promoted," *Chicago Defender,* 22 Jan. 1921; William A. Sundstrom, "The Color Line: Racial Norms and Discrimination in Urban Labor Markets, 1910–1950," *Journal of Economic History* 54 (1994): 389.

21. "Two Pullman Employees" to director general, 3 June 1918.

22. The *Pullman Car Works Standard,* for instance, highlighted engagements and marriages of women workers but not those of men, even as it noted that the plant needed more women workers because it "lost a number recently to marriage" (*Pullman Car Works Standard,* May 1917, 4, 14–15, and July 1917, 15).

23. According to the samples, no black men or women were hired as clerical workers at the Calumet, Richmond, or Wilmington shops before the railroad shopmen's strike of 1922. See "Julius N. Avendorph, Who Is Doing Things," *Chicago Defender,* 10 Aug. 1918. The men named in this article are

listed on the central office payroll for the first half of August 1918, but most disappear by mid-1919. See Payrolls, General Office, PP; Sharon Hartman Strom, *Beyond the Typewriter* (Urbana: University of Illinois Press, 1992), 302–3; Sundstrom, "The Color Line," 389–91.

24. List of Delegates Present at Convention of Carmen, 06/01/01, Box 1, File 10, PANL; 1942 Annual Conference of the Repair Shops and Pullman Co. Management, 27–29 Aug., 141, 06/01/04, Box 26, File 695a, PANL; Florence Clark, "Interview with Shop Committee from BRC Shop local re Seamstresses," 21 Aug. 1919.

25. Inspection of Columbia, S.C., Yard, 16 Feb. 1920; memorandum, St. Louis Series 2–8 and 11–16, pp. 5–6; Garret Rice, president, Local 16351 Car and Coach Cleaners, Chicago, to Mr. Carter, 1 Feb. 1919, E-38-3, General File 1918–22, USRA.

26. Inspection reports of Pullman yards, Box 97, Files 196–202, Women's Service Section, USRA.

27. Memorandum from Florence E. Clark to Miss Goldmark, 16 Jan. 1920, Box 97, File 199, Women's Service Section, USRA. See McCartin, *Labor's Great War*, 112–13, on Clark.

28. Investigation at Council Bluffs, Iowa, Pullman C & NW, 9 Feb. 1920, Box 97, File 202, Women's Service Section, USRA.

29. Barrett, *Work and Community*, 203–19; McCartin, *Labor's Great War*, 108–18; Spero and Harris, *The Black Worker*, chaps. 9–12.

30. Memorandum, St. Louis 41, 3, Box 97, File 198, Women's Service Section, USRA.

31. Memorandum, St. Louis Series 2–8, 11–16, pp. 5–6.

32. "Pullman Co. Tries to Get by with Wage Cut," *New Majority*, 8 Jan. 1921. Chambers is quoted in *Report of Proceedings of the Fortieth Annual Convention of the American Federation of Labor* (Washington, D.C.: Law Reporter Printing Co., 1920), 311 (see also 272–73, 351–52); *Report of Proceedings of the Thirty-ninth Annual Convention of the American Federation of Labor* (Washington, D.C.: Law Reporter Printing Co., 1919), 228, 305; *Report of Proceedings of the Forty-first Annual Convention of the American Federation of Labor* (Washington, D.C.: Law Reporter Printing Co., 1921), 230–31, 431–32.

33. Arnesen, "Charting an Independent Course," 291–93; Reid, *Negro Membership*, 33–38. The Railway Men's International Benevolent Industrial Association viewed such moves to open membership to black workers as a farce and continued to attack the AFL.

34. Brody, *Steelworkers in America*, chap. 12; McCartin, *Labor's Great War*, 171–94.

35. Eligibility to vote at Pullman required employment for at least sixty days; only those who had been in service for two years were eligible to be representatives. Even this seemingly small narrowing of the franchise meant that in 1924 only 89 percent of Car Works employees were eligible to vote in ERP elections. See Statement in Regard to the Plan of Employe Representation, 1, 5–6, 06/01/01, Box 2, File 43, PANL; printed copies of plan provi-

sions for 1920, 1924, 1927, with proposed revisions written in, 06/01/01, Box 4, File 68a, PANL; *Pullman News*, June 1924, 62; Barrett, *Work and Community*, 248–54; Brody, *Steelworkers in America*, 226–28; Davis, *Power at Odds*, 49–52; McCartin, *Labor's Great War*, 205, 212–17; David Montgomery, *The Fall of the House of Labor: The Workplace, the State, and American Labor Activism, 1865–1925* (New York: Cambridge University Press, 1987), 411–17; Daniel Nelson, "The Company Union Movement, 1900–1937: A Reexamination," *Business History Review* 56 (1982): 344–46.

36. Hines, *War History*, chap. 17; Davis, *Power at Odds*, 48–49; Zakson, "Railway Labor Legislation," 355–56.

37. Pullman managers violated the national contract with the shopcraft unions, and Pullman officials used every tactic to delay resolution of outstanding differences. By February 1920 the union and company officials disagreed on almost sixty issues. See F. L. Simmons, memo for C. S. Pflager, 8 Dec. 1919; Issues Raised by Pullman Company re National Agreement, Feb. 1920, Box 12, Agreements Between Railroads and Labor Organizations, USRA; Hines, *War History*, 174–75; O'Brien, *Workers' Paradox*, chap. 5; Harry D. Wolf, *The Railroad Labor Board* (Chicago: University of Chicago Press, 1927), 40–43.

38. All the women hired in the unskilled jobs were immigrants from southern and eastern Europe, as were two-thirds of those hired in the helper-level positions. All the women hired as paint scrubbers, laborers, or as members of the woman's labor gang began in 1920. For differences in pay rates see Payrolls, Calumet Repair Shop, 31 May 1920 and 31 July 1920, PP. Daczkowska's and Benicky's employee service records are part of the Calumet database. In *Women, War, and Work*, 93, Greenwald notes that women's employment in the railroad industry as a whole peaked in October 1918, and thereafter more women were laid off than hired in new positions.

39. Payroll, Calumet Repair Shop, 15 Sept. 1920, PP; 1942 Annual Conference of the Repair Shops, 141; memorandum, St. Louis 41, 4; Index of Complaints by Name of Road, Pullman Company, #79; Fifth Weekly report (14–20 Apr. 1922), John F. Nelson, 5478, Box 8, File 10, AFLRED; Davis, *Power at Odds*, 42–43; Wolf, *The Railroad Labor Board*, 60–61, 107.

40. All the women except Daczkowska who had been hired as paint scrubbers, laborers, or for the woman's labor gang left the shop by 1922, most by 1921. See Payrolls, Calumet Repair Shop, 31 July 1920, 15 Sept. 1920, and 30 June 1921 through 30 Apr. 1922, PP; Greenwald, *Women, War, and Work*, 133, 138.

41. F. L. Simmons, memo for J. S. Runnells, 14 Oct. 1920, 06/01/04, Box 1, File 30, PANL.

42. F. L. Simmons to Edward Carry, 21 Jan. 1922, and Plan of Employe Representation, 1 June 1920, revised effective 1 June 1923, 06/01/01, Box 2, File 34, PANL; F. L. Simmons, memo to Clive Runnells, 1 Dec. 1920.

43. Copy of letter from Walter N. Abrams to C. F. Carruthers, 23 Mar. 1921, 1, 06/01/01, Box 5, File 93, PANL.

44. "Pullman Workers Get Sample of 'Company Union' Tactics," *New Majority*, 5 Mar. 1921.

45. The Pullman Company hired a small number of black women as maids on some of its most exclusive trains. Its workforce included ninety-two hundred porters and sixty-seven maids on March 31, 1921. See Statement in Regard to the Plan of Employe Representation, 9; F. L. Simmons to Phil H. Brown, 5 Apr. 1922; "Pullman Car Men Ask Raise," *Chicago Evening Journal*, 5 Jan. 1921, and "Pullman Conductors Request Increased Wages," *Railway Age*, 14 Jan. 1921, both in PS A34; *Pullman News*, Nov. 1922, 227; W. Harris, *Keeping the Faith*, 17–18; Spero and Harris, *The Black Worker*, 440–44.

46. Statement to Mr. Chairman and Gentlemen of the Board by F. L. Simmons, n.d., 06/01/01, Box 1, File 19, PANL; John F. Nelson, general chairman, System Federation #122, to B. M. Jewell, president, AFLRED, 6 Feb. 1922, 5478, Box 8, File 10, AFLRED; "Pullman Co. Tries to Get by," *New Majority*, 8 Jan. 1921; "Pullman Shop Crafts Fight for National Agreement Conditions," *New Majority*, 18 June 1921.

47. J. E. Flannery to F. J. Boeckelman, 17 July 1962, 06/01/03, Box 24, File 537, PANL; John F. Nelson, general chairman, System Federation #122, to E. F. Carry, president, Pullman Company, 19 Mar. 1923, 5478, Box 107, File 4, AFLRED; "2,000 Employes of Pullman Co. to Work 9 Hours," *Chicago Tribune*, 17 Jan. 1921, and "Pullman Company Wage Reduction," *Railway Age*, 28 Jan. 1921, both in PS A34; Davis, *Power at Odds*, 49–58.

48. *Pullman News*, May 1922, 31.

49. "Pullman Co. Tries to Get by," *New Majority*, 8 Jan. 1921; "Pullman Company Wage Reduction," *Railway Age*, 28 Jan. 1921, 267, "Pullman Unions Declare Pay Cut Move Is Illegal," *Chicago Evening Journal*, 10 June 1921, and "Unions Attack Pullman Move," *Chicago Daily News*, 10 June 1921, all in PS A34.

50. Copy of letter from Louis Morelli et al. to U.S. Labor Board, 18 May 1921, 06/01/01, Box 5, File 93, PANL.

51. "Pullman Shop Workers Fight Wage Cuts," *Chicago American* 7 Jan. 1921.

52. Transcript of Proceedings, 1946 Representation of Pullman Employees, National Mediation Board R-1625, 71, 74, 06/01/05, Box 4a, PANL; "12,000 Pullman Shop Employes Voting on General Strike," *Chicago Evening Journal*, 6 June 1921, PS A34; "Pullman Shop Crafts Fight" *New Majority*, 18 June 1921; "Pullman Car Signs Up with Rail Unions," *New Majority*, 17 Sept. 1921; untitled article, *Industrial Solidarity*, 11 June 1921. The service record of employee W101 reveals the contract's effect. W101 began work on August 13, 1917, and was classified as a battery helper and paid at the helper's rate. He was given the mechanic's rate under the USRA order to the Pullman Company in February 1920; his job title was changed to battery electrician in September 1921 upon the signing of the contract with the system federation. See Service record of W101, Wilmington Repair Shop, 06/02/03, PANL. Haydu uses the RLB decision in September 1921 as an example of how the board often supported unions and how companies often complied with its rulings. From Pullman's perspective, however, signing a contract was mere-

ly a tactical move in a war that it had no intention of losing. See Davis, *Power at Odds*, 52–55; Haydu, *Making American Industry Safe*, 112–14.

53. The system federation was stronger at some Pullman shops and yards than others: 86 percent of the St. Louis repair shop workers belonged, as did 71 percent of those at the Buffalo and Wilmington shops, but only 49 percent of those at the Richmond shop, which had just voted for the ERP. See Simmons, Statement to Mr. Chairman and Gentlemen, n.d. See also John F. Nelson to B. M. Jewell, 6 Feb. 1922; Document #213, Minutes of Executive Council Meeting, Railway Employes Department, 23 Feb. 1922, 2–3; Committee (J. E. Nichols et al.), New York City, to Charles P. Ford, international secretary, International Brotherhood of Electrical Workers, 27 June 1922; First Weekly Report (17–24 Mar. 1922), 2; Fifth Weekly Report (14–20 Apr. 1922); and Fourth Weekly Report, Western Tour (6–13 June 1922), John F. Nelson, all in 5478, Box 8, File 10, AFLRED; Davis, *Power at Odds*, 56–57.

54. Nelson was the only leader of the shopcraft unions at Calumet whose employee service record is part of the Calumet database. See J. F. McGrath, vice president, AFLRED, to John F. Nelson, 24 Feb. 1922, and Nelson to McGrath, 16 May 1922, both in 5478, Box 8, File 10, AFLRED.

55. Second Weekly Report (24–31 Mar. 1922), Third Weekly Report (1–7 Apr. 1922), Fourth Weekly Report (7–14 Apr. 1922), Fifth Weekly Report (14–20 Apr. 1922), Third Weekly Report, Western Tour (30 May–6 June 1922), Fourth Weekly Report, Western Tour (6–13 June 1922), John F. Nelson, all in 5478, Box 8, File 10, AFLRED.

56. First Weekly Report, Western Tour (16–23 May 1922), John F. Nelson, 5478, Box 8, File 10, AFLRED.

57. *Pullman News*, June 1922, 48.

58. Wages may well have been relatively high, because the Pullman Company's frequent corporate ally on the Chicago labor scene, International Harvester, found it difficult to get workers at its West Pullman plant because of the higher rates paid at Pullman's Calumet shop and the Illinois Central's Burnside shop. See Davis, *Power at Odds*, 58–63; Robert Ozanne, *Wages in Practice and Theory: McCormick and International Harvester, 1860–1960* (Madison: University of Wisconsin Press, 1968), 46–47.

59. The maintenance-of-way workers, whose wages also were cut by the Railroad Labor Board, began to strike in conjunction with the shop workers but quickly returned to work. See Davis, *Power at Odds*, 62–63; Margaret Gadsby, "Strike of the Railroad Shopmen," *Monthly Labor Review* 15, no. 6 (Dec. 1922): 4–5, 13.

60. Minute Book 1, Executive Committee, Board of Directors, Pullman Company, meeting of 18 July 1922, 02/01/02, vol. 15, PANL.

61. "Pullman Plant to Lay Off Men," *(Wilmington, Del.) News*, 21 June 1922, PS A34; "Prosperity Hits at Pullman Shops; 10 Days Holiday Given," *Richmond (California) Daily Independent*, 30 June 1922; "Pullman Workers Stay Out," *Richmond Daily Independent*, 8 July 1922; "Pullman Men to Strike Monday," *(Wilmington, Del.) Every Evening*, 8 July 1922; John F. Nelson to Edward F. Carry, 19 Mar. 1923; 1937 Conference Proceedings, 281, 06/01/04, Box 25, File 677, PANL; Davis, *Power at Odds*, 66–68.

62. Samples of those in the Calumet, Wilmington, and Richmond shops during June 1922 show 96 percent or more of mechanics went on strike. At Calumet 94 percent of helpers and 88 percent of laborers went on strike, and those who were black were even more likely than white workers to strike. At Wilmington 86 percent of helpers struck but only 57 percent of laborers. Black men were concentrated at the laborer rank, but they were as likely to strike as white laborers. The one black mechanic at Wilmington went on strike too. On July 28 the company reported 31 workers at the St. Louis shop, 25 at Buffalo, 54 at Wilmington, and 18 at Richmond, with Calumet completely closed. See Typed Reports on Conditions at the Repair Shops and Yards, July–October 1922, 06/01/01, Box 5, File 103, PANL; from *Every Evening:* "Pullman Workers at Buffalo Almost All Out on Strike," 10 July 1922, "Little Change in Strike at Pullman's," 11 July 1922, "Pullman Strike Shows No Change," 12 July 1922, "Central Union Pledges Support to Striking Shopmen," 19 July 1922; "Railroad Strike Sweeps Nation," *Richmond Daily Independent*, 1 July 1922; B. M. Jewell to John F. Nelson, 26 July 1922, 5478, Box 107, File 8, AFLRED.

63. Twenty men in the sample of Calumet shop workers had been strikers at the Car Works in 1894 and were employed at the shop in June 1922. Four had become leaders or foremen and did not strike in 1922. The other sixteen struck in 1922. See Typed Reports on Conditions, July and Aug. 1922. The following argument can also be found in Susan Hirsch, "The Search for Unity Among Railroad Workers: The Pullman Strike in Perspective," in *The Pullman Strike and the Crisis of the 1890s*, ed. Richard Schneirov, Shelton Stromquist, and Nick Salvatore (Urbana: University of Illinois Press, 1999).

64. Job histories of members of the Calumet sample—among them, Bernier, who worked at the Car Works during 1922—reveal no evidence of strike activity. Bernier's employee service record is part of the Calumet database. See also Davis, *Power at Odds*, 73–75; Peterson, "The Intellectual World of the IWW," 153–72.

65. Of Wilmington sample members who were in the shop in June 1922, 98 percent were white men and 80 percent were born in the United States. Of those born in the United States for whom precise birthplaces are given, 93 percent were born in Delaware or contiguous states. Sixty percent had been hired before 1911, and 18 percent were in the shop during the 1894 strike. Herdman's employee service record is part of the Wilmington database. See also *Pullman Car Works Standard*, Mar. 1917, 11; "Pullman Workers Went on Strike at Local Plant Today," *Every Evening*, 10 July 1922; Second Weekly Report, John F. Nelson, 31 Mar. 1922.

66. Carol Hoffecker, *Corporate Capital: Wilmington in the Twentieth Century* (Philadelphia: Temple University Press, 1983), 5–39, 85, 87, 94; Charles N. Lanier Jr., "Labor in Delaware," in *Delaware: A History of the First State*, ed. Henry Clay Reed (New York: Lewis Historical Publishing Co., 1947), 2:565; Yda Schreuder, "The Impact of Labor Segmentation on the Ethnic Division of Labor and the Immigrant Residential Community: Polish Leather Workers in Wilmington, Delaware in the Early-Twentieth Century," *Journal of Historical Geography* 16 (1990): 412, 417–18.

67. "Pullman Plant to Lay Off Men," *(Wilmington, Del.) News*, 21 June 1922, PS A34.

68. Colin J. Davis, "The 1922 Railroad Shopmen's Strike in the Southeast: A Study of Success and Failure," in *Organized Labor in the Twentieth-Century South*, ed. Robert Zieger (Knoxville: University of Tennessee Press, 1991), 113–34, argues that while community support and women's auxiliaries helped strikers to hold out, the degree of intransigence of the companies and the effectiveness of the structure of each railroad's system federation determined the success or failure of the strike on any particular line. See also "Pullman Strikers Say They Are Gaining," *Every Evening*, 14 July 1922; Davis, *Power at Odds*, 66–68, 272.

69. The shopcraft unions sought to capitalize on the civic and political power of workers by backing a candidate for county sheriff who promised to deputize strikers to keep the peace. From the *Richmond Daily Independent:* "Support Is Lent Strikers in This City," 10 July 1922, "Pullman Shop Men Out; Post Picket Lines," 11 July 1922, and "Pullman Shop Men Endorse Stand of Rev. Paul Little," 10 Aug. 1922.

70. "A Justifiable Strike," *Richmond Daily Independent*, 10 July 1922.

71. Of the Richmond workers in the sample who were on strike in 1922, 45 percent were born in the United States, and 56 percent lived in Richmond. Reeves's employee service record is part of the Richmond database. See also "Pullman Bar License Taken Away," 15 May 1917, and "Pullman Bar Case Is Put over a Week," 29 May 1917, both in *Richmond Record-Herald*.

72. "Now Picketing Homes," *Chicago Daily News*, 17 July 1922; from *Richmond Daily Independent:* "Pullman Shop Men Out; Post Picket Lines," 11 July 1922, "Pullman Workers Maintain Pickets at Shops Here," 15 July 1922, "Pullman Pickets Are Enjoined," 24 July 1922, and "Pullman Shop Men Endorse Stand of Rev. Paul Little," 10 Aug. 1922; from *(Wilmington) Every Evening:* "Pullman Strikers Say They Are Gaining," 14 July 1922, "Little Change in Pullman Situation," 17 July 1922, "Pullman Strikers are Marking Time," 19 July 1922, "Central Union Pledges Support to Striking Shopmen," 19 July 1922, "Pullman Strike May Be Settled Soon," 21 July 1922, "Pullman Situation," 26 July 1922, "Striking Shopmen Say They Will Win Fight," 2 Aug. 1922, and "Striker Says He Can Not Meet Support Order," 5 Aug. 1922. The Typed Reports on Conditions at the Repair Shops and Yards note picketing "as usual" from July through the third week of September. See also Davis, *Power at Odds*, 78–80, 96.

73. "Telegram to Stephens Says Troops Are Not Needed," *Richmond Daily Independent*, 21 July 1922; from the *(Wilmington) Every Evening:* "To Notify All Men at Pullman to Quit," 13 July 1922, "Accused of Annoying Railroad Workers," 15 July 1922, "G. M. Gilkey is Attacked by Mob, Dragged from Car," 28 July 1922, "James B. Stevenson Brutally Assaulted," 5 Aug. 1922, and "P.R.R. Fourteenth St. Bridge Dynamited at 2:35 This Morning," 31 Aug. 1922. Numerous articles in the *Daily Calumet* include "Shop Strikers are Arrested," 14 July 1922, "Strikers Fire on Car Filled with Strikebreakers," 19 July 1922, "Rioting in Burnside, One Man Badly Beaten," 26 July

1922, "Two Are Attacked by Men Thought to Be Striking Shopmen," 26 July 1922, "Imported Shop Worker Beaten by Four Men," 28 July 1922, "Two Men Shot in Burnside Strike Riots," 29 July 1922, "Non-Union Shopman Victim of Trio of Sluggers Here," 29 July 1922, "Burnside Shopman Slain by Sluggers on Way to Work," 3 Aug. 1922, "Non-Union Shopman Victim of Assault by Strikers," 4 Aug. 1922, "Colored Man Attacked and Beaten by 'Crew,'" 25 Aug. 1922, and "Two Strikebreakers Attacked by Sluggers," 31 Aug. 1922. See also Davis, *Power at Odds*, 71–73, 75, 83–89, 96–98.

74. "Now Picketing Homes," *Chicago Daily News*, 17 July 1922.

75. The woman is quoted in "Women Join Burnside Rioters," *Chicago Daily News*, 7 July 1922. See also "Burnside Shopmen Slugged," *Chicago Daily News*, 8 July 1922.

76. "Smothering a Strike by Injunction," *Literary Digest* 74, no. 12 (16 Sept. 1922), 7–9; Gadsby, "Strike of the Railroad Shopmen," 3, 6, 9–10; Zakson, "Railway Labor Legislation," 357–58.

77. Davis, *Power at Odds*, 133–39; Gadsby, "Strike of the Railroad Shopmen," 11–12.

78. "Appeal Made to Stephens to Stop Use of Japs," *Richmond Daily Independent*, 8 July 1922; "Colored Men at the B.&O. R.R. Shops Here," *Daily Calumet*, 8 July 1922; "Armed Workers Anger Local Railroad Worker," *Daily Calumet*, 30 Aug. 1922; Davis, *Power at Odds*, 69–71, 117–26, 158–59; Spero and Harris, *The Black Worker*, 308. In Milwaukee public concern about the possibility of a race riot pressured railroads to stop using black strikebreakers. See Joe William Trotter Jr., *Black Milwaukee: The Making of an Industrial Proletariat, 1915–1945* (Urbana: University of Illinois Press, 1985), 56–57.

79. Typed Reports on Conditions, Aug. and Sept. 1922.

80. According to the samples of those in the shops in June 1922, 42 percent of Wilmington strikers returned to the shop eventually, as did 71 percent of Calumet strikers and 63 percent of Richmond strikers. See Typed Reports on Conditions, 14 and 16 Oct. 1922; L. S. Hungerford, memo to F. A. Cooke, 26 Sept. 1922, 06/01/03, Box 26, File 607, PANL; John F. Nelson to B. M. Jewell, president, AFLRED, 11 Sept. 1922, 5478, Box 107, File 7, AFLRED; Nelson to Jewell, 19 Oct. 1922, 5478, Box 107, File 6, AFLRED; Nelson and Harry Smith to J. F. McGrath, vice president, AFLRED, 22 Nov. 1922, 5478, Box 107, File 5, AFLRED; "Tag Day for the Railroad Strikers," *Daily Calumet*, 18 Sept. 1922; "Rail Strike Tag Day," *New Majority*, 7 Oct. 1922; "Shop Crafts Tag Day Tomorrow," *Richmond Daily Independent*, 20 Oct. 1922; Davis, *Power at Odds*, 138–39, 152–57.

81. John F. Nelson and Harry Smith to J. F. McGrath, 22 Nov. 1922.

Chapter 4: Restoring the Open Shop

1. Reports from the Mutual Industrial Service, 24 Nov. 1922–23 Apr. 1923, 06/01/01, Box 3, File 52, PANL.

2. Forty-four percent of Calumet strikers returned between October and December 1922, as did 43 percent of Richmond strikers and 39 percent of Wilmington strikers; some returning strikers retired on company pensions in the 1920s and 1930s. See F. L. Simmons, memo to L. S. Hungerford, 10 Dec. 1923, 06/01/01, Box 2, File 37; 1937 Conference Proceedings, 281, 06/01/04, Box 25, File 677, and service records of employees W103–W107, Wilmington shop, 06/02/03, all in PANL; *Pullman News,* Oct. 1922, 163, Nov. 1922, 195–96, and Dec. 1922, 238. Other railroads, such as the Pennsylvania, also lured workers back with pension benefits. See *(Wilmington) Every Evening,* 10 Aug. 1922. One might have expected to see age discrimination to weed out older workers who would demand pensions. The average ages of returnees and nonreturnees were virtually identical, however, except at Wilmington, where returnees were actually older on average than those who did not return. Average age of returnees versus nonreturnees: Wilmington, 45.9 years/42.9 years; Richmond, 38.4/37.2; Calumet, 41.7/42.4.

3. Comment in service record of employee W108, Wilmington shop, 06/02/03, PANL. See also L. S. Hungerford, vice president and general manager, to E. C. Morris, general auditor, 7 Aug. 1923 and 8 Apr. 1929, 06/01/04, Box 25, File 655, PANL; 1941–42 Conference with Company Representatives, 149, 06/01/04, Box 26, File 695, PANL. All mechanics who returned to Wilmington and Richmond got mechanic-level jobs; 95 percent of those at Calumet did. See also Milton Nadworny, *Scientific Management and the Unions, 1900–1932* (Cambridge, Mass.: Harvard University Press, 1955), chap. 8.

4. "Conditions at Buffalo Shops, Nov. 24, 1922," Box 1, File 16, and Weekly Report on Conditions of the Repair Shops, 16 Oct. 1922, Box 5, File 103, both in 06/01/01, PANL; *Pullman News,* Jan. 1950, 24, 27, and Apr. 1950, 19; U.S. Bureau of the Census, *Fourteenth Census of the United States (1920)* (Washington, D.C.: Government Printing Office, 1922), 3:table 8.

5. Of the men hired between September 1922 and December 1923 at the Calumet Shop, 43 percent of whites and 4 percent of blacks were mechanics; 41 percent of whites and 50 percent of blacks were helpers. At Wilmington 33 percent of whites and 2 percent of blacks were mechanics, while 51 percent of whites and 80 percent of blacks were helpers.

6. Spread Sheet, Employment in Shops, Nov. 1919, 06/01/01, Box 1, File 10; 1939 Annual Conference, 14–25 Aug., 143, 06/01/04, Box 25, File 688; and 1940 Conference Proceedings, 20–23 Aug., 156, 06/01/04, Box 26, File 690, all in PANL.

7. The employee representative is quoted in 1937 Conference Proceedings, 60, 06/01/04, Box 25, File 677, PANL. See also John F. Nelson to John Scott, secretary/treasurer, AFLRED, 23 Mar. 1923, 5478, Box 107, File 4, AFLRED.

8. L. S. Hungerford to Luis Lopez, 9 Feb. 1924, Lopez's employee service packet, Calumet shop, 06/02/03, PANL; David Brody, *Steelworkers in America: The Nonunion Era* (New York: Harper and Row, 1960), 265–69; Lizabeth Cohen, *Making a New Deal: Industrial Workers in Chicago, 1919–1939* (New York: Cambridge University Press, 1990), 165–67; Edward Greer, *Big Steel: Black Politics and Corporate Power in Gary, Indiana* (New York: Monthly

Review Press, 1979), 85–86; Rick Halpern, *Down on the Killing Floor: Black and White Workers in Chicago's Packinghouses, 1904–1954* (Urbana: University of Illinois Press, 1997), 75; Paul Taylor, *Mexican Labor in the United States* (Berkeley: University of California Press, 1932), 2:34–37, 57.

9. According to the samples, women comprised 3.6 percent of those hired between September 1922 and December 1929 at the Calumet shop, 3.0 percent at Wilmington, and 6.6 percent at Richmond. Virtually all these women were clerical workers, seamstresses, nurses, or cooks. Calumet hired a few women in seemingly nontraditional helper jobs, but the women did not stay in those jobs more than a few months. See C. W. Pflager, memo to F. L. Simmons, 5 May 1930, W. J. Keville, memo to C. W. Pflager, 1 May 1930, shop manager, St. Louis, memo to C. W. Pflager, 1 May 1930, shop manager, Wilmington, to C. W. Pflager, 8 May 1930, Richmond Shop Statement re Negro Employment as of 31 Dec. 1928, and "Information Concerning the Negro in Industry," 9 May 1930, all in 06/01/01, Box 1, File 23, PANL.

10. The supervisor of industrial relations is quoted in Minutes of Meeting Held at Chicago, 4–6 Dec. 1922, 8, 06/01/01, Box 3, File 55, PANL; Alba Edwards, *A Socio-Economic Grouping of the Gainful Workers of the United States, 1930* (Washington, D.C.: U.S. Bureau of the Census, 1938), 100–101.

11. *Pullman News*, Aug. 1923, 111, and Oct. 1924, 173; Chicago Commission on Race Relations, *The Negro in Chicago* (Chicago: University of Chicago Press, 1922), 365–66; Thomas N. Maloney, "Degrees of Inequality: The Advance of Black Male Workers in the Northern Meat Packing and Steel Industries before World War II," *Social Science History* 19 (1995): 31–62; Robert Ozanne, *The Negro in the Farm Equipment and Construction Machinery Industries* (Philadelphia: University of Pennsylvania Press, 1972); Howard W. Risher Jr., "The Negro in the Railroad Industry," in *Negro Employment in Land and Air Transport*, Herbert Northrup, Howard W. Risher Jr., Richard D. Leone, and Philip W. Jeffress (Philadelphia: University of Pennsylvania Press, 1971), 45–46; Sterling Spero and Abram Harris, *The Black Worker: The Negro and the Labor Movement* (New York: Columbia University Press, 1931), 152–57, 308–9.

12. Spero and Harris, *The Black Worker*, 167.

13. Ibid., 309.

14. "Information Concerning the Negro in Industry," 9 May 1930; A. Edwards, *A Socio-Economic Grouping*, 100–101; William H. Harris, *Keeping the Faith: A. Philip Randolph, Milton P. Webster, and the Brotherhood of Sleeping Car Porters, 1925–1937* (Urbana: University of Illinois Press, 1977), 55.

15. Minute Book 1, Executive Committee, Board of Directors, Pullman Company, meeting of 29 Mar. 1922, 02/01/02, vol. 15, PANL; A. P. O'Leary, memo to F. L. Simmons, 7 Dec. 1923, 06/01/01, Box 2, File 42, PANL; John F. Nelson to John Scott, 23 Mar. 1923, and newspaper article attached to letter from John F. Nelson to B. M. Jewell, president, AFLRED, 30 Mar. 1923, 5478, Box 107, File 4, both in AFLRED; *Pullman News*, May 1929, 3.

16. Cohen, *Making a New Deal*, 205; Halpern, *Down on the Killing Floor*, 87.

17. John F. Nelson, general chairman, System Federation #122, to Edward F. Carry, president, Pullman Company, 19 Mar. 1923, 5478, Box 107, File 4, AFLRED.

18. A. P. O'Leary to F. L. Simmons, 7 Dec. 1923; John F. Nelson to John Scott, 23 Mar. 1923; newspaper article and letter from Nelson to Jewell, 30 Mar. 1923; Spero and Harris, *The Black Worker*, 310.

19. Steinle's and Elbring's employee service records are part of the Calumet database. See John F. Nelson and Harry Smith to J. F. McGrath, vice president, AFLRED, 22 Nov. 1922, 5478, Box 107, File 5, AFLRED; "Roads Have 150,000 Still Locked Out," *New Majority*, 31 Mar. 1923; Colin J. Davis, *Power at Odds: The 1922 National Railroad Shopmen's Strike* (Urbana: University of Illinois Press, 1997), 154.

20. The figures on promotion are for those in helper or helper-apprentice positions between September 1922 and December 1926. Among those hired at the unskilled level during that period, 75 percent of white men rose to the helper level, on average in 0.4 years, while 91 percent of black men did, on average in 0.4 years.

21. Many more Italians came to work at the shop in the 1920s than would have been expected from their share of the local population. Whether fewer of them were racially prejudiced or not, supervisors also alleged that the foreman of the large Labor Department preferred to hire Italians. In 1930, 50 percent of adult males in the four community areas that comprised the Pullman area were foreign-born whites; in 1920, 10 percent of foreign-born whites were Italian and in 1930, 19 percent were (computed from U.S. Bureau of the Census, *Fourteenth Census of the United States [1920]*, vol. 3 [Washington, D.C.: Government Printing Office, 1922], and Edward Burgess and Charles Newcomb, *Census Data of the City of Chicago, 1930* [Chicago: University of Chicago Press, 1933], 628). The federal government estimated that an urban family needed $2,088 for an adequate standard of living in the mid-1920s. Those earning 70 cents per hour would bring home only $1,500 if they experienced six weeks of layoff; those earning 75 cents per hour would bring home $1,800, even if they had only two weeks off. The government estimate is quoted in Harris, *Keeping the Faith*, 17. Gagatek's and De Antoni's employee service records are part of the Calumet database. See also F. L. Simmons, confidential memo to L. S. Hungerford, 13 Mar. 1925, 06/01/01, Box 2, File 37, PANL.

22. In 1930 only 1.6 percent of the adult male population of the four community areas around Pullman was black. Seventy-two percent of black men hired in the 1920s at Calumet were born in southern states; another 20 percent might have been, because they listed their birthplace as the United States but did not specify a state. Heard's employee service record is part of the Calumet database. See Burgess and Newcomb, *Census Data of the City of Chicago*, 635; Ozanne, *The Negro in Farm Equipment*, 22; Thomas Lee Philpott, *The Slum and the Ghetto: Immigrants, Blacks, and Reformers in Chicago, 1880–1930* (Belmont, Calif.: Wadsworth, 1991), 128–29, 146, 183; from the *Daily Calumet*: "Klan Visits Local Church: Donates $208," 18 Dec.

1922, and "South Chicago Baptist Church Receives Visit from Ku Klux Klan," 23 Jan. 1923.

23. Cohen, *Making a New Deal*, chaps. 2, 3; Philpott, *The Slum and the Ghetto*, 140–41, 186–89; Peter Rachleff, "The Dynamics of 'Americanization': The Croatian Fraternal Union between the Wars," in *Labor Histories: Class, Politics, and the Working-Class Experience*, ed. Eric Arnesen, Julie Greene, and Bruce Laurie (Urbana: University of Illinois Press, 1998), 345–47.

24. Cohen, *Making a New Deal*, 123; Michael Homel, *Down from Equality: Black Chicagoans and the Public Schools, 1920–1941* (Urbana: University of Illinois Press, 1984), 46–47; Philpott, *The Slum and the Ghetto*, 193–94, 218–29; Janice L. Reiff, "Rethinking Pullman: Urban Space and Working-Class Activism," *Social Science History* 24 (2000): 21.

25. See James Grossman, *Land of Hope: Chicago, Black Southerners, and the Great Migration* (Chicago: University of Chicago Press, 1989), for the factors that attracted black migrants to Chicago and for the nature of the community that they created in the 1910s. For Bronzeville in the 1920s see St. Clair Drake and Horace Cayton, *Black Metropolis: A Study of Negro Life in a Northern City*, rev. ed. (New York: Harcourt, Brace and World, 1970), chaps. 5, 14. For a discussion of voluntary separatism in a different context, see Howard Kimmeldorf and Robert Penney, "'Excluded' by Choice: Dynamics of Interracial Unionism on the Philadelphia Waterfront, 1910–1930," *International Labor and Working-Class History* 51 (1997): 66–67.

26. Beth T. Bates, *Pullman Porters and the Rise of Protest Politics in Black America, 1925–1945* (Chapel Hill: University of North Carolina Press, 2001), chap. 2; Leila Houghteling, *The Income and Standard of Living of Unskilled Laborers in Chicago* (Chicago: University of Chicago Press, 1927), 25.

27. F. L. Simmons, memo to L. S. Hungerford, 29 June 1923, 06/01/03, Box 15, File 317, PANL. Pflager did not apply this plan to the seamstresses, the skilled women, and he continued to pay them at a lower "women's" wage scale. See Cohen, *Making a New Deal*, 169–70.

28. No A-level mechanics but 1 percent of B-level and 5 percent of C-level were demoted. Average cumulative service for white workers hired between September 1922 and December 1929 was twenty-six years (s.d. 13); for black workers it was twenty-five years (s.d. 14). See 1937 Conference Proceedings, 60.

29. Simmons to Hungerford, 13 Mar. 1925.

30. The percentage of black workers is calculated from the actual number of black workers on December 31, 1928, and the total employment in the shop in January 1929. See shop manager, St. Louis, to C. W. Pflager, 1 May 1930; Statement "B," Average Number of Men Working—Repair Shops, 1929, 06/01/04, Box 25, File 656, PANL.

31. Only another 3 percent of Wilmington strikers were ever rehired. See F. L. Simmons to L. S. Hungerford, 10 Dec. 1923.

32. Between the strike and December 1926, 80 percent of new black workers were hired as helpers and 2 percent as mechanics. Black men comprised 13 percent of Wilmington's adult males in 1930. See Carol Hoffecker, *Cor-*

porate Capital: Wilmington in the Twentieth Century (Philadelphia: Temple University Press, 1983), 85–88, 94; Pauline A. Young, "The Negro in Delaware, Past and Present," in *Delaware: A History of the First State,* ed. Henry Clay Reed (New York: Lewis Historical Publishing Co., 1947), 587–89, 597; U.S. Bureau of the Census, *Fifteenth Census of the United States (1930)* (Washington, D.C.: Government Printing Office, 1932), 3:table 15.

33. Employee service record of W106, Wilmington shop, 06/02/03, PANL. "Tried on several benches" means he was moved from one work group to another within the department.

34. Only 12 percent of those hired at Wilmington between September 1922 and December 1926 took jobs as helper-apprentices, although 48 percent did at Calumet. Those hired at Wilmington in the 1920s stayed with their jobs for an average of eighteen years. White workers had slightly longer average cumulative service than black workers: nineteen years (s.d. 11) versus sixteen years (s.d. 11). See List of Scheduled Working Hours in the Various Repair Shops, 8 Mar. 1930, 06/01/02, Box 1, File 13, H. R. Lary, memo to J. M. Carry, 24 Mar. 1947, 1, 06/01/03, Box 3, File 44, and H. R. Lary, memo to T. S. Hopkins, 29 May 1941, 06/01/03, Box 12, File 240, all in PANL; 1936 Conference Minutes, 06/01/04, Box 25, File 668, PANL; 1940 Conference Proceedings, 61; 1941–42 Conference with Company Representatives, 193.

35. Johnson's employee service record is part of the Wilmington database.

36. Twenty-seven percent of black helpers at Wilmington were downwardly mobile versus 8 percent of white helpers. See Risher, "Negro in the Railroad Industry," 45.

37. Seventy-nine percent of the white shop workers in 1926 lived in Wilmington, as did 90 percent of black workers. See Susan Mulcahy Chase, "The Process of Suburbanization and the Use of Restrictive Deed Covenants as Private Zoning, Wilmington, Delaware, 1900–1941" (Ph.D. diss., University of Delaware, 1995), 264, 304–16; Alice Dunbar-Nelson, "'These "Colored" United States': No. 16—Delaware: A Jewel of Inconsistencies," *Messenger* 6, no. 8 (Aug. 1927): 244–45, and no. 9 (Sept. 1927): 277–79; Hoffecker, *Corporate Capital,* 88–93.

38. John C. Saylor, "Organized Labor in Delaware," *American Federationist* 33 (1926): 1081.

39. Of those hired in the 1920s, 47 percent were native-born whites, 40 percent were foreign-born whites, and 12 percent were nonwhite. All the latter were black except for one Native American. Only 14 percent of newly hired workers were born in California; the others (157 people) had been born in twenty-nine different states and twenty foreign countries. Only 53 percent lived in Richmond. In 1930 the black population of Richmond was 48, out of a total of 20,093. See Marilyn S. Johnson, *The Second Gold Rush: Oakland and the East Bay in World War II* (Berkeley: University of California Press, 1993), 16–17.

40. 1937 Conference Proceedings, 217; Shirley Ann Wilson Moore, *To Place Our Deeds: The African American Community in Richmond, California, 1910–1963* (Berkeley: University of California Press, 2000), 12, 16, 23–25, 33;

Robert Wenkert, *A Historical Digest of Negro-White Relations in Richmond, California* (Berkeley: University of California Survey Research Center, 1967), 12–14.

41. Employee service records of R002–R004, Richmond Shop, 06/02/03, PANL; Davis, *Power at Odds,* 152–53; Moore, *To Place Our Deeds,* 13.

42. Percentage calculated as in note 30; C. W. Pflager to F. L. Simmons, 5 May 1930; Statement "B," 1929; *Pullman News,* Jan. 1951, 24–29, and Oct. 1952, 37; Samuel L. Adams, "Blueprint for Segregation: A Survey of Atlanta Housing," *New South* 22 (1967): 81; Christopher Silver and John V. Moeser, *The Separate City: Black Communities in the Urban South, 1940–1968* (Lexington: University of Kentucky Press, 1995), 21–22, 34.

43. F. L. Simmons, memo to L. S. Hungerford, 2 May 1928, Box 2, File 37, and F. L. Simmons to Edward Carry, 12 Mar. 1928, Box 2, File 34, both in 06/01/01, PANL; 1939 Annual Conference, 78; 1941–42 Conference with Company Representatives, 191; *Pullman News,* Oct. 1952, 37. Information on the integration of departments and job levels comes from a comparison of payrolls for the Atlanta repair shop for October 21, 1931, and June 6, 1936 (PP) and social security application cards (06/03/04, PANL) for workers listed on those payrolls. See also Ronald H. Bayor, *Race and the Shaping of Twentieth-Century Atlanta* (Chapel Hill: University of North Carolina Press, 1996), 94–112.

44. Of those employed in 1926, 47 percent of Calumet workers had been hired before the strike, as had 43 percent of Richmond workers and 48 percent of Wilmington workers. The percentages of black workers are calculated as in note 30. The Richmond shop force was 7 percent black, whereas Buffalo's was 15 percent black; Calumet, 16 percent; Wilmington, 19 percent; Atlanta, 44 percent; and St. Louis, 47 percent. See C. W. Pflager, memo to F. L. Simmons, 5 May 1930; W. J. Keville, memo to Pflager, 1 May 1930; shop manager, St. Louis, memo to Pflager, 1 May 1930; shop manager, Wilmington, to Pflager, 8 May 1930; Richmond Shop Statement re Negro Employment; Statement "B," 1929. In 1930 the percentages of adult males in each city who were black were 30 percent, Atlanta; 2 percent, Buffalo; 2 percent, Pullman area (four census tracts); 0.2 percent, Richmond; 12 percent, St. Louis; 13 percent, Wilmington (Census Bureau, *Fifteenth Census,* table 15).

45. Day's employee service record is part of the Calumet sample. See L. S. Hungerford to E. C. Morris, 3 Apr. 1929 and 8 Apr. 1929, 06/01/04, Box 25, File 655, PANL; U.S. Department of Labor, *Wage Chronology: Railroads—Nonoperating Employees, 1920–62,* B.L.S. Report #208 (Washington, D.C.: Government Printing Office, 1963), 3.

46. At the Calumet shop 16 percent of workers (including supervisory and clerical) had deductions for the stock purchase plan. See Payroll, Calumet Repair Shop, 30 June 1926, PP; Questionnaire from National Industrial Conference Board re Employee Stock Purchase Plans, March 1930, 06/01/01, Box 3, File 64, PANL; *Pullman News,* May 1926, 356, and Jan. 1946, 111; Spero and Harris, *The Black Worker,* 442; Leroy Stinebower, "Employee Stock Ownership in Chicago" (master's thesis, University of Chicago, 1927), 11, 31, 39, 76.

47. *Pullman News,* May 1922, 3, June 1922, 48, and Sept. 1922, 160; Cohen, *Making a New Deal,* 179.

48. *Pullman News,* June 1922, 48.

49. *Pullman News,* Sept. 1922, 148, Oct. 1922, 171, Nov. 1922, 228, Dec. 1923, 268, May 1924, 8, June 1924, 45, Aug. 1924, 123, Mar. 1926, 368, Apr. 1926, 392, Oct. 1926, 209, Jan. 1927, 297, June 1927, 65, May 1929, 35, July 1929, 101, Oct. 1929, 219, Apr. 1930, 459, May 1930, 43, Jan. 1931, 388, and Oct. 1933, 63.

50. "Information Concerning the Negro in Industry," 9 May 1930; Dennis C. Dickerson, *Out of the Crucible: Black Steelworkers in Western Pennsylvania, 1875–1980* (Albany: State University of New York Press, 1986), 104–7; Spero and Harris, *The Black Worker,* 440.

51. Minute Book 1, executive committee meeting, 8 Sept. 1922, and Minute Book 3, executive committee meeting, 9 Oct. 1929, 29, 02/01/02, vol. 17, both in PANL; *Pullman News,* Feb. 1924, 321, Dec. 1928, 286, and Sept. 1929, 147–48.

52. The company also provided reduced-rate passes for the families of workers. See 1937 Conference Proceedings, 275–76; 1940 Conference Proceedings, 205–6; 1941–42 Conference with Company Representatives, 223.

53. Harden's employee service record is part of the Calumet database. See also Spero and Harris, *The Black Worker,* 130.

54. Terrence Hines to J. P. Carey, 17 Dec. 1925, in Hines's service record, Calumet shop, 06/02/03, PANL.

55. At the Calumet shop the average cumulative service for black workers hired in the 1920s was 25 years, for white workers 26 years. At Richmond black workers averaged 19 years and white workers 18 years. At Wilmington black workers averaged 16 years and white workers 19 years. The variation by race at Wilmington was explained by the shop manager as a consequence of the concentration of black men at the helper level. Black helpers and laborers were more likely to quit than white ones, but black mechanics were less likely to quit than white ones because they had so few opportunities elsewhere. See manager, Wilmington shop, to C. W. Pflager, 8 May 1930, and "Information Concerning the Negro in Industry," 9 May 1930. In *The Black Worker,* 167–68, Spero and Harris report some discriminatory layoffs but insist that most were due to lesser seniority. In *Making a New Deal,* 205–6, Cohen notes discriminatory layoffs at Armour, and William Sundstrom, "Last Hired, First Fired? Unemployment and Urban Black Workers during the Great Depression," *Journal of Economic History* 52 (1992): 415–29, argues that such layoffs were widespread.

56. F. L. Simmons, memo, 12 Mar. 1925, 06/01/01, Box 2, File 37, PANL; List of Scheduled Working Hours, 8 Mar. 1930.

57. Halpern, *Down on the Killing Floor,* 78; Harris, *Keeping the Faith,* 17; Spero and Harris, *The Black Worker,* 454.

58. *Pullman News,* May 1922, 11.

59. Statement in Regard to the Plan of Employe Representation, 9, 06/01/01, Box 2, File 43, PANL; Spero and Harris, *The Black Worker,* 442–44. At

the highest level of the grievance system only eighty of 239 cases by porters asking for reinstatement were decided in their favor. See Summary of Cases Heard by the Joint Bureau of Industrial Relations Between Nov. 8, 1926 and Nov. 12, 1930, 06/01/01, Box 3, File 67a, PANL.

60. Melinda Chateauvert, *Marching Together: Women of the Brotherhood of Sleeping Car Porters* (Urbana: University of Illinois Press, 1998), 1–6, chap. 1; Harris, *Keeping the Faith*, 79.

61. Jervis Anderson, *A. Philip Randolph: A Biographical Portrait* (New York: Harcourt Brace Jovanovich, 1972), 127–28, 137, 168, 174, 207; Herbert Garfinkel, *When Negroes March: The March on Washington Movement in the Organizational Politics for FEPC* (Glencoe, Ill.: Free Press, 1959), 130; Harris, *Keeping the Faith*, 17–18, 34–35, 94; Theodore Kornweibel Jr., *No Crystal Stair: Black Life and the "Messenger," 1917–1928* (Westport, Conn.: Greenwood Press, 1975), 188–89.

62. *Pullman News*, May 1924, 6, Mar. 1926, 357, and July 1929, 78; from the *Federation News:* "Charge Pullman Co. with Intimidation," 25 May 1929, "Generous Pullman Co. Grants 16 Cent Raise," 15 June 1929, "Pullman Hits Back at Union Porters," 3 Aug. 1929, and "Pullman Porters Expose Company Union Scheme," 25 Oct. 1930; Bates, *Pullman Porters*, chap. 3; Chateauvert, *Marching Together*, 41; Harris, *Keeping the Faith*, 18–22, 43–54, 63, 80–83, 147–49; Kornweibel, *No Crystal Stair*, 98, 225.

63. Harris, *Keeping the Faith*, 39; Barbara Posadas, "The Hierarchy of Color and Psychological Adjustment in an Industrial Environment: Filipinos, the Pullman Company, and the Brotherhood of Sleeping Car Porters," *Labor History* 23 (1982): 355–56.

64. Harris, *Keeping the Faith*, 71–72, 84–96; Laurence S. Zakson, "Railway Labor Legislation, 1888 to 1930: A Legal History of Congressional Railway Labor Relations Policy," *Rutgers Law Journal* 20, no. 2 (1989): 358–80.

65. Harris, *Keeping the Faith*, 98–112, 141, 153–56.

66. Pullman Company Manufacturing Department, "Some Interesting Notes and Views of Pullman Car Works Located at Pullman, Chicago," Chicago, 1924, 17–18, Chicago Historical Society; "Pullman Strike Cripples Shops," *New Majority*, 10 May 1924; Brody, *Steelworkers in America*, 276–78.

67. F. L. Simmons to Edward Carry, 13 Mar. 1922, 06/01/01, Box 2, File 34, PANL; Business Training Corp., *Course in Pullman Production Methods* (Chicago: for the Pullman Car and Manufacturing Corp., 1926), 1:1–2, 28, 37, 49, and 2:1–13, 26, 37–44, 53.

68. Bureau of Industrial Relations Decisions, 13 Sept. 1926–9 Sept. 1930, #243, #288, #289, 06/01/07, Box 1, File 3, PANL; notes re "do not rehire" on service records of employees W110–W115, Wilmington shop, 06/02/03, PANL.

69. Summary of Cases Settled by the Bureau of Industrial Relations, 1 June 1920–20 June 1927, 06/01/01, Box 3, File 67a, PANL; Statement "B," 1929; *Pullman News*, Feb. 1927, 334–35.

70. F. L. Simmons, memos to Edward Carry, 5 Mar. 1923 and 14 May 1924, 06/01/01, Box 2, File 34, PANL.

71. From the *New Majority:* "Pullman Strike Cripples Shops," 10 May 1924, "Car Strikers Spurn Pullman Boss Union," 17 May 1924, and "Pullman Strike Ends," 24 May 1924.

72. *Carbuilder*, Mar. 1955, Chicago Historical Society, provides a history of the manufacturing company and those it absorbed.

73. *Pullman News*, July 1924, 69; Statement in Regard to the Plan of Employe Representation, 17.

Chapter 5: A New Deal for Pullman Workers?

1. At the Calumet Repair Shop 68 percent of workers experienced at least one layoff between 1930 and 1940; 37 percent experienced two or more. At the Richmond shop 63 percent were laid off at least once and 25 percent more than once. At the Wilmington shop 70 percent were laid off at least once and 21 percent more than once. See Minute Book 3, Executive Committee, Board of Directors, Pullman Company, meeting of 9 Oct. 1929, 27, 47, 02/01/02, vol. 17, and Minute Book E, board of directors meetings, 28 Mar. 1918–31 Dec. 1934, meeting of 19 Nov. 1930, 76, 02/01/02, vol. 6, PANL; F. L Simmons, "Number of Employes on the Rolls of the Pullman Company, 1 Sept. 1929," 4 Oct. 1929, 06/01/01, Box 2, File 48a, PANL; Pullman Monopoly Anti-Trust Suit Defense, 8–9, 06/01/03, Box 20, File 462, PANL; typescript of meeting where wage agreements negotiated, 23 Jan. 1933 meeting, 7–8, 06/01/03, Box 6, File 136, PANL; from the *Calumet Index:* "Over 1,500 on Pullman Payroll," 7 Dec. 1933, "3,000 to be Busy in Pullman Shops by Feb. 1," 3 Jan. 1935, and "Pullman Shops to Start a 6 Day Week," 7 Mar. 1935.

2. Minute Book E, meetings of 19 Nov. 1930, 76, 18 Apr. 1932, 173–74, 15 Nov. 1933, 232–33; Minute Book 3, meeting of 10 Oct. 1934, 97–98; *Pullman News*, Feb. 1931, 404; David Brody, *Workers in Industrial America: Essays on the Twentieth Century Struggle*, 2d ed. (New York: Oxford University Press, 1993), 71; Lizabeth Cohen, *Making a New Deal: Industrial Workers in Chicago, 1919–1939* (New York: Cambridge University Press, 1990), 239–40; Brian Gratton, "'A Triumph of Modern Philanthropy': Age Criteria in Labor Management at the Pennsylvania Railroad, 1875–1930," *Business History Review* 64 (1990): 653; Carol Hoffecker, *Corporate Capital: Wilmington in the Twentieth Century* (Philadelphia: Temple University Press, 1983), 102.

3. At the Calumet, Richmond, and Wilmington shops 97 percent of those who were laid off at least once returned to their jobs. Of those laid off at least twice, 99 percent at Calumet and 96 percent at Wilmington returned but only 62 percent at Richmond returned. Of those laid off three or more times, 99 percent returned at Calumet, 95 percent at Wilmington, and 47 percent at Richmond. The employee service records of Carter and Panozzo are part of the Calumet database. See also "$30,000 Given by Calumet Shop to Aid Ex Employees," *Calumet Index*, 28 Apr. 1932; Cohen, *Making a New Deal*, 314–16.

4. Payrolls of 31 Oct. 1931, Calumet, Richmond, and Wilmington shops, PP, show the forty-eight-hour week was in force; employee W001, interview

by author, 26 Jan. 1981, Chicago; Minute Book 3, meeting of 17 Aug. 1932, 58; Cohen, *Making a New Deal,* 243–45.

5. Cohen, *Making a New Deal,* 242–43; Hoffecker, *Corporate Capital,* 101–2; Howard W. Risher Jr., "The Negro in the Railroad Industry," in *Negro Employment in Land and Air Transport,* Herbert Northrup, Howard W. Risher Jr., Richard D. Leone, and Philip W. Jeffress (Philadelphia: University of Pennsylvania Press, 1971), 46; William Sundstrom, "Last Hired, First Fired? Unemployment and Urban Black Workers during the Great Depression," *Journal of Economic History* 52 (1992): 415–29.

6. 1941–42 Conference with Company Representatives, 81, 06/01/04, Box 26, File 695, PANL.

7. Employee W001 interview; Elyce J. Rotella, *From Home to Office: U.S. Women at Work, 1870–1930* (Ann Arbor, Mich.: UMI Research Press, 1981), 21, 119–23.

8. *Pullman News,* Feb. 1929, 366.

9. Clerical Employes—Agreement of 16 Aug. 1935, Exhibits 2–5, and Maids' Agreement of 1 June 1929, Exhibit 11, of Series 1–12, Affidavits re Furloughed Employes due to Change in Railroad Retirement Act, 06/01/03, Box 21, File 474, PANL.

10. Employee W001, interviews by author, 26 Jan. and 19 Mar. 1981, Chicago.

11. 1938 Annual Conference Proceedings, 8–12 Aug. (Union), 14, 06/01/04, Box 25, File 685, and H. R. Lary, memos to Champ Carry, 17 Feb. 1940, 06/01/03, Box 17, File 358, both in PANL; Cohen, *Making a New Deal,* 242–43; Ruth Milkman, "Female Factory Labor and Industrial Structure: Control and Conflict over 'Woman's Place' in Automobile and Electrical Manufacturing," *Politics and Society* 12 (1983): 177.

12. "Sleeping Car Porters Hold Huge Gathering," *Federation News,* 1 Feb. 1930; William H. Harris, *Keeping the Faith: A. Philip Randolph, Milton P. Webster, and the Brotherhood of Sleeping Car Porters, 1925–1937* (Urbana: University of Illinois Press, 1977), 163–64, 179.

13. F. L. Simmons, memo to D. A. Crawford, 19 Mar. 1930, 2–3, 06/01/04, Box 25, File 656, PANL; W. B. Bentley, memo, 29 Nov. 1954, 06/01/04, Box 26, File 656, PANL; 1940 Conference Proceedings, 20–23 Aug., 92–93, 06/01/04, Box 26, File 690, PANL; Milton Nadworny, *Scientific Management and the Unions, 1900–1932* (Cambridge, Mass.: Harvard University Press, 1955), 124–25; Leonard Painter, *Through Fifty Years with the Brotherhood Railway Carmen of America* (Kansas City, Mo.: Brotherhood Railway Carmen of America, 1941), 192–93.

14. Minute Book E, meeting of 17 Feb. 1932, 152; W. B. Bentley, memo, 4 May 1938, 06/01/03, Box 6, File 134, PANL; W. Harris, *Keeping the Faith,* 176.

15. Minute Book E, meetings of 11 Oct. 1933, 224–25, and 20 June 1934, 276–77; memorandum on wage reductions effective 1 Feb. 1932, no date or name, 06/01/03, Box 6, File 134, PANL; Risher, "The Negro in the Railroad Industry," 27; U.S. Labor-Management Services Administration, *Railroad*

Shopcraft Factfinding Study (Washington, D.C.: Government Printing Office, 1968), 1:112, 140.

16. F. L. Simmons, memo, 30 Mar. 1934, 06/01/03, Box 6, File 139, PANL.

17. About two-fifths of railroad workers still belonged to company unions in 1934. From the *Federation News:* "The Pullman Porters' Plight," 3 Feb. 1934, and "Car Porters Labor Rally Sunday Nite," 16 June 1934; Irving Bernstein, *Turbulent Years: A History of the American Worker, 1933–1941* (Boston: Houghton Mifflin, 1970), 205–15; Bureau of Information of the Eastern Railways, *Railroad Wages and Labor Relations, 1900–1946* (New York: Bureau of Information of the Eastern Railways, 1947), 96; Walter Galenson, *The CIO Challenge to the AFL: A History of the American Labor Movement, 1935–1941* (Cambridge, Mass.: Harvard University Press, 1960), 566–68; W. Harris, *Keeping the Faith,* 162, 175, 180–88.

18. Mary MacKinnon, "Providing for Faithful Servants: Pensions at the Canadian Pacific Railway," *Social Science History* 21 (1997): 67–68; Bureau of Information, *Railroad Wages,* 98–99; David Schreiber, *The Legislative History of the Railroad Retirement and Railroad Unemployment Insurance Systems* (Washington, D.C.: Government Printing Office, 1978), 3.

19. H. R. Lary, memo to C. S. Williston, 9 Jan. 1936, 06/01/03, Box 11, File 235, PANL; W. Harris, *Keeping the Faith,* 188; Risher, "The Negro in the Railroad Industry," 30; Laurence S. Zakson, "Railway Labor Legislation, 1888 to 1930: A Legal History of Congressional Railway Labor Relations Policy," *Rutgers Law Journal* 20, no. 2 (1989): 387.

20. "Porters Asking Pay Conference," *Federation News,* 24 Nov. 1934; Rick Halpern, *Down on the Killing Floor: Black and White Workers in Chicago's Packinghouses, 1904–1954* (Urbana: University of Illinois Press, 1997), 106–7; W. Harris, *Keeping the Faith,* 165, 201–7; 1938 Annual Conference Proceedings, 28; *Pullman News,* Jan. 1933, 139, Jan. 1934, 70, Jan. 1936, 78, and Jan. 1937, 89.

21. W. Harris, *Keeping the Faith,* 181–82, 207–8.

22. E. K. Hogan to B. M. Jewell, 20 Nov. 1934, 1, 5478, Box 8, File 11, AFLRED; Galenson, *The CIO Challenge,* 566–68.

23. Everett Hill, Committee B, Ft. Worth, Texas, to Mr. R. Stewart, Toronto, Canada, 25 June 1934, 06/01/03, Box 11, File 236, PANL; E. K. Hogan to B. M. Jewell, 20 Nov. 1934, 2, J. H. Gutridge, acting international president, International Brotherhood of Boiler Makers, Iron Ship Builders, and Helpers, to B. M. Jewell, 25 Oct. 1935, and C. J. McGlogan, international vice president, International Brotherhood of Electrical Workers, to George Fuller, Alhambra, Calif., 5 June 1937, all in 5478, Box 8, File 11, AFLRED.

24. Minute Book E, meeting of 21 Nov. 1934, 304–5; *Pullman News,* July 1935, 7; Cohen, *Making a New Deal,* 350–51.

25. In 1931, 45 percent of Wilmington workers were at the helper level; in 1936, 27 percent were. See H. R. Lary, memo to C. W. Pflager, 4 Nov. 1936, 06/01/04, Box 25, File 667, PANL, and 1939 Annual Conference, 14–25 Aug., 28, 06/01/04, Box 25, File 688, PANL.

26. The average age of workers in 1937 was 41.9 (s.d. 11.2) at the Calumet

shop, 41.3 (s.d. 12.5) at Richmond, and 41.3 (s.d. 12.6) at Wilmington. See C. W. Pflager to Champ Carry, 12 Sept. 1940, 1, 06/01/04, Box 26, File 691, PANL; W. B. Bentley, memo, 29 Nov. 1954; 1937 Conference Proceedings, 18, 82–83, 86–87, 06/01/04, Box 25, File 677, PANL; 1938 Annual Conference Proceedings, 42–43; 1939 Annual Conference, 374–75; 1940 Conference Proceedings, 92–93; 1941–42 Conference with Company Representatives, 143, 145–46; Calumet Council Meeting of the CEA of the Repair Shops, 15 Feb. 1938, 8, 06/01/04, Box 25, File 684, PANL.

27. Charles Gartelman, memo to L. Hyry, 26 May 1941, in service record of employee Co10, Calumet shop, 06/02/03, PANL.

28. 1939 Annual Conference, 387–88.

29. 1937 Conference Proceedings, 250, 254; 1939 Annual Conference, 399; 1940 Conference Proceedings, 5e; C. W. Pflager to Champ Carry, 12 Sept. 1940.

30. 1939 Annual Conference, 387–88.

31. C. W. Pflager to Champ Carry, 12 Sept. 1940; 1939 Annual Conference, 133–37, 383–84, 391, 393, 399.

32. Minute Book F, Board of Directors, Executive Committee, and Stockholders Meetings, Pullman Company, 17 Apr. 1935–20 Dec. 1939, meeting of the board, 21 Oct. 1936, 02/01/02, vol. 7, and employee Co11 to Mr. Carey, 28 July 1936, in service record of employee Co11, Calumet shop, 06/02/03, both in PANL; 1938 Annual Conference Proceedings, 15–16; 1939 Annual Conference, 99–100, 104, 318, 329, 463.

33. 1939 Annual Conference, 441; Mechling is quoted on p. 392.

34. Ibid., 391.

35. 1937 Conference Proceedings, 289–90.

36. 1941–42 Conference with Company Representatives, 154.

37. The supervisor of industrial relations counseled Pullman executives to accept the code for laundry workers in this spirit. Even though the sleeping-car service, as a common carrier, did not come under the act, he advised accepting its provisions because the code was more favorable to employers than he had expected it to be. See F. L. Simmons, memo to L. S. Hungerford, 18 Aug. 1933, 06/01/03, Box 12, File 246, PANL; Ruth O'Brien, *Workers' Paradox: The Republican Origins of New Deal Labor Policy, 1886–1935* (Chapel Hill: University of North Carolina Press, 1998), 178.

38. Code of Fair Competition for Railway Car Building Industry, 7 Apr. 1934, 06/01/03, Box 12, File 246, PANL; E. K. Hogan to B. M. Jewell, 20 Nov. 1934, 2.

39. Transcript of Case #111-15984-D, Pullman Standard Car Manufacturing Co. and USWA Local 1834, National War Labor Board, 16 July 1945, 113–14, Box 160, File 30, USWA; Halpern, *Down on the Killing Floor*, 140–45; Sanford M. Jacoby, *Employing Bureaucracy: Managers, Unions, and the Transformation of Work in American Industry, 1900–1945* (New York: Columbia University Press, 1985), 223, 242, 244; O'Brien, *Workers' Paradox*, 181, 190–91.

40. The quote is from Mario Manzardo, "Liberi Cuori (Liberated Hearts),"

in *Rank and File: Personal Histories by Working-Class Organizers*, ed. Alice Lynd and Staughton Lynd (Boston: Beacon Press, 1973), 133; from the *Calumet Index*: "Legion and Labor Council Unite in Search for Jobs," 18 Feb. 1932, "Reds Fail in Attempt to Incite Riot When Police let them Talk," 7 July 1932, "Vet Returns to Organize Local Bonus Army Unit," 28 July 1932, "Legionnaires Halt Crowd Angered by Reds' Jeers," 4 Aug. 1932, "Police Break Up Demonstration on Michigan Ave.," 8 Sept. 1932, and "Police Forced to Suppress Third Red Disturbance," 15 Sept. 1932; Harold Lasswell and Dorothy Blumenstock, *World Revolutionary Propaganda: A Chicago Study* (New York: Alfred A. Knopf, 1939), 168–70.

41. Statement of Men Working at Repair Shops, Year 1936, 06/01/04, Box 25, File 666, PANL; 1939 Annual Conference, 98; *Pullman News*, Apr. 1941, 146; transcript of Case #111-15984-D, 107–8.

42. H. R. Lary, memo to Champ Carry, 10 May 1937, 06/01/04, Box 25, File 651, PANL; 1937 Conference Proceedings, 22; 1939 Annual Conference, 165–66, 374–75; Calumet Council meeting, 15 Feb. 1938, 24; transcript of Case #111-15984-D, 112–18; minutes of staff meetings, USWA—District 31, 29 Apr. 1937 to 14 June 1937, Box 124, File 6, and typed lists of SWOC members at the Calumet shop, Box 184, File 3, both in USWA. Employee service records exist for 100 of the 160 Calumet shop workers listed in SWOC files as members of Lodge #1721. Of these 100, 57 had not been employed at the shop before 1936, suggesting that manufacturing workers formed the core of support for SWOC.

43. Propaganda Reports of CIO Activities in Car Shops, etc., 19 Apr. 1937–16 Dec. 1937, 06/01/04, Box 25, File 651, PANL; Lawrence Crouchett, Lonnie Bunch III, and Martha Winnacker, *Visions toward Tomorrow: History of the East Bay Afro-American Community, 1852–1977* (Oakland, Calif.: Northern California Center for Afro-American History and Life, 1989), 37; W. Harris, *Keeping the Faith*, 114–15.

44. H. R. Lary, memo to Champ Carry, 10 May 1937; Beth T. Bates, *Pullman Porters and the Rise of Protest Politics in Black America, 1925–1945* (Chapel Hill: University of North Carolina Press, 2001), 138–40; Bernstein, *Turbulent Years*, 453–55; Cohen, *Making a New Deal*, 325–36; Halpern, *Down on the Killing Floor*, 158; Manzardo, "Liberi Cuori," 137–39.

45. Thirteen percent of Calumet's male workers in 1937 were black. Of those who were mechanics, about one-third held jobs at each level: A, 35 percent; B, 36 percent; C, 29 percent. While the Pullman Porters Benevolent Association lost many members in the 1930s, the Calumet branch remained strong, an indication both of the more consistent employment at the shop and the separate identification of black and white shop workers. See U.S. Bureau of the Census, *Fifteenth Census of the United States: 1930: Unemployment*, (Washington, D.C.: Government Printing Office, 1931), 2:371; *Pullman News*, Jan. 1937, 89; from the *Calumet Index*: "Colored Pupils from Morgan Pk. Crowding Fenger," 16 Feb. 1933, and "Minstrel Show Proceeds to Be Used in Welfare," 16 Nov. 1933.

46. Minutes of SWOC staff meeting, 14 June 1937.

47. Bernstein, *Turbulent Years*, 485–90; Barbara Newell, *Chicago and the*

Labor Movement: Metropolitan Unionism in the 1930s (Urbana: University of Illinois Press, 1961), 135–44; Robert Slayton, "Labor and Urban Politics: District 31, SWOC, and the Chicago Machine," *Journal of Urban History* 23 (1996): 36–38.

48. 1947 Annual Conference—Minutes, 15–19 Sept., 19, 06/01/04, Box 26, File 719, PANL.

49. Bernstein, *Turbulent Years,* 455–57; Galenson, *The CIO Challenge,* 96.

50. 1937 Conference Proceedings, 226.

51. Calumet Council meeting, 15 Feb. 1938, 6, 12.

52. 1939 Annual Conference, 98; Bernstein, *Turbulent Years,* 727–29; Brody, *Workers in Industrial America,* 111.

53. Although most manufacturing workers left the Calumet shop at the end of the air-conditioning project, fifty-two of the one hundred Calumet workers identified as SWOC members remained at the shop. One former SWOC member even became a foreman in the 1950s.

54. Only 14 percent of PCEARS leaders served on the old ERP. At Wilmington the new representative to the national leadership had been a striker in 1922. Names of ERP and PCEARS leaders were culled from all documents in the Pullman Archives relating to those organizations and checked against employee service records. See Minute Book F, Executive Committee meeting, 9 Aug. 1937, 509–10; handwritten note attached to Repair Shop Agreement, 1 Sept. 1937, 06/01/04, Box 25, File 678, PANL; 1937 Conference Proceedings, 89–92, 118; U.S. Department of Labor, *Wage Chronology: Railroads— Nonoperating Employees, 1920–62,* B.L.S. Report #208 (Washington, D.C.: Government Printing Office, 1963), 15.

55. Ben H. Lewis, chairman, PCEARS, to G. M. Williams, assistant mechanical superintendent, 25 Jan. 1937, Box 39-260 (old numbering), PANL.

56. Typed notes attached to the Repair Shop Agreement, 1 Sept. 1937.

57. 1937 Conference Proceedings, 245; 1939 Annual Conference, 87; 1941–42 Conference with Company Representatives, 280.

58. 1937 Conference Proceedings, 68.

59. Handwritten note attached to 1937 Repair Shop Agreement.

60. 1937 Conference Proceedings, 81; 1941–42 Conference with Company Representatives, 58–59.

61. 1937 Conference Proceedings, 68.

62. "To All Repair Shops," 20 Aug. 1937, 06/01/04, Box 25, File 667, PANL; 1937 Conference Proceedings, 26–27; 1939 Annual Conference, 161–62.

63. Helper-apprentice contract, 6 July 1937, in service record of employee Co13, Calumet shop, 06/02/03, PANL; 1937 Conference Proceedings, 11, 13, 57, 88, 95–99, 120–21, 264; 1938 Annual Conference Proceedings, 8, 11; 1939 Annual Conference, 103–6, 131, 139, 143–44, 278.

64. At Calumet in 1937, 16 percent of mechanics and 9 percent of supervisors were returned strikers. At Richmond 21 percent of mechanics and 19 percent of supervisors were, while at Wilmington 21 percent of mechanics and 10 percent of supervisors were returned strikers. See 1937 Conference Proceedings, 104.

65. Calumet Council meeting, 15 Feb. 1938, 6.

66. Ibid., 8.

67. At Calumet the proportion of newly hired white workers who were foreign born fell below 50 percent for the first time between 1934 and 1936 (41 percent). In the next five years the percentage declined even further (to 21 percent). At Richmond, where the foreign born had been nearly half of all white men hired, they comprised less than 25 percent between 1930 and 1942. See H. R. Lary, Confidential and Personal Memo to All Repair Shops, 3 Sept. 1937, 06/01/02, Box 1, File 13, PANL; 1937 Conference Proceedings, 217.

68. 1940 Conference Proceedings, 46.

69. Calumet Council meeting, 15 Feb. 1938, 3, 20, 24; 1937 Conference Proceedings, 207–8, 286; 1939 Annual Conference, 385.

70. 1937 Conference Proceedings, 200, 202. Milkman, "Female Factory Labor," 177.

71. 1938 Annual Conference Proceedings, 14; 1941–42 Conference with Company Representatives, 173.

72. Service record of employee W116, Wilmington shop, 06/02/03, PANL.

73. One way of splitting the shops was differential layoffs. For example, in October 1934 the Atlanta shop had 35 percent fewer workers than it did in October 1929. Richmond had 40 percent fewer, St. Louis, 55 percent fewer, and Wilmington 30 percent fewer. At the same time Calumet experienced only a 6 percent decrease and Buffalo a 2 percent decrease. See handwritten note, Number of Employees in Repair Shops, 31 Oct. 1934, 06/01/02, Box 1, File 13, PANL; Statement "B," Average Number of Men Working—Repair Shops, 1929, 06/01/04, Box 25, File 656, PANL; Calumet Council meeting, 15 Feb. 1938, 3, 5, 18–20, 24; 1937 Conference Proceedings, 207–8, 286; 1939 Annual Conference, 98, 165–66, 385, 387–88.

74. 1937 Conference Proceedings, 225; 1940 Conference Proceedings, 127–29, 131. The CIO was also gaining in Wilmington, to the dismay of AFL leaders there. By 1940 the CIO's communist-led International Fur and Leather Workers had organized three firms in Wilmington's largest industry, in which the AFL had tried for years to gain a foothold and failed. Kelleher's employee service record is part of the Wilmington database. See Yda Schreuder, "The Impact of Labor Segmentation on the Ethnic Division of Labor and the Immigrant Residential Community: Polish Leather Workers in Wilmington, Delaware in the Early-Twentieth Century," *Journal of Historical Geography* 16 (1990): 412, 417–19.

75. Pullman Inc., *Annual Reports, 1927–1949,* 11/00/02, Box 2, PANL; Minute Book 3, meetings of 9 Oct. 1929 and 19 Aug. 1931, 27, 47; Minute Book E, meeting of 18 May 1932, 174; typescript of 23 Jan. 1933 meeting, 3; *Pullman News,* Jan. 1931, 352, and Jan. 1934, 73.

76. "Brotherhood of Sleeping Car Porters Wins Million and a Quarter Wage Increase for Porters!" *Federation News,* 6 Sept. 1937; Jervis Anderson, *A. Philip Randolph: A Biographical Portrait* (New York: Harcourt Brace Jovanovich, 1972), 224; W. Harris, *Keeping the Faith,* 207–15.

77. Calumet Council meeting, 15 Feb. 1938, 30–31.

78. Employee service record of David Knox, St. Louis repair shop, 06/02/03, Box 263, PANL.

79. The quote may be found in Ben Lewis to H. R. Lary, 6 Nov. 1936; see also PCEARS St. Louis, memo to H. R. Lary, stamped "arrived 12 Dec. 1936," and H. R. Lary to Officers of PCEARS St. Louis, 17 Dec. 1936, all in 06/01/04, Box 25, File 674, PANL; Ben Lewis to H. R. Lary, 7 July 1937, 06/01/04, Box 25, File 678, PANL.

80. 1937 Conference Proceedings, 275–76.

Chapter 6: The War at Home

1. "Porters Winner of Rights on N.W.," *Federation News*, 15 Apr. 1939; St. Clair Drake and Horace Cayton, *Black Metropolis: A Study of Negro Life in a Northern City*, rev. ed. (New York: Harcourt, Brace and World, 1970), 1:237–42; Howard W. Risher Jr., "The Negro in the Railroad Industry," in *Negro Employment in Land and Air Transport*, Herbert Northrup, Howard W. Risher Jr., Richard D. Leone, and Philip W. Jeffress (Philadelphia: University of Pennsylvania Press, 1971), 52–56.

2. Charles Gartelman to C. W. Pflager, 11 Apr. 1940, in service record of Tillman Davis, Calumet shop, 06/02/03, PANL. Davis worked at the shop from October 1922 until February 1967. His employee service record is part of the Calumet database.

3. 1941–42 Conference with Company Representatives, 219–28, 06/01/04, Box 26, File 695, PANL.

4. Ibid., 219 (Knox quote), 222 (Meyer quote); Rick Halpern, *Down on the Killing Floor: Black and White Workers in Chicago's Packinghouses, 1904–1954* (Urbana: University of Illinois Press, 1997), 146–47, 169.

5. 1941–42 Conference with Company Representatives, 222.

6. Jervis Anderson, *A. Philip Randolph: A Biographical Portrait* (New York: Harcourt Brace Jovanovich, 1972), 243–48, 254. Herbert Garfinkel, *When Negroes March: The March on Washington Movement in the Organizational Politics for FEPC* (Glencoe, Ill.: Free Press, 1959), gives the best single overview of the March on Washington Movement.

7. Memorandum of features to be considered in the employment of new porters, 27 Jan. 1941, 06/01/03, Box 24, File 557, PANL; Lowell M. Greenlaw to Hotterman Rauch, director, Fair Employment Division, Wisconsin Industrial Commission, 1 Aug. 1946, 06/01/03, Box 12, File 243, PANL.

8. In 1940–41, 47 percent of Calumet shop workers were laid off at least once, as were 48 percent of Richmond workers and 43 percent of Wilmington workers. Nine percent of Richmond workers left the shop for other jobs in those years. On average these men were thirty-eight years old and had ten years of cumulative service at the shop. Only 6 percent of Calumet workers and 3 percent of Wilmington workers left then, reflecting fewer opportunities in those cities. See 1940 Conference Proceedings, 20–23 Aug., 136, 153, 06/01/04, Box 26, File 690, PANL; 1941–42 Conference with Company Representatives, 22–23, 44, 82; 1942 Annual Conference of the Repair Shops

and Pullman Co. Management, 27–29 Aug., 12, 17, 06/01/04, Box 26, File 695a, PANL; H. R. Lary, memo to Champ Carry, 20 Oct. 1942, 2, 06/01/03, Box 2, File 32, PANL; H. R. Lary, M. R. Wendt, and C. H. Poole Jr. to Champ Carry, 16 Mar. 1943, 1, 06/01/04, Box 25, File 655, PANL.

9. Formal Complaint of Otis Chappell against Pullman Standard Car Company, undated; Austin Scott, memo to Robert C. Weaver re complaint of Sidney Fieldon, 19 May 1942; William Kunhing to Malcolm S. McLean re refusal of employment at Pullman Standard, 24 Nov. 1942, all in FEPC; John M. Blum, *V Was for Victory: Politics and American Culture During World War II* (New York: Harcourt Brace Jovanovich, 1976), 183–84; Merl E. Reed, *Seedtime for the Modern Civil Rights Movement: The President's Committee on Fair Employment Practice, 1941–1946* (Baton Rouge: Louisiana State University Press, 1991), 41.

10. Memo, 10 Nov. 1943, re case 6-BR-97, FEPC. See also pictures in wartime issues of the *Pullman Standard Log* (Calumet Shipyard), and *Carbuilder*, Dec. 1943, 64, Chicago Historical Society; Statement #1, Pullman Company Payrolls, 21 May 1943, 06/01/03, Box 2, File 32, PANL; William H. Harris, *The Harder We Run: Black Workers since the Civil War* (New York: Oxford University Press, 1982), 121–22; Maureen Honey, *Creating Rosie the Riveter: Class, Gender, and Propaganda during World War II* (Amherst: University of Massachusetts Press, 1984), 21; M. Reed, *Seedtime for the Modern Civil Rights Movement*, 347–48.

11. Charles Gartelman, memo to C. W. Pflager, 26 Feb. 1943, in service record of employee Co14, Calumet shop, 06/02/03, PANL; H. Guilbert, Confidential Inquiry for the Benefit of the Personnel Officers Working Group, 27 Nov. 1943, 06/01/03, Box 12, File 243, PANL; "Breakdown of Repair Shops Employes as of June 21, 1946," 06/01/03, Box 15a, File 328a, PANL; 1941–42 Conference with Company Representatives, 221. In "The Negro in the Railroad Industry," 74, Risher notes that black employment increased on the railroads despite widespread discrimination.

12. Carol Hoffecker, *Corporate Capital: Wilmington in the Twentieth Century* (Philadelphia: Temple University Press, 1983), 8, 112–15; Andrew Kersten, "A Tale of Two States: The FEPC in Illinois and Ohio, 1941–1946" (unpublished paper, Organization of American Historians, 1996), 8–9.

13. The California Minor's War Employment Act allowed sixteen- and seventeen-year-olds to work full time and attend continuation school at night. On average, teenagers stayed only one year with the Pullman shop, while older men hired at the same time stayed eleven years. See James N. Gregory, *American Exodus: The Dust Bowl Migration and Okie Culture in California* (New York: Oxford University Press, 1989), 15–17, 175–76, 179; Marilyn S. Johnson, *The Second Gold Rush: Oakland and the East Bay in World War II* (Berkeley: University of California Press, 1993), 4–5, 48–50, 95, 105, 107; Robert Wenkert, *A Historical Digest of Negro-White Relations in Richmond, California* (Berkeley: University of California Survey Research Center, 1967), 17, 22, 27–28; Shirley Ann Wilson Moore, *To Place Our Deeds: The African American Community in Richmond, California, 1910–1963* (Berkeley: University of California Press, 2000), 44.

14. Alice Kessler-Harris, *Out to Work: A History of Wage-Earning Women in the United States* (New York: Oxford University Press, 1982), 287, 290; Ruth Milkman, "Female Factory Labor and Industrial Structure: Control and Conflict over 'Woman's Place' in Automobile and Electrical Manufacturing," *Politics and Society* 12 (1983): 191–92; Michael Nash, "Women and the Pennsylvania Railroad: The World War II Years," *Labor History* 30 (1989): 608–21; Bruce Nelson, "Organized Labor and the Struggle for Black Equality in Mobile during World War II," *Journal of American History* 80 (1993): 960–62.

15. No women were hired in nontraditional positions at Wilmington, but at Richmond, where the labor shortage was most severe, 71 percent of women who began at unskilled jobs were upwardly mobile during the war; at Calumet 46 percent were. Hedlund's employee service record is part of the Calumet database. The average age of women hired in unskilled or helper level jobs was thirty-eight. See C. W. Pflager, General Letter to All Repair Shops, 9 Sept. 1943, 06/01/04, Box 26, File 701, PANL.

16. No black women were found in the Calumet shop oversample for women, while the Richmond and Wilmington samples each contained one black woman hired for janitorial work. See *Martha Dennis v. The Pullman Company and R. Bucherati, General Foreman*, Case #CSF-12682-66, 29 Nov. 1966, State of New York, State Commission for Human Rights, 06/01/03, Box 30, File 693, PANL; "Sister Maggie Hudson," *Black Worker*, Oct. 1944, 5; Karen T. Anderson, "Last Hired, First Fired: Black Women Workers during World War II," *Journal of American History* 69 (1982): 82–97; Melinda Chateauvert, *Marching Together: Women of the Brotherhood of Sleeping Car Porters* (Urbana: University of Illinois Press, 1998), chap. 5; Honey, *Creating Rosie the Riveter*, 54–55.

17. Nancy Gabin, *Feminism in the Labor Movement: Women and the United Auto Workers, 1935–1975* (Ithaca, N.Y.: Cornell University Press, 1990), chap. 2.

18. C. W. Pflager, General Letter to All Repair Shops, 9 Sept. 1943, 2.

19. Karen Anderson, *Wartime Women: Sex Roles, Family Relations, and the Status of Women during World War II* (Westport, Conn.: Greenwood Press, 1981), 61–62; Thomas Doherty, *Projections of War: Hollywood, American Culture, and World War II* (New York: Columbia University Press, 1993), 155; Honey, *Creating Rosie the Riveter*, 47–51; Kessler-Harris, *Out to Work*, 288.

20. *Pullman News*, Jan. 1944, 103.

21. In the Calumet shop sample the only case of a worker's being warned for use of profanity was a woman war worker. See service record of employee Co16, Calumet shop, 06/02/03, PANL; K. Anderson, *Wartime Women*, 43, 51–53; Honey, *Creating Rosie the Riveter*, 155.

22. Among workers in the Calumet samples, women requested two-thirds of leaves to care for sick family members; the men who requested such leaves were almost always caring for a sick wife. See Charles Gartelman to C. W. Pflager, 20 Apr. 1945, in service record of employee Co15, Calumet shop, 06/02/03, PANL; pamphlet on Pullman's voluntary insurance plan with the Pru-

dential Company, Box 7, File "Sept.–Dec. 1943," BSCP; K. Anderson, *Wartime Women*, 6, 49–51, 177; Honey, *Creating Rosie the Riveter*, 174–75; David Schreiber, *The Legislative History of the Railroad Retirement and Railroad Unemployment Insurance Systems* (Washington, D.C.: Government Printing Office, 1978), 56, 61, 77.

23. In 1943 hourly rates were as follows: mechanic A, 91 cents; mechanic B, 96 cents; helpers, 68 to 81 cents; laborers, 61 to 67 cents; seamstresses, 81 cents. See Payroll, Calumet Repair Shop, 3 Apr. 1943, PP; employees' proposals to company, 1944, 1–2, 06/01/04, Box 26, File 711, PANL; K. Anderson, *Wartime Women*, 44–47.

24. In the Richmond shipbuilding plants, for instance, many women were slotted into lighter indoor jobs, while black men found openings in hard outdoor work. See K. Anderson, "Last Hired, First Fired," 86; Johnson, *The Second Gold Rush*, 63; Wenkert, *Historical Digest*, 20.

25. According to the samples, no black men (or women) held clerical positions at Calumet, Richmond, or Wilmington, except those specified. In 1946, 11.5 percent of supervisors were black at St. Louis (where 57.8 percent of blue-collar workers were black), as were 1.5 percent of supervisors at Buffalo. Overall, about 4 percent of clerical workers were black, but at Atlanta 11.4 percent were. See Breakdown of Repair Shop Employes as of 21 June 1946; Honey, *Creating Rosie the Riveter*, 54; Johnson, *The Second Gold Rush*, 55, 65; Susan E. Hirsch, "No Victory at the Workplace: Women and Minorities at Pullman during World War II," in *The War in American Culture: Society and Consciousness during World War II*, ed. Lewis Erenberg and Susan Hirsch (Chicago: University of Chicago Press, 1996), 252–56.

26. Emilio Evangelista to President Franklin D. Roosevelt, 29 May 1943, and Formal Complaint, 2 July 1943, case #6-BN-52, FEPC.

27. M. R. Wendt, memo to Lowell M. Greenlaw, 19 June 1943, 06/01/03, Box 12, File 243, PANL.

28. Emilio Evangelista to Harry L. Barron, chief, Division of Compliance, War Manpower, FEPC, 20 Aug. 1943, and Joy Schultz, memos to Elmer Henderson, 11 Oct. to 30 Oct. 1943, re #6-BN-52, FEPC.

29. Elmer A. Henderson, regional director, President's Committee on Fair Employment Practices, to Louis Taylor, vice president, Pullman Company, 20 Oct. 1943, 06/01/03, Box 12, File 243, PANL; memo re 6-BR-166, 15 Sept. 1943, FEPC.

30. Champ Carry to David A. Crawford, 27 Oct. 1943, 06/01/03, Box 12, File 243, PANL.

31. Ibid.

32. David A. Crawford to Champ Carry, 1 Dec. 1943, 06/01/03, Box 12, File 243, PANL.

33. Joy Schultz, memo to Elmer Henderson, 3 Dec. 1943, re 6-BR-166, and Clarence Mitchell, assoc. dir. field operations, memo to Elmer Henderson, 5 Feb. 1944, FEPC; Kersten, "A Tale of Two States," 6; M. Reed, *Seedtime for the Modern Civil Rights Movement*, 136, 155; Risher, "The Negro in the Railroad Industry," 61–64.

34. Memo, 31 Jan. 1945, re 6-BR-166, 2, FEPC.

35. David A. Crawford to Champ Carry, 1 Dec. 1943.

36. Women became stockkeepers, packers, and stock record clerks in the storerooms for the first time. Other new jobs included messenger and junior clerk. See employee Woo1, interview by author, 26 Jan. 1981, Chicago; 1942 Annual Conference of the Repair Shops, 20; Honey, *Creating Rosie the Riveter*, 22–23; U.S. Bureau of the Census, *Historical Statistics of the United States*, pt. 1 (Washington, D.C.: Government Printing Office, 1975), 139–40.

37. AFL unions in general, not just the railroad unions, discriminated. In the Richmond shipyards AFL unions kept blacks and other new workers in auxiliary unions wherever possible, and in Chicago the FEPC found that it could do nothing to open the lily-white AFL steamfitters' and plumbers' unions to minorities. See Johnson, *The Second Gold Rush*, 61; Kersten, "A Tale of Two States," 7.

38. In the election at the Car Works, SWOC garnered 943 votes to the company union's 1,119. See minutes of district staff meetings, SWOC, 21 and 28 Aug. 1941, Box 124, File 6, USWA; Stephen Levitsky to Raymond Sarocco, 27 Oct. 1941; letter to Philip Murray and Joseph Germano, 6 Sept. 1942, first page only, no signatures; and Report of Consent Election, 20 Jan. 1944, NLRB case #13-R-2175, all in Box 184, File 3, USWA; "Pullman Co. Forces Men to Strike for Rights," *Federation News*, 15 Feb. 1941; Irving Bernstein, *Turbulent Years: A History of the American Worker, 1933–1941* (Boston: Houghton Mifflin, 1970), 727–29.

39. Austin Scott, memo to Robert C. Weaver re complaint of William H. James, 22 Apr. 1942, FEPC; Johnson, *The Second Gold Rush*, 61, 71–72, 75.

40. John Beecher, field representative, memo to George Johnson, assistant executive secretary, Committee on Fair Employment Practice, 15 April 1942, 2, Box 21, File 2, BSCP; Robert J. Norrell, "Caste in Steel: Jim Crow Careers in Birmingham, Alabama," *Journal of American History* 73 (1986): 674; Judith Stein, "Southern Workers in National Unions: Birmingham Steelworkers, 1936–1951," in *Organized Labor in the Twentieth-Century South*, ed. Robert Zieger (Knoxville: University of Tennessee Press, 1991), 187–91.

41. Proceedings before Arbitrator, Pullman Standard Car Manufacturing Co., and USWA Local 2534, 3 Feb. 1943, 297–98, Box 108, File 1, USWA; radio script, USWA CIO Station KJOB Hammond, Indiana, 19 Jan. 1944, 3, Box 184, File 3, USWA; Official Report of Proceedings, National War Labor Board, Case #111-5948D, Pullman Standard Car Manufacturing Co. and United Steelworkers of America, 22 Feb. 1944, 12, Box 160, File 29, USWA; National War Labor Board, verbatim transcript, "Public Hearing, The Pullman Standard Car Manufacturing Co., et al.," 16 Mar. 1944, 7, Box 160, File 28, USWA; Milkman, "Female Factory Labor," 180–85; K. Anderson, *Wartime Women*, 56; Gabin, *Feminism in the Labor Movement*, chap. 2; Kessler-Harris, *Out to Work*, 289.

42. The quote is from "Pullman Dynasty Falls," *Keel*, 28 Jan. 1944, Box 188, File 6, USWA. The USWA received 1,295 votes, while the company union got 611 in the Car Works election. Interestingly, one-fifth of eligible workers did

not vote. Some may still have been intimidated; others might have been uninterested. See Report of Consent Election, 20 Jan. 1944.

43. Radio script, 19 Jan. 1944, 3.

44. Gary Gerstle, "The Working Class Goes to War," in *The War in American Culture,* ed. Erenberg and Hirsch, 117–18; Halpern, *Down on the Killing Floor,* 169; Harris, *The Harder We Run,* 114–15; George Lipsitz, *Rainbow at Midnight: Labor and Culture in the 1940s* (Urbana: University of Illinois Press, 1994), chap. 3.

45. Arnold Hirsch, *Making the Second Ghetto: Race and Housing in Chicago, 1940–1960* (New York: Cambridge University Press, 1983), 45–55; Robert Ozanne, *The Negro in the Farm Equipment and Construction Machinery Industries* (Philadelphia: University of Pennsylvania Press, 1972), 25; Janice L. Reiff, "Rethinking Pullman: Urban Space and Working-Class Activism," *Social Science History* 24 (2000): 25–26.

46. Harris, *The Harder We Run,* 118–21.

47. Elmer Henderson, memo, 20 Dec. 1944, re 6-BR-681, FEPC; see also files for cases #6-BR-681 and #6-BR-686, FEPC.

48. "The Pullman Car Manufacturing Company, Shipbuilding Division Strike, December 5–13, 1944 Chronology," 3, 4, 6; Elmer Henderson, memo, 6 Dec. 1944, re 6-BR-681; Harry C. Gibson, memo to Elmer Henderson, 7 Dec. 1944, re 6-BR-681, all in FEPC.

49. Letter to Philip Murray and Joseph Germano, signatures missing, 6 Sept. 1942.

50. NWLB, "Public Hearing," 16 Mar. 1944, 58, 91–94; typescript, Arbitration Panel in the Case of Al Franklin, Discharged for Insubordination and Causing a Work Stoppage July 19, 1944, at the Calumet Harbor Yard, Box 188, File 6, USWA; transcript, National War Labor Board, Case 111-15984-D, 16 July 1945, Box 160, File 30, USWA; from *Federation News:* "Pullman Co. Forces Men to Strike for Rights," 15 Feb. 1941, and "Pullman Co. Signs Pact," 18 Oct. 1941; Galenson, *The CIO Challenge,* 117–18.

51. Filing Agreements with U.S. Department of Labor, 06/01/03, Box 10, Files 208, 209, 212, PANL.

52. Blum, *V Was for Victory,* 92–95; Johnson, *The Second Gold Rush,* 36.

53. 1941–42 Conference with Company Representatives, 12–14.

54. At Calumet 51 percent of white helpers and 30 percent of black helpers became mechanics or trainees; 56 percent of white laborers and 41 percent of black laborers were upwardly mobile. At Wilmington 37 percent of white and 35 percent of black helpers advanced, as did 25 percent of white and 33 percent of black laborers. At Richmond 23 percent of white and 50 percent of black helpers advanced, but only 13 percent of white and 9 percent of black laborers did so. See C. W. Pflager, General Letter to All Repair Shops, 9 Sept. 1943; Chateauvert, *Marching Together,* chap. 4.

55. BSCP Brief to the National Mediation Board in Case R-1625, 12–14, 06/01/05, Box 4a, PANL; Philip S. Foner, *Organized Labor and the Black Worker, 1619–1981* (New York: International Publishers, 1981), 214; A. Philip Randolph, "The Crisis of the Negro Railroad Workers," *American Federationist* 46 (1939): 815; Risher, "The Negro in the Railroad Industry," 65–66.

56. Garfinkel, *When Negroes March*, 140; Harris, *The Harder We Run*, 89–92; Ray Marshall, *The Negro and Organized Labor* (New York: John Wiley and Sons, 1965), 27–28; Genna Rae McNeil, *Groundwork: Charles Hamilton Houston and the Struggle for Civil Rights* (Philadelphia: University of Pennsylvania Press, 1983), 158–63; Joseph E. Wilson, *Tearing Down the Color Bar: A Documentary History and Analysis of the Brotherhood of Sleeping Car Porters* (New York: Columbia University Press, 1989), 183–84.

57. "Sleeping Car Porters Assail Reds, Hear Speakers Ask Barring of All Communists from Unions," *Federation News*, 21 Sept. 1940; J. Anderson, *A. Philip Randolph*, 5–6, 233–35.

58. About one-third of the Chicago red caps were white men. See Drake and Cayton, *Black Metropolis*, 237–42; Marshall, *The Negro and Organized Labor*, 47; Herbert Northrup, *Organized Labor and the Negro* (New York: Harper, 1944), 91; Risher, "The Negro in the Railroad Industry," 52–56.

59. Willard S. Townsend to I. S. Hopkins, personnel manager, 25 Sept. 1942, 06/01/03, Box 2, File 32, PANL.

60. Minutes of Chicago Division meeting, 27 Nov. 1942, 2, Box 7, BSCP.

61. Copy of newspaper clipping, "UTSEA Cancels Drive," 28 Sept. 1942, Box 7, BSCP; Garfinkel, *When Negroes March*, 140; Northrup, *Organized Labor and the Negro*, 92; Risher, "The Negro in the Railroad Industry," 48–49, 52–55.

62. "Pullman Porters . . . Attendants Attention! Beware of Greeks Bearing Gifts" (flyer), Box 10, File 3, BSCP.

63. Chateauvert, *Marching Together*, 82–85.

64. "UTSEA Opens Pullman Laundry Drive," *Bags and Baggage*, July 1942.

65. Statement of Condition, UTSE, 28 Sept. 1943, Box 61, File "UTSE, 1943," UTSE; "Pullman Laundry Employees Hold National Confab," *Bags and Baggage*, Feb.–Mar. 1943; "UTSEA Girds for Nation Wide Pullman Laundry Poll," *Bags and Baggage*, Apr. 1943.

66. The union is quoted in "A New Day at Pullman," *Bags and Baggage*, Jan. 1943. See also "Pullman Shop Workers Open National Drive," in the same issue.

67. The employee service records of three of the six leaders of the local—Ensley L. Moseley, John Rimutis, and Robert E. Mason—are part of the Calumet database. The other leaders were Edward Sheahan, Herberto Rodriguez, and N. Blazak. See Complainant to Committee on Fair Employment Practice, 25 Dec. 1942, and Complainant to Harry Barron, 23 Jan. 1943, re #012042, case #6-BC-172, FEPC.

68. Employee service records of Mosley, Mason, and Davis in Calumet database.

69. 1941–42 Conference with Company Representatives, 304, 307. Another point of contention was that job vacancies were not posted. Managers consulted with representatives of the company union in assigning promotions, but the senior worker did not always get the job. See "Employee Proposals to Company, 1944," 1, 06/01/04, Box 26, File 711, PANL; International Brotherhood of Electrical Workers, 1948 Agreement, Rule Change Discussion Summaries, 1947, meeting of 10 Dec. 1947, 29–30, 06/01/04, Box 23, File 622,

PANL; "A New Day at Pullman," *Bags and Baggage,* Jan. 1943, and "At the Pullman Shops" and "Pullman Company's Vacation 'Racket' Exposed by UTSEA," *Bags and Baggage,* Feb.–Mar. 1943.

70. "Analysis of the Passenger Traffic Report Prepared by the Section of Transportation Service and Issued by the Federal Coordinator of Transportation, January 17, 1935," Pullman Company, Chicago, 1935, and Lowell M. Greenlaw, "Memorandum on Anti-Trust Questions Related to the Pullman Group of Companies," typescript, 23 Sept. 1938, both in Lowell M. Greenlaw Papers, Chicago Historical Society; Meeting Book G, Board of Directors, Executive Committee, and Stockholders Meetings, Pullman Company, meeting of board, 16 Feb. 1944, 1014–15, 02/01/02, vol. 8, PANL; Felix Knight to B. M. Jewell, 29 May 1945, 5478, Box 8, File 11, AFLRED.

71. H. R. Lary, memo to J. F. Lane, 5 Dec. 1942, 06/01/03, Box 9, File 194, PANL; C. W. Pflager to Champ Carry, 18 Oct. 1943, 06/01/04, Box 26, File 706, PANL; "Employee Proposals to Company, 1944."

72. Flyer, Pullman UTSEA–CIO Local 80, 14 Feb. 1945, 06/01/03, Box 20, File 462, PANL.

73. Guilbert, Confidential Inquiry, 27 Nov. 1943; Statement of Condition, UTSE, 28 Sept. 1943; National Mediation Board Certification Case No. R-1238, 25 Mar. 1944, 5478, Box 8, File 11, AFLRED.

74. *Pullman News,* Apr. 1942, 70; *Carbuilder,* Mar. 1955.

75. B. M. Jewell to Executive Council Members, 18 Apr. 1945, 5478, Box 8, File 11, AFLRED.

76. *Black Worker,* July 1943, Sept. 1943, Dec. 1943, Feb. 1944, Apr. 1944, Sept. 1944, Oct. 1944, and Jan. 1945; names of members appear in Minutes of Provisional Committee of the BSCP for the Organization of Pullman Car Cleaners and Yard Forces, Chicago Division Headquarters, 7 June 1945, Box 7, BSCP; "We'll Tell the World," flyer from Pullman Organizing Committee, AFL; B. M. Jewell to Thomas. E. Bickers, secretary, National Mediation Board, 17 May 1944; Eugene Frank to J. J. Duffy, 26 Mar. 1945; Felix Knight to William Green, president, AFL, 15 May 1945; Roy Horn, general president, International Brotherhood of Blacksmiths, Drop Forgers and Helpers, to William Green, 5 July 1945; and B. M. Jewell to All Organizers Assigned to the Pullman Company, 10 Sept. 1945, all in 5478, Box 8, File 11, AFLRED; Marshall, *The Negro and Organized Labor,* 27–28; Paula Pfeffer, *A. Philip Randolph, Pioneer of the Civil Rights Movement* (Baton Rouge: Louisiana State University Press, 1990), 135.

77. IPWF Brief to National Mediation Board re Case R-1625, 22 July 1946, 9, 06/01/05, Box 4a, PANL; lists of racial breakdown of Pullman employees attached to letter from B. M. Jewell to executive council members, 18 Apr. 1945; Felix Knight to B. M. Jewell, 27 Apr. 1945; J. W. Seabolt to Felix Knight, 2 May 1945; memo on discussions re 8-219, 21 May 1945; Fred N. Aten to executive council members, 1 June 1945; B. M. Jewell to All Organizers Assigned to the Pullman Company, 10 Sept. 1945; "Pullman Workers! Are You Receiving the Benefits Obtained by the Bonafide Collective Action of Your Fellow Railroad Workers?" circular, all in 5478, Box 8, File 11, AFLRED; Marshall, *The Negro and Organized Labor,* 27–28.

78. BSCP circular attached to B. M. Jewell to Pullman organizers, 10 Sept. 1945.

79. Roy Horn to William Green, 5 July 1945.

80. Circular #1418, 4 June 1945, from Railway Employes Department to general chairmen, System Federation Officers and Railroad Field Staff, 5478, Box 8, File 11, AFLRED.

81. Flyers (no dates) from PCEARS, Box 13, and IPWF, Box 10, File 3, BSCP.

82. Flyer from BSCP to "Pullman Car Cleaners and Yard Forces," attached to Eugene Frank to J. J. Duffy, 26 Mar. 1945; Felix Knight to B. M. Jewell, 29 May 1945; and B. M. Jewell to Felix Knight, 11 July 1945, all in 5478, Box 8, File 11, AFLRED; Willard Townsend to A. Philip Randolph, 18 Apr. 1946, Box 61, File "UTSE, Jan. to June 1946," UTSE; 1946 Representation of Pullman Employees, National Mediation Board, R-1625, "Determination of Craft or Class," 30 Sept. 1946, 3, 10, 06/01/05, Box 4a, PANL.

83. UTSEA's strength in Richmond may have reflected the large number of black workers recently hired by the shop. This new interest in black workers reflected the shop's experience with the white teenagers whom it had hired previously and who left quickly for jobs elsewhere. Only 5 percent of those hired at Richmond in 1943–44 were black men, but 30 percent of those hired in 1945 were.

84. Minutes of UTSE staff meeting, 28 May 1945 and 19 June 1945, Box 143, File "Executive Board and Staff Meetings, 1945–1947," UTSE; R. B. Collins to L. M. Wicklein, 6 Apr. 1945; Felix Knight to B. M. Jewell, 27 Apr. 1945; R. H. Moran to B. M. Jewell, 6 May 1945; Fred N. Aten to executive council members, 24 May 1945; Carl K. Smith to J. J. Duffy, 22 July 1945; Fred N. Aten to executive council members, 30 July 1945; R. Leonard Jones to Fred Aten, 3 Aug. 1945, all in 5478, Box 8, File 11, AFLRED.

85. B. M. Jewell to executive council members, 22 Aug. 1945; B. M. Jewell to Robert F. Cole, secretary, National Mediation Board, 5 Sept. 1945; B. M. Jewell to All Organizers Assigned to Pullman, 10 Sept. 1945, all in 5478, Box 8, File 11, AFLRED.

86. PCEARS Brief re Case R-1625, 6 Aug. 1946, 06/01/05, Box 4a, PANL.

87. Application for Extension of Financial Aid, Box 61, File "UTSE June–September 1947," UTSE; Risher, "The Negro in the Railroad Industry," 48–49, 135–49.

88. These storeroom positions, primarily stockkeeper, packer, and checker, were termed "nonclerical" in the industry at large, but they had been considered clerical positions by the Pullman Company and were discussed as such in previous chapters.

89. Board of Directors, Pullman Company, Minute Book H, meeting of 16 Oct. 1946, 1226, 02/01/02, vol. 9, PANL.

90. H. R. Lary, memo to Shop Managers, Superintendents . . . , 23 Oct. 1946, 2, 06/01/03, Box 15a, File 328a, PANL.

91. H. R. Lary to J. M. Carry, 21 Jan. 1947, 06/01/03, Box 18, File 388, PANL; C. M. Fitzgerald, district superintendent, confidential memo to L. R. Armstrong re organizing meeting held by BSCP in Los Angeles, 1 Apr. 1947, 06/01/04, Box 29, File 847, PANL; 1947 Annual Conference—Minutes, 15–19 Sept., 19, 06/01/04, Box 26, File 719, PANL.

92. See picture in *Black Worker*, May 1948, 5.

93. Application for Extension of Financial Aid, UTSE; *Black Worker*, Nov. 1946, 1, Jan. 1947, 6, Oct. 1947, 1, Feb. 1948, 6, Mar. 1948, 1, and Apr. 1948, 1; B. M. Jewell to H. H. Schwartz, chairman, National Mediation Board, 2 July 1945, 5478, Box 8, File 11, AFLRED.

Chapter 7: The Last Pullman Workers

1. Karen Anderson, "Last Hired, First Fired: Black Women Workers during World War II," *Journal of American History* 69 (1982): 82–97; Philip S. Foner, *Organized Labor and the Black Worker, 1619–1981* (New York: International Publishers, 1981), chap. 18; Nancy Gabin, *Feminism in the Labor Movement: Women and the United Auto Workers, 1935–1975* (Ithaca, N.Y.: Cornell University Press, 1990), chap. 3; Edward Greer, *Big Steel: Black Politics and Corporate Power in Gary, Indiana* (New York: Monthly Review Press, 1979), 94–95; William H. Harris, *The Harder We Run: Black Workers since the Civil War* (New York: Oxford University Press, 1982), 125.

2. Joy Schultz, memo to Elmer Henderson, 24 Oct. 1945, re Conference with Mr. H. V. Sherman, re ES-270, FEPC.

3. *Pullman News*, July 1945, 21. Only at the Wilmington shop did black mechanics employed in 1945 show significant downward mobility after the war. Forty-four percent of black mechanics but only 5 percent of white ones were downwardly mobile. Wilmington helpers fared better: 19 percent of black helpers and 30 percent of white ones were upwardly mobile, and few (8 percent and 5 percent, respectively) were downwardly mobile. At the Calumet shop the picture was brighter. Only 18 percent of black mechanics and 8 percent of white ones were downwardly mobile. Thirty-eight percent each of the white helpers and black helpers were upwardly mobile after the war, while 24 percent of white helpers and 13 percent of black helpers were downwardly mobile. Chances for advancement were the best at Richmond. Of those employed in 1945, 81 percent of white helpers and 63 percent of black helpers were upwardly mobile; only 3 percent of white mechanics and 17 percent of black mechanics were downwardly mobile. See Howard W. Risher Jr., "The Negro in the Railroad Industry," in *Negro Employment in Land and Air Transport*, Herbert Northrup, Howard W. Risher Jr., Richard D. Leone, and Philip W. Jeffress (Philadelphia: University of Pennsylvania Press, 1971), 74.

4. Felix Knight, general president, Brotherhood of Railway Carmen of America (BRCA), to the "Pullman Crew," 27 July 1945, 2, 5478, Box 8, File 11, AFLRED. Women hired at the Calumet shop between 1943 and 1945 remained in the shop only 4.8 years on average, whereas men hired in those years worked for 14.6 years.

5. By 1947 only four women worked as electricians in all the Pullman shops and none in the yards, although this had been one of the most common jobs opened to women during the war. Seventy-five percent of the women hired at the Calumet shop after the war were clerical workers; another 14 percent

were hired in traditionally women's blue-collar jobs. See International Brotherhood of Electrical Workers, 1948 Agreement, Rule Change Discussion Summaries, 1947, meeting of 10 Dec. 1947, 56, 06/01/04, Box 23, File 622, PANL; Alice Kessler-Harris, *Out to Work: A History of Wage-Earning Women in the United States* (New York: Oxford University Press, 1982), 286–87; Ruth Milkman, "Female Factory Labor and Industrial Structure: Control and Conflict over 'Woman's Place' in Automobile and Electrical Manufacturing," *Politics and Society* 12 (1983): 191–92.

6. Of the women hired at the Calumet shop between 1943 and 1945, 79 percent in unskilled jobs and 69 percent in clerical positions quit before 1949. In contrast, 57 percent of those in mechanic positions and 43 percent of helpers were laid off or disciplined; only 29 percent of mechanics and 36 percent of helpers quit. The remaining either retired or left because of illness. See Kessler-Harris, *Out to Work*, 286–87; Sherrie Kassoudji and Laura Dresser, "Working Class Rosies: Women Industrial Workers during World War II," *Journal of Economic History* 52 (1992): 431–46.

7. "Sister Maggie Hudson," *Black Worker*, Oct. 1944, 5.

8. Esque A. Iles, secretary, Shop Committee, Calumet Council, PCEARS, to Charles Gartelman, shop manager, 7 Jan. 1947; and Charles Gartelman, memo to C. W. Pflager, 8 Jan. 1947, both in service record of employee Co17, Calumet shop, 06/02/03, PANL.

9. D. M. Cohee, Wilmington shop manager, to L. F. Munson, 30 Oct. 1953, letter attached to service record of employee W116, Wilmington shop, 06/02/03, PANL.

10. Charles Gartelman, memos to C. W. Pflager, 4 Sept. 1946 and 10 Sept. 1946, in service record of employee Co18, Calumet shop, 06/02/03, PANL.

11. Lowell M. Greenlaw to David A. Crawford, 5 Sept. 1946, and Clair W. MacLeod, attorney, to W. S. Greenlaw, assistant general attorney, Pullman Co., 30 Aug. 1946, both in 06/01/03, Box 12, File 243, PANL; "Does State FEPC Hamper You?" *Business Week*, 25 Feb. 1950, 114–17; Foner, *Organized Labor and the Black Worker*, 269–71; Greer, *Big Steel*, 94; Merl E. Reed, *Seedtime for the Modern Civil Rights Movement: The President's Committee on Fair Employment Practice, 1941–1946* (Baton Rouge: Louisiana State University Press, 1991), 164–65.

12. Carol Hoffecker, *Corporate Capital: Wilmington in the Twentieth Century* (Philadelphia: Temple University Press, 1983), 8, 118–23; Marilyn Johnson, *The Second Gold Rush: Oakland and the East Bay in World War II* (Berkeley: University of California Press, 1993), 199–201, 211; Shirley Ann Wilson Moore, *To Place Our Deeds: The African American Community in Richmond, California, 1910–1963* (Berkeley: University of California Press, 2000), 95, 100–101; Charles Tilly, Wagner Jackson, and Barry Kay, *Race and Residence in Wilmington, Delaware* (New York: Teachers College, Columbia University, 1965), 31; Robert Wenkert, *A Historical Digest of Negro-White Relations in Richmond, California* (Berkeley: University of California Survey Research Center, 1967), 34, 76.

13. Another example of discrimination in the repair shops was that all cler-

ical workers, male or female, hired at the Calumet, Richmond, and Wilmington shops after the war were white. See J. M. Carry to Lowell M. Greenlaw, 2 Aug. 1946, and Lowell M. Greenlaw to J. M. Carry, 3 Aug. 1946, both in 06/01/03, Box 12, File 243, PANL; Moore, *To Place Our Deeds*, 106–8; Risher, "The Negro in the Railroad Industry," 68.

14. Charles Gartelman, memo, 23 Jan. 1946, in service record of employee C020; L. R. Hyry, memo, 19 June 1946, in service record of employee C019; Report of Investigation of Work Injury, 22 July 1946, in service record of employee C021; Charles Gartelman, memo, 8 Apr. 1947, in service record of employee C022; remarks in service records of employees C023–C025, Calumet shop, all in 06/02/03, PANL.

15. 1947 Annual Conference—Minutes, 15–19 Sept., 1–2, 06/01/04, Box 26, File 719, PANL.

16. Application for Extension of Financial Aid, Box 61, File "UTSE June–September 1947," UTSE; C. M. Fitzgerald, district superintendent, confidential memo to L. R. Armstrong, re organizing meeting held by BSCP in Los Angeles, 1 Apr. 1947, 06/01/04, Box 29, File 847, PANL; Robert Korstad and Nelson Lichtenstein, "Opportunities Found and Lost: Labor, Radicals, and the Early Civil Rights Movement," *Journal of American History* 75 (1988): 804.

17. Benjamin F. McLaurin, International field organizer, BSCP, open letter to New York Division Carmen, n.d., 06/01/03, Box 15a, File 328c, PANL.

18. 1947 Annual Conference, 22; Minute Book I, Executive Committee, Board of Directors, and Stockholders, Pullman Co., Meetings 1947–1952, meetings of 15 Sept. 1947, 1, and 20 Oct. 1947, 1, 02/01/02, vol. 10, PANL; A. F. Lanka, national president, IPWF, to Frank Douglas, chairman, National Mediation Board, 13 May 1948, 06/01/03, Box 15a, File 328c, PANL.

19. In December 1946, 8,233 carmen were eligible to vote; in July 1948 only 6,264 were. See tables 10 and 12; Felix Knight to "Pullman Crew," 27 July 1945.

20. H. R. Lary, memo to superintendents, 20 Dec. 1946, 06/01/03, Box 15a, File 328a, PANL; Report of Election Results, National Mediation Board Case R-2020, 27 July 1948, 06/01/03, Box 15a, File 328c, PANL. UTSEA members were still employed in the shops at the time of the election, including two of the three leaders of the UTSEA local at Calumet. (The third leader had just retired.) See service records of employees C026–C028, Calumet Repair Shop, 06/02/03, PANL. Stanley Meyer became an official in the system federation, as did John Di Gregorio, who had been national treasurer of the Independent Pullman Workers Federation.

21. H. R. Lary, memo to shop managers, 22 Jan. 1949, 05/03/01, Box 13, File 293, PANL; Filing Agreements with U.S. Dept. of Labor, 06/01/03, Box 10, Files 208, 209, 212, PANL; List of Railroad Labor Organizations at Pullman Company, 1959, 06/01/03, Box 10, File 209, PANL. The BSCP also gave up the storeroom nonclerical workers to the Brotherhood of Railway and Steamship Clerks.

22. Memos, letters, and reports, 1953–54, re case of George C. Greenidge, 06/01/03, Box 30, File 693, PANL.

23. Melinda Chateauvert, *Marching Together: Women of the Brotherhood of Sleeping Car Porters* (Urbana: University of Illinois Press, 1998), chap. 9; Harris, *The Harder We Run,* 140–41; Harris P. Shane, former vice president for industrial relations, Pullman Standard, interview by author and Janice Reiff, 27 June 1988, Chicago.

24. Memos, Box 137, File 16, BSCP; see records of the Denver case, 01/01/06, Box 4, File 41, PANL.

25. Employee W001, interview by author, 19 Mar. 1981, Chicago. Service records for sample workers reflect pay increases for all seamstresses at the Calumet, Richmond, and Wilmington repair shops in 1951 as well as their reclassification as upholsterers.

26. *Martha Dennis v. The Pullman Company and R. Bucherati, General Foreman,* Case #CSF-12682-66, 29 Nov. 1966, State of New York, State Commission for Human Rights, 06/01/03, Box 30, File 693, PANL; G. S. Holland, regional superintendent, to F. X. Giaccone, commissioner, State of New York Commission for Human Rights, 31 Mar. 1966, 06/01/04, Box 28, File 794, PANL.

27. In 1948 Calumet had 139 separate job titles, Wilmington had 100, and Richmond, 107. In 1952 Calumet had 89, Wilmington had 83, and Richmond had 71. See D. M. Cohee, manager, to L. F. Munson, 30 Oct. 1953, and Munson to Cohee, 4 Nov. 1953, attached to service record of employee W116, Wilmington shop, 06/02/03, PANL; Summary of Conference Held December 13, 1949, Between Representatives of the Railway Employes Department, A.F. of L. and Representatives of the Pullman Company for the Purpose of Discussing the Agreement to Settle Jurisdictional Disputes on all Railroads between Organizations Comprising the Railway Employes Department, A.F. of L., 8, 06/01/04, Box 27, File 724, PANL.

28. In 1947 the company had 29,804 employees, in 1953 only 22,757. See Minute Book I, executive committee meetings of 15 Sept. 1947, 1; 20 Oct. 1947, 1; and 4 June 1951; David Crawford, draft of letter to Willard F. Place, 5 Apr. 1947, 06/01/03, Box 3, File 44, PANL; J. P. Leach Jr., office memo, 10 July 1953, Box 39-313-1 (old numbering) PANL.

29. The employment level at each Pullman shop remained virtually stationary until the last few months before closing, then all were let go. See Board of Directors meeting of 14 May 1951, Minute Book I; Minute Book J, 1953–57, Pullman Co.; Board of Directors meetings of 1 Feb. 1954, 3; 7 May 1956, 4; and 6 May 1957, 3; and executive committee, meeting of 6 Dec. 1954, all in 02/01/02, vol. 11, PANL; Pauline Lesley Cook, *Railway Workshops: The Problems of Contraction* (London: Cambridge University Press, 1964), 27–35.

30. Minute Book K, Board of Directors, Executive Committee, and Stockholders Meetings, 1958–1964, board of directors, meetings of 3 Feb. 1958, 6; 4 Aug. 1958, 3; 2 Nov. 1959, 3; 1 Feb. 1960, 2, 02/01/02, vol. 12, PANL; Report to the President by the Emergency Board (Emergency Board #155, Washington, D.C., 2 Nov. 1963), 47–48, 72/132 C, Box 32, C. L. Dellums Papers, Bancroft Library, University of California, Berkeley.

31. Bureau of Information of the Eastern Railways, *Railroad Wages and Labor Relations, 1900–1946* (New York: Bureau of Information of the Eastern Railways, 1947), 96–98.

32. M. B. Osburn to E. P. Schwotzer, 28 June 1948, C. R. Harding, president, to H. E. Jones, chairman, Joint Conference Committee, 12 Mar. 1952, and E. J. McDermott, International Brotherhood of Electrical Workers, to F. J. Boeckelman, 8 May 1952, all in 06/01/03, Box 9, File 194, PANL; B. M. Jewell to Felix Knight, 28 June 1945, 5478, Box 8, File 11, AFLRED.

33. Twenty-eight percent of Atlanta shop workers had fifteen or more years of seniority; another 45 percent had five to fourteen years. See Atlanta Shops Employes Seniority as of 11 Feb. 1954, 06/01/03, Box 21a, File 479a, PANL; System Federation #122 to F. J. Boeckelman, 23 Mar. 1954, 06/01/02, Box 1, File 18, PANL; E. J. McDermott to John F. Murray, mediator, 8 Dec. 1954, 06/01/02, Box 1, File 7, PANL; H. R. Lary to R. F. Walsh, executive secretary, Association of Western Railways et al., 17 Dec. 1954, 06/01/03, Box 21a, File 479a, PANL; minutes, executive committee meeting of 1 Mar. 1954, 3, Minute Book J; Report . . . of Emergency Board #155, 43–44.

34. In 1957 the average age of shop workers was fifty-one at Calumet, fifty at Richmond, and fifty-three at Wilmington. See Labor Situation Reports, 27 Jan. 1955, 25 Apr. 1955, 21 July 1955, and 9 Oct. 1956, all in 06/01/02, Box 1, File 23, PANL. The median age of skilled shop employees on all railroads was forty-nine in 1948. See U.S. Railroad Retirement Board, *Annual Report of the Railroad Retirement Board, 1948* (Washington, D.C.: Government Printing Office, 1949), 165.

35. Labor Situation Reports, 16 July 1959; Memorandum of Agreement with System Federation #122, 24 Feb. 1958, 06/01/04, Box 28, File 817, PANL; service records of employees R005–R013, Richmond repair shop, 06/02/03, PANL.

36. The mechanics' rate was $3.60 per hour in 1969. See Labor Situation Reports, 29 Jan. 1960–Oct. 31, 1962; F. J. Boeckelman, memo to Managers—District Operations et al., 28 July 1966, 06/01/03, Box 24, File 537, PANL; Calumet Shop Employees in Active Service on 1 Jan. 1969, 06/01/04, Box 29, File 844, PANL; Public Law Board #512, Statement of Claims, 13 Apr. 1970, Box 134, File 32, BSCP; Report of Emergency Board #155, 44–48. See Risher, "The Negro in the Railroad Industry," 15, for the decline of employment in the railroad industry.

37. "Chicago Railway Carmen Achieve Impressive Contract Gains," *Federation News*, 29 June 1946; *Carbuilder*, Mar. 1955, 2; Shane interview.

38. Merrill Lynch, Pierce, Fenner and Beane, *Investor's Reader*, 25 Aug. 1954, 10–11.

39. Memos on shutdowns at Hammond and Worcester, Box 108, File 2, and Memorandum of Agreement attached to 1960 contract, 3–4, 8, Box 108, File 3, all in USWA; *Carbuilder*, Mar. 1955, 2; Greer, *Big Steel*, 99; Merrill Lynch, *Investor's Reader*, 25 Aug. 1954, 12.

40. Harris, *The Harder We Run*, 137–41; Carolyn Hernandez, "Integration of the Workforce in the Steel Industry: The Inland Steel Experience, 1945–

1960" (master's thesis, Loyola University Chicago, 1990), 67–68, 101–2; Korstad and Lichtenstein, "Opportunities Found and Lost," 800–801.

41. Shane interview; Hernandez, "Integration of the Workforce," 86–89; Arnold Hirsch, *Making the Second Ghetto: Race and Housing in Chicago, 1940–1960* (New York: Cambridge University Press, 1983), 7–8, 30–36, 41–56, 186–99; Robert Ozanne, *The Negro in the Farm Equipment and Construction Machinery Industries* (Philadelphia: University of Pennsylvania Press, 1972), 25; David Roediger, *Towards the Abolition of Whiteness: Essays on Race, Politics, and Working Class History* (New York: Verso, 1994), 187–90.

42. Shane interview.

43. Allen T. Woods and thirteen cosigners to David McDonald, president, USWA, 14 May 1963, Box 187, File 2, USWA; *Swint v. Pullman-Standard*, 539 F.2d 77 (1976). For the role of the USWA in the Birmingham steel industry, see Robert J. Norrell, "Caste in Steel: Jim Crow Careers in Birmingham, Alabama," *Journal of American History* 73 (1986): 669–94; Judith Stein, "Southern Workers in National Unions: Birmingham Steelworkers, 1936–1951," in *Organized Labor in the Twentieth-Century South*, ed. Robert Zieger (Knoxville: University of Tennessee Press, 1991), 208–9, asserts that in the late 1940s and 1950s the USWA provided a vehicle for black workers to exert influence that they had not possessed previously. This does not seem to have been the case at Pullman Standard.

44. Shane interview. Shane provided me with copies of his journal for 1968 that documented many details of the integration process at Bessemer. In "Caste in Steel," 675–79, 685, Norrell describes how white workers at nearby steel plants used USWA contract provisions on seniority to control the best jobs and resisted any pressure from the national union leadership to integrate local union affairs.

45. Shane interview and journal.

46. The managers are quoted in R. J. Gorski to G. L. Green, 23 Aug. 1967. See also F. B. Snyder to Eugene Luening, 10 June 1966, F. B. Snyder, confidential memo to R. J. Gorski, 24 Aug. 1967; draft press release, 9 Sept. 1967; memo for Law Dept., File #42–69, NAACP Inquiry, 21 Feb. 1968; and draft letter #2 from F. B. Snyder to Lee Williams, 28 Jan. 1970, all in Box 15, Files 42–69, Pullman Archives, Calumet Regional Archives, Gary, Indiana.

47. Jenny Rohrer, ed., *The Last Pullman Car Study Guide* (Chicago: Kartemquin Educational Films, 1985), 8–10; David Young, "Morrison Knudsen Risks Its Life by Riding Rails," *Chicago Tribune*, 9 July 1995.

48. Rohrer, *The Last Pullman Car Study Guide*, 4.

49. Ray Robles, secretary, Local 1834, USWA, in the film *The Last Pullman Car* (Kartemquin Films, 1985); Rohrer, *The Last Pullman Car Study Guide*, 21–24.

50. John Bowman, president, Local 1834, USWA, in film *The Last Pullman Car*.

INDEX

SUSAN ELEANOR HIRSCH is a professor of history at Loyola University of Chicago and the author of *Roots of the American Working Class.* She has also contributed essays to *The Public Historian, Radical History Review, Women's Studies International Quarterly,* and the *Journal of Social History,* among others. With Lewis Erenberg she edited *The War in American Culture: Society and Consciousness during World War II.*

The Working Class in American History

The University of Illinois Press
is a founding member of the
Association of American University Presses.

Composed in 9.5/12.5 Trump Mediaeval
by Jim Proefrock
at the University of Illinois Press
Manufactured by Thomson-Shore, Inc.

University of Illinois Press
1325 South Oak Street
Champaign, IL 61820-6903
www.press.uillinois.edu